The Voyage of the Slave Ship *Hare*

The Voyage of
the Slave Ship *Hare*

A Journey into Captivity from
Sierra Leone to South Carolina

SEAN M. KELLEY

The University of
North Carolina Press
CHAPEL HILL

*Published with the assistance of the Anniversary
Fund of the University of North Carolina Press*

Set in Charter and IM Fell
by codeMantra
Manufactured in the United States of America
The paper in this book meets the guidelines for permanence and
durability of the Committee on Production Guidelines for
Book Longevity of the Council on Library Resources.

The University of North Carolina Press has been a member of the
Green Press Initiative since 2003.

Cover illustration: Bance Island in 1748 (The National Archives of the U.K.,
ref. CO700/SIERRALEONE1A [1]), with a background texture courtesy of Bittbox

Library of Congress Cataloging-in-Publication Data
Names: Kelley, Sean M., 1966– author.
Title: The voyage of the slave ship Hare : a journey into captivity
from Sierra Leone to South Carolina / Sean M. Kelley.
Description: Chapel Hill : The University of North Carolina Press, [2016] |
Includes bibliographical references and index.
Identifiers: LCCN 2015039986|
ISBN 9781469627687 (cloth : alk. paper)
ISBN 9781469654768 (pbk. : alk. paper)
ISBN 9781469627694 (ebook)
Subjects: LCSH: Hare (Ship) | Slave ships—United States—History—18th century. |
Slaves—South Carolina—18th century. | Slave trade—South Carolina—History—
18th century. | Slave trade—Sierra Leone—History—18th century.
Classification: LCC E445.S7 K45 2016 | DDC 306.3/620975709033—dc23
LC record available at http://lccn.loc.gov/2015039986

To Kathleen

CONTENTS

FIGURES AND MAPS

ACKNOWLEDGMENTS

When I began research on this book, I scarcely understood just how much I would depend on others for advice, criticism, and support. To start, I owe a tremendous debt of inspiration to Robert Harms, whose own study served as a model for this one, and who reassured me over lunch that there was room in the world for more than one such book. This study also benefitted immeasurably from the wide-ranging expertise of many other scholars. Paul Lovejoy in particular supported the project from the start and has offered invaluable guidance. Bruce Mouser read an entire draft and shared his vast knowledge of the Rio Pongo and Northern Rivers with me. Jane Landers and Bob Olwell each took time out from their busy schedules to read complete drafts and offer their perspectives. Jim Oakes and his students at the CUNY Graduate Center read the entire manuscript and provided extensive and valuable critique, as did an anonymous reader for UNC Press.

I am also very grateful to Doug Bradburn, Diane Sommerville, Dave Hacker, and all of the members of the Upstate Early American History Workshop for reading an 87-page section without complaint. Thank you also to Bill Ashbaugh, Ed Baptist, José Curto, Lisle Dalton, Dora Dumont, Jeff Fortin, Matthew Hendley, Joanne Melish, Robin Mitchell, Kenneth Morgan, Philip Morgan, Anthony Parent, David Richardson, Heather Schwartz, Suzanne Schwarz, David Trotman, and Larry Yarak, each of whom commented on smaller sections as chapters, conference papers, or article drafts. Roark Atkinson, David Eltis, Michael Jarvis, Kristin Jones, Walter Kamphoefner, Peter Kolchin, Jonathan Roberts, Jim Sidbury, and Tom Thurston each provided sources, advice, or support. I owe a special thanks to Joseph Opala and Phil Misevich, who advised me on my visit to Sierra Leone, and to Alpha Kanu and Ibrahima Bangura, who made my visit a successful and memorable one. Thanks are also due to David Klempner for hosting me in London on several occasions and to Lance and Melissa Schacterle for opening their home to me during my time in Worcester.

This project has also benefitted from the financial support of the National Endowment for the Humanities and the American Antiquarian Society (AAS). Special thanks are due to Paul Erickson for making my fellowship year at AAS an especially productive and rewarding experience. I can think of no better home for an Early Americanist than AAS, where the collections are surpassed only by the expertise and helpfulness of the entire staff. Thanks also to Hartwick College for awarding me Trustee Research Grants from 2008 to 2011, the funds from which allowed me to visit archives on three continents. I was also fortunate to work with several outstanding archivists and librarians, including Jane Aldrich of the South Carolina Historical Society, Graham Duncan of the South Caroliniana Library, Bert Lippincott of the Newport Historical Society, and Elizabeth Pope and Jackie Penny of AAS. Dawn Baker, Peter Riesler, and Sue Stevens of the Interlibrary Loan Department at Hartwick's Stevens-German Library worked miracles on a regular basis. Sir Archibald Grant very kindly allowed me access to the Grant of Monymusk Papers in the National Archives of Scotland. Finally, and most importantly, thank you to Vicki and Kathleen for supporting the project without reservation and for tolerating my frequent absences.

The Voyage of the Slave Ship *Hare*

Introduction

They had names, the seventy-two people Caleb Godfrey purchased on the Upper Guinea coast in late 1754, but we do not know what they were. They were mothers and fathers, sons and daughters, brothers, sisters, and cousins. They surely possessed as wide a range of characteristics as can be found in any collection of seventy-two people, but we will never know what those were. The very existence of the seventy-two men, women, and children Godfrey packed onto the sloop *Hare* is revealed to us solely as a consequence of their enslavement. They enter the historical record as a mere tally of goods to be purchased and sold: twenty-eight men, twenty-five women, twelve girls, and seven boys.

It is no accident that the *Hare* captives' names were never recorded. Slaves are people whose right to kinship has been extinguished. Names speak to kinship, belonging in a community, and personhood before the law. Godfrey's elision was an intrinsic part of the process through which fathers, mothers, and children were transformed into commodities, the new property tie to the slave owner displacing the former ties of family and community. None of this means that the *Hare* captives or any other slaves actually ceased to be people or forgot who they were simply because someone did not consider it important to record their names, and none of it means that they failed to establish new family and community bonds. Still, we could say so much more about them if we knew their names.[1]

This book reconstructs the voyage of a single Rhode Island sloop that carried captives from Sierra Leone to South Carolina in 1754–55. It seeks to answer a seemingly straightforward question: who were the *Hare* captives? The hope is that grappling with that problem—even if definitive answers should prove elusive—will yield new insight into the old question of the African experience in the New World, an issue that lies at the center of American history and identity. Most Americans are accustomed to thinking of their country as a historical extension of Europe. Few realize that by 1775, enslaved Africans constituted 30 percent of all Old World migrants arriving in British North America, or that the number of coerced migrants from Africa surpassed the number of free migrants to New England during the so-called Great Migration of the seventeenth century by a factor of nearly fourteen. By the time the legal slave trade ended in 1808, the number of African Muslims arriving in North America almost certainly surpassed the number of Puritan Congregationalists coming to their City Upon a Hill, and by a wide margin.[2]

The *Hare* captives' experience offers a chance to revisit the long-standing historical question of African identities and cultures in the New World. With the inauguration of the modern debate in the 1990s, most historians, anthropologists, and linguists have championed one of two positions. On one side have stood proponents of what might be termed the Creolization thesis, the classic statement of which came from anthropologists Sidney Mintz and Richard Price in 1976 (and in a revised edition in 1992). Based largely on fieldwork done in the mid-twentieth century, Mintz and Price argued that it had not been possible for Africans to reconstitute specific cultures and identities in the Americas. The slave trade had recombined Africans of diverse linguistic and ethnic backgrounds to the extent that they constituted crowds more than coherent groups. New World plantations were therefore populated by an "aggregate" of randomly selected Africans with little in common. In that regard, Mintz and Price's vision of cultural disruption and discontinuity bore a passing resemblance to the older arguments of E. Franklin Frazier, even though in their vision of African American cultures as creative, dynamic, and sharing African-derived "grammatical principles," they saw themselves as working in the tradition established by Melville J. Herskovits. Unable to form speech communities, they argued, Africans abandoned their languages and devised creoles. Lacking "priesthoods and temples," they improvised new approaches to the sacred. As Mintz and Price stressed, the history of African American culture was one of dynamism and creativity. And given the conditions of the slave trade and the New World plantations, that dynamism and creativity played out primarily in the Americas. The result was a variety of hybridized, regional African American cultures, with an emphasis on the American.[3]

The Creolization paradigm dominated most work on North America in the 1970s and 1980s.[4] By the 1990s, however, some historians began to discern shortcomings, their criticisms revolving around a simple point: Creolization scholarship left little room for a discussion of Africa as a historical entity or of Africans as historical agents with actual, discoverable pasts. A new, Revisionist school of interpretation emerged to challenge the Creolization argument. The Revisionists differed from the Creolization theorists in significant ways. The early proponents of Creolization based many of their conclusions on fieldwork undertaken in the Americas, often working backward in time using anthropological and linguistic models. Revisionists emerged out of the field of African history; employing historical and ethnographic methods that centered on Africa and working inductively, Revisionists relied more heavily on archival work. At the heart of their critique was an insistence that the African past was both discoverable and germane to New World history.[5]

One of the Revisionists' first targets was the notion that the slave trade was a randomizing process, along with the corresponding argument that New World plantations were cultural and linguistic "aggregations" of Africans of diverse backgrounds. Drawing on existing studies of the slave trade, Revisionists argued that most ships purchased a majority of their captives at only a few locations along the coast. The diversity of slave cargoes, they argued, and consequently of New World plantations, had been overstated. The Revisionists' arguments found support with the release of the Transatlantic Slave Trade Database (TSTD1) on CD-ROM in 1999 (with the updated TSTD2 version published online in 2008). TSTD1 recorded approximately 75 percent (80 percent in TSTD2) of all the slave-trading voyages that crossed the Atlantic. The data confirmed that many regions of the Americas received the bulk of their captives from only one or two African regions, and moreover that relationships between specific regions of Africa and America often persisted over decades, if not longer. There was, to be certain, a great deal of variation in the structure of the slave trade over time and space. In addition, because TSTD1 essentially connected ports with ports, it could not provide definitive answers to questions about the geographic distribution of captives within the New World colonies. One thing, however, was clear: the slave trade was not quite the random or randomizing process that the Creolization literature had imagined it to be. It was a highly structured business that was shaped by elaborate (if not always streamlined) networks.[6]

Though the new data seemed to imply that African cultures in the Americas were potentially more coherent than the Creolization literature imagined, historians on all sides of the debate still acknowledged the need for further empirical research. New work began to use the data to explore not a generalized "African" culture in the Americas, but the histories of specific African ethnic and linguistic groups in specific New World settings. These studies eventually developed a more nuanced framework for thinking about Africans in the Americas, one centered less on demonstrating pure cultural transplantations than on using specific African cultures and histories as a starting point for discussions of Africans in specific New World locations. To some extent, the new emphasis on cultural dynamism and transformation in the Revisionist literature represented a convergence with Creolization scholarship: Africans created new cultures and identities in the Americas, but out of specific African historical and cultural materials and at a much more gradual pace than Mintz and Price implied.[7] At the same time, Creolization scholars began to shift their focus from the Americas to Africa as the primary locus of "ethnogenesis."[8]

Surveying the field in 2011, historians James Sidbury and Jorge Cañizares-Esguerra called the Creolization-Revisionist debate "overtheorized" and increasingly "meaningless." Historians, they suggested, should focus on the "local variables (contingency, geography, demography, and other material conditions) as they modified the beliefs that people from [Europe, Africa, and the Americas] brought to their interactions." This fundamentally empirical task should be undertaken with theoretical and conceptual awareness, but it is difficult to imagine a new emphasis on empirical research resulting in any kind of consensus. Historians will likely continue to differ in their emphasis on the African versus New World terms of the equation, the timing and nature of cultural transformation, and the level of disruption created by the slave trade.[9]

Despite the outpouring of new work inspired by TSTD1 and TSTD2, scholars of North America (with notable exceptions) have been slow to initiate a similar reexamination. It is not difficult to understand why. As significant as their numbers may be in North American history, Africans are far more central to the history of Brazil and the Caribbean. It is hardly an exaggeration to suggest that the histories of some New World regions are not merely inseparable from the history of the African diaspora—they are almost synonymous with it. The Catholic colonies have generated some of the deepest research; scholars have drawn heavily on ecclesiastical records that detail African lay fraternities, marriages, baptisms, and god-parentage. Inquisition records, especially, have proven to be among the richest sources available. Comparable studies for Protestant regions, like British North America, where even the reach of the Anglican Church was limited, are simply not possible.[10]

Another explanation for the relative paucity of recent studies on North America has to do with the continent's aberrational history of slavery. For most New World slave societies, the institution of slavery and the transatlantic slave trade were nearly coterminous. In many cases, the time elapsed between the effective end of the slave trade and the end of slavery was a few decades: less than four for Brazil, a bit less than three for the British West Indies, and two for Cuba; in Haiti, both were terminated at the same time. For places like these, slavery and the transatlantic slave trade were nearly synonymous. But in the case of South Carolina, the total time elapsed between the close of the slave trade and the end of slavery was almost six decades. In Virginia's case, it was about nine. It is therefore understandable that many U.S. historians say little or nothing about the slave trade. After all, on the eve of the Civil War less than 1 percent of U.S. slaves had been born in Africa. In contrast, when slavery ended in Brazil and Cuba, there were still large numbers of Africans residing in Rio de Janeiro and Havana. Many survived into the twentieth century, attracting attention from ethnographers and historians. For all of these reasons, the experiences of Africans on the North American mainland have frequently proven more elusive than those of Africans in other places.

The study of individual slaving voyages represents a potentially fruitful, if difficult, way to approach the question of African cultures in the Americas. Most slave-ship documents—logbooks, commercial accounts, and mercantile correspondence—do not lend themselves to the pursuit, since they deal mostly with the particulars of the ship and voyage. Given their nature, it is difficult to glean much about the lives of the captives before or after their transatlantic passage. Ships' records typically list only the name of the port where the captives embarked and rarely include sales lists with the names of the individuals who purchased them in the New World.[11] Only twenty-three slave sale records are known to have survived for the nearly 500 vessels that carried captives from Africa to South Carolina before 1776. Of the twenty-three, the *Hare*'s 1754–55 voyage, the records for which are housed at the New-York Historical Society, is the most thoroughly documented slaving voyage to eighteenth-century North America and is among the best documented for any time or place. This is true despite the fact that no logbook or ship's journal for the *Hare* survives. American captains tended to hold on to logs and journals for future reference, so they are seldom found among the merchants' papers that form the bulk of the documentation for the slave trade. However, many of these other documents, which for the *Hare* include ship's accounts, crew pay records, and a set of letters written by the captain from the coast of Africa, are actually more revealing than logs. Perhaps most important, the surviving records include a list of twenty-four individuals along the Upper Guinea coast who sold captives to the *Hare* and a sales record with the names of the twenty-six individuals who purchased the captives in South Carolina. These records not only reveal the workings of the colonial Rhode Island slave trade in great detail, but also allow for the drawing of connections from specific geographic locations along the Upper Guinea coast to specific North American slaveholdings.[12]

The same rare combination of documents also allows for an exploration of many poorly understood aspects of the slave trade, which can in turn shed light on African lives in the Americas. Important questions concerning the structure of slave sales, the shipmate relationship, and the geographic distribution of captives have seen little analysis, which is surprising because there has been much debate about whether Africans lived in culturally and linguistically heterogeneous communities or in more coherent clusters.[13]

The *Hare* captives' experience offers indirect support for the Revisionist school of interpretation, suggesting the strength and endurance of specific African—in this case, Mande—worldviews and cultural practices in the Americas. Like many recent studies, however, this one finds that specific ideas and lifeways did not remain unchanged. The conditions of enslavement and the environment of the New World demanded some accommodation. The *Hare* captives, like most migrants, likely confronted their challenges by drawing not upon a generalized African culture or "grammar," but upon their own historically and culturally specific experiences. As they acted upon these experiences, they inevitably altered their thoughts and practices to suit the American environment, resulting in recognizable variants of the African cultures they had left behind.

In addition to providing a focal point for the discussion of African cultures in the Americas, a well-documented voyage like the *Hare*'s permits a weighing of all the variables of the slave trade and diaspora. Unlike a composite study, which draws from a wide variety of sources, a single voyage allows us to monitor the many historically specific conditions—that is, the overall temporal, geographic, political, and economic contexts—that together shaped the outcome of the voyage and, in the process, the movement of Africans into the Americas.[14] Instead of demonstrating the norms of the slave trade, it allows us to see how things came together in *this* instance. The result sometimes confirms standing interpretations, but just as often it reveals previously unknown problems that force us to reconsider earlier certainties. The story of the *Hare* captives, then, opens a window to the Atlantic slave trade and the lives of African captives in colonial South Carolina.

Still, no voyage, however well documented, can settle all debate in the field. For one thing, although South Carolina (along with Georgia) was the largest importer of African labor in North America, accounting for about 54 percent of the total, there was little about the *Hare*'s voyage that was typical.

Statistically speaking, the typical slave ship sailed from Brazil, purchased captives in West Central Africa, and carried them back to Brazil.[15] North American–owned vessels like the *Hare* carried only 2.4 percent of the Africans who crossed the Atlantic as part of the slave trade. North American slave traders, moreover, took most of their captives to the larger West Indian slave markets (60 percent overall and 73 percent before 1776) rather than to the lesser ones on the North American mainland. Finally, three-quarters of the Africans in South Carolina (or 96 percent prior to 1776) arrived aboard British, not North American, vessels.[16]

A more important blind spot has to do with the cultural legacy of the nearly 100,000 Upper Guineans who came to South Carolina and Georgia prior to 1808. A number of valuable studies on the Gullah/Geechee language and culture have appeared over the years, all noting the importance of the Upper Guinean contribution. Most, however, are not primarily concerned with the experiences of the migrant generation itself. With feet firmly planted in some later time period, usually in the nineteenth or twentieth century, the discussion of Africans typically amounts to an effort to reverse engineer Gullah, or to disentangle the various cultural inputs of a later, more unified, and coherent creole language and culture. Lorenzo Dow Turner's pathbreaking study of the Gullah language, Charles Joyner's historical ethnography of the All Saint's Parish, and Margaret W. Creel's analysis of Gullah religious culture in the antebellum period are prominent examples of works in this mode. For studies like these, the migrant generation figures primarily as the "African background," heritage, or origin of latter-day "survivals" or "Africanisms." The particulars of the slave trade, the distribution of Africans throughout the colonies, and even the patterns of eighteenth-century life generally receive little attention.[17] Studying the *Hare* captives also sheds precious little light on the debate over the origins of Carolina rice culture, or the "Black Rice" thesis. Rice culture had been established in the Low Country for a half century before the *Hare* captives arrived, so while many of them helped to perpetuate the rice complex by employing their agricultural and other skills in the New World, they were not involved in the initial transfer.[18]

In sum, the present work is concerned with the experiences of newly arrived Africans more than with their impact on future generations. The two questions are closely related, both in the historical sense as African migrants laying the foundation of a later creole culture, and in a methodological sense, as historians study Gullah culture for clues to the early experiences of Africans in the Low Country. It is worth emphasizing, however, that these are two distinct approaches trying to answer two different questions, one concerning the African (or Upper Guinean, or Central African) contribution to a later antebellum African American culture, the other interested in the experience of the captives themselves for what it reveals about a specific place in time.

That place, the Low Country of the 1750s, was experiencing a major transformation in its relationship to the wider world. Stimulated by European demand for New World products and made possible by several historical developments, including the stabilization and maturation of the plantation regime and a pause in the seemingly endless progression of dynastic-turned-colonial conflicts that afflicted the entire Atlantic rim, the volume of the slave trade was about to ascend to unimagined heights. The next half century would see more Africans carried across the ocean than any other fifty-year period, in spite of three extended periods of warfare. The years 1751–1800 also saw a shift in the regions sending captives across the ocean, especially in the case of Upper Guinea, the area visited by the *Hare*. During the first half of the eighteenth century, Upper Guinea was a minor contributor to the diaspora, accounting for about 8 percent of all captives sold into Atlantic slavery. Over the second half of the century, the number of captives shipped from Upper Guinea tripled, while its share of the overall slave trade doubled to 16 percent. As such, the *Hare* captives were taken from a part of Africa that was experiencing unprecedented upheaval, which will be explored in greater detail in the chapters that follow.[19]

The destination of many, the "Rice Kingdom" of South Carolina, was one of the plantation colonies that had matured in the decades prior to 1750. Historians generally recognize three major phases in the transatlantic slave trade to South Carolina. The first lasted from about 1700 to 1740. Prior to this, the colony imported most of its captives indirectly, from Caribbean colonies like Barbados. With the success of rice planting, Carolinians began direct importations, and most of these—perhaps 70 percent—came from the Central African region of Kongo-Angola. Then, in 1739, slaves of probable Kongolese origin staged the largest slave rebellion in colonial American history, near the Stono River. The following year, the legislature passed a restrictive Negro Act and raised the import duty on foreign slaves, which, in combination with war from 1739 to 1748, effectively ended importations. When peace returned, Carolinians eagerly sought African labor. This time, however, most of the captives—almost 60 percent in the years leading up to the Revolution—came from Upper Guinea, a region very distant and very different from Central Africa. The Upper Guinea phase of the Carolina slave trade lasted for over twenty-five years and ended only when the Continental

Congress passed an import ban in 1774. Importations picked up again during the mid-1780s and 1790s, with a majority again coming from Upper Guinea, but the third major phase of the slave trade came when the state of South Carolina re-legalized importations in 1804. Driven by the demand in cotton-growing areas, the numbers of imported slaves spiked to unprecedented levels. Even then, Upper Guinea supplied a plurality of the migrants. The influx of Africans then fell drastically once the slave trade was banned by federal law as of January 1, 1808, effectively closing a chapter of North American history. It is hardly surprising that students of Gullah culture have discerned a very strong Upper Guinean influence.[20]

Because the *Hare* helped to connect three continents (and Barbados), the voyage yields additional insight into still other historical debates, such as New England's involvement in the slave trade. Over the past few decades, historians have methodically dismantled the old notion of New England as a marginal, even reluctant participant in slavery. Bondage in the New England colonies shared many features with systems elsewhere, including violence, exploitation, and a growing emphasis on color.[21] More important, the New England economy depended heavily on trade with slave systems in other parts of the globe, especially the Caribbean. In light of these developments in the literature, we might expect historians to revisit the issue of the New England–based transatlantic slave (or "triangular") trade, which a generation of nineteenth-century abolitionists and antiquarians saw as the driver of the New England economy. That reexamination has not taken place, however, as historians continue to view New England as a fringe participant in the transatlantic slave trade, operating at a level well below that of major powers, such as England. The slave trade, they point out, accounted for only sixteen voyages per year between 1730 and 1775, less than 1 percent of all clearances from New England ports.[22]

Though these views rest on empirically sound foundations, they do need to be placed in proper perspective. New England may well have trailed the mother country as a transporter of captive Africans, but old England had a much larger population. In fact, on a per capita basis the slave trade was more important to New England, which dispatched one slaver per 1,000 inhabitants annually over the period 1730–75, than it was to England, which sent out one ship for every 1,400 residents. Even so, counting voyages is not the best way to gauge the regional impact of what one historian has appropriately called "the slave-carrying trade." It is far more useful to calculate the value of slave trading to the economy. As chapter 1 will show, slave trading contributed at least as much to the New England economy as lumber and whale product exports, and possibly even as much as livestock and meat exports. The only export that contributed more was fish, which in turn was exceeded by the (nonhuman) carrying trade. Looking at it that way, slave trading was more important to the New England economy than previously thought, not only in Rhode Island, where it was quite significant, but to the New England economy as a whole.[23]

The voyage of the *Hare* also sheds light on the face-to-face workings of Atlantic trade. It is easy to get the impression from the literature that the commercial connections undergirding the Atlantic World ran smoothly and efficiently. This tendency is most visible in the familiar textbook graphs, charts, and maps depicting ever-increasing numbers of Africans transported across the Atlantic over the eighteenth century, but it also comes across in descriptions of the far-flung, complex mercantile networks that orchestrated the trade. Few historians make this argument explicitly, but to the extent that we stress the connective qualities of the Atlantic, we risk overlooking important complicating factors. Researchers in the field frequently encounter frayed connections in otherwise smooth-running transoceanic networks. All of this highlights a central tension in the Atlantic World: commercial networks that were efficient for their time were simultaneously riddled with seemingly inefficient disjunctures. The transatlantic slave trade is a case in point. Merchants found it difficult to get good information on markets, both in Africa and in the Americas. Mistrust between buyers and sellers on the African coast made the extension of credit from Europe to America to the African interior a challenge. Ultimately these problems would find a solution, though one rooted in violence. The slave trade was also complicated significantly by the fact that the commodities in play were humans, and unwilling humans at that. By examining the connections between the three regions central to this study—New England, Sierra Leone, and South Carolina—our account of the voyage of the *Hare* provides a basis for commentary on these and other incongruities of the Atlantic World.

Tracing the *Hare* as it knit together three disparate locations along the Atlantic rim requires some familiarity with regional languages, place names, and ethnonyms. Some of these entail a certain level of controversy or dispute, which in most instances is addressed within the text or footnotes. For readers unfamiliar with these terms, a glossary of geographic, linguistic, and ethnological terms may be found in appendix 1. One particularly confusing term is "Upper Guinea," which has already appeared here and is worth addressing in detail. Historians of the slave trade have customarily divided the slave-trading portions of the African coast into seven or eight different "embarkation regions." These regional designations originated among slave traders and later received a certain official sanction in historical circles, figuring prominently in works like Philip Curtin's seminal *The Atlantic Slave Trade: A Census* (1969) and TSTD2.[24] While useful, several things must be kept in mind when invoking the designations. The most important is a recognition that these are largely commercial and nautical terms—Windward Coast, Gold Coast, Slave Coast, Bight of Benin, and Bight of Biafra—which make the most sense on shipping charts. The boundaries of these regions bore no relation to the manner in which Africans organized themselves politically, economically, culturally, or linguistically. "Sierra Leone" was a name given by the Portuguese to a mountainous peninsula that was easily visible from the sea, but the indigenous people did not identify themselves as "Sierra Leonean." In fact, a single embarkation region might contain multiple polities, languages, and identities; indeed, trade routes channeling captives to the coast frequently extended hundreds of miles inland. Coastal designations, therefore, often imply a greater degree of unity and integration than was really the case.

At the same time, the opposite is true: the act of drawing a coastal boundary can imply an unwarranted measure of difference and understate the level of integration. This tendency has informed numerous older discussions of the African cultures in the Americas, including the Creolization thesis, with many works portraying Africa as a babel of language, culture, and religion. This led many historians to view Africans in the New World in similar terms: fragmented and unable to communicate with each other. This view was compounded by the fact that Africans in the New World had been removed from all things familiar. More recent studies have discerned a greater integration both within and among the embarkation regions. This change in perspective has been most significant for the region where the *Hare* captives embarked. Though it still appears in TSTD2 and most of the literature as "Sierra Leone," if the goal is to find out who the *Hare* captives were in cultural and linguistic terms, it makes more sense to consider Senegambia, Sierra Leone, and the Windward Coast together as either "Greater Senegambia," "Western Africa," or the term that will be used here, "Upper Guinea." Although historians differ on the precise boundaries, most agree that the region shared a common history and enjoyed a greater cultural and linguistic integrity than the coastal designations or later colonial partitions would imply.[25]

"Mande" is another term requiring clarification. Not to be confused with Mende, which is the name for an ethnic group and a language of modern

Sierra Leone, Mande is the name for a large subset of the Niger-Congo language family that covers much of Western Africa. The Mande languages are spoken widely and include Mandinka, Susu, Koranko, Kono, Dyula, Yalunka, Mende, Vai, Loko, and Soninke, with some so close as to be mutually intelligible. Mande, however, is not a language itself. Not all residents of Upper Guinea speak Mande languages. Most Upper Guinean speakers of non-Mande languages (referred to hereafter as "non-Mande speakers") live near the coast and speak one of the Atlantic languages, including Wolof, Fulfulde, Serer, Nalu, Banyun, Diola, Limba, Gola, Papel, Balanta, Baga, Bullom, and Temne. There is, however, some justification for speaking of a Mande culture. Mandinka was the language of Mali, a vast empire that encompassed much of the region during the fourteenth century. Though it did not always displace local cultures, it exerted a varying influence upon them, a process sometimes called "Mandingization." The implications of this for the *Hare* captives will be explored in detail in chapter 4.[26]

The book follows a chronological and geographic organization. Chapters 1 and 2 center on Rhode Island and examine the organization of the *Hare*'s voyage. Their goal is to analyze the place of the slave trade in the Rhode Island and New England economies. Chapters 3 and 4 shift to the Upper Guinea coast and detail the *Hare*'s activities there. Their principal task is to pinpoint the locations where the *Hare* purchased its captives, and they retrace the captives' footsteps back up the routes that carried them to the coast in order to shed light on what the captives' lives were like before they encountered Captain Godfrey. The Middle Passage and the *Hare*'s stop at Barbados are the focus of chapter 5. The sale and dispersal of the captives in South Carolina are the subjects of chapters 6–8. By tracing the *Hare* captives to specific slaveholdings, at its core an exercise in historical geography, this book tries to address questions relating to African cultures and identities in the eighteenth-century Low Country.

Admittedly, there are problems with using a slaving voyage to explore African lives in colonial America. It can be argued that doing so places Europeans (or white North Americans) at the center of a story that should focus on Africans. Moreover, it creates a situation in which only the Europeans emerge as individuals, while the *Hare* captives themselves appear at most as a group or a cohort, lacking individuality or agency. It is difficult to rebut those criticisms, except to point out that much of what we know of slavery comes from documents created by the non-enslaved. As far as agency is concerned, this book happens to center upon a moment when the captives' ability to influence their own fates, if perhaps not entirely absent, was at its ebb.

To suggest otherwise would be to trivialize the nature of their captivity. It is of course possible to imagine alternative ways of framing the *Hare* captives' experiences—for example, by starting the narrative in Africa rather than in Rhode Island. Another strategy would be to push the sources a bit farther in order to view events from the perspective of the captives. However, while this book does present events in that way occasionally, much of the material is presented in chronological narrative form. None of this is to suggest that the study of the diaspora can be accomplished solely through European sources, as several recent oral histories and ethnographies have demonstrated.[27] Indeed, certain truths can only be accessed through feats of imagination, as in the fiction of Caryl Phillips, Barry Unsworth, Maryse Condé, and especially Lawrence Hill, whose 2007 novel *Book of Negroes* traces a path very similar to the one here.[28] A key difference between that book and this one can be found in its U.S. title: *Someone Knows My Name*. The *Hare* captives had names, of course, but we do not know them.

CHAPTER ONE

The Port

There was nothing remarkable about the vessel moored at Malbone's Wharf in late June 1754. A single-masted sloop of about fifty feet in length, the *Hare* was just one of dozens of shallops, schooners, brigs, and three-masted square-riggers lining the quayside at Newport, Rhode Island, that summer. The *Hare*'s master, a forty-eight-year-old veteran of the sea named Caleb Godfrey, had been hired only a few weeks earlier. He now busied himself supervising the lading of casks, hogsheads, barrels, and kegs of all sizes and inspecting the work of the various sailmakers, carpenters, and riggers who serviced his ship, all while readying his paperwork for the king's customs officials. That task involved listing each item in the outbound cargo, recording the markings, contents, and quantity of the barrels and containers, the names of the shippers, and the names of the consignees, as well as providing a declaration of the ship's tonnage and destination and attesting that the owners were British subjects. As he did these things, Godfrey assembled a crew, a chore he completed just before the end of the month.[1]

Godfrey's employers, the brothers Samuel and William Vernon, lived only blocks away and probably visited their vessel regularly. At this moment, they had more than the usual incentive to check on the progress of Godfrey's preparations. Slaving voyages like the one the *Hare* was about to undertake were high-risk, high-reward enterprises. The better the preparation, the better the chances for success. At the beginning of the month, with things apparently coming along satisfactorily, they wrote to Thomlinson, Trecothick, and Company in London, asking to purchase insurance for the voyage. "Capt Godfrey is an experienced comander on the [African] Coast," they informed their correspondents, hoping that bit of information might keep their insurance charges to a minimum. The Vernons had been involved in slaving voyages before, but now, with business picking up after a four-year recession, they were plunging into the African trade with the same vigor they previously expended on privateering and West Indian ventures. This

14

was the third slave ship in which they were concerned and their second since the end of King George's War in 1748. In the latter voyage, however, they had been only investors and had not overseen matters. In charge of the entire operation this time, they probably devoted more attention to the *Hare* than to their previous ventures. If this voyage went well, there would be others.[2]

By the middle of the eighteenth century, people like Godfrey and the Vernons had made Newport into the slave-trading capital of British America. No other colonial port on the North American mainland or in the Caribbean outfitted as many slaving voyages as Newport. Between 1700 and 1775, more slave ships sailed from Rhode Island (most often Newport) than from all other mainland colonies combined, with more than three times as many departures as second-ranked Boston. Newport's dominance of North American slaving was not inevitable. It possessed no significant advantages over any of the other colonial ports. The town entered the slave trade early in the century and became the leading North American slave-trading port because it served as a gathering point for the commodities and for the people necessary to carry on the trade. By midcentury, no other place in British America possessed the necessary experience and goods for the trade in captives. Newport's rum distilleries produced a product in demand on the African coast. The town also possessed a large population of maritime tradesmen, experienced merchants with connections in Africa and the Caribbean and well-tuned information networks, a large and rotating pool of ordinary seamen, and—perhaps most important—a large number of shipmasters and ships' officers who knew how to operate on the African coast. By 1754, the slave-trading infrastructure was firmly established and self-perpetuating.[3] Slave trading was not Newport's primary economic activity, but it was so deeply entwined with the town's overall economy that a sudden halt to it would have affected the entire region.

The town of Newport is situated in a sheltered notch on the southwestern shore of Aquidneck Island. With a population of only 6,753 in 1755, this diminutive metropolis was the fifth-largest port in North America. Stretching for about a mile on a north–south axis, Thames Street was the principal thoroughfare, "so straight," one traveler described it, "that standing at one end of it you may see to the other."[4] More than four dozen wharves of all sizes and shapes jutted from Thames Street into the harbor like the teeth of a comb. "Merchants," wrote a visitor, "can load and unload their vessels at their own doors."[5] Toward the north end lay the town's biggest dock, the Long Wharf, eight hundred feet long, which ran out to a spit of land known as "the Point" to form an enclosed pool where smaller vessels could

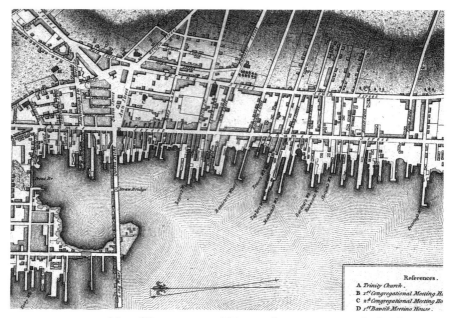

FIGURE I.I. *Map of Newport, 1777. This map shows Newport at the height of its prosperity as British North America's leading slave-trading port and fifth-largest port overall. To the left is the Long Wharf, which runs out to the Point. The triangular plaza across from the Long Wharf is the Parade, the site of the legislature and several coffee houses. (Library of Congress)*

find shelter from winter storms. Warehouses, chandlers, and retail shops crowded the quayside and even lined the docks. In 1761, Newport resident Ezra Stiles counted 439 warehouses and estimated the port's total wharfage at 177,791 feet, or 33 miles.[6]

Thames Street opposite the docks featured a mixture of commercial and residential buildings. Toward the southern end, or "court end of town," stood a row of mansions owned by the upper stratum of merchants.[7] There were also two public market houses, one at the corner of Thames and King Streets right beside the *Hare*'s berth at Malbone's Wharf, the other on the quayside between Tillinghast's and Carr's Wharves.[8] Sloping uphill from the docks was the rest of the town, a collection of one- and two-story clapboard buildings with broad, non-gabled sides fronting the streets. Amid these were several notable public buildings. The State House, a three-story Georgian brick structure with a clock in the pediment and topped by a hexagonal cupola, stood at the head of a square known as "the Parade," opposite the Long Wharf. Farther uphill stood the Redwood Library, a Palladian structure

FIGURE 1.2. *View of Newport, ca. 1730. This image shows
Newport just as the transatlantic slave trade was emerging as a
major economic pursuit. (Yale University Art Museum)*

recently built by Newport merchant and sometime slave trader Abraham
Redwood. One block off the waterfront sat the elegant Trinity Anglican
Church, its steeple visible from far out on Narragansett Bay. Toward the
northern end of town just off Farewell Street sat a large wooden building
that served as the meetinghouse for the town's large Quaker population.
Several Baptist, Seventh Day Baptist, and Congregational meetinghouses
were scattered throughout, a testament to Rhode Island's history of religious
toleration. One of North America's most vibrant Jewish communities still
worshipped in private residences, but in just a few years it would erect the
classically inspired Touro Synagogue, the first on the continent, a few blocks
uphill from the harbor.

Newport—and for that matter, Rhode Island—was dominated by a small
group of wealthy merchants, who, in addition to their economic power,
wielded great political power. The governor—who was elected, rather than
appointed, according to the 1663 charter—was usually a Newporter who
catered to mercantile needs. In 1754, the town's elite families—the Wan-
tons, Champlins, Tillinghasts, Malbones, Taylors, Redwoods, Gardners, and
Vernons—were on the verge of a long-term increase in their share of the
town's wealth. In 1760, Newport's thirty-three highest taxpayers (who made
up the top 3.4 percent and included the Vernons) paid 27 percent of the taxes;

by 1775, the top thirty-three paid 34 percent of the taxes. Eight of the top ten payers in 1772 owned slave-trading vessels.[9] The rich were about to become richer, and slaving voyages like the *Hare*'s would play no small part in that.

In and among the town's houses and places of worship was working Newport. The town bustled with practitioners of every maritime-related occupation: seamen, longshoremen, coopers, caulkers, glaziers, braziers, sailmakers, riggers, and porters. In 1754 there were a dozen or so rum distilleries scattered about, some on Thames Street near the dockside, others sandwiched between residences on side streets. Distilleries employed many people in substantial buildings that contained multiple rooms for the still, cisterns, storage of molasses, wood fuel, and the finished product. On the outskirts of town were several ropewalks, or cordage manufactories. These were located away from the dense area of settlement, both because they required a great deal of space—the ropewalks were narrow strips of land over seven hundred feet long and sheltered by a long roof—and because the distance reduced the risk to the surrounding community, should fire break out. Beyond the ropewalks stood a number of small farms. Though the soil could not support an export-oriented cash-crop economy, it did manage to supply the town with corn, rye, oats, peas, hemp, flax, fruit, and meat. Also on the road out of town was an almshouse, built in 1723 when Newport began its rise to commercial center with a growing population of transients, widows, and disabled sailors. A second "workhouse" was built nearby during the 1750s. There, under the overseers of the poor, Newport's indigent were set to work at a variety of menial tasks to offset the cost of their maintenance.[10]

A significant portion of Newport's workforce was enslaved. At the time of the *Hare*'s voyage, almost one in five residents was black, although not all black residents were enslaved. Many had arrived in small numbers aboard Newport's African and West Indian vessels, but during the 1750s, about one thousand captives arrived in Rhode Island on ten slave ships directly from Africa. Most worked on farms and in workshops elsewhere in Rhode Island and New England, but some remained in town. Newport's slaves worked in every possible occupation, skilled and unskilled, maritime and shoreside. Half of the town's slaveholders owned a single bondperson; two-thirds owned two or fewer. Ownership of ten or more slaves was confined to a wealthy few who probably distributed them over multiple residences and businesses.[11] Although they worked alongside whites, Newport's slaves lived in the town's marginal spaces, in garrets, cellars, and outbuildings. Because so few slave owners held more than one bondperson, enslaved couples were often forced to reside apart. Primus, a slave belonging to the merchant

Thomas Cranston, was probably typical in this respect, residing at the Cranston house and working at his master's distillery. Primus's wife, whose name is unrecorded, was a slave of Evan Malbone's; she lived in his garret. We know about them because early one morning in 1772, Primus attempted to kill his wife for refusing to lend him money. Hearing calls of "murder and fire," Malbone found part of the house ablaze and quickly put it out. He then ran upstairs to discover Primus in the process of strangling his wife. Primus fled, and Malbone ran to tell Cranston. The two men soon discovered that Primus had set fire to Cranston's nearby still-house. Forcing open the door, they found that he had committed suicide by drowning himself in one of the vats. The episode illustrates the close proximity of blacks to whites in Newport, as well as the peripheral, hiding-in-plain-sight existence of most slaves. We would never know about Primus if he had not died in such a newsworthy fashion.[12]

With a well-protected, deep-water harbor, it would be easy to suppose that Newport had always been a major maritime trading center, but it had not. Newport owed its position as a leading slave-trading port to a confluence of historic and economic circumstances. British policy makers of the era, guided by a set of ideas now known as "mercantilism," imagined the world as a place of struggle among the major military and economic powers. In the first half of the seventeenth century, policy makers fixated on the accumulation of specie to raise, equip, and pay the armies that projected the realm's power and defended it against potential enemies. By the early eighteenth century, full employment had supplanted simple accumulation of gold and silver as the primary policy objective. They sought to accomplish this goal by maintaining a favorable balance of trade, an objective that demanded a state sell commodities to its rivals while minimizing its own purchases from the same rivals.[13]

Colonies were central to the economic well-being of the major powers. The ideal colony possessed several attributes: it produced commodities that were in demand in the mother country (also known as the "metropolis") and its rivals, it supplied commodities that could not be produced at home and therefore did not compete with the metropolis, and it did not trade with rival powers or colonies on its own. These policies were articulated in the Navigation Acts, which had governed overseas trade since the 1650s. Under them, certain "enumerated" goods could be shipped only to Britain, where they would be either consumed or re-exported to continental rivals. At the same time, no foreign goods could be shipped directly to the British colonies— they needed to go through Britain for re-export to the colonies. Finally, all colonial commerce was reserved for British ships, which included British North American ships.

At first glance, these policies would appear to hamper economic development. Their authors envisioned the colonies as producers of agricultural and raw goods. They believed it was in the British interest to prevent the growth of colonial industries that might compete with the mother country in order to preserve an exclusive market for British manufactures. The most valuable British colonies, the Caribbean islands, were essentially plantations writ large, churning out sugar, molasses, coffee, and indigo for consumption in Britain and for re-export. As plantation colonies, the Chesapeake and Lower South functioned similarly, which led to extensive growth but little intensive development. The Middle Colonies combined the production of staples, mostly grains, with a nascent mercantile and manufacturing sector. But New England, with its poor soil and short growing season, did not conform to the ideal. New England produced commodities, of which fish and lumber were the most important, but the New England colonies were problematic in the calculus of empire. Much of what they produced could be had in Britain, minus the shipping costs.[14]

New England eventually found its economic niche within the British imperial system. New Englanders could turn a profit by building ships and—even more profitable—by carrying other colonies' produce. Obeying the merchant's timeless imperative to buy low and sell high, New Englanders swapped whatever lumber and fish they could for Portuguese wines, Carolina rice and naval stores, Pennsylvania wheat, and, most important, West Indian sugar and molasses. The latter product they distilled into rum, which they both consumed and used as an article of commerce. Exchanging these commodities in markets around the Atlantic basin, New Englanders were able to satisfy their demand for British manufactures.[15] These "baubles of Britain," the buckles, broadcloth, china, and innumerable other articles shipped over from the mother country, became tokens of cultivation and refinement.[16] Thus, lacking a marketable agricultural staple of their own, New Englanders became the consummate trading people. And if circumventing the Navigation Acts became necessary to maximize profits, Yankee traders viewed it as entirely excusable and perhaps even beneficial in the long run.

Newport labored under the same economic debilities as the rest of New England, but with the added hindrance of being hemmed in by Boston. Newport's none-too-fertile agricultural hinterland was small to begin with, but the encroachment of Boston's wealthier merchants made it even smaller.

Well into the eighteenth century, Newport merchants found themselves unable to attract direct shipments from Britain. They were forced to purchase goods, with the inevitable markup, from their rivals in the Bay Colony. Overshadowed by Boston, Newporters had to work harder to earn credits and to attract direct trade.[17]

Smuggling was one way to gain advantage. All New Englanders evaded the Navigation Acts, but Rhode Islanders were masters of the art. The primary object of most smuggling was molasses, which New Englanders bought in the French Caribbean. In 1733, Parliament, at the behest of British West Indian planters, amended the Navigation Acts by passing the Molasses Act, which specifically sought to drive out non-British molasses by imposing a prohibitive sixpence per gallon duty. The new legislation did little to stop the importation of contraband molasses. New Englanders continued to import the cheaper French product through bribes to customs officials and a sizable repertoire of evasive ploys. In 1739, the governor of Bermuda informed the Board of Trade that there was an "open trade" between Rhode Island and Martinique and charged that the customs officers at Newport regularly disregarded the violations. In 1750, the Board of Trade heard testimony alleging that Yankee skippers routinely filed false papers in the British West Indies declaring they were bound for Boston with rum, and then sailed with empty casks to the Dutch island of St. Eustatius, a notorious rendezvous point for illicit trade. There they filled the casks with foreign rum and molasses and returned to the mainland. Another scheme involved clearing customs in Newport when taking lumber to the West Indies; once there, however, the vessels demanded payment in specie, rather than exchanging the lumber for outbound cargo. They then ran to St. Eustatius and exchanged the specie for contraband. Another ruse involved running staves, lumber, and other produce to Barbados and trading them for specie. Rhode Islanders would then buy empty barrels, fill them with water, and obtain customs papers under the pretense that the casks were filled with rum. They would then sail to St. Eustatius, purchase rum and molasses, and land their cargoes in Newport, using the papers obtained at Barbados.[18]

Alongside the often-illegitimate West Indian trade, the "Guinea trade" became integral to the Rhode Island economy. Its essential function was to earn credits with British merchants that could be used to finance importations of manufactured goods. Although the Caribbean molasses and other nonhuman-carrying trades were the most important fields of New England commerce, the slave trade was much more important to the regional economy than some recent historians have suggested.[19] Statistics for the years

1768–72, the most complete of surviving data, illustrate the point. If we suppose that the captives carried on New England ships sold at an average price of twenty-five to thirty-five pounds sterling, they would have grossed between sixty thousand and eighty-nine thousand pounds sterling annually for their sellers (see table 1 in appendix 3).[20] However, as with the statistics for the other export commodities, this figure does not take into account such costs as shipping, insurance, interest, physical plant, trade goods, and crew wages. Nor do we have reliable statistics on earnings from the carrying trade, which surely outstripped the slave trade and export trades by a wide margin, perhaps amounting to 62 percent of all payments. Lastly, the years 1768–72 represented a higher-than-average period in the colonial-era slave trade. In some previous years, no New England ships sailed for Africa. Nevertheless, it is difficult to argue, at least for the late colonial period, that the slave trade was insignificant to the New England economy, because its gross earnings were at least as valuable as those of lumber and whale products and may have rivaled those of livestock and meat products.[21] In Rhode Island, a colony that accounted for over two-thirds of New England slave voyages with a population less than one-sixth that of Massachusetts, the slave trade was disproportionately significant. This is not to say that Newport was a single-commodity port—it clearly was not. The West Indian and other trades were responsible for more clearances and probably generated more profits, but slave trading was integral to the local economy. It is no accident that in 1754, when the Vernon brothers were outfitting the *Hare*, they were able to locate a captain, officers, vessel, and trade goods within a mile's radius of Newport.[22]

BY THE MIDDLE OF THE eighteenth century, Newport's economy had reached maturity. In peacetime, the town's merchants turned great profits by running goods produced elsewhere (as well as captive laborers) around the Atlantic rim, ignoring all inconvenient restrictions. In times of war, they outfitted privateers and plundered enemy (and sometimes friendly) ships. Godfrey Malbone, a native of Virginia, exemplified the pattern. Arriving in the colony in the early part of the century, he smuggled, raided, and traded his way to wealth. The country house he built outside of town was Newport's most opulent, a three-story mansion of stone made to look like marble. Malbone and the other merchants of Newport gathered in the town's coffee houses, clearing houses for all things mercantile, where they exchanged information on commodities, politics, world events, and shipping. In Newport, several coffee houses lined the Parade, while another, the White Horse, stood a block north on Marlborough Street. By the mid-eighteenth century, however, more formal institutions began to supersede the coffee house as gathering spots for men of commerce. The Philosophical Club was one of them. One visitor to the club was surprised to find that "no matters of philosophy were brought upon the carpet," the members instead discussing "privateering and building of vessels." And unlike a public tavern or coffee house, the more exclusive Philosophical Club was a place where the town's aristocracy could speak freely about the "raggamuffin company of cowherds and other such trash," a group that made up a majority of the population.[23]

In 1754, Samuel and William Vernon, third-generation Rhode Islanders, were Newport's most promising up-and-coming entrepreneurs. Their paternal grandfather, Daniel Vernon, had been a prosperous merchant in London before coming to the colony sometime before 1670. Newport antiquarians would later suggest that his migration was brought about by a business failure, perhaps connected in some way with the Great Fire of London in 1666. Daniel Vernon married Ann Dyre, a descendant of Anne Hutchinson. Their son Samuel, the brothers' father, was a silversmith by trade; but he was politically ambitious and eventually named judge on the Rhode Island Superior Court of Judicature. His son, Samuel Jr., was born in 1711. Virtually nothing is known of Samuel's early life, and a relative dearth of correspondence means that we know little of his later life as well. Brother William was born in 1719.[24] Samuel and William had two more brothers in addition to four sisters; one brother, Thomas, served as register of the Court of Vice Admiralty in Newport and became a Loyalist during the American Revolution.[25] Little of the Vernons' personality comes out in surviving correspondence. After 1755, both were members of Ezra Stiles's Second Congregationalist Church, and judging by the frequency with which Stiles dined with them, they were quite active members. Both were slaveholders, each with five bondpeople in 1774. And they, like most merchants, cultivated a reputation for cosmopolitan gentlemanliness. William would later purchase one of Newport's finest mansions, which he would decorate with Italianate frescoes. He also participated in public scientific experiments, such as an effort by Stiles, a future president of Yale University, to chart the transit of Venus in 1769. Through endeavors like these William presented himself to the world as a man of taste and learning.[26]

It is uncertain exactly how and when the Vernons got their start in business. Their earliest known venture was a 1737 slaving voyage, but it is likely that other voyages to the Caribbean preceded it. African voyages were expensive and risky and required a great deal more planning than a simple West Indian run, making it unlikely the brothers would undertake an African voyage without having completed Caribbean runs. The brothers also backed a voyage to the Caribbean and Britain in 1738. After the outbreak of war in 1739, however, the Vernons turned to privateering. In 1744, they partnered with Godfrey Malbone in the raider *Duke of Marlborough*. In 1746, they backed the privateer *Vernon Galley*. Both ventures wound up in litigation. At one point, with one of the *Vernon Galley*'s prizes the subject of a legal dispute in South Carolina, William Vernon lamented that "thefes and Robbers" on the court were preventing them from being "able to come at our own Right."[27] But William did more in South Carolina than handle the privateer. It was on that same trip that he discovered South Carolina's commercial potential, something he and his brother would exploit for many years to come. He took advantage of his time there to establish a relationship with Charles Town merchant Gabriel Manigault, which lasted for ten years. He then instructed Samuel to send a second vessel loaded with osnaburg cloth, used in slave clothing, to trade for rice and turpentine. In subsequent years, they shipped products ranging from potatoes to British manufactured goods to rum. It was one of their more reliable branches of trade.[28]

When King George's War ended in 1748, the Vernons turned from privateering back to commerce. Despite the litigation spawned by their privateering ventures, they seem to have done well, using the proceeds to finance a series of trading voyages to all parts of the Atlantic. It was in these years that they developed a relationship with Michael Bland's London trading house. In 1753 they invested in a slaving voyage by the sloop *Sierra Leone*, which was owned by Abraham Redwood. But by far the bulk of their trade was with the West Indies, as it was for most Newport merchants. A majority of the Vernons' vessels ran down to the islands, where they exchanged local produce for sugar and molasses. The brig *Mary*, which sailed for Antigua in 1757, carried a typical assortment of outbound cargo, consisting of boards, planks, flour, ship bread, tobacco, pork, soap, and cheese. The *Mary* would certainly have taken on sugar and molasses and returned to Newport, had it not been intercepted by a French privateer.[29] Although no customs records survive for the 1750s, those from 1768–72, a time when the Vernons may actually have been scaling back on their activities, reveal some fifteen Vernon-owned vessels (about three per year) were entered at Newport. All of the ships had come from the Caribbean, nine from Jamaica and three each from Surinam and Hispaniola. The trade in logwood at the Bay of Honduras constituted a second, if relatively minor, branch of the Vernons' Caribbean enterprise.[30]

Although most of the Vernons' Caribbean dealings seem to have been with the British islands, the brothers, like most New Englanders, were by no means above smuggling goods into and out of the ports of imperial rivals. William Vernon once opined that the laws restricting trade were "oppressive and unjust, and therefore to evade them is no crime."[31] The Vernons actually inserted smuggling instructions into the written orders to one of their captains. "When you come on [the Rhode Island] Coast," they told Nathaniel Hammond, "avoid speaking with any Vessil, and go in at the East Side of the Island," which was to say on the opposite side from Newport and well outside the gaze of the customs officers. "Let us know of your Arrival as soon as possible," they instructed, "and where you intend to anchor . . . send a man on shore to us, charge him not to let any one see him."[32]

The coastwise trade in North America was another, if somewhat less important, endeavor for the Vernons. On more than one occasion the Vernons purchased sugar from Philadelphia, which boasted several refineries during the colonial period. On another occasion the brothers shipped rum there with instructions to their correspondent to store the goods until prices rose. And though direct evidence is lacking, they almost certainly purchased grain there for transshipment to Europe and the Caribbean. But more important than Philadelphia for the Vernons was South Carolina, where they had been dealing with Gabriel Manigault since 1745.[33]

Europe was another leg in the Vernons' trading enterprise, but it was less busy than the others. For several of the commodities they handled, like rice, sugar, coffee, logwood, and tar, Europe was the principal market. They exchanged these goods for silks, woolens, and other textiles, tools, and all types of manufactured items. Most of the Vernons' European trade went to Britain, where it was handled by one of two London houses, Thomlinson, Trecothick, and Company or Michael Bland. The Vernons had accounts with both of these houses, which enabled them to draw bills of exchange, financial instruments essential to their business. Both houses also underwrote insurance policies on the Vernons' vessels and cargoes; not until after the American Revolution did Newport merchants regularly insure their own shipping.[34] The Vernons also explored trading flaxseed and rum to Ireland for the explicit purpose of earning pounds sterling, but whether they ever did so is unclear. In this branch of trade, however, they appear to have relied primarily on ships owned by other, probably British, merchants. Indeed, few Newport merchants used their own vessels to trade with Great Britain. During the entire decade of the 1750s, only two Newport ships per year sailed to Britain, none of them, it appears, owned by the Vernons.[35]

London was not the only European port with which the Vernons dealt. Lisbon was an important market for New England fish. After 1730, when

Parliament permitted direct shipment of rice from the colonies to Europe south of Cape Finisterre, "Carolina gold" became an important export, which the brothers exchanged for wine and other goods. Like most British subjects, the Vernons did business with one of the many British firms in Lisbon, dealings which were made possible by the Methuen Treaty of 1703.[36] In addition to the Portuguese trade, they sold coffee in Amsterdam, received bills of exchange drawn on Hamburg, and in 1770 attempted to swap rice, sugar, and ginger in Gothenburg, Sweden, for canvas, rope, and untaxed, contraband tea.[37]

The Vernons, like all merchants involved in transatlantic commerce, confronted a common set of problems revolving around information and risk. The tremendous distances involved and the communications technology of the era placed limits on what people like the Vernons could do to manage their affairs. They required a network of correspondents and agents on whom they could depend to act intelligently and in their economic interests. These contacts made up the mercantile infrastructure that allowed for the enslavement, removal, and sale of millions of captive Africans in the Americas. These contacts also enabled the delivery of British manufactures to North American consumers. At the heart of the matter lay the problems of information and trust. No concern could operate without reliable agents in key ports or good intelligence on market conditions. To a great extent, these two things were closely related, in that they came together in the business correspondent and the shipmaster. These two figures acted as the eyes, ears, and mind of merchants like the Vernons and were indispensable to their activities.

The Vernons took full advantage of their extensive network of correspondents to receive the latest news, leveraging information with information. One season, they arranged to have each of their several ships on the African coast sail for Barbados, where they would find further instructions directing them to the best New World markets. Barbados made an ideal dispatch point because in sailing ship terms it lay roughly midway between Rhode Island and West Africa. Barbados also lay to windward of the rest of the Caribbean, which allowed ships stopping there to sail virtually anywhere with ease. And with vessels plying the waters between Newport and the Caribbean on a near-continual basis, the Vernons could receive and send the latest intelligence and use it to redirect their ships. But there were problems with this sort of information, too. In theory, a merchant always worked in the interest of his correspondent. In practice, merchants had many correspondents, some more important than others. This could lead to conflicts of interest and the withholding of valuable information. Barbados, which was used by many merchants as a collection point, had a reputation in some quarters as a center of bad intelligence. As one shipper complained, "At Bdoes they have an abominable practice of some times keeping up Letters for Guinea ships." He went on to recommend sending multiple copies of all letters, "one to a Mercht & another to a Friend, [and another to] an Attorney, on whom [you] can depend."[38]

Experienced, reliable ship captains were every bit as essential to the Vernons' commercial activities as trustworthy correspondents. Merchants not only relied on their captains' maritime skills, but also depended on them to exercise good judgment and act in their interests. Occasionally, shipowners asked their captains to find dependable merchants in distant ports. "Get the best information you possibly can," the brothers told Nathaniel Hammond, "[on] what house is the most likly to do your business the best, and give you the quickest dispatch, when you have determined what Merchant to addres your self too, deliver him our Letter."[39] The Vernons' relationships with their shipmasters varied. Some, such as Thomas Teakle Taylor, seem to have been considered near equals. Beginning simply as a shipmaster in the employ of the Vernons and other Newport merchants, Taylor progressed to the rank of investor, partnering with the Vernons on at least four occasions.[40] Most other captains remained employees, but for certain favored shipmasters, the brothers provided steady employment. Drawing repeatedly from the same pool of experienced, reliable shipmasters contributed to the effectiveness of their mercantile infrastructure. John Duncan made six trips to Africa for the Vernons, and three others made at least three. Other veterans of the African trade also made runs to the Caribbean, which may have helped the Vernons retain their services in between slaving voyages. Captain Peter Dordin, for example, made at least seven voyages for them in the coastwise, Caribbean, and Honduran trade, along with two trips to the Gold Coast.

NO IMAGE OF THE *Hare* survives and it left little trace in official records, but it is possible to put together a basic sketch.[41] One thing is certain: the *Hare* was a sloop. Newspaper announcements and merchant records describe it as such with perfect consistency. The term "sloop," as applied to merchant shipping in the eighteenth century, generally meant a small, single-masted vessel. Sloops were fore-and-aft rigged, with their mainsail running lengthwise, rather than across the beam, as a square-rigged sail would. Rhode Island merchants frequently employed single-masted sloops, and many were built in the colony. Deeply concerned in the coastal and West Indian trades, Rhode Islanders wanted fast vessels that could easily navigate the many islands and hazards of Narragansett Bay, the Carolina coast, and the Caribbean. Sloops fit the bill. The fore-and-aft rig allowed the sloop to sail in unfavorable winds (or "close to the wind"), while the small size, sternward incline of the mast, and sleek lines allowed it to travel faster than larger ships. Oceangoing sloops often added a square topsail, which allowed them to sail with great speed with a stern breeze, or "before the wind." The combination of a fore-and-aft mainsail and a square topsail would have allowed the *Hare* to make headway in different types of winds, and it is therefore likely that it carried both.[42]

The same characteristics that made the sloop a good choice for the coastal and Caribbean trades made it well suited to the slave trade, especially on the Upper Guinea coast. With many offshore sandbars and with a coastal estuary honeycombed by rivers, mangroves, and salt marshes, the area around Sierra Leone posed a challenge to larger vessels. Large ships generally had to anchor in the deep water of the Sierra Leone River and send out smaller boats to trade. The shallow draft of a sloop allowed it to enter small streams and estuaries, although even vessels like the *Hare* had to send out boats to reach more remote areas. The compact dimensions of the sloop also meant that it took less time to fill to capacity with slaves. The less time spent on the coast, the lower the mortality rate for captives and crew alike. Similarly, the ability of the sloop to sail swiftly translated into fewer captive deaths and greater profit for the owners.

Two other pieces of information about the *Hare* appear in contemporary documents. A deposition sworn out in 1759 describes the *Hare* as "of the Burthen of Sixty Tons or thereabouts."[43] This was small, though well within the established norms of the era. Those Rhode Island–based sloops that carried roughly the same number of captives as the *Hare* averaged about 88 tons burden, ranging from a low of 30 to a high of 128 tons.[44] A second piece of information emerges from a letter written by the owners to an insurance agent in London. In it we learn that the *Hare* was "double bottomed," which is to say that the hull had two layers of planking to protect against the worms and parasites found in tropical waters. These pests could cause severe damage to wooden vessels, causing leakage and necessitating repairs or even abandonment. The double bottom was valuable—the *Hare* was able to embark on a second African voyage a few months after returning in 1755 and was also fit to undertake two more tropical voyages later on.[45]

The other features of the *Hare* can only be conjectured based on descriptions of similar vessels. Sloops of comparable tonnage had decks measuring less than fifty feet, with the vessel's bow bringing the total length (not including bowsprit) to just less than sixty feet. They boasted a beam of something less than twenty feet and drew between seven and ten feet of water. In other words, the *Hare* was about the same length as one of today's smaller private yachts. At the stern would have been an elevated cabin, often with a rounded roof, that housed the captain's quarters. The mates' quarters would have been in this section of the ship as well. Most sloops were steered with a tiller, which would have projected upward from the rudder and over the roof of the stern cabin. There was probably no forecastle—sloops of this size generally did not have them—but there would have been a capstan in the bow to handle the anchor. The *Hare* probably carried armament of some sort, though it is impossible to know whether it was just a few light carriage guns on deck behind closeable gun ports, small but deadly swivel guns (mounted firearms of a caliber somewhere between a shotgun and a small cannon), or a combination of the two. In the unlikely event that the *Hare* mounted no guns at all, the crew would have carried a complement of small arms. Weapons were essential to preventing insurrection, maintaining control of the captives, and fending off attacks from land and sea. The *Hare* also carried a longboat of less than twenty feet in length, which would have been elevated on a cradle, crosswise and aft of the mast. The longboat may even have carried its own armaments, swivel guns, or small carriage guns. The yawl, a smaller craft, would have been nestled within the longboat.[46]

Belowdecks the *Hare* was likely very cramped, with a hold measuring ten feet in depth, possibly less. This is where the outbound cargo and stores were kept. Access was through a companionway, or ladder through an opening in the deck. A "platform" would have divided the hold horizontally into two separate spaces of less than five feet in height. On regular merchant ships the platform was toward the bow, but on sloops engaged in military or transport operations—and almost certainly slaving—an extended, center platform was installed to accommodate the extra bodies. Seamen would have stowed their gear and slept toward the bow. The ship's stove was also kept on the forward section of the platform. A smaller galley hatch allowed access from the deck.[47] A grate over the main hatch would have been the principal source of air for the captives, perhaps supplemented by a few small ports. Sloops appear in many of the maritime-themed images of the era. One of the more detailed surviving images shows a sloop in the West Indies trade. It likely bears a close resemblance to the *Hare*, along with numerous other New England sloops.[48]

FIGURE 1.3. *Sloop. This vessel probably resembled the* Hare *very closely. The term "sloop" signified a single-masted vessel with a fore-and-aft rigged mainsail, which was well suited to sailing "close to the wind." The* Hare *also likely carried a square topsail, which would have allowed it to perform well "before the wind." Generally small—the* Hare *was about fifty feet long—these vessels were built for speed and enjoyed the favor of many North American slave traders. (Courtesy of the American Antiquarian Society)*

THE HOLD OF THE *Hare* was filled with rum, the principal trade good used by Rhode Islanders on the African coast. European slave traders had access to a wide range of manufactured goods and, because of their metropolitan location, were able to receive and re-export Eastern goods like textiles and cowries. In contrast, North American traders had to furnish their own trade goods. Most North American exports, like fish, lumber, and grain, were not only bulky—they were produced in Africa and therefore not in demand. The exception was tobacco, which was in demand despite the fact that it, too, grew in Africa. It ranked a distant second as a trade good among New England slavers.

New England rum had a number of advantages as a trade good. It was popular enough on the African coast, although it was more popular in some areas than in others. A manufactured, value-added product, rum's value-to-weight ratio was higher than for most raw goods; it was not as bulky as most of the other commodities available to colonial traders. Some 22 percent of all available rum in Rhode Island (the overwhelming majority of which was distilled locally) was exported overseas, mostly to Africa. Africa thus provided a market for Rhode Island's distillers that, though insufficient to finance all of the colony's British imports, was nevertheless vital to the increasingly significant slave trade.[49]

Seven different merchants and distillers supplied rum to the *Hare*, and the Vernons appear to have purchased from them directly.[50] There is no evidence that the suppliers shared in the proceeds of the voyage as investors, though the Vernons and other Newport traders often did sell shares in voyages as a way of distributing risk. Rather, these suppliers were provisioners who undoubtedly profited by supplying a slave ship but belonged in the same category as the other merchants and artisans who sold goods and services to the *Hare*. Two of the seven rum suppliers came from the middle 50 percent of Newport property owners. Though that may seem to indicate that the slave trade functioned with the broad participation of Rhode Island's middle class, the evidence from the *Hare* suggests that the colony's elite were, in fact, the primary beneficiaries of the slave trade. Four of the six named suppliers, who together accounted for 79 percent of the rum carried on the *Hare*, ranked among the wealthiest fifth of Newport's taxpayers (who, as property owners, were wealthier than the population at large). But while most of the suppliers were comparatively well off, they were far from equal. The richest was more than eighteen times wealthier than the poorest and owned more than twice the property of the second wealthiest. So while middling Newporters were sometimes concerned in slaving voyages, their involvement with the *Hare* was limited to small-scale provisioning.[51]

Thomas Cranston delivered seventeen hogsheads of approximately one hundred gallons each to the *Hare*, more than any other provisioner. He was also the wealthiest supplier, with a tax assessment of eighteen pounds in 1760. Thirty-four years old at the time of the *Hare*'s voyage, he was the grandson of Samuel Cranston, a longtime governor and dominant figure in Rhode Island politics for the first quarter of the eighteenth century. A birthright Congregationalist, he gravitated toward the Anglican Church as his fortune grew, as did many of Newport's mercantile elite. He married Elizabeth Coggeshall, a member of one of Newport's oldest families, and was admitted a freeman in 1731. He learned the sailmaking trade as a young man, and at the age of twenty-one he was aboard a brig that survived a damaging gale on the way back from Surinam. A few years later, during King George's War, he served on a privateer. He eventually took command of one as master, seizing at least three prizes. By the mid-1740s, however, his career began to transcend the usual maritime activities, no doubt aided by his pedigree and connections. In 1746 he was elected to the Rhode Island legislature for the first time, a seat he would not relinquish for twenty-eight years. By 1748 he operated a distillery—a venture that demanded a level of capital investment well beyond the reach of most ordinary mariners—and began trading with Jamaica, Honduras, and the Netherlands. He is on record as investing in at least one slaving voyage, which delivered approximately 165 captives from the Gold Coast to South Carolina in 1765. As he prospered, he acquired two houses on Thames Street and, like nearly all wealthy Newporters, became a slave owner.[52]

The Vernons' rum accounts show that a John Thurston delivered eight barrels to the *Hare*, while a Jonathan Thurston delivered six. As many as five John and Jonathan Thurstons were active in Newport at the time.[53] The most likely provisioners with those names included a father and two sons, all named Jonathan or John, who began as ship captains and became merchants and distillers. The line between mariner, merchant, and distiller was often a fine one, and an individual could easily act in all three capacities, especially over the course of a long career. It is unknown which two John or Jonathan Thurstons supplied rum to the *Hare* in 1754, but we can still delineate three likely careers, which in some combination almost certainly related to the actual suppliers.

The earliest and most abundant references are to at least two mariners named Jonathan Thurston, one of whom—probably the father—was the brother of merchant Peleg Thurston. Bills of exchange drawn on Boston and registered in Newport show that a "Capt. Jona. Thurston" was operating out of Newport as early as 1731. In 1744 a Jonathan Thurston commanded the sloop *Defiance*, owned by Peleg Thurston, on a run down to Jamaica. That same year a Jonathan Thurston commanded a privateer, and the following year a person by that name served as quartermaster on the Vernons' and Godfrey Malbone's privateer, *Duke of Marlborough*. Following King George's War in 1749, a Jonathan Thurston skippered the eighty-five-ton brig *Unicorn* on a voyage to Jamaica. A 1753 notarial registry for a bill of exchange drawn on a merchant in Bath Town, North Carolina, indicates that a Jonathan Thurston—probably the father—undertook a voyage there for his brother, Peleg Thurston. Jonathan Sr. died in 1755, less than a year after the embarkation of the *Hare*. The Town of Newport inventoried his estate: at the time of his death, Thurston owned one male slave and £528 in personal property, and his debits exceeded his credits by about £670. Jonathan Jr. continued to sail out of Newport into the 1760s. In 1761 he rescued the crew of the distressed snow *Olive Branch* and delivered them safely to Charles Town, South Carolina.[54]

While some combination of the father-son, mariner-merchant Jonathan/ John Thurstons supplied the *Hare* with fourteen hogsheads of rum, it is impossible to know exactly who did. The most likely combination is Jonathan Thurston Sr., who was still alive when the *Hare* sailed, and his son John, who was bequeathed a still in his father's 1749 will. The only distiller named Thurston listed in the 1760 rate assessment was John, who owed £4.10. This was less than a quarter of the amount owed by Thomas Cranston but still enough to place him in the top quintile of Newport's taxpayers.[55]

Nathaniel Coggeshall, who supplied ten hogsheads, was descended from one of Newport's founding families. There were two Nathaniel Coggeshalls active at the time, a father and son. The elder was fifty-two years old in 1754 and worked as both a merchant and a distiller. His 1760 tax assessment was £4.15, once again falling into the top 20 percent of Newport taxpayers. Coggeshall was a deacon in the Second Congregational Church, the membership of which included the Vernons. In 1740, he was also among the Newport "gentlemen" who published a letter in a Boston newspaper warning the city's mercantile community that they would not accept any notes on the financier John Colman. The younger Coggeshall was twenty-five and married to the daughter of Thomas Cranston, the *Hare*'s wealthiest rum supplier. Of the two, it seems probable that it was the elder Nathaniel, the one listed as a merchant-distiller, who supplied rum to the *Hare*, rather than his son. Nathaniel Coggeshall Sr., moreover, had prior involvement in the Guinea trade, serving in 1749 as one of the backers of a voyage by the sloop *Fanny*, the outcome of which is unknown. Two years later and three years before the embarkation of the *Hare*, he was elected deputy to the Rhode Island General Assembly. At the time of his death in 1784, he owned two slaves, a man named Cato and a woman named Sarah.[56]

A person listed only as "Richardson" contributed four hogsheads. While several Richardsons operated as merchants in Newport during the time period, it is likely that the person in question was either Thomas Richardson Sr. or Jr. The elder Richardson, listed in various records as "Thomas Richardson, Esq.," was one of Newport's commercial pioneers and treasurer of Rhode Island at the time of the *Hare*'s departure. A native of New York who had worked as a merchant in Boston, Richardson came to Newport in 1712 at the age of thirty-two. Richardson was the first to try to break the hold of the Boston merchants on Newport by initiating direct trade with Britain. His efforts met with mixed results—Boston always overshadowed Newport—but he was able to dispatch vessels to Lisbon, Surinam, Jamaica, the Netherlands, New York, and North Carolina from his wharf on Thames

Street. Thomas Richardson Jr. was a shipowner and master. When he died in 1785, his insolvent estate included a large still worth three hundred fifty dollars and a smaller one worth twenty dollars. Either father or son could have supplied the *Hare*. Thomas Sr.'s account book continues up to 1754, the year the *Hare* sailed, although the book contains no mention of the Vernons for that year. Thomas Jr. was still sailing in the 1760s, and there is no mention of him as a distiller before then. In either case, the 1760 tax assessments for father and son place each squarely in the top quintile—so whoever supplied the rum, here is yet another path leading directly back to Newport's wealthiest residents.[57]

The remaining suppliers were not among Newport's elite and, consequently, left scant trace in the record. David Earl, who supplied five hogsheads, apparently on the account of Thomas Cranston, appears in the 1760 Newport tax list as owing nine shillings, just one shilling above the minimum assessment. In 1744 he was admitted a freeman of Portsmouth, a small town just north of Newport on Aquidneck Island. It seems probable that he was a mariner, although the evidence is slim. A David Earl appears in the *Newport Mercury* as a shipmaster in the West Indian trade in 1774. Assuming he was about twenty-one years old in 1744, he would have been fifty in 1774; fifty was old for a seaman but far from unheard of, as the example of Caleb Godfrey shows. Other evidence points toward a maritime career for Earl. After merchants, sailors had the best chance of acquiring significant quantities of rum through their privileges and individual "adventures." The fact that Earl's rum was on Cranston's account also suggests he may have been employed by Cranston, perhaps as a mariner.[58] George Gardner, who supplied eight hogsheads, may have been a poor relation to the prominent Newport mercantile clan headed by Caleb Gardner. In 1760, George Gardner's tax assessment of £1.4 placed him in the broad middle 50 percent of Newport freemen. A Baptist and the owner of a 700-acre "plantation" on Block Island, twenty miles southwest of Newport, Gardner may have been an influential figure in the vicinity of Shoreham, where he carried the title "Esq." and likely had relatives in Boston. Though it is unknown exactly what his mercantile activities were, he appears to have run a distillery since at least 1742. He supplied rum to a Vernon-owned slave ship on at least one other occasion, in 1752. He also seems to have run a general mercantile business, as evidenced by a 1741 receipt for flour, but little else is known about him.[59] The remaining two hogsheads are listed only as coming "from Providence," which we may assume refers to an unnamed merchant in Rhode Island's second city and not God's guiding hand.

With no professional, full-time longshoremen on the waterfront, the Vernons probably relied on the crew and casual hired labor to load the *Hare*, all under the supervision of Caleb Godfrey and mate John Arnold Hammond. The fifty-nine hogsheads of rum contained 6,078 gallons, a mean volume of 103 gallons each, and had an approximate market value of £788 sterling. The Vernons insured the cargo for only £350, a small gamble that would save on the premium but provide only a partial indemnification in the event of a loss. Rum was by far the most valuable good carried on the outbound voyage. Unlike many Rhode Island vessels, which frequently carried significant amounts of tobacco as a secondary trade good, the *Hare* carried only a single hogshead of the sot weed. The Vernons also shipped a hogshead of sugar that may have been intended for trade on the African coast, along with a dozen individual loaves for the crew's consumption. Like all oceangoing vessels, the *Hare* also packed naval stores: six barrels of tar and 605 feet of boards. The lumber could serve as a trade good at the European forts, but it was also necessary for general repairs and maintenance. Slavers also used it in the construction of a wall, or "barricado," athwartship to separate male from female captives. The remaining cargo consisted largely of provisions, some of which underscore the integration of the Vernons' slave and non-slave trading operations: forty-two barrels of beef (six of which came from "Carilona"), twenty-two barrels of flour, twelve barrels of pork (including two from "Corrolina"), twelve loaves of sugar (almost certainly from the Caribbean), two quarter casks of wine (probably from the Portuguese wine islands), four hogsheads and eight kegs of bread, one barrel of beans, one tierce of hams, and one barrel of "Irish corn" (which may have been barley, wheat, or oats). Though there is no record of it, it is very likely that the *Hare* also carried livestock of some sort—chickens, sheep, or goats, perhaps—for meat and milk. The record of later events reveals that Godfrey also brought a large dog with him. Exactly what experience prompted him to do that remains a mystery, but he would find use for it on this trip. All told, the non-rum cargo of the *Hare* was probably worth between one hundred and two hundred pounds sterling.[60]

CHAPTER TWO

The Crew

The Vernons hired Caleb Godfrey to captain the *Hare*. In an industry that was dominated by the young, Godfrey, at age forty-eight, was venerable. Born in Newport in 1706, Godfrey married Abigail Prince in 1730, and the couple's first child, Caleb Jr., was born in 1732. Over the next twenty years, Abigail would bear eight more children.[1] During this time, Godfrey seems to have prospered and improved his position in the community. He acquired property as early as 1728, when he owned a town lot on the west side of Thames Street. While the records are literally fragmentary, it is clear that Godfrey engaged in periodic buying and selling of real estate through the 1740s.[2] His ownership of property allowed him to be admitted as a freeman of Newport, a title for which only half of all the adult men in Newport qualified.[3] Godfrey also owned at least two slaves, one man and one woman, which was typical for a Newport sea captain.[4]

Godfrey was active in Newport's civic life. He was an Anglican, and to all evidences an observant one. He was admitted a vestryman of Trinity Church in 1737 and in 1750 appeared on a list of subscribers to a book of sermons preached in South Carolina.[5] Documents elsewhere confirm that he enjoyed the respect of the community. In 1740 he was one of the Newport "gentlemen" who published an announcement in the *Boston Weekly News Letter* warning subscribers not to accept any of John Colman's bank notes, and in 1747 the Vice-Admiralty Court called upon him to inspect a vessel for damages and submit a report.[6] Godfrey's rise to respectability would have been unblemished, except for his troubled finances. He had clearly done well in his early career, but something deteriorated later. Exactly how bad his situation was in 1754 is impossible to know, but in 1756 William Vernon told a correspondent that Godfrey's "Late misfortunes" had "reduc'd his circumstances Extreem Low," all of which were aggravated by "a large Family of Children to Support."[7] This explains in part why a prominent member of Newport's seafaring fraternity would undertake a dangerous Guinea voyage at an age when most of his peers were retiring. Skippering the *Hare* was a bid to reverse his "low" circumstances.

Godfrey rose steadily in his profession. In many respects, his career embodied maritime New England in the eighteenth century—a young man stood a fair chance of advancing from seaman to mate to captain as long as he avoided becoming one of the 30 percent of sailors who perished before the age of thirty. Like most Rhode Islanders, he spent much of his career sailing to and from the Caribbean. He almost certainly began his life at sea either as a ship's boy, apprenticed to a shipmaster at about age twelve, or as an ordinary seaman at about age fifteen. Starting out as an ordinary seaman was the more common route in New England, as an apprenticeship required a payment from the parents to the master and was thus limited to those with means. However, the fact that Godfrey was sailing as second mate by the age of eighteen suggests that he may have been an apprentice.[8] The first mention of his maritime career dates to 1724, when he embarked on a Jamaican voyage as mate aboard William Wanton's vessel the *Wanton*. Driven off course by a storm, the *Wanton* was captured by a Spanish vessel. The ship's company was taken to the Bay of Honduras, where they were accused of smuggling and treated "very barbarously and inhumanly perticularly in hanging up some of [the] sailors by the neck to make them confess where they were bound." Captain Wanton and some of the crew, including Godfrey, were then taken to Campeche on Mexico's Yucatán peninsula and imprisoned "with very little cloaths." Six crew members, probably the ordinary seamen and those who were not officers, were placed in a boat, presumably to make their way home. Wanton, Godfrey, and the others were then transferred to Vera Cruz where they were imprisoned in a cell "that was almost knee-deep with water." They were eventually released after a local British merchant and passing shipmaster intervened.[9]

By 1728 Godfrey had become a shipmaster, skippering the sloop *Little George* on another eventful run to Jamaica. Before reaching Kingston, he was once more taken by a Spanish vessel. He remained aboard for two months, then was placed aboard a second vessel that brought him to Trinidad, Cuba; from there he made his way home.[10] In 1729–30 he was in the employ of Godfrey Malbone, Newport's colorful merchant-privateer, carrying boards, shingles, staves, candles, beef, pork, flour, bread, and hoops to Jamaica aboard the sloop *Dimond* in exchange for sugar, salt, iron, copper, and cotton.[11] Two years later, in 1732, he was master of yet another sloop, the *Jolly Hanna*, on a run from Hispaniola to New York to Rhode Island. From 1747 to 1749, he was master of John Banister's brig *Abigail,* carrying cargoes of bricks, fish, onions, beans, water, candles, staves, hoops, boards, grain, livestock, and meat across Caribbean waters.[12] On many of these voyages, Godfrey probably engaged in the sort of smuggling that was typical of Rhode Islanders. In 1736, the governor of the Leeward Islands accused him of attempting to thwart the enforcement of trade restrictions. When the commander of a British vessel cruised the waters near St. Eustatius in search of smugglers, Godfrey ordered him to "follow him and had his guns ready," using what the British skipper termed "gross language." Lightly armed, the coast guard vessel "made off and outsailed Godfrey."[13]

During the 1730s, between West Indian runs, Caleb Godfrey began to make periodic trips to Africa. It is unknown exactly when he entered the slave trade and how many voyages he made because John Godfrey, a probable relation, captained several slavers at roughly the same time, and the documents did not always distinguish between them. Between 1733 and 1749 a Godfrey made no fewer than five voyages to Africa. It is probable that Caleb Godfrey made at least a few of these, but his first confirmed voyage to Africa occurred in 1737 when he took a sloop there on behalf of Godfrey Malbone.[14] The following year, he was involved in an incident that showed him to be a skilled seaman who could keep his head under pressure. Somewhere off the coast of Africa and with a hold full of captives, the sloop he commanded "was totally consum'd by Lightning." Godfrey and his crew "saved their Lives by taking to the Long Boat," leaving, it would appear, most, if not all, of the captives to perish in the burning ship.[15] Despite losing the vessel and, probably, the slaves, Godfrey's quick thinking may have helped his reputation among Newport's merchants. When one shipowner was weighing whether to engage Godfrey or a Captain Stanton to skipper his "Guinea Vessel," John Banister advised him that "Cap [sic] Godfrey is as good a Master and Sutable for Such a voyage, being well acquainted as any man in the Country."[16] The Vernons likewise told their insurers that "Capt Godfrey is an experienced comander on the Coast."[17] Later, on the Hare, the Vernons' instructions would give Godfrey great latitude in choosing a location in Africa to trade for captives, proving their trust and confidence in him.

The various newspaper squibs and shipping records that document Godfrey's life provide little sense of his personality, but his later actions, aboard the Hare and in retirement, suggest that he was thin-skinned, prone to self-pity, and quick to anger. He was also capable of being both obsequious and assertive, especially in matters of money. His correspondence with shipowners and business partners was salted with deferential phrases designed to take the edge off his dogged pursuit of what he considered his rightful share. When Godfrey sued a Boston merchant in a dispute over some spoiled molasses, he was quick to say that he was "very sorry that their has bin any occation of a Dispute," explaining that he was under legal advice to do so.[18] As we will see later in his dealings with the Vernons, he pursued his interests doggedly, playing skillfully on the Vernons' sense of patronage. He was also, despite his apparent religiosity, capable of great cruelty. This was hardly a unique trait among slave-ship captains. Although the most spectacular expression of his inhumanity would occur on the *Hare*, his indifference to human suffering was already apparent in his readiness to abandon a lightning-struck ship full of men, women, and children. And as we will see, his indifference was not reserved exclusively for Africans. In a world in which an extreme level of violence was the norm, Godfrey practiced a trade distinguished in its brutality.[20]

COMPARED WITH SLAVE SHIPS from Liverpool and London, Rhode Island ships carried few officers. British ships generally carried a first and second mate, with a third and even fourth mate on the larger vessels. In 1788, Parliament mandated that each slaver carry a surgeon, but many were already doing so well before then, if for no other reason than to keep the captives alive. In addition, British ships often carried a carpenter, a gunner or armorer, a cooper, a cook, and a ship's boy.[19] While their crews were larger than those of nonslaving vessels, the Rhode Island Guineamen sailed with much smaller and less-specialized crews than did their British counterparts. Surgeons, armorers, and ships' boys were rare. Boatswain, cooking, and carpentry jobs were more likely to be distributed informally among the crew.[20]

In the maritime hierarchy, ships' officers were much closer to the captain than to the crew. Experienced mates could, in due time, become masters. Most had ascended to mate status from the rank of ordinary seaman, and those who managed to become mates often benefited from family and community ties. Moreover, the status gap between mates and men was reflected in their compensation. In addition to a higher wage, officers often were allowed to earn extra money by trading for a small number of captives on their own account. Often, the value of these "privilege slaves" exceeded the mates' total wages for the voyage. Still, the gap between officers and crew was narrower on Rhode Island vessels than on British ones. American captains generally earned only slightly more than seamen and sometimes even received the same wage, while captains' wages on British ships were about five times more than crew wages.[21]

Three days after signing on for the voyage, Captain Godfrey recruited John Arnold Hammond (often rendered as "Hamond") to serve as his chief or first mate. At twenty pounds Rhode Island money per month (about one pound, five shillings, and sixpence British sterling), his wage was equal to Godfrey's.[22] This was logical because Hammond would become the skipper if Godfrey became incapacitated or died. Hammond took a small advance of eight pounds, twelve shillings, and sixpence Rhode Island currency, which suggests that he was not desperate for money. In addition, Hammond was almost certainly allowed two privilege slaves—the same number the Vernons gave Gilbert Phillips, mate on the *Hare*'s 1755–56 voyage—to sell on his own account.[23] The privilege slaves were worth approximately seventy pounds sterling, without taking into account what the trade goods necessary to purchase them would have cost.

Hammond's early life is obscure. There were several John Hammonds in Newport during the mid-eighteenth century, and distinguishing among them is difficult. He was born in Newport in 1730, which means he was about 24 years old when he sailed on the *Hare*. From this it seems reasonable to infer that Hammond went to sea in his late teens, learned his craft well, and worked his way up to mate. It is impossible to know whether he commanded other vessels before the *Hare*'s voyage, but the Vernons' decision to pay him a captain's wage and his appearance as a skipper in 1757 both suggest that he had done so or expected to very soon. Hammond was also a newlywed, having married Mary Scott on June 6, 1754, just one month prior to sailing.[24]

Almost six weeks later, well after he had hired most of the crew, Godfrey signed Richard Cole as second mate and cooper at twenty-five pounds per month (about one pound, twelve shillings in British sterling), five pounds more than he and Hammond earned as skipper and first mate. Cole's salary probably reflected his barrel-making duties; it was common for Rhode Island ships to merge specialists' with seamen's work. In addition to the extra pay, Cole was entitled to one privilege slave.[25] Exactly where he came from and how he learned his trades is unknown—no record of his birth or marriage has emerged. Cole's broader career suggests that he was primarily a professional mariner who acquired carpentry and barrel-making skills along the way. In 1751, he sailed as mate aboard the sloop *Ranger* from Sassafras, Maryland, to Boston. Laden with wheat and flour, the *Ranger* encountered "very Violent gales of Wind & Great Seas" and was forced to put in at Newport. Though the cargo was damaged, the sloop pulled through, due no doubt in part to Cole's skill and experience. Despite some later difficulties aboard the *Hare*, Cole took command of a vessel in his own right just a few weeks after leaving the *Hare* and skippered several Newport ships through the 1750s. Like Hammond, then, Cole appears to have been an established member of Newport's maritime fraternity.[26]

Very little is known about the ordinary seamen who sailed on the *Hare*. The lack of documentation is directly related to the lowly position of sailors in the eighteenth-century Atlantic World; they ranked just above the captives they transported. Though free, seamen labored under conditions that were unfree in many respects. On the one hand, they signed on to the *Hare* of their own accord. On the other hand, maritime law and custom treated them almost as indentured laborers. They had to obey the captain's every order, were not allowed to leave the ship until formally discharged, and were subject to physical punishment, including whipping, for infractions.[27] Rhode Island law even allowed towns to force young, troubled men to go to sea as an alternative to binding them out locally.[28] But perhaps the most telling indicator of the rank of the seamen on a slaver relative to that of the captives they tended is revealed in the surviving records. The sailors' names, wages, and length of time served are listed in the *Hare*'s portledge bill (which Godfrey called a "portage bill"), which speaks to their personhood before the law, their status as free men, and the finite term of their service. In contrast, the only information on the *Hare*'s captives derives from a sale record that lists sex, age category (adult or child), and price paid, which speaks to the captives' lack of legal personhood, lifelong servitude, and commodity status.

All sailors, of course, worked under difficult conditions, but some historians have suggested that a daily routine saturated in violence and brutality made service on a Guineaman particularly odious, with sailors acting as both the perpetrators and objects of extreme cruelty. In addition, high death rates from disease—which averaged between 15 and 22 percent during the eighteenth century—and the risk of being killed during an insurrection could make it very difficult to find willing crew members. For these reasons, British slavers had a reputation for attracting only the most abject, vicious, and dissipated of seamen, along with similarly inclined and incompetent landsmen. At times, merchants in Liverpool and London relied on an auxiliary network of tavern and boardinghouse keepers, prostitutes, and crimps to procure labor for their ventures. In a typical situation, a crooked boardinghouse keeper would allow a sailor to run up an impossibly high liquor tab and then sell the debt to the agent of the shipowner, who would offer the seaman a choice between jail and a trip to Africa.[29]

No evidence of institutionalized trickery and peonage exists for Newport, which raises the question of how Rhode Island slavers were able to find sailors. John Hoxse, whose memoir is the only one penned by a native Rhode Island slave-ship sailor, simply grew tired of his life as a shipwright and, in 1795, decided to "try [his] fortune" as ship's carpenter aboard one of the D'Wolf family's vessels.[30] It is possible that a few wayward youths were forced to work on slavers by the town councils, but for the most part the ability of Rhode Island slave ships to attract crews without coercion or trickery had to do with the structure of New England society, in which an increasing number of young men in need of work outstripped the supply of accessible farmland. A stint or career as a sailor was one option for the poor or propertyless, but the men who took it found that wages were low and that it was easy to run out of money, even without indulging in the six-week spree of sailors' lore.[31] Sailors constituted a significant proportion of those who took advantage of Rhode Island's early bankruptcy law, and their long absences often left family members destitute.[32] Maritime employment and wages fluctuated greatly, soaring in times of war, as privateers and press-gangs scooped up able-bodied mariners, and ebbing during periods of depression. New England maritime labor was also seasonal, with clearances rising during the late spring thaw and dropping again as the fall hurricane season approached.[33] For a young Rhode Islander, the decision to sign on to an African voyage required weighing many factors: his current employment and domestic situation; the wages offered; the availability of alternatives, including shoreside work; and the likelihood of surviving the trip.

At the same time, Newport drew upon a wider Atlantic maritime labor market in which New England vessels appear to have enjoyed a better reputation than their British counterparts. New England merchants seem to have had a reputation for paying well. "Ramblin' Jack" Cremer, an Englishman who sailed in the 1710s and 1720s, discussed jumping ship at Boston with some of his mates because of the "great wages given for Sailors." This was probably true, at least for his time, although the wages paid aboard the *Hare* were certainly not high. Other factors may have made Rhode Island vessels attractive to British and foreign sailors. Irish-born Nicholas Owen, who made three voyages aboard Newport slavers in the 1750s, reported that "every man recev[ed] the reward of his toils with honour" and that his employer "always orderd good usage in all his vessels, particularly charging all his officers to be moderate to his people." Owen also noted that on at least one voyage he and other crew members were allowed "large privileges in the cargo and what we pleased to purchace in slaves upon our return." This, however, may have been a unique condition and was not the case aboard the *Hare*. Yet Owen's experience raises the possibility that Rhode Island had a segmented

maritime labor market in which residents used kinship and personal connections to secure berths on coasting and West Indian voyages, leaving
transients—especially those who found themselves stuck in Newport—to
the riskier African voyages.[34]

The task of recruiting sailors for the *Hare* belonged to Captain Caleb
Godfrey. He probably turned first to local acquaintances and then searched
more widely. The sailors who were not from Rhode Island probably came
from any number of boardinghouses located within a block or two of
Newport's wharves. Boardinghouse proprietors understood their clien-
tele and catered to the seaman's pragmatic worldview. Outside one boardinghouse hung a sign that read, "Come, brother sailor, make a stop / And lend
a hand to strap the block / And if the work is neatly done / You shall have a
glass of rum."[35] Newport's many taverns—as opposed to its merchant coffee
houses—functioned not only as drinking and social spots but also as general business centers for a population in motion, mail collection spots, and
unofficial employment offices where a captain might crew his ship. One tavern was described as occupying a "commodious Dwelling-House" on Broad
Street near the Town House, and included a yard, barn, and "out house."
This particular watering hole was "known by the sign of the White Bear";
others included the "Marquis of Granby" and, slightly later, "Pitt's Head."[36] A
second method for recruiting sailors was to "beat up for seamen," in which
the ship's owners hired a man to walk the streets with a drum, announcing
the voyage and any expected benefits, such as a share in the prize money of a
privateer.[37] It is unknown exactly which of these methods Godfrey employed.
However, the demand for sailors at the time was probably small, as it often
was in peacetime due to the reduced impressment of merchant sailors into
the Royal Navy, so it is likely that Godfrey was able to avoid the expense of
hiring a drummer.

The *Hare* began its voyage with six seamen. The first of these, William
Jones, joined on June 11, 1754, with the *Hare* still tied up at Malbone's
Wharf in Newport. He signed on for a monthly wage of sixteen pounds
Rhode Island money (slightly more than one pound sterling) and received
an advance of one month's pay.[38] Eleven days passed before a second seaman signed on. The delay was likely due to two factors. First, Godfrey and
the Vernons wanted to avoid paying new seamen until there was work for
them. Second, they may have had minor difficulties procuring men, perhaps due to competition from other ships. The New England economy was
just recovering from the 1750–54 recession that had followed King George's
War. As a result, the wages of the *Hare*'s crew were slightly low by historical

standards, but upward pressure on wages may have been building as trade picked up.[39] Thus, when William Burling took his berth on June 24, he signed on for seventeen pounds per month (one pound and two shillings sterling) and received slightly more than a two-month advance. William Ball signed for the same wage on June 26, taking no advance, and on June 28, William White signed for seventeen pounds per month with a fifty-one pounds and nineteen shillings advance. William Baggott signed on June 28 as well, receiving an advance of thirty-three pounds and nine shillings. The signing of John Batty on June 29, for seventeen pounds and with an advance of thirty pounds and fourteen shillings, completed the outbound crew. Over the course of the voyage some crew members would be discharged and six more men would sign on.[40]

It is unclear from where, precisely, the *Hare*'s crew came. In one of his letters, Godfrey mentioned that William White was from Boston.[41] Other than that, crew members left scant trace in local records. John Batty may have come from Providence. Genealogical and military records show that a "John Battey" or "John Batte" was born in 1720 in Warwick, Rhode Island, married Priscilla Westcott in Providence in 1741, sailed as master of a privateer in 1744, was admitted a freeman of Providence in 1747, and died in 1797, but these references may or may not have been to the correct individual.[42] Moreover, a man would have to be extremely desperate to sail as an ordinary seaman on a Guineaman at the age of thirty-four, ten years after serving as master of a privateer. A "John Battey" also appeared as a shipmaster several times in the shipping news and newspapers during the 1760s, but it is impossible to say whether he was the same John Batty who sailed on the *Hare*—perhaps so. A William Jones sailed on a Rhode Island privateer in the 1740s, and a William White stood guard at Newport during King George's War, joining a militia company during the French and Indian War, but these names were both very common and it is impossible to know whether they were the same men who served on the *Hare*.[43] Finally, while a tiny percentage of Rhode Island slave-ship crewmen were black, it is probable that there were no African American sailors aboard the *Hare*. The odds are against it, and the documentary record contains none of the common markers—the exclusive use of a first name, any obvious "Negro" names, such as Scipio, Cato, or Primus, or any explicit references to race.[44]

The sparse documentation suggests two things about the *Hare*'s outbound crew. First, it suggests that the *Hare*'s crew, like most seamen, came from the ranks of the poor. Property ownership generated a great deal of paperwork in the form of deeds, tax bills, wills, and probate inventories, but none of the ordinary seamen who worked on the *Hare* seems to have left any such traces. This points toward a second probability, namely, that several of the *Hare*'s seamen were transients from elsewhere in the Atlantic World. This conclusion runs counter to some historians' findings. Jay Coughtry has shown that 75 percent of slave-ship crew members in 1803–7 resided in Newport and 95 percent lived in the state. Sixty percent were native Rhode Islanders, and fully half were born in Newport.[45] Similarly, Daniel Vickers and Vince Walsh found that 80 percent of the men who sailed out of Salem, Massachusetts, were local residents.[46] But there is reason to question whether the crew lists of 1803–7 were representative of Newport's prerevolutionary "Golden Age," when Newport was not only a much more significant port but also a part of a larger British–Atlantic network. Lacking a parallel collection of crew lists, it is difficult to say for certain. Additionally, over 43 percent of the Rhode Island crews that sailed to Britain during the 1750s consisted of men who were not even British subjects, which points to a colonial-era maritime labor force that was far more international than its early republican counterpart.[47] There is, of course, strong evidence that sailors from the smaller ports, such as Salem, were more likely to be native sons, but as British North America's fifth-largest port, Newport's maritime labor force probably more closely resembled that of Boston.[48] The *Hare*'s crew, then, was probably drawn from the lowest echelons of the Atlantic World's free population and was international in its origins, perhaps even anational in its outlook.[49]

SOMETIME BEFORE EMBARKING, the crew of the *Hare* may have carried out one last piece of business: casting a horoscope. Astrology was extremely popular in colonial New England, arriving during the migrations of the seventeenth century. The practice had reached a high point in England during the Civil War and Interregnum and was common among Puritans and Anglicans alike. Astrology was generally divided into two branches. The first, "natural astrology," concerned itself largely with phenomena such as weather and harvests, and though it always had its skeptics, it was at least politically and theologically uncontroversial. It entered a phase of decline during the Restoration and was moribund by the middle of the eighteenth century. The second branch, "judicial astrology," caused more acrimony. Concerned with the fate of individuals, it verged on conjuring and other dark arts, and for that reason was often condemned by religious authorities and by the usual doubters. For all of its controversy, judicial astrology required a great deal of knowledge. Practitioners were required to master the movements and positions of the various heavenly bodies and to interpret them according to an elaborate and open-ended set of guidelines. They used this knowledge to cast horoscopes calibrated to the moment of an individual's birth or to the moment of a crucial decision. By the mid-eighteenth century, the practice of astrology in England had declined to the point where it existed only in popular form among the rural and urban laboring classes. But for unclear reasons, it persisted in colonial America, and for reasons that are even murkier, all surviving maritime horoscopes come from Rhode Island.[50]

There is no direct evidence to suggest that anybody associated with the *Hare* cast a pre-voyage horoscope, but they were very common. One nineteenth-century Newport historian claimed to have seen "hundreds" of eighteenth-century horoscopes, which were generally used to determine the optimal moment to embark on a voyage. Several astrologers, or "conjurers," worked in the Newport area. One, a Mr. Stafford, lived in Tiverton on the shore of Narragansett Bay opposite the northern tip of Aquidneck Island. He reputedly was "wont to tell where lost things might be found and what day, hour, and minute was fortunate for vessels to sail &c."[51] Another was John Sherman, a seaman who lived in Newport and kept a record of thirty-four horoscopes cast for various Newport vessels in the late 1750s and early 1760s. The entry for each vessel in his notebook consisted of an astrological diagram followed by a short narrative of the voyage. It is unclear whether he cast the horoscopes before the vessels departed or whether he did so retroactively. The notebook seems to have been kept for personal use as a way of testing or proving his method, so he may have cast them after the voyages. The fact that the horoscopes and voyage narratives appear close together yet uncrowded on the page also suggests that they were written at the same time, following the voyage. Because Sherman kept his book during the Seven Years' War, many of the trips ended in failure—capture by privateers, interception by the Royal Navy for trading with the enemy, as well as the usual causes of disease, poor markets, and foul weather. Most of the voyages in Sherman's book were to the West Indies. Only one was to "Affrica": the *Little Betsey*, commanded by Benjamin Hicks. The narrative, which was typical of most, read in its entirety: "This sloop sailed for the coast of Affrica under the command of Benjamin Hicks Where he arrived in a short Passage and began to slave, when a French Frigate came down the Coast & took many vessels, & fired many shott over her but by fortune & the help of a Reef of Rocks which which [*sic*] she Runover made her escape the frigate not chusing to follow her[.]"[52] The *Little Betsey* later sold its captives in Virginia.[53]

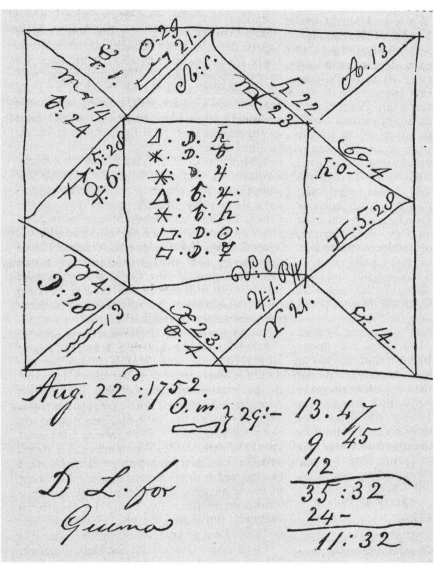

FIGURE 2.1. *Slave-ship horoscope, 1752. Many Rhode Island mariners had horoscopes cast before setting out on their voyages. This horoscope was probably cast on behalf of David Lindsay, who skippered thirteen slave ships from 1740 to 1761. Lindsay undertook one of these voyages in the summer of 1754, arriving in Sierra Leone just days ahead of the* Hare. *(Courtesy of the American Antiquarian Society)*

If Godfrey or a member of the *Hare*'s crew had a horoscope cast, it would indicate several things about the men on the ship. On the one hand, it would point to a flexible and pragmatic cosmology that grew out of the needs of the seamen. Most New England sailors were at least nominally Christian. Most would have been baptized or, in the case of Rhode Island's Baptists, taught the basic tenets of their respective denominations in childhood. However, most of them probably occupied a spectrum ranging from unbeliever to what one historian has termed "horse-shed Christian," or one whose devotion was limited to intermittent church attendance.[54] The isolation of a ship from society at large weakened the hold of established religion, as did the need to labor on the Sabbath. The general absence of clergy allowed sailors to pursue their own heterodoxies. Contact with people from other cultures and religions, including Africans, may have changed their views. The inherent danger of the sea, moreover, may have fostered a pragmatic outlook, rather than an idealistic one, on life and fate.[55]

Eschewing a formal, established Christianity, many sailors followed what church authorities characterized as "superstition," a category that included astrology and other divination practices. As one prominent historian has argued, "The seaman's worldview was an amalgam of religion and irreligion, magic and materialism, superstition and self-help."[56] Astrology may have come naturally to many sailors, given the amount of time they devoted to studying the sky. Making their living in an extremely risky and capricious industry, they needed all the help they could get, divine or otherwise. For Newport's seamen, astrology was probably just a way to seek control over their fates. It followed logically that what could be known could be influenced. Moreover, the prominence of slave trading, which was even more dangerous than ordinary merchant service, may help explain the peculiar popularity of astrology in Rhode Island.

Still, none of this necessarily conflicted with Christian beliefs held by Rhode Island's seamen. While most clergy would have frowned upon astrological conjuring, practitioners often found ways to reconcile it with formal religion. The system was open enough to allow practitioners to elide any conflicts. One English astrologer saw his horoscopes as a way to discern the workings of Providence. Whenever his horoscopes foretold a misfortune that never arrived, he simply believed that God's will had superseded the stars' will.[57] This urge to test the heavens against divinely ordained fate may in fact have been John Sherman's reason for casting horoscopes for voyages he never undertook. Newport, thus, in addition to providing one-stop shopping for the slave traders, provided a supporting cast of clergy and conjurers to serve the spiritual and cosmological needs of their employees.

WITH THE CREW HIRED and the outbound cargo stowed, the Vernons delivered written instructions to Godfrey. All merchants did, not merely to specify their wishes, but because the instructions played a significant role in assigning liability in case something went wrong. Shipmasters who deviated unnecessarily from their instructions could find themselves financially responsible for damages and losses. The instructions addressed a range of issues, such as the captain's commission as well as how many privilege slaves he and the mates would be allowed. They told the captain—in greater or lesser detail, depending on his experience—where to trade on the African coast, and they generally provided very specific instructions on where to take the cargo, which merchants to contact, what prices to seek, and where to go if market conditions at the first port of call were poor.

The instructions for the *Hare*'s 1754–55 voyage do not survive, but a copy of the instructions for its nearly identical 1755–56 voyage does, and we can assume that they were similar in most respects. Many of the orders were standard for all slavers: try to purchase young, male captives; feed them well so they will survive the journey; complete the voyage as quickly as possible to minimize the number of deaths from disease; keep the peace between officers and men. If anything were to happen to the slaves or vessel, Godfrey was to make out a "protest," or declaration, before a notary at the nearest British port.

Communication during the voyage was another area of interest for the Vernons. Information on markets and ships took, at minimum, several weeks to cross the ocean and often took many months. Staying on top of their far-flung enterprises was paramount to the Vernons. Therefore, they specified that, while in Africa, Godfrey should take advantage of any departing vessel to send them updates on his progress. They instructed him to forward all bills of lading "by the first Vessels from the Coast." At the same time, however, they told Godfrey to "Speak with no Vessels at Sea," presumably for safety's sake and to prevent any valuable economic intelligence from falling into the hands of competitors. Lastly, the Vernons warned Godfrey to "Keep a watchful Eye over 'em [the captives] and give them no Opportunity of making an Insurrection." Here was a reminder that slaving was not like other branches of trade.[58]

There are two areas in which the 1755 instructions probably differed from the 1754 instructions. For the later voyage, the Vernons ordered Godfrey to sell his captives in South Carolina. However, for the earlier voyage they seem to have had somewhere else in mind. When writing to Thomlinson, Trecothick, and Company for insurance a few weeks earlier, William Vernon said that the *Hare* would be sailing "To the Island of Jamaica with Liberty to touch at the Windward Islands," which probably included Barbados. If Godfrey were to "make his Trade to Windward," the Vernons asked that he be insured to Carolina. (Here they meant the Windward Coast of Africa, an imprecise term, which, in the eighteenth century, could encompass Senegambia to the Gold Coast.) Thus, the Vernons appear to have handed Godfrey conditional instructions. If he purchased his captives along the Gold Coast, he should try to sell them in the Caribbean, starting at Barbados and progressing westward toward Jamaica if prices were not good. However, if he purchased captives on the Windward Coast, including at Sierra Leone, it is likely he was under orders to carry them to South Carolina. If so, the Vernons were expressing a belief, widespread at the time, that South Carolina was particularly receptive to Africans from that region. The promotion of South Carolina to a first-choice destination in the 1755 instructions was probably a result of the Vernons' satisfaction with the outcome of the 1754 voyage.[59]

A second difference between the 1754 instructions and the 1755 orders probably concerned the location at which the captives should be purchased. The Vernons generally gave their captains great latitude in deciding where to trade, and Godfrey's 1755 instructions were no exception: "You are at Liberty to trade . . . at such Places as you think most for our Interest." However, worried that war between France and Britain might break out, the Vernons took special care to suggest that Godfrey trade on the "Windward Coast," likely in hopes of keeping their vessel away from areas frequented by French ships.[60] Another stipulation—that he avoid trading at a place known as "Port Dally"—may also have been prompted by wartime fears, since it was close to the French forts at St. Louis and Goree in Senegal. There was, however, another reason beside war to order Godfrey to avoid that part of the coast: the high level of violence that prevailed in slave-trading regions. In August 1754, a month after the *Hare* departed, word arrived in New York that two British ships had been taken and plundered by "natives" at Portudal, just south of Goree. One crew member escaped and the other vessel was retaken. The news reached the Vernons through either the New York or Charles Town, South Carolina, papers, prompting their instruction to Godfrey in 1755. But in early July 1754, war was still unforeseeable and news of the attacks at Portudal had not yet reached North America, so Godfrey's instructions probably did not mention them.[61]

Cargo stowed, horoscopes potentially cast, customs declarations filed, and instructions received, the *Hare* set sail sometime between June 29 and July 5, 1754.[62] Sailing with the tide, the *Hare* would have passed Fort George, a thirty-six-gun installation guarding Newport Harbor on Goat Island, staying close to the Aquidneck Island side to avoid the "grassy, choaky ground."

Once past the fort, Godfrey would have given plenty of leeway to Maykril Cove on Conanicut Island, which, sailing instruction books warned, "is shoal and dangerous at its entrance." Avoiding the "great many sunken rocks" that dotted the bay, "some of which are above Water," Godfrey and the crew would have caught their final glimpse of Rhode Island: a lighthouse on a spit of land to starboard known as the "Bever's Tail." Ahead would have lain open ocean.[63]

If by any chance Godfrey had taken the latest Boston papers with him (Newport would not have its own newspaper until 1758), he would have encountered a number of interesting stories. He would have read with great interest the account of a Boston vessel that was struck by lightning off Cape Hatteras, having once been through the experience himself. In this instance, a lightning bolt "ran down the Mast and stove a hole thr[ough] the Deck, and struck down two of the Men," leaving them "stunn'd for some time." Although one of the men "had the Skin on the Back Part of his Head rip'd from the Skull, and was scorch'd on his Back quite down to the Waste Band," both victims managed to recover thanks to a bloodletting administered by another crew member. Also of potential interest would have been an account of an uprising among Protestant peasants in France. A military official had tried to force the Protestant mayor of a small town to cooperate in the arrest of a local minister. The mayor raised the alarm in the surrounding area, drawing a large number of country folk to his side. Reports that twenty thousand troops were required to quell the *jacquerie* were probably exaggerated, no doubt appealing to the anti-Catholic and anti-French prejudices of New England readers. The rest of the news was of little interest: the king made a speech to Parliament, offering bland praise for showing "the most attentive Regard to every Branch of Publick Service"; an editorial from London criticized the king for pursuing "Don Quixote Projects" on the Continent; and a certain Mr. Whitefield had returned to the colonies to continue his religious revival, this time in Georgia.

If Godfrey noticed the story on page two of the *Boston Gazette* at all, he probably did not attach much significance to it. The account, dateline Annapolis, told of a clash in the Ohio country between the French and the English. The English got the better of the encounter. But against the wishes and efforts of a "Major Washington," an Indian ally known as the "Half King" buried a tomahawk in the head of a captured French officer, Ensign Joseph Coulon de Villiers de Jumonville. The account did not speculate on what the ramifications might be, but hindsight reveals it to be the opening skirmish of the French and Indian War, which would ultimately transform North America. As he set out for Africa, however, the clash was probably the furthest thing from Godfrey's mind.[64]

CHAPTER THREE

Long Knives

Mild weather makes June and early July the best time for a North Atlantic crossing, and the *Hare* seems to have had a speedy and uneventful passage. But the small sloop did much more than sail from one point to another: it remade the ties that bound three continents together, even though the connections were not material. The ocean was eternally "trackless," and the reams of paper carried on ships across the sea were important not in themselves but as markers of the abstract profits, losses, and capital that served as the primary connectors between continents. Yet the linkages represented in bills of exchange, shipping instructions, and insurance policies, to say nothing of the decrees of state, were real, yielding stubbornly material consequences, moving produce and people over great distances.

The links between continents were many, far more than the term "triangular trade" would imply. The *Hare*'s voyage joined the trading systems of two continents. The rum, tobacco, and other goods carried by the *Hare*, the products as well as the means of maintenance of these intercontinental connections, came to rest in the Vernons' hold courtesy of a network of slave-worked plantations, commercial correspondents, regional producers and artisans, and capital accumulated through years of transactions. In Africa, the *Hare* would complete the articulation between the produce and capital of the New World and the Old. The *Hare*'s trade goods would reach distant consumers by means of coastal middlemen and indigenous commercial networks. The trail led ultimately to a powerful African state that paid for the goods in human beings, defined as "outsiders" and sent back down the chain.

In the abstract, these connections seemed to compose a well-integrated, smoothly functioning system—an "Atlantic World"—and that was true, at least in the sense that the system managed to channel eleven million Africans to the Americas. But a closer look reveals that these links were more tenuous than they appeared. Relationships between African and European traders were fraught with violence. Trust of the sort that facilitated long-distance commercial transactions was in short supply. Crews deserted and slaves rebelled. Those with captives to sell did not always choose to sell them to Europeans. The supply of slaves could dry up with little warning due to factors unrelated to the demand for labor. Finally, European traders faced great challenges in catering to the tastes of African consumers. But even accounting for considerable slippage, the system worked. Understanding how its parts fit together is essential, because only by reconstructing the links in the chain is it possible to address the most important question: who were the *Hare* captives? Arriving at some understanding of the captives' backgrounds is essential to understanding the links between Africa and North America.

With no surviving logbook, we cannot know exactly what course the *Hare* took to Africa. Like other New England slave ships, the *Hare* probably charted a southeasterly course after it left Newport Harbor. After sailing that course for a week or two, the *Hare* most likely scudded eastward along the southern edge of the North Atlantic Current, bypassing Bermuda and continuing southeastward at between 25 and 32 degrees north latitude, turning south at between 20 and 25 degrees north latitude.[1] Though we cannot know the precise route, in all likelihood neither did Caleb Godfrey. The art of navigation had advanced significantly in his lifetime, but at the time of the *Hare*'s departure, the most important development—the ability to determine a vessel's longitude—still lay several years in the future, at least for modest, provincial merchant captains like Godfrey. A practical, precise, and widely available solution to "finding the longitude" eluded navigators and astronomers until John Harrison, a Yorkshire watchmaker, devised a chronometer that retained its accuracy in rough seas, in temperatures warm and cold, and in areas of high and low air pressure. His revolutionary device, however, was not perfected until the 1760s and, due to skepticism and high cost, was not widely used for many years. Until then, a ship could miss its destination by dozens, or even hundreds of miles, sometimes with disastrous consequences.

Godfrey, therefore, probably used some form of "dead reckoning" to navigate the *Hare* across the Atlantic. Dead reckoning had been in use since the time of Columbus, though by Godfrey's time there had been significant improvements. The method required two pieces of information to determine a vessel's location. First, the navigator needed to determine the direction the ship was sailing using a compass. Second, he needed to estimate the ship's speed. This was commonly done by heaving overboard a "Dutchman's log," a quadrant-shaped piece of wood, and allowing it to float in place as the ship passed it by. The log was tied to a rope with knots at regular intervals, which unwound from a spool, so that as the ship passed the floating log, the number of knots played out over fifteen to thirty seconds (timed with a sandglass) and provided a measurement of the vessel's speed. The practice, of course, gave rise to the terms "logbook" and "knots" (as a measure of speed). Having determined the vessel's course and speed, the navigator plotted the vessel's position on a chart or board. For example, if a vessel was sailing eastward at a speed of five knots, the navigator would draw a line in an eastward direction for a distance of five nautical miles, multiplied by the number of hours since the previous estimate. Even in Columbus's time, mariners were able to supplement their reckonings with readings on latitude, which could be determined by measuring the angle of the sun as it reached its noon apex: the higher the sun, the closer the vessel was to the equator. This allowed shipmasters to "sail the latitude" by heading to the parallel of their ultimate destination and then sailing along the imaginary line all the way across the ocean.[2]

Godfrey's generation saw a number of technological advances, all of which improved navigational accuracy, but it is unknown whether he was able to take advantage of them all. Since the end of the sixteenth century, navigators had used an instrument known as the backstaff to measure the angle of the sun at its highest point. By Godfrey's time, backstaffs sported small lenses that allowed for observations in cloudy weather. In 1731 the backstaff was superseded by the octant, which allowed its user to determine latitude within two minutes of arc at two different times of day, instead of just at noon. Octants, however, cost approximately fifteen times as much as backstaffs, so it is improbable that Godfrey would have owned one. Compasses, too, improved with the introduction of a heavier, more magnetically sensitive needle, although such instruments were just becoming widespread by the time of the *Hare*'s voyage. One innovation that Godfrey likely did employ was the sea atlas, which came into use at the end of the previous century. A sea atlas combined nautical charts with rutters, or textual descriptions of coastlines with instructions for sailing. The most common of these, the *English Pilot*, was first published in 1671 and underwent multiple updates in the eighteenth century, with volumes eventually covering Europe, the Americas, Africa, and the Mediterranean.[3]

None of these improvements, however, provided a definitive solution to the problem of longitude. While "sailing the latitude" could certainly have gotten Godfrey where he wanted to go, he probably also made attempts to determine the *Hare*'s longitude, however inaccurately. Before the widespread use of the marine chronometer, sailors employed two methods to determine longitude. The first of these involved plotting the position of the moon, which is close to the earth and moves relatively quickly across the sky, against the more distant and comparatively fixed stars. Octants could be used for this, but as mentioned, they were quite expensive. The navigator then consulted a complex book of tables to calculate the longitude based on the moon's position. Godfrey, however, more likely employed a second, less complicated method, which was originally devised in the seventeenth century and revived by the Dutch after 1740. This method took advantage of the variation between magnetic and true north. The difference between true north and the reading on a compass differed by several degrees, depending on the vessel's location. In Godfrey's time, special charts mapped this variation, which, given knowledge of a vessel's latitude, could provide a rough estimate of its longitude. In the final analysis, however, mariners like Godfrey had no way to determine the position of their vessels with any real confidence and therefore had to call upon experience and instinct to reach their destinations.[4]

As Godfrey and mate John Arnold Hammond navigated the vessel, they also supervised the work of the crew. Customarily, work aboard a sailing vessel was organized according to two shifts, known as the starboard and larboard watches, one commanded by the master, the other by the mate. Each watch lasted four hours, with all hands working the two two-hour shifts in the 4–8 P.M. "dog watch," during which each watch swapped daily schedules to ensure that neither would have an advantage in daytime hours. There were occasional departures from this routine. All hands worked in foul weather, and vessels with small crews probably observed a less formal routine. With three officers and six ordinary seamen on the outbound voyage, the *Hare* probably adhered to this schedule most of the time.[5]

Seamen put out more sail in weak to moderate breezes and "reefed," or took in sail, when the wind grew too strong. One member manned the helm while another heaved the log. In fair weather, seamen were put to a near-limitless variety of chores. Tasks aboard the Connecticut snow *Africa* on its outbound voyage in 1757 included: "scraping sterage & areing sails"; "Gitting Top Gal[lant] Masts & yards a Cross"; "Painting Roaps" with tar; "Roping Boats Sails"; "Piking Ocum" for caulking; "Scraping Quarter Deck"; and "Making Quarter Netting & Making Sinnet," which was a type of cordage made from rope yarn. Ships' carpenters—aboard the *Hare* this would have been Richard Cole, the second mate and cooper—had special work to do. They were responsible for maintaining the longboat and yawls. The *Africa's* carpenter caulked the longboat on the outbound voyage and strengthened the masts with two shrouds known as "swifters." He was also responsible for the good condition of the many barrels and casks aboard, a duty that took on special importance aboard New England vessels, which risked losing money from leakage of their primary trade good, rum.[6]

South of the Azores, the *Hare* likely picked up the Canary Current, which sweeps down the northwestern coast of Africa past the Canary Islands. It does not appear, however, that the *Hare* called at the Canaries; rather, Godfrey likely charted a more direct and southerly course toward Cape Verde.[7] It would be difficult to overstate the significance of Cape Verde to eighteenth-century Atlantic commerce. Situated at the juncture of the Canary Current and the trade winds, the archipelago straddled all of the major shipping routes between Europe, Africa, and the Americas. The islands were also difficult to miss, blessed as they were with a natural beacon, the perpetual inferno atop the volcanic island of Fogo. Rising over nine thousand feet above the sea and visible from a distance of 120 miles, the crew of the *Hare* would have welcomed it as a harbinger of a completed Atlantic crossing.[8]

A Portuguese possession since 1455, Cape Verde was another of those small but significant places scattered along the Atlantic rim whose history, like Newport's, was intimately bound up with slavery. Situated some three to four hundred miles off the coast of Senegal and consisting of ten major islands, the archipelago had once been a sugar-planting colony; it was a market for enslaved African labor even before Columbus and his successors made it possible to extend the plantation system across the Atlantic. The arid climate, however, proved unsuitable for large-scale cane cultivation, and by the time of the *Hare*'s visit, Cape Verde's plantation economy had long since withered. Residents now earned their living supplying ships, with slavers comprising a major portion of their business. The islands' herders sold salted beef and goat, while farmers found a ready market for fresh fruits and vegetables. Islanders also did a brisk business in naval stores, dispensing timber, sails, rope, and tar to battered vessels, all at notoriously high prices. Textiles constituted a third branch of the Cape Verdean economy. In the fifteenth century the Portuguese had introduced cotton, but like sugar, it never blossomed as an export. Instead, local artisans wove the cotton into bolts of cloth, known as *panos*, which were prized as trade goods along the African coast. Ship captains often traded for cloth in order to improve their assortment of goods. At the time of the *Hare*'s visit, cotton textiles described by one sailor as "very finely wrought" were worth fifteen pence in Cape Verde but sold for up to four times that amount on the African coast.[9] Godfrey did not purchase any textiles, however. He may have judged the price too high, as did the captain of a Connecticut slaver on a voyage in 1757.[10]

Having sailed to Africa before, Caleb Godfrey was almost certainly familiar with Cape Verde, and if the 1755–56 records are any guide, he brought the *Hare* to two different islands. The first was the island of "St. Jago," which was the contemporary English rendering of "Santiago." The island's principal port was Ribeira Grande, seat of both the government and a Roman Catholic bishopric whose territory encompassed the entire Upper Guinea coast. Historically, Ribeira Grande had been Cape Verde's largest town, but in the mid-eighteenth century, the town of Praia, on the other side of the island, was in the process of overtaking its rival in both population and economic significance. Godfrey did not record which of the two ports he visited, but his payment of twelve shillings and sixpence for a "Present to the Gov." strongly suggests that he visited Ribeira Grande, situated on the southern, leeward shore of Santiago, at the foot of two flat-topped hills and backed by mountains that rose to 4,566 feet.[11] At the time of the *Hare*'s visit, Ribeira Grande consisted of approximately one hundred fifty buildings and a crumbling cathedral; it was commanded by a fort perched on the hillside. A stream ran down from the mountains, through a narrow valley, and into the town. Residents had constructed a dam of pebbles at the mouth, which formed an inexhaustible pool of excellent fresh water. The floor of the harbor, however, was extremely rocky, with sufficient anchorage for only three ships at a time, and even three ships rode too close to be safe.[12] Godfrey and other members of the crew likely went ashore here, spending three Spanish dollars for anchorage.[13]

As the crew members made their way around Ribeira Grande, they would scarcely have failed to notice that most of the residents, from the government officials to the clergy to the common laborers, were black. The *Hare*'s crew was accustomed to the sight of black people. One-fifth of Newport's population was of African descent, and most, if not all, of the crew members had visited the West Indies, where up to 90 percent of the population was black. Cape Verde's population was largely descended from the Africans who were brought to work the cane fields in the fifteenth and sixteenth centuries. Although in the eyes of most New Englanders Cape Verde's population would have appeared similar to the population of Jamaica, there were significant differences. While most Cape Verdeans would have appeared "black" to the *Hare*'s crew, their skin color and features varied tremendously, the result of three centuries of European-African intermarriage. Many residents who would have been considered "negroes" in Rhode Island, where any known African ancestry "blackened" an individual, considered themselves—and indeed *were*—white in Cape Verde. Both the attitudes of the Portuguese and the history of the islands contributed to this particular racial formulation. With no plantation economy and little demand for slave labor, many masters had manumitted their bondmen rather than spend the money to maintain them. By the mid-eighteenth century, there were four times as many free residents on Santiago as there were slaves. Ironically then, slavery, while firmly embedded in the local economy and society, did not define race as completely in Cape Verde as it did in British America. This underscores the close, but nondeterministic relationship between labor and race. The *Hare* was about to enter a dramatically different racial environment, one in which "black" people wielded a great deal more power than the crew was used to on the other side of the Atlantic.[14]

After provisioning at Santiago, the *Hare* likely made for a second island in the Cape Verde archipelago, the island Godfrey called "Isle May," or Maio. A bit more than ten miles east of Santiago, Maio was easily visible from there in clear weather. It was ringed with sandy inlets broken up by occasional outcroppings of rocks. Two mountains rose from the interior, one flattening into a bluff, the other peaking at 1,430 feet. The anchorage was on the western side in a small bay fronted by a broad, sandy beach. Beyond this lay the engine of the local economy, a vast salt pond that yielded what one visitor described as "huge heaps of salt like drifts of snow." Although the salt was free, residents earned a living hauling it to the ships anchored in the roadstead. The British codfish fleet usually visited on its way to Newfoundland to collect the salt required to preserve their catch. Other ships carried salt to North America and the Caribbean, where it was used to preserve meat. Maio had a population of only 230 at the turn of the eighteenth century, and probably not much more at the time of the *Hare*'s visit. On the 1755–56 voyage, Godfrey dispensed ten Spanish dollars' worth of "presents" to the island's officers, all of whom, including the governor, were Luso-African, and purchased six dollars' worth of "Stock, Grass and Corn." He likely did the same this time, then set sail for the coast.[15]

Sailing time from Cape Verde to the Upper Guinea coast was just a few days, so the *Hare* probably sighted land on about August 15, somewhere between Senegambia and Sierra Leone. From the sea, the coastline between those two points is, as one traveler put it, "low and level, the trees with which it is fringed appearing to reach to the water's edge."[16] Another English visitor agreed, noting that this part of the coast had "less variety in the observance than most other countrys. Almost a universal sameness runs through the whole."[17] On a clear day it was possible to glimpse the inland mountains, but this being the rainy season, the mountains were probably obscured by clouds. From Cape Verde, the *Hare* sailed southward, past the Isles de Los, an archipelago about three miles off the coast of present-day Conakry, the two long, narrow islands enclosing the third like parentheses around a period. From the *Hare*, Godfrey would have glimpsed a narrow strand giving way to dense palm forest that climbed up a steep bluff, above which were several palm-topped hills. The Isles de Los were in the process of becoming a major slave-trading entrepôt.[18] If Godfrey stopped here on the way down the coast, it was not for long, for there is no record of it. The *Hare*, however, would return in the coming months.

Continuing southward along the coast for a few miles, Godfrey and the crew could hardly have missed the dramatic change in the landscape, as the "universal sameness" of the low-lying coast gave way to what appeared from the sea to be an island dominated by rich green slopes that rose gracefully to heights of over two thousand feet. But this was no island; it was the "Lion Range," or as the Portuguese had named it, "Serra Lyoa." Occupying a twenty-mile-long peninsula and running in a northwest–southeast direction parallel to the coast, the mountains marked the entrance to a massive natural harbor, where the Mitombo, or Sierra Leone River, met the Atlantic to form Sierra Leone Bay. Entrance to the bay was partially obstructed by extensive shallows several miles offshore. Nautical atlases like the *English Pilot* warned vessels to keep twelve to fifteen miles from the coast until the cape bore east by south, at which point it was safe to steer for the bay. Once inside the cape, vessels were well advised to "keep within one or two Cable's Length on the Starboard-side . . . [and] keep the high Land as near as you can," avoiding the shallows around Tagrin Point on the northern shore. The mountainous southern shore of the harbor was punctuated by a series of smaller bays: Pirate's Bay, Maria's Bay, Cockle Bay, White Man's Bay, Frenchman's Bay, and Fourah Bay.[19] Visitors were advised to keep a lookout for an inlet with reddish sand and "an abundance of Banana Trees," which indicated that the vessel had reached "the Watering Place." This was usually the first stop for most European vessels arriving at Sierra Leone. Here a ship could anchor comfortably in fourteen to sixteen fathoms while sending the boat for wood and water. There was also a village nearby, where, according to the *English Pilot*, a skipper could always ask directions.[20]

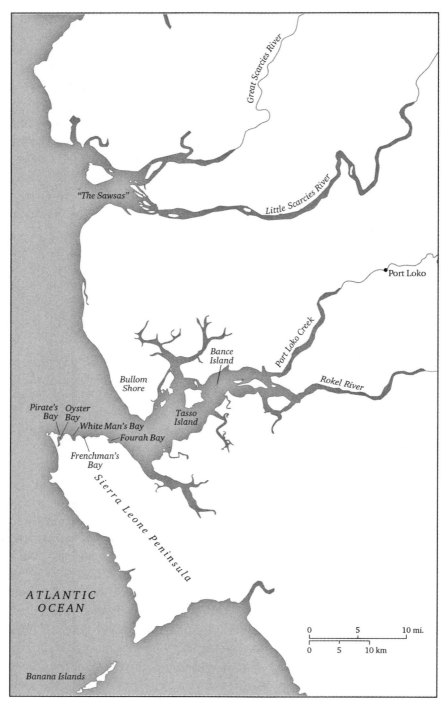

MAP 3.1. *Sierra Leone and vicinity*

Acting on all of this advice, however, would have been much easier said than done. Although the decision to set sail in midsummer made for, in Godfrey's words, "very Pleasant wether for six weeks after we Saild," it put the *Hare* on the African coast at the height of the rainy season. Coastal Sierra Leone averages 160–80 inches of rain annually, with some 70 percent falling in July, August, and September. In a typical August, the month of the *Hare*'s arrival, twenty-eight of thirty-one days are considered "wet," and the sun breaks through the clouds for only two hours per day. With a mean morning temperature of 90 degrees Fahrenheit, the humidity would have been overwhelming to the New Englanders.[21] In addition to the sheer volume of the rains, this part of the African coast was subject to what travelers referred to as "tornadoes," or extremely violent storms that blew in from the northeast. One visitor described the "dense lurid sulphureous looking mass" of clouds that gathered before a tornado, followed by "vivid flashes of forked lightning, in rapid succession, and thunder claps which give one the idea of the crash of brazen clouds, for the din is more like that which the encounter of great metallic bodies would occasion."[22] Godfrey must have experienced something similar, for he told the Vernons in his first letter from the coast that he had witnessed "the Greatest floods of Rain I ever Saw . . . it has Raind this ten days allmost without Intermition and very Strong winds." Nothing remained dry during the rainy season. After ten days on the coast, the *Hare*'s sails were encased in mildew, which proved impervious to repeated dousings with saltwater. Godfrey also discovered that the longboat was in poor condition, though it is doubtful that the rains were responsible. It seems instead to have been poorly constructed, tippy and unable to carry full sail, although eventually some of these defects were corrected. There was one saving grace, from Godfrey's point of view: no water had seeped into the rum casks. The *Hare*'s principal trade good remained undamaged.[23]

The *Hare* arrived in Sierra Leone on August 18, 1754, to find nine other vessels riding out the weather and trading when they could: three from Liverpool, one from London, three from France, one from Barbados, and another from Rhode Island. The latter was the schooner *Siraloon* (yet another rendering of "Sierra Leone"), skippered by veteran captain David Lindsay and owned by William Johnston & Co. Lindsay had sailed from Newport a few weeks before Godfrey but arrived only three days ahead of him, so he may have made other stops.[24] Despite being in need of both wood and water, Godfrey chose not to venture upriver to the main trading fort at Bance Island, the heavy rains and winds making any attempt to sail a risky proposition. He remained instead near White Man's Bay, where he paid King

Peter, a local ruler, three bottles of snuff as customs so that he could trade for fish, peppers, and limes. The weather prevented him from taking on wood or water. It also prevented the crew from beginning the task of readying the sloop for captives.[25]

At this point, possibly from conversations with the other captains, Godfrey learned that his rum was not worth much. Africans, like consumers everywhere, had particular likes and dislikes, all of which fluctuated according to time and place. Certain items were in demand for a while, only to be spurned as markets became glutted. Resident traders were attuned to these trends and always tried to inform their correspondents in Europe and North America. With communications taking several months to reach home, though, many merchants found it a challenge to synchronize their mix of wares—often referred to as an "assortment"—with African demand. Having a well-sorted cargo was analogous to getting a good currency exchange rate. The slave trade at Sierra Leone was conducted in a local currency known as "bars." These were originally iron bars manufactured in the Mande interior and traded with coastal residents for salt and other commodities. The Portuguese, recognizing a demand, began trading iron there in the sixteenth century. By the eighteenth century, bars were still the de facto currency of the slave trade, though as one trader put it, more "an imaginary value" than a commodity.[26] Before conducting trade, Europeans first negotiated the bar value of their goods with local merchants. Vessels therefore usually carried a variety of items in hopes that some would be in demand. It was the captain's job to get the most for his employers' money, and he often did so by swapping goods with other captains before trading for slaves.

This seems to be exactly what Godfrey had hoped to do, and it was particularly crucial for North American captains because they carried mostly rum, as opposed to the multiple trade goods, the textiles, guns, pans, cowries, and spirits, carried by European vessels. Rhode Islanders were at a particular disadvantage in Upper Guinea, where the Muslim influence lessened the demand for alcohol.[27] The thirty-four hogsheads, ten tierces, eight barrels, and six half barrels of rum landed by David Lindsay just a few days before, which apparently followed several other shipments, turned out to be all the local market could handle. The other shipmasters, who Godfrey had hoped might trade some of their goods for some of his rum, had little interest either, since they were hoping to buy captives in the same market. Despite the poor conditions, Godfrey did test the market by purchasing two boys, whom he described as being "above four feet" tall, and for whom he was "forst to give" ninety-five gallons of rum each.[28]

Godfrey did learn one bit of encouraging news. "I hear theirs some Whites Comeing from the Sawsa's," he related, "and hope I may Git of some rum to them." This was a reference to a group of traders on the coast north of Sierra Leone, and Godfrey was clearly pinning his hopes on rum being scarce up there. That turned out to be the case: within a few days he received confirmation that the traders were "in Great want of provisions and that I can Git of[f] my Rum with them." For the moment, he resigned himself to swapping rum for food and water, albeit at inflated prices, and waiting for the weather to clear before making any other moves.[29]

THE FOCAL POINT for all trade in Sierra Leone was Bance Island.[30] Located some twenty miles up the Sierra Leone River at the limit of deep water navigation, the island featured the largest slave-trading fort over the 1,300-mile stretch between the Gambia and the Gold Coast. The location made Bance Island a common provisioning station for southbound vessels, yielding the fort's owners a tidy supplement to their slaving income. The island itself lay about a mile from the nearest riverbank. The original fort had been built by the Royal African Company, the English slave-trading monopoly, in the 1670s. The fort was the successor to an earlier installation on nearby Tasso Island, erected in 1662 and destroyed by the Dutch in 1664, and another on Konkaw Island, which also proved vulnerable to attack. Not that Bance Island was impregnable. In the 1690s, Royal African Company officials deemed it indefensible, consolidated operations one hundred miles to the south on York Island in the Sherbro River, and maintained only a skeleton crew for the next ten years. In 1704, the French destroyed the fort; in 1705, they attacked it again. Pirates, who were a persistent menace to shipping in the area, briefly occupied the island in 1719 and again in 1720.

The biggest blow to the Royal African Company's activities came in 1728, struck by José Lopez, a Luso-African trader. Lopez had a complicated relationship with the Royal African Company. He competed with it but at the same time did business with it, supplying slaves, ivory, and dyewoods in exchange for the company's trade goods, often on credit. In fact, during the 1720s, Lopez was the company's largest non-European debtor in Sierra Leone, which may have been a factor in his decision to attack it. During the night of October 25, 1728, several hundred of Lopez's forces stormed the fort at Bance Island. Aided by African servants and slaves within the walls, they expelled the company's agent and all of its employees. The Royal African Company would never return to Sierra Leone, and the island sat abandoned for over a decade.[31]

British presence on the island was reestablished in 1744, when a Captain Boyce, acting as agent for London merchant George Fryer, paid Bai Samma, a Bullom ruler, for the privilege of operating a trading fort there. Bai Samma agreed only after Boyce gave reassurances that he did not represent the hated Royal African Company. Boyce rebuilt the fort's magazine and walls and mounted twenty-two cannons. He and Fryer conducted business there until about 1748, when they sold out to a partnership of Scottish merchants residing in London. The new proprietors, Grant, Oswald, & Co., devoted most of their capital to continuing Fryer and Boyce's construction program, purchasing boats for local trade and hiring agents and employees. They also had to contend with uncertainty regarding their right to trade at Bance Island. Technically, the Royal African Company had never relinquished its rights, even though the sure opposition of Bai Samma and other regional rulers would have rendered reoccupation impractical. In 1751, however, with the Royal African Company reorganized as the Company of Merchants Trading to Africa, Parliament allowed Grant, Oswald & Co. to keep Bance Island. With their trading rights confirmed by both Whitehall and their Bullom landlords, the proprietors began the slow process of building up a slave trade. As of 1752, they had dispatched two shiploads.[32]

Bance Island was about one-third of a mile long by five hundred feet wide, with a towering stand of trees at the northern tip. The island's narrow strand led to a short bluff, atop the northern end of which sat the fort. The exact condition of Bance Island is difficult to know. When the *Hare* arrived in the summer of 1754, the island had just begun its ascent from dereliction to profitability. Grant & Oswald's chief agent reported in 1751 that "this Fort is quite out of Repair," while another visitor noted that "The Walls in many places [are] ready to fall." By 1756, however, a military survey of British installations along the African coast pronounced Bance Island "in Good Repair," so at the time of the *Hare*'s visit its condition was likely somewhere between these two points.[33] A thick, castellated wall was the fort's main defense, at the bottom of which was a smaller "Pallisado" made of upright tree trunks. A stone jetty was the main landing point, but only smaller craft could dock there. Larger vessels had to anchor about five hundred yards away, so slaves and supplies were transported in shallops and longboats. The trip could be quite risky. Tornadoes and storms could make navigation very dangerous, and sharks and crocodiles could attack sailors and captives. Sharks and reptiles were not the only animal hazards, however: in 1723 an elephant attacked a shallop that was lightering six captives out to a snow. Three died.[34]

FIGURE 3.1. *Bance Island in 1748. In 1748, Bance Island's new owners were making repairs after almost two decades of neglect. The structure to the immediate left of the flag is the agent's dwelling, and to its left are the ruins of the Royal African Company governor's residence, which was destroyed in the 1728 attack that forced the abandonment of the island. "Shipping slaves" were kept in rooms built into the wall on the far side of the fort, while "castle slaves" lived in the small houses outside the walls, to the right. (The National Archives, U.K.)*

The entrance into the castle was uphill from the jetty, along a path and through a gate beside one of two large cylindrical bastions. In the center of one bastion was a flagpole topped by a massive Union Jack, visible at a great distance. The gate opened into a large courtyard. Directly ahead was the former company agent's residence, a two-story brick structure with a large, sweeping staircase, a crumbling ruin by 1754. A short distance from this stood the new agent's dwelling house, a two-story L-shaped structure built by Boyce and Fryer just a few years earlier. The upstairs apartments were supported by four stone pillars and featured a formal dining room, lodging for visitors, and a shaded balcony overlooking the yard. Below these were warehouses, and behind them were the kitchen, cook's stores, and a sizable garden. Near the garden, at a safe distance from the dwelling house, stood the thick-walled powder magazine.[35]

Along the southeastern edge of the courtyard ran a long, mud-walled structure consisting of four rooms, each with its own entrance and windows. The island's white employees—accountants, bookkeepers, the surgeon and his mate, sailors, and skilled tradesmen—lodged here. Next to this lodging and against the edge of the courtyard stood a row of five adjoining houses constructed of hefty mangrove spars, covered in plaster and topped with a terra-cotta roof. The "shipping slaves," those captives awaiting sale and transport, were kept in these houses. At times when there were too many captives to house indoors, the overflow spilled outdoors into the courtyard. Adjoining the shipping-slave houses and jutting into the courtyard was a "palaver house," where company agents and African merchants negotiated prices. However, only a fraction of Bance Island's captives were brought directly to the fort by African dealers. As one employee described the process, company agents and African merchants negotiated with "small shells which they use as Counters . . . every peice of European goods has it's fixed price." The reasons for holding talks in the palaver house rather than in the agent's dwelling are not clear. The choice of the palaver house probably stemmed from security concerns but perhaps also represented a concession to local custom, with the palaver house a more neutral site than the enclosed office. Almost every village featured a palaver house in which all manner of trade and civil affairs were conducted.[36]

Distinct from the shipping slaves and housed outside the walls of the fort were the "castle slaves," or "factory slaves." In 1751, there were thirty-four on the island; in 1756, after several years of increased slaving, their numbers had grown to ninety-three. These laborers occupied a tenuous position on Bance Island. They could generally expect to work and live on the island for life. Castle slaves were allowed families and learned skilled trades, which they passed on to their children; this gave them more stability and predictability than the shipping slaves were afforded. Shipping slaves would labor and die in foreign countries after they were sold. Historically, not all of the black laborers at Bance Island were enslaved—a certain number were "gromettas" or "gromettos." The word *grometto* was borrowed from the Portuguese, originally referring to a ship's boy. Along the African coast, it doubled as a term for black wage laborers, but it is difficult to determine the precise line between gromettos and castle slaves at Bance Island. During the 1720s, two dozen gromettos worked there and were clearly distinct from the forty or so castle slaves. Later descriptions of the fort, such as the naval surveys of the 1750s, mention only the slaves, while other observers used the terms interchangeably or noted only the "black men" without specifying their legal status. All of this suggests that slave labor may have supplanted waged labor at Bance Island before 1750, perhaps as a result of the 1728 rebellion. Similarly, the boundary between castle slaves and shipping slaves was permeable, with agents occasionally selling castle slaves as shipping slaves, a fate gromettos also feared. When one agent asked a group of gromettos to help sail a company vessel to South Carolina, nine of them fled with their wives and children in a canoe, suspecting they would be sold once in America. When one of the fugitives was recaptured, he shot himself in the head with a pistol.[37] Bance Island was not the only place that employed gromettos; they were present at virtually every slave-trading establishment, large and small, on the coast. Godfrey, in fact, hired two of them for three months, apparently from King Peter while at White Man's Bay.[38]

Bance Island was a trading fort, but it is perhaps better to think of it as a constellation of trading forts and a commercial empire unto itself. While agents purchased some slaves and other goods from traders who brought them to the island, they acquired many more at the several smaller trading posts they maintained, which were known as "out-factories."[39] During the 1720s, Bance Island was supplied by at least four out-factories, three to the north of Sierra Leone Bay, at the Rio Pongo, the Rio Nuñez, and Mania, and a fourth to the south at Cape Mount. These establishments were probably quite modest and impermanent camps; in fact, it is unclear whether there were any installations there or whether Bance Island's traders simply lodged with local merchants. After Grant & Oswald acquired the fort, the supply network expanded considerably. By 1763, proprietors operated seven out-factories, most of which were at least semipermanent establishments located north of Sierra Leone Bay in the area known as the Northern Rivers.[40]

Bance Island's out-factories were staffed by employees known as "factors," who, in some cases, were assisted by "under factors." Factors were generally ex-sailors who had been lured from visiting ships by the job's thirty- to forty-pound salary to purchase slaves and to safeguard trade goods. James Low, a bookkeeper who was involved in recruiting, took a dim view of the factors, describing them as barely literate and "not worth Victualls."[41] A few of them were African, possibly trusted employees and interpreters who had been promoted or prominent locals, including the sons of Eurafrican and African traders, who had been placed by their families to solidify commercial connections. Once hired, a new factor was sent out with a veteran in order to learn how to conduct the trade—a wise policy considering the many ways in which deals could go wrong.

A factor was allowed a small number of assistants, black or white, and was served by one of Bance Island's several shallops or sloops. One of the agents in charge made periodic visits to the out-factories to check on operations and to bring a change of crew. It appears doubtful that the factors were paid

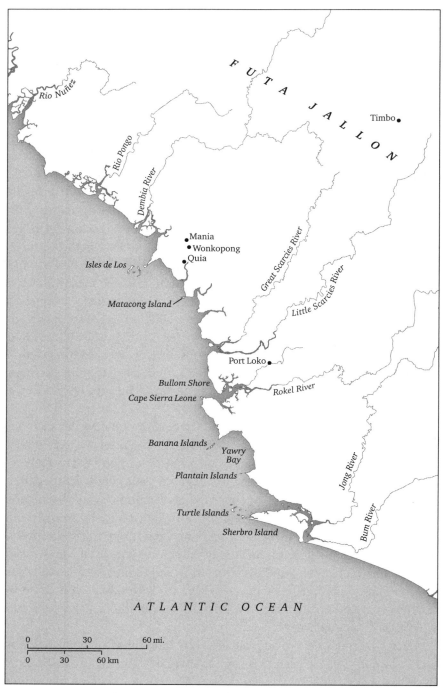

MAP 3.2. *The Upper Guinea coast from Cape Verga to Cape Mount*

any commission; instead, their salary was intended to suffice. As a book-keeper, James Low was too valuable to send out as a factor, but he did imply that he stood to make more money, albeit dishonestly, if he had been one. "I will hardly have any Chance for one of those Factorys," he told his patron back home in Scotland, "as I will always [be] necessary on the Island, nor Indeed would I much Choose [to work as a factor], as I don't see they can honestly gain more than their wages."[42] Because of this—or perhaps despite it—Grant & Oswald had a very difficult time with their factors. Many of them used their positions to accept inducements from their suppliers or to trade on their own account using the company's goods. And once they had gained experience in the trade, many of them abandoned their employers and either set up shop for themselves or negotiated a better deal with the competition.[43]

Aside from the out-factories, Bance Island supplied itself with captives through its fleet of small watercraft. In 1751, the fort owned one sloop, one shallop, two small boats, two canoes, and a schooner that was "out of repair." Grant & Oswald also owned a larger snow, which they presumably used for long-distance voyages to England or the Americas. A 1756 inventory describes a comparable flotilla of five vessels of 140, 35, 20, 15, and 10 tons burden, all in "good repair" and each with a shipmaster on the payroll. These vessels sailed the region's many rivers and estuaries in search of slaves and other goods. Each carried a cargo of trade goods and a factor, who was recruited and trained in a manner similar to the training of those who manned the out-factories. Between these vessels and the out-factories, Bance Island was able to influence commerce, if not actually dominate it, over a radius of about two hundred miles.[44]

Bance Island's economic reach crowded out many slave-ship captains. With out-factories and trading vessels buying up so many captives, the supply was small and the price high. In fact, at the time of the *Hare*'s visit, most of Grant & Oswald's business was devoted to supplying their own American plantations, or those of their associates. In later years, large-scale contracting would dominate, mostly with the French. The fort's agents had a strong disincentive to sell to independent captains because the agents were liable for penalties if they failed to fulfill their contracts. Often, captives were not available to noncontracted ship captains because they were promised to other vessels. For these reasons, relatively few of the Bance Island captives were sold to "private" vessels. Over the years 1748–84, the period of Grant & Oswald's proprietorship, only about 18 percent of the fort's captives were sold to independent slave ships, with none at all recorded for 1754 or 1755.[45]

The *Hare* therefore purchased few if any captives at Bance Island on this voyage, buying instead from the many smaller dealers who dotted the Upper Guinea coast. Still, we know that Godfrey did visit Bance Island. Among his expenses was a payment to "Capt. Stephens People," a reference to Jonathan Stephens, Grant & Oswald's agent in charge of Bance Island. The exact nature of the payment is unclear, but it was probably for provisions, naval stores, or lighterage.[46]

Godfrey's other visit to Bance Island was slightly less routine. On August 30, he boarded the snow *Honorable Friend*, which had put in at Sierra Leone with a leaky hull and was headed upriver to the fort for repairs. The crew had captured a "large tygar"—in reality probably a leopard—which they chained to the taffrail atop the poop deck. While aboard, Godfrey went aft to speak with someone in a small boat. With the cat behind him and out of view, Godfrey drifted too close to the animal. Suddenly the leopard seized him, digging its claws into each arm and sinking its teeth into the soft flesh below his ear. The cat, he later recounted, "had me down on the deck in an Instant[,] but through the Mercy of God the Capt and his People Resqued me of his Jaws[,]" a feat accomplished at "considerable hurt" to Godfrey. With blood streaming from six "prety Deep" holes in his throat, Godfrey was taken to Bance Island, where the surgeon of a British slave ship bandaged his wounds. A few days later, with the holes in his neck leaking blood and pus, Godfrey prevailed upon a French surgeon from one of the nearby vessels to lance them. Although the attack left him "very ill," his injuries seem to have been minor. After only four days at the fort, Godfrey pronounced himself "very well" and reassumed active command of the *Hare*.[47]

Leopards were far from the only problem Godfrey encountered on the coast. A more serious problem was his relationship with the *Hare*'s crew. Tension among shipmates was a near-universal fixture of maritime life. Trouble started at the end of August or the beginning of September, when several crew members attempted to desert, though the specific circumstances are murky. Godfrey told the Vernons in a letter that a Captain Gardner, commanding a sloop out of London, had instructed his mate to "invegeile" two of his people to leave the *Hare* by offering them fifty shillings per month. Several days later, with Godfrey away recuperating from his wounds on Bance Island, five of the *Hare*'s seamen attempted to abscond in the longboat. Mate John Arnold Hammond heard the men lowering the boat and managed to stop them. When Godfrey returned, he clapped the five into irons, but released three of them upon securing their promise not to flee again. Godfrey kept William White, whom he called "as great a Villain as any in the world," and William Jones locked up for a longer time.[48] It is not certain how long they remained confined, but the fact that White was discharged on October 28 and Jones on December 12 suggests that the men either were put off or left on their own accord after a few weeks. With a third of his seamen confined, Godfrey was now "forst to keep watch myself and hardly dare go from the Vessel for fear of their Giting away." Some relief came on September 21, when Barnt Hartwick, who may have been German, Dutch, or Scandinavian, signed on as an ordinary seaman.[49] Tensions like this rarely found their way into the written record; they reflected poorly on the captain's ability to command his vessel. Godfrey, though, was concerned that the Vernons might blame him for the voyage's slow progress, and he wanted it in the record that any delay was due to problems with "my people and the misfourtune with the Tygar." Future events would nonetheless call into question Godfrey's ability to manage a crew.[50]

While it is unknown what specific circumstances inspired the men to jump ship, desertions of this sort were very common. Conditions aboard slave ships were notoriously bad, and sailors went ashore—either permanently or temporarily—for a variety of reasons: to procure alcohol, to find women, to trade, to escape an abusive captain, to avoid punishment or prosecution for crimes, to find a better situation aboard another vessel, or to earn more money as factors. Nicholas Owen deserted off the coast of Sierra Leone in 1752. Earlier, his ship failed to salvage a French vessel that had been crippled by a slave revolt, and the crew "devided" over the competency of the captain and officers. This, in turn, sparked "sevare usage without respect" and a punitive cut in the men's rations. Seeking to "obtain that liberty which every Europain is intitle to," Owen and four confederates stole the longboat and sailed to Cape Mount. After a period of foraging and begging along the coast, Owen fell ill with a fever. The men then decided to surrender at Bance Island. It was not unusual for slave forts to serve as houses of detention for deserting sailors, although in most instances they did not arrive voluntarily. In fact, seamen were often housed in them for longer periods of time than slaves, for the simple reason that ships were always more eager to pick up captives than refractory tars. But instead of facing punishment when he recovered, Owen was allowed to sign on to a Rhode Island vessel. Through his actions he escaped a bad situation, earned a respite from the tyranny of maritime life, and secured a presumably better position for himself.[51]

Slave-ship crews thus turned over, even in the middle of a voyage. The loss of too many sailors could delay operations and imperil the profitability of the voyage. Safety was an issue because slave ships needed more than a full complement of sailors to guard against insurrection; in fact, a few months before the *Hare*'s arrival, captives aboard the London ship *Adventure* seized control of the vessel a few miles outside the bar, killed one crew member and wounded a second, drove the ship onto the shore, and destroyed it.[52] Godfrey was careful never to leave fewer than eight men aboard the *Hare*. But the most common reason for turnover in crew members was the need to replace seamen lost to disease. With no immunity to tropical parasites like the *Plasmodium falciparum*, which causes malaria, and the yellow fever virus, European sailors succumbed in great numbers. At the end of the eighteenth century, crew mortality averaged about 18 percent, and it was not unprecedented for a ship to lose an entire crew to disease.[53] Although Godfrey made no mention of illness in his letters, it is virtually certain that most, if not all, of the crew contracted malaria or another tropical disease and spent some portion of the voyage incapacitated with fever. Remarkably, however, not a single member of the *Hare*'s crew seems to have died while employed aboard the *Hare*. The only two members who did not accompany the vessel back across the Atlantic were William White and William Jones, both of whom, as mentioned earlier, appear to have either deserted or been put off the ship by Godfrey. The *Hare*'s captives would not be so fortunate.

GODFREY'S PAYMENT to open trade with King Peter signaled that he would observe regional custom. It was a wise choice. Europeans who traded on the African coast entered an environment that was emphatically not in their control, but rather in the control of their hosts. At the heart of this situation was the simple fact that, at least on the shore, Africans were militarily more powerful than their European visitors. They could muster large forces and expel Europeans almost at will, as José Lopez had done to the Royal African Company. And while the British had reoccupied Bance Island, the Africans still retained this advantage. In the words of proprietor Richard Oswald, Europeans depended "chiefly upon a good understanding with the Natives[,] without which the strongest Fortification in Africa would be of very little Service."[54] Captains like Godfrey thus had every incentive to comply with local and regional conventions. The outer limit of Godfrey's power scarcely extended beyond the range of the *Hare*'s guns, and in many respects, not even that far. Shipmasters who ignored the custom of the country took a gamble, one that sometimes paid off but that more often brought disaster.

Violence was endemic along the African coast, and the slave trade was responsible for a great deal of it. Enslavement, after all, usually occurred through an act of violence. Resistance and rebellion by the enslaved were fixtures in those areas where the trade was significant.[55] Yet while violent resistance by slaves was unquestionably a concern for Europeans once they took on their cargoes, trade entailed risk from a different quarter: the people who supplied the captives. Disputes between shipmasters and private traders, on the one hand, and African suppliers, on the other, frequently turned deadly. In 1742, two Luso-Africans, backed by twenty-two soldiers, "cut off" (which is to say, attacked) a Massachusetts vessel in Sierra Leone Bay, seizing seventy-five captives and executing the captain.[56] Numerous similar occurrences led one trader to recommend: "Make it a general rule always to be upon your guard among all natives whether you know them to be good or bad." He suggested ordering the watch to call out "all is well" every half hour while at anchor, erecting a barricade athwart the vessel for defensive purposes, forbidding "natives" to carry arms onboard, manning the swivel guns at all times, and keeping all but a few principal traders off the quarter deck (the primary site of trade negotiations).[57] John Newton, the British slaver who would later oppose the trade and write the words to "Amazing Grace," summed up matters: "We trade under arms; and they are furnished with long knives."[58]

To outside observers, this sort of violence appeared random and senseless, but it was a part of the trading system. The violence had a logic of its own, sustaining a "warlike peace," as Newton called it; it had a common if informal code of justice, punishment, and retaliation, worked out over the course of two centuries of European-African interaction.[59] Dealers, middlemen, and captains all understood its basic workings. In many respects, this culture of violence constituted a "middle-ground," a brutal but functional pidgin or border language through which Africans, Eurafricans, and Europeans conducted their business. The slave markets may have been more efficient had there been no violence, but they may not have existed without it, given the role of retaliation as a facilitator of the trade. If nothing else, the soaring numbers of captives exported from Upper Guinea in the second half of the eighteenth century, all traded according to these customs, testify to the system's paradoxical commercial efficiency. It was in this environment that the links were forged between the African interior and the larger Atlantic World.[60]

Relationships between Europeans and Africans were structured by a set of long-established conventions, which, when followed, usually kept tensions to a minimum.[61] The most fundamental of these was the landlord-stranger relationship, which prevailed throughout Upper Guinea and long predated the arrival of the Europeans. It was, in essence, a way of ordering economic and political relations in a multicultural environment. Under its terms, non-native visiting merchants (or "strangers") were allowed to trade in the land-lord society as long as they acknowledged the priority and sovereignty of the landlord through the payment of tribute, in addition to whatever other terms might be negotiated. The landlord, for his part, owed the stranger protection from threats to his person and goods. This obligation was taken quite seriously. In fact, a fair proportion of the violence along the coast stemmed from the imperative to retaliate for thefts and assaults committed against one's clients. The landlord-stranger relationship extended to other areas. Landlords were envisioned as father figures, whose authority came with reciprocal obligations. It was expected, for example, that the landlord would be consulted in such matters as matrimony, and strangers could beg provisions in times of famine. When the Europeans arrived, they assimilated into this framework, though with some modifications. Older stipulations that agreements were not transferrable or inheritable were often, though not always, ignored. Europeans also reserved the right to administer justice to their own. Nevertheless, large proprietors like Grant & Oswald (and the eventual Sierra Leone Company of the 1790s) and the hundreds of small traders paid a ground rent to live and work on the Upper Guinea coast.[62]

The institution of "palaver"—which signified a dispute—was another important framework for European-African interaction. Although the word itself was a corruption of the Portuguese "palavra," or "word," palaver orig-inated in Africa and existed independently from any European influence. As with the landlord-stranger relationship, Europeans were expected to adhere to its basic tenets. Europeans habitually likened the palaver to the suit at law. When, for example, misunderstandings occurred between landlords and tenants, they would "make a palaver." But palaver meant more than just a dispute; it also implied an effort to reach a resolution and to restore lost comity. Even something like trade negotiation fell under the heading of palaver, indicative of the degree to which West Africans viewed such deal-ings as essentially conflictual. One visitor recounted that "a palaver is held over every thing they have for barter . . . every tooth of ivory requires a new palaver, and they will dispute for a whole day . . . with the most determined firmness." Bance Island even featured a palaver house, the sole purpose of which was to serve as a dedicated site for trade negotiations.[63]

Palavers were generally conducted quite formally, usually in a ceremonial building dedicated to the purpose. Special "palaver talkers" argued for each side, with the actual parties to the dispute remaining silent. Proceedings gen-erally began with a ceremonial salute, after which the palaver talkers would present their cases over the course of two or more hours. Palaver entailed an aesthetic tradition of its own, and one European described the talkers as speaking with "such dignity of action, force, and energy of elocution, as would do honour to an English orator."[64] The local ruler presided indirectly over the affair. Palaver talkers made their case to the village elders, who then presented it, along with a recommendation, to the ruler.[65]

Any number of things could bring about a palaver: gunpowder casks with false barrelheads, watered spirits, textiles folded to hide large holes, delays in furnishing goods, or indiscretions with local women. One of the most common events to instigate a palaver was the practice known as "panyarring." Like the term "palaver," "to panyar" originated in the Portuguese and described a practice that existed before the arrival of the Europeans in Africa. The word initially referred to an action of distrain or the seizure of property for debt. Customarily, if a person failed to fulfill a debt, the creditor was entitled to seize him or a member of his household or family and hold the person until restitution was made. European traders soon learned to abide by the custom of the country, as both initiators and objects of panyarring. The old Royal African Company at Bance Island frequently saw its employees and retainers panyarred by its local trading partners. In 1722, the company paid 450 bars to redeem seven women and nine children held by José Lopez. As time passed and the slave trade grew increasingly important, panyarring seems to have lost some of its connection with debt and came to signify the opportunistic abduction of Africans by slave-ship crews. John Atkins invoked both the original and later meanings in 1725 when he said, "*Panyarring*, is a Term for Man-stealing along the whole Coast: Here it's used also, for stealing any thing else, and by Custom (their Law) every Man has a right to seize of another at any Conveniency, so much as he can prove afterwards, at the Palaaver-Court, to have been defrauded of, by any body in the same place he was cheated."[66]

Slave trading was further structured by the closely related institution of pawnship. The institution seems to have developed out of a desire to avoid the violence associated with panyarring. European merchants and ship captains accepted pawns, usually family members or dependents of coastal dealers, as security for goods received on credit. When the debt was settled, the pawns were redeemed, but there was a great deal of room for slippage. For example, if a debtor missed the deadline for redeeming his pawns, the pawns could be permanently enslaved and sold in the Americas.[67] In other circumstances, African elites used pawnship to circumvent the prohibition against selling domestic slaves (that is, those born locally) to traders by simply "pawning" the slaves in question without intending to redeem them.[68] By custom, ships were expected to provide three to four weeks' notice before sailing with any pawns, in order to give relatives and debtors a chance to redeem them. Many captains adhered to the practice, hesitating to antagonize powerful coastal figures, in order both to maintain good trade relations and to avoid provoking violent retaliation. The proportion of pawns in any cargo seems to have varied. Paul Cross, a Briton who, as a slave dealer, routinely advanced goods to his suppliers, once delivered thirty-four captives, of whom fourteen were pawns, to a shipmaster. On other occasions the proportion was much lower. Of the twenty-three captives Cross delivered to the brig *William* in 1772, only one was a pawn, and among the thirty-five captives he sold to an unnamed vessel in 1773, only two were pawns. Some captains, especially those who did not expect to return to Africa, sailed with pawns aboard in flagrant violation of coastal convention.[69]

Disputes over panyarrings and departed pawns were among the greatest sources of strife on the Upper Guinea coast. "In one place or another, trade is often suspended, all intercourse cut off, and things are in a state of war," wrote John Newton, "till necessity, either on the ship's part, or on theirs, produces overtures of peace, and dictates the price, which the offending party must pay for it."[70] Some of these disagreements were settled peaceably in the forum of the palaver, but with little choice but to participate, Europeans complained that they rarely received justice. "In their disputes with white men," wrote John Mathews, "they are not very rigid observers of justice; and . . . if a white man should succeed in his suit . . . they never adjudge any recompense to be made him on any occasion." When Mathews complained to his hosts about an unfavorable verdict, they told him, "White men get so much money; they cannot want their money."[71] Another trader warned that ship captains who went ashore to negotiate with Africans risked being seized themselves on dubious grounds. "They can bring a palaver against you for looking only," he reported, warning that captains "must pay a quantity of goods to gain your liberty."[72] The practices of panyarring, pawnship, and palaver reveal a great deal about the dynamics of power along the Upper Guinea coast. The fact that Europeans felt obliged to participate in, indeed submit to, local customs and perceptions of justice suggests their political and military weakness. However, the Europeans' bending of these institutions to deliver ever-growing numbers of captives is testament to their economic power.

Rhode Islanders were full participants in this culture of violence, both as victims and as perpetrators. In fact, given the tendency for disputes to escalate into ever-widening circles of retaliation, it was often hard to distinguish between victims and perpetrators. Nicholas Owen was panyarred while serving aboard a Newport slaver. Having gone ashore with five other crew members, he was suddenly "secur'd by the natives, put into irons, and hove down upon the ground in a barborous manner, striping us of all our cloaths." When the seamen asked the reason for their capture, they were told it was in retaliation for the panyarring of several local residents by a Dutch ship. When the men protested that they were British, not Dutch, their captors released them but confiscated all of their goods, which, according to Owen, amounted to four years' pay.[73] The violence often escalated considerably further. In 1754, just south of the Gambia, a Liverpool skipper panyarred a number of free subjects of the Damel of Cajor. The damel (whom the British called the "king") responded by seizing a South Carolina vessel captained by John Ruff and imprisoning him, four crew members, and his interpreter, all with the support of the local French trader. Ruff managed to escape, and the French redeemed the remaining British captives for 211 Spanish dollars, with the expectation of compensation. Ruff, however, wanted his vessel and cargo returned, so he panyarred several additional free subjects to gain leverage. Hall, a British slave dealer from Sierra Leone, and a Newport vessel captained by William Ellery came to Ruff's aid. Together, they "went on the Domel Coast and have been seizing & killing all the people they met with." The damel responded by seizing another British vessel and crew, while the governor petitioned for more soldiers and weapons.[74] Ellery's involvement shows that Rhode Island skippers were fully conversant in the system of retaliatory violence. In a short while, Godfrey would show that he was, too.

CHAPTER FOUR

Traders and Captives

Few if any of the captives purchased by the *Hare* came from Bance Island. In the summer of 1754, the proprietors were still building up their trade, and what slaves they had generally stocked their own American holdings or those of their friends. Even at its peak, Bance Island supplied only a portion of the captives taken from Sierra Leone. In 1768, a longtime employee of the Company of Merchants Trading to Africa estimated that 80 percent of all captives from greater Sierra Leone (defined as the area south of Cacheu to Cape Mount) were sold by traders not affiliated with Grant & Oswald (see table 2 in appendix 3).[1] Moreover, with the market for spirits saturated around Sierra Leone Bay, Godfrey realized he needed to look elsewhere to sell rum for slaves. Fortunately for him, there were plenty of alternatives. Unlike some of the other parts of Africa, such as the Gold Coast and Ouidah, where trade was channeled through a small number of forts (and hence known as the "fort trade"), the Upper Guinea coast was dotted with dozens, if not hundreds, of small European and Eurafrican dealers (the "private trade"). From the perspective of a slave-ship captain, these dealers provided a welcome alternative to the larger entrepôts like Bance Island. The main disadvantage was that they could only deliver a small number of captives at a time, occasionally up to sixty or seventy, but more often fewer than a half dozen. The smaller numbers meant that vessels had to patronize multiple dealers in order to complete their cargoes. Shuttling between suppliers and waiting for them to deliver captives added to the total time spent on the coast, which in turn increased mortality for both slaves and sailors. Some localities would eventually build themselves into large-scale bulking centers that rivaled Bance Island. The Isles de Los is the best example. This trend, however, was just beginning in the 1750s, so Godfrey was not able to take full advantage.

Many of the small-scale slave dealers of the Upper Guinea coast were descendants of European resident traders, Portuguese *lançados* in the

78

sixteenth century and agents of the Royal African Company in the seventeenth and eighteenth centuries. Often, they married into prominent local families and managed to establish lineages while enhancing their connections, prospects, and power. Successive generations of Eurafricans continued and expanded the business. Many of the second generation were comfortable in two worlds, which made them ideal brokers. Some had been baptized, and several had gone to Europe for formal education. "With a White Man he is a White Man," said an Englishman of one of the more successful Anglo-African traders, "with a Black Man [he is] a Black Man." Prominent families in Sierra Leone included the Caulkers, descended from a Royal African Company factor named Thomas Corker, who came to Sherbro in 1684. The lineage he founded became one of Sierra Leone's most enduring and powerful. The Cleveland, Rogers, and Tucker families followed similar paths. Still other dealers were former sailors, pirates, and employees of the forts who thought they stood better chances as independent operators. Familiar with intricacies of trade, palaver, panyarring, and pawnship, they founded numerous small establishments along the region's creeks and rivers and on several of the nearby islands.[2]

Private traders made their living by purchasing captives from African and Eurafrican dealers and selling them either to ship captains or to the larger entrepôts like Bance Island and the Isles de Los. In contrast to the forts and barracoons of the larger establishments, the private traders tended to live in much smaller houses built in the local style, with outbuildings to house trade goods and captives and a small landing for watercraft. Nicholas Owen, who worked first for a private trader, then on his own account, described one of his houses as being built "of long sticks muded over and whitewash'd, haveing the inside line with mats and well thatched aloft." His sketch shows a small house in a clearing, with two windows and surrounded by a small fenced garden.[3] The private traders' operations varied in scale. Owen was assisted by a few hired gromettos and perhaps some slaves. At the other end of the spectrum was Paul Cross, who had between fifty and sixty slaves.[4] Benjamin Hore, one of Cross's neighbors, had a comparable retinue of thirty slaves and gromettos. For Hore, having that many slaves caused problems. Unable to produce enough food one year, he was forced to use some of his proceeds to trade for rice with nearby villages.[5]

Like all merchants, the private traders made money by buying low and selling high. They preferred to do business with ship captains rather than with the fort. During periods of scarce shipping, however, Bance Island's status as the biggest buyer of slaves allowed it to exert a monopsonistic power, with private traders forced to sell to the fort for less than they wished. Moreover, small-scale dealers had few, if any, slaves close at hand and ready for sale. The costs of maintaining them and the risk that they might die before a willing buyer arrived discouraged the practice. They might have a half dozen or fewer on hand, but selling captives in larger numbers, which is what most captains preferred, generally required the buyers to trade goods in advance of delivery. In turn, the private trader would advance the goods to an African supplier, a loan usually secured with pawns.[6] The shipmaster and trader would agree on a number of slaves and a time for delivery, although it is doubtful that they actually made a formal agreement, including late penalties, as was the practice with contract sales at the large forts. Assembling the captives usually took several months, as they were acquired sporadically, in ones and twos. It took Paul Cross from January 23 to May 27, 1773, to assemble thirty-five captives for delivery to the *Little Will*.[7] Sometimes the captives were brought in canoes or on foot by African dealers. As Nicholas Owen described the process, "you are obliged to treat them all to liquer before you purchase anything or not." These exchanges were made "very troublesome" by the need to put up with the African traders' "noise and bad language." And, generally speaking, slaves were sold in lots, on a take-it-or-leave-it basis, which often forced traders to accept less desirable captives. At other times, traders ranged over hundreds of miles of coastline and riverfront, visiting numerous dealers in search of captives. Owen sailed "continually from one place to another" in his shallop, suggesting that this sort of travel absorbed a majority of his time. Paul Cross did, too, although he seems to have employed people to do the trading.[8]

Private trading could be very lucrative. For example, two private traders who each shipped ten slaves to South Carolina on their own accounts cleared nearly $60,000 each in today's money in just one transaction.[9] Paul Cross told an old patron that he had been "Blest with my share of success" and reckoned the value of his slaves at £2,400 sterling, or nearly $400,000 today.[10] Eurafrican trader Henry Tucker's wealth "sets him above the Kings," and John Newton was attracted to the trade upon learning that his master had "acquired considerable wealth," having bought a quarter share in Newton's former ship, and was able to make visits to England.[11] Wealth aside, life in Africa changed the traders in complex ways. Most, if not all, had relationships with African women, but their engagement with African people and culture often ran beyond sex to embrace larger, cosmological practices.[12] After dismissing Mande methods of divination as black magic, Nicholas Owen found himself employing it in his own affairs. And John

Newton, who was chagrined to admit that he actually enjoyed the trader's life, noted that "There is a significant phrase frequently used in those parts, That such a white man is grown black." This did not entail any changes in "complection," he was quick to add, but in "disposition." "I have known several," he elaborated, "who, settling in Africa at the age of thirty or forty, have . . . been gradually assimilated to the tempers, customs, and ceremonies of the natives." Some even preferred Africa to England, having become "dupes to all the pretended charmes, necromancies, amulets, and divinations of the blinded negroes."[13]

The *Hare* purchased all, or nearly all, of its captives from twenty-four small private traders like these (see table 3 in appendix 3). The names of all twenty-four survive in an account kept by Godfrey, which also lists the number of men, women, girls, and boys and the amount of trade goods paid.[14] The account does not give the dates of purchase or the locations of the dealers. However, by using other documents, it is possible to locate almost half of them. As it happens, Godfrey listed the dealers in rough geographic order, from north to south, along approximately two hundred miles of coastline. In all likelihood, the *Hare* bought its captives in something resembling the order in which they are listed, since the account follows the prevailing winds and currents, which run down the coast. An account of Godfrey's other expenditures generally confirms the basic north–south route.[15] The account, however, probably does not list the dealers in the precise order of purchase. From Godfrey's letters we know his first stop after Sierra Leone Bay was the Scarcies, yet the first dealers listed appear to be a bit farther north, at the Dembia River and the Isles de Los. But accounting for the inevitable crisscrossing and backtracking, it seems the *Hare* worked its way southward from the Isles de Los and the Scarcies toward Sherbro during the final four months of 1754.

As table 3 in appendix 3 suggests, a large proportion, perhaps just short of half, of the *Hare*'s captives came from dealers to the north of Sierra Leone Bay on the Scarcies, Dembia, and Rio Pongo, an area that included the ports of Wonkopong, Quia, Mania, and the Isles de Los. Godfrey went there in early September and stayed there at least until late October. The *Hare* accounts show that he paid for a boat off the Isles de Los in December and paid customs at several trading ports in the Northern Rivers, so Godfrey either remained to the north for that entire time or went south and returned.

The terrain of the Northern Rivers, home to people of Baga, Nalu, and Susu backgrounds, consisted largely of mangrove swamps amid a serpentine maze of slow-flowing streams, sloughs, low islands, and lush tropical vegetation. The residents subsisted largely on tidal rice, using a cultivation technique that took advantage of the twice-daily ebb and flow of fresh river water to flood their fields. The best river landings housed what one visitor called the "many Villages in the habits of considerable trade"—the various traders' compounds.[16] The private traders in the Northern Rivers tended to live relatively close to one another, creating European-Eurafrican enclaves devoted to the slave trade. Though competitors, and occasionally mortal enemies, they often socialized with one another over lavish dinners, described by one visitor as "high frolics," and exchanged food and other supplies as required.[17]

The Susus controlled trade in the region, including trade on the Scarcies. The words "Sawsas," "Souses," and "Sussias" were all English corruptions of "Susu." The Susu people speak a Mande language that is very close to Yalunka, a language of the Futa Jallon highlands several miles to the northeast. The Susus were, in fact, recent migrants to the Northern Rivers, having only arrived in the seventeenth century, with a second wave arriving after 1726. Political strife caused their migration, and by the eighteenth century they had displaced many of the local Baga people, though in places Bagas remained as landlords to Susu strangers. The Susu elite owed additional tribute and political allegiance to the Muslim Fula rulers of the Futa Jallon. In 1754, most Susus in the Northern Rivers area still practiced traditional religions, but the number of Muslim converts was increasing as religious teachers, known as *marabouts*, established schools and spread the faith. Some of the Susus were members of a Mande Muslim trading clan known as the Juula, whose connections stretched throughout Upper Guinea. It was through this network that most captives were funneled from the interior to the coast.[18]

The *Hare* arrived at the Scarcies estuary on September 10, 1754, three days after Godfrey's previous letter from Sierra Leone and eleven days after the leopard attack. It could not have taken very long to get there, despite the weather, although the *Hare* would have had to tack some in order to make headway. There are several islands at the mouth of the Scarcies, the largest of which is Kortimaw. Godfrey would have known it by the "extensive mudbanks" visible from the north and west. Sailing directly into the mouth of the river from the sea was risky due to the seven miles of shifting shoals and banks, but then again, that was why small vessels like the *Hare* were so useful. There was also a safer approach that involved sailing north of Kortimaw Island toward swampy Yallaboi Island, then southeast along a channel toward the mouth.[19] Exactly how far upriver the *Hare* traveled is not certain, but since two of Godfrey's letters carry the dateline "at the mouth of the Sawsas," it likely was not far. Furthermore, despite the fact that the Great and Little Scarcies are actually two different rivers, Godfrey referred to them as if they were only one, suggesting he remained at the bay, which formed where both rivers empty into the sea, never venturing far enough to see the split.

Although all of the private traders of the Northern Rivers maintained residences in one of the trader enclaves, they traveled widely up and down the coast between Sierra Leone and the Rio Nuñez in various small crafts, in search of slaves and other merchandise. They regularly sold captives and bought supplies at Bance Island and, more often, the Isles de Los. Their mobility makes it difficult to determine their precise locations at any given moment, but in most cases it is possible to know their basic theater of operations. Godfrey bought at least six captives, likely more, from traders who were based on the Scarcies itself. The first of these was John Wallace, who sold Godfrey one man and two women. In all probability, this is the same Wallace mentioned by John Newton in his 1751 ship's journal. Newton encountered Wallace at Bance Island, when Newton sent a cargo back to the "Sussias" in a yawl under Wallace's care. Unlike most private traders, who sold their captives to ship captains, Wallace sometimes sold slaves in the Americas on his own account. The move was risky—he lost money if a captive died or sickened on the voyage—but it was potentially much more profitable, since it cut out the middleman. In 1753, he shipped ten captives to South Carolina on the snow *Africa*; they sold for £283 sterling. That the *Africa* was from Lancaster raises the possibility that Wallace might have been too, since merchants often preferred to deal with people they knew, but there is no direct evidence to support the notion.[20]

James Tweed, another of the Scarcies traders, sold two men and a woman to Godfrey. A native of Scotland, Tweed was near the beginning of what was to prove a long career in the slave trade, culminating in his service as one of the chief agents for Grant & Oswald at Bance Island during the late 1750s and early 1760s. In 1754, however, Tweed appears to have been a private trader near the Scarcies; as late as April 1757, while anchored at the Isles de Los, John Easton of the *Africa* recorded that a "Mr. Twead came in from the Suses." Tweed's status as a private trader during these years is confirmed by the fact that he does not appear on a Bance Island personnel roster until 1758. Tweed's post–Bance Island career is obscure. He may have been the same James Tweed who purchased several tracts of land in South Carolina during the 1760s and 1770s. The strong connection between Sierra Leone and the Carolina Low Country makes that a plausible, if unconfirmable, possibility; although even if he were the same person, it is not certain that he ever resided on his holdings. What is certain is that Tweed had returned to England by 1771 and authored a pamphlet criticizing the Company of Merchants Trading to Africa as a waste of public money. The fact that he survived his years on the coast to have a public career suggests that he did quite well.[21]

Godfrey bought several more captives farther up the coast at the river ports of Wonkopong, Quia, and Mania. The timing and duration of his visit are uncertain: on the one hand, it would have made sense for him to go there at the same time he went to the Scarcies (that is, in September and October) because of proximity, and the traders on his list of purchases are lumped together with the Scarcies traders. On the other hand, his accounting of customs payments (he paid sixteen gallons of rum to "Masseboy King of Nunko," five gallons at "Mongoyallaw," three gallons at Quia, and two and one-half each at "Wongopong" and Mania) seems to indicate that he visited in mid-December.[22] In any event, like the Scarcies, the area around Quia, Wonkopong, and Mania featured a cluster of private traders in an environment of winding rivers and mangrove swamps. And like the Scarcies, this was another Susu area, tributary to the Futa Jallon state in the highlands to the east.

A description of the area two years prior to the *Hare*'s arrival survives, courtesy of Thomas Thompson, an Anglican missionary. Thompson sketched a region in the early stages of what would eventually be a thorough Islamization. On the one hand, Thompson described the town of Wonkopong as a stable bastion of Islam. He described the town itself as approximately three miles in circumference, with houses scattered about. The houses were not clustered together behind a fortified perimeter, which suggests that residents had little fear of slave raids, as they did in many other parts of West Africa. Their relative security was due to the progress of Muslim proselytization: Muslims were forbidden to enslave fellow Muslims. "The Mosques," noted Thompson of nearby Quia, "are built of Clay, in an hexangular Form; and are both neatly fabricated, and kept very clean." Worshippers sat on "an earthen Bench that goes round," both on the inside and outside. The roof was supported by six wood pillars, each capped with an "ornament." He also noted an "old Mundingo teaching some Children in the Street, who had their Lesson written in Arabick, on a Board," and seemed surprised to learn that the man did so "out of Charity, and for God's Sake, not for Fee or Reward." And he noted the careful observance of the *salah*, the prayers said five times a day, one of the pillars of Islam. Yet despite this demonstration of religious devotion, the local landlord to the British traders struck Thompson as something short of devout. Known as Mongo (an honorific that Thompson analogized to "King") Dandi and "reputed to be rich in Slaves," Thompson described him as an "unprincely Character," who "commonly went in a very ordinary Garb." Worse still, in Thompson's telling, Mongo Dandi was "almost always drunk, and often laid out in the Streets all Night." This sketch suggests that Mongo Dandi was a non-Muslim of Baga and Bullom background. Within a few years, however, this area would fall to a coastal jihad carried out by Mandes connected to the Futa Jallon. Non-Muslim rulers would eventually be replaced with ones more compatible with Futa Jallon's brand of Islam.[23]

Godfrey purchased two men, one woman, and one girl from William Ord, one of Mongo Dandi's resident "strangers," at a cost of 347 gallons of rum, along with smaller quantities of beef, pork, ham, wine, and sugar.[24] Ord resided at Wonkopong along with "several" other English and Scottish traders. Reverend Thompson had actually lodged with Ord two years earlier and baptized one of his Anglo-African children, for which he received three pieces of gold and "an handsome Piece of Goods."[25] Ord's modus operandi, like that of most traders, was to travel up and down the coast in a shallop in search of captives to buy. John Newton reported that he was active on the Scarcies and at Sherbro, over a hundred miles to the south. In other respects, though, Ord was different from the mass of private traders, at least more ambitious and perhaps more successful. It was he who, along with Scarcies-area trader John Wallace, shipped a cargo of ten captives to South Carolina on his own account, essentially cutting out the ship-owning middleman and pocketing the difference. Three years later, he carried eighty-two captives to Barbados as master of the brigantine *Swallow*. He may have been helped in these pursuits by a relative: a London merchant named James Ord was a member of the Company of Merchants Trading to Africa at about the same time, although there is no evidence of a connection.[26]

Shortly after the *Hare* was at Wonkopong and Quia, it entered the Dembia River, which lay just north of the Isles de Los in the present-day Republic of Guinea. This too was a Baga- and Susu-dominated area, very similar to the Scarcies and Wonkopong-Quia areas in its culture, economy, and landscape. The Dembia had a large and active population of private traders who made their living supplying captives to the factories of the Isles de Los. Either here or on the islands, Godfrey met John Holman and bargained 510⅔ gallons of rum, 25 barrels of pork, 1 barrel of flour, 9½ gallons of wine, 12 loaves of sugar and some ship's bread for two men and three women.[27] Holman had come to the area a few years earlier to start what would be a long and successful career in the slave trade. In the 1770s he was apparently shipping cargoes of slaves on his own account to South Carolina, where Henry Laurens handled his affairs.[28] At some point, probably early on, he established a strong local connection through his marriage with a Baga woman, with whom he had at least two sons, the eldest of whom he sent to Britain for his education. In 1790, with his business in the Pongo threatened by a charismatic religious movement, he fled to South Carolina, where his family had purchased property three years earlier. He died the following year, but his sons continued to operate in both South Carolina and the Rio Pongo. In 1807 John Jr. was an investor in a Charleston-based slaving venture to the Rio Pongo, and he accompanied the vessel to Africa. The ship did not sail from the Pongo until January 1808, at which time a ban on slave trading came into effect for U.S. citizens and vessels. A British Admiralty Court condemned the ship and its cargo, but Holman continued his activities until at least 1813. His descendants, considered black in the United States, established themselves as planters in South Carolina and as traders on the Rio Pongo.[29]

Godfrey purchased captives from several other traders in the Northern Rivers, though their precise locations are not certain. Many traders frequently shuttled back and forth between the mainland and the new factories at the Isles de Los. Several appear in various records on the islands, but whether they were full-time residents or simply there on business is impossible to say. A case in point is George Dowdall, who furnished the *Hare* with three men and two girls in exchange for 483 gallons of rum, a barrel of flour, 15 barrels of ham, 12 pounds of sugar, some ship's bread, 107 feet of wooden boards, and a pair of oars.[30] A transaction between Godfrey and Dowdall on the *Hare*'s second voyage places Dowdall at the Isles de Los. On that occasion, Dowdall gave Godfrey a cake of beeswax to satisfy a debt, it appears.[31] The following year, Dowdall was mentioned several times in a Connecticut ship's journal, all at the Isles de Los.[32] Another trader, listed by Godfrey as "Wm Harriss," may also have been active around the Isles de Los. A William Harrison had dealings with Paul Cross there in the early 1780s; it could be the same person or a namesake, but that is far from certain.[33]

Another trader of unknown base who operated in the Northern Rivers was "Jo'n Langston," from whom Godfrey purchased two women for 217 gallons of rum, 7½ pounds of brown sugar, 9 gallons of wine, and 9 pounds of loaf sugar.[34] This was almost certainly Jonathan Langton, twice encountered by John Newton on his voyages in the 1750s. Their first meeting took place in

1751 at White Man's Bay at Sierra Leone proper. Newton went aboard Langton's shallop to examine some slaves and bought three. His next dealing with Langton came in 1752, also in Sierra Leone Bay, when Langton arrived in his shallop from Kissy in the Northern Rivers with six slaves. Whether Langton was based primarily at Sierra Leone or Kissy is impossible to say, but it is clear that he purchased his captives in the Northern Rivers. Langton may have had connections with a mercantile firm back home, like some of the other traders. In 1756, Henry Laurens of South Carolina did business with the firm of Langton, Shepherd, & Co., which was headed by a John Langton and based in Kirkham, Lancashire, midway between Liverpool and Lancaster. It is probable that the two were either the same person, with Langton returning to England after a stint in Africa, or relatives.[35]

These seven traders accounted for almost a third of the *Hare*'s total captives and seem to account for almost all of those purchased in the area north of Sierra Leone Bay. In a letter from the Scarcies dated October 26, 1754, Godfrey informed the Vernons that he had twenty-seven captives aboard.[36] The seven traders listed above accounted for twenty-three captives in all, leaving only four untraced. Three of the remaining four can be accounted for if we assume that Godfrey listed his dealers in rough geographic order, from north to south. If that is correct, then Andrew Morrison (who furnished a woman, a girl, and a boy), or some combination of Alexander Ross, Robert Simson, William Harriss, and one other trader probably furnished the remaining captives from the north. After them, Godfrey's account lists traders from points south.

THE *HARE* PROBABLY headed back toward Sierra Leone in the late fall of 1754, retracing its original inbound passage. There is a small possibility that Godfrey purchased three captives at Bance Island then. Andrew Morrison, mentioned above, furnished three captives to the *Hare* in exchange for 209⅔ gallons of rum, along with other goods. Of all the traders who sold captives to the *Hare*, only Tweed and Morrison appear in the record as employees of Bance Island. Like Tweed, however, Morrison seems not to have been employed in 1754: he appears on a 1751 personnel roster as a trader in "sickly" condition and is not listed on the next roster, which dates to 1756.[37] His placement among the Northern Rivers traders on Godfrey's account suggests that by 1754 he had left Grant & Oswald's service and set up on his own, as did so many others. Grant & Oswald's sales records lend support to the hypothesis, recording no captives furnished to independent ship captains in 1754. Still, without a personnel roster for 1754, we cannot be completely certain that

Morrison was not at Bance Island, so there is a small chance that the *Hare* did more than just purchase supplies there.

Resupplied and with twenty-seven captives now aboard, the *Hare* continued southward off the Sierra Leone peninsula, past "a Mountain of prodigious Height, whose Top is continually cover'd with Clouds."[38] Mariners were well advised to stay at least three miles away from the shore and to take regular soundings with the lead. Twenty-five miles and several hours later, the *Hare* would have reached the Banana Islands, which lay about five miles off the southwestern tip of the peninsula. Taking care to avoid the foul ground off the largest island's eastern shore, Godfrey likely anchored on the ocean side in ten or more fathoms and rowed ashore in the longboat. Resplendent in tropical color, the largest island was about four miles long and between three hundred and one thousand yards wide. Two hills dominated the islands, one about 450 feet and the other about 680 feet high. Each hill was blanketed by trees which, in the words of Nicholas Owen, "furnish'd . . . all kinds of tropical freuts, such as plantains, bananas, pineaples, limes, papas, [and] watermelons," but was also "much infested by snakes."[39] The islands had long been a hideaway for pirates and escaped sailors, like Owen. After King George's War, with the entire region becoming a major source of captives, more slave traders began to use the Bananas as a base, attracted by the belief that sea breezes made them healthier than did the climate of the mainland. One of these new traders was Robert Wright, from whom Godfrey purchased one man and one woman for 213⅓ gallons of rum. Wright, listed in Godfrey's account as "Mr. Wright," came to the Bananas in about 1749 after trading on the mainland for seven years. When Captain Daniel of the HMS *Assurance* called at the Bananas in 1751 or 1752, Wright was the only European trader he encountered there. He apparently enjoyed a good relationship with his Bullom landlords, having very probably married into a prominent family. Shortly thereafter, Wright caused consternation at Whitehall by inviting French merchants to base themselves there, promising to use his influence with his landlords to maintain the peace. The outcome of Wright's bid is not known, but when Nicholas Owen visited a few years later he reported "several malatos, tradeing men that lives upon the low grounds and lords it over the rest of the island." Whether these were relatives and allies of Wright, or whether he had died or been ousted by this time is unknown.[40] In addition to Wright, the *Hare* may have bought seven more captives at the Bananas from the partnership of Baillie and Key. The two are all but untraceable, though at least one traveler in the 1770s noted the existence of a "Bailly's Port" on one of the islands.[41]

Just south of the Bananas were the Plantains, another small archipelago. The islands were the bailiwick of William Cleveland, one of the wealthiest and most powerful Anglo-African traders in the region. Godfrey purchased eighty bars worth of "sundries" from Cleveland, but no slaves.[42] While at the Plantains, however, he did buy eight captives (two men, one woman, one girl, and four boys) from Patrick Clow, another private trader. Clow is best known as the one-time master of John Newton, who worked for him in the late 1740s. Worried that he would be impressed by a man-of-war, Newton had jumped ship "with many golden dreams, that here I should find an opportunity for improving my fortunes." At the Plantains were several traders who made their livings by purchasing captives along the rivers of the mainland, much as those in the Northern Rivers did. Clow had initially traded on the mainland near Cape Mount but had moved to the Plantains and now inhabited a "low sandy island, about two miles in circumference and almost covered with palm trees." Clow's Bullom wife, dubbed "P.I." by Newton, had a great hand in the operation and was in complete charge during her husband's frequent absences. During those periods, Newton was effectively enslaved to P.I., and she treated him with "scorn and contempt," working him hard and withholding food. Clow would eventually treat Newton with similar cruelty. After living as a virtual slave for over a year, Newton managed to get a letter to his father in Liverpool, who prevailed upon a merchantman to rescue his son. Newton visited Clow and P.I. a few years later as master of a slave ship, by which time his ill feelings seem to have subsided. In fact, when a member of Newton's crew attempted to kill one of Clow's gromettos with an axe, P.I. intervened to save Newton from the prescribed retaliation by the man's "people." Newton would later credit his time on the Plantains with bringing down his "haughty heart," but he noted that upon his departure he was still some distance from the "wholesome repentance" that characterized his later life.[43]

Opposite the Plantains and just off the mainland was Sherbro, a thirty-mile-long island that resembled a tilted triangle. The tip of the island marked the wide entrance to Sherbro Bay, which narrowed into a small estuary on the eastern end. Hazardous shoals guarded the entrance to Sherbro; one navigational atlas recommended hiring a pilot at Sierra Leone, though there is no evidence that Godfrey did so. Proceeding along the northern, inner edge of Sherbro Island, Godfrey sailed to the trading compound of Richard Hall. There he purchased a single captive, a woman, for ninety-six gallons of rum.

Born in England, Hall had once been a gentleman of means but had squandered his fortune in the classic, debauched manner. Deciding to start over anew—whether in Africa or America is uncertain—he took passage out of London. In Hall's telling, his vessel was becalmed at Cape Verde, so he and several others went on an exploratory excursion in a rowboat. The party was blown off course in the direction of the Gambia River and washed up on some islands, probably the Bijagos. Hall lived the next three years as the pampered slave of the local ruler, marrying his daughter and serving as a "doctor." A European slave trader from Sierra Leone eventually rescued him, and some time afterward he apparently set up as a private trader at Sherbro. Described as "always generous," "seldom out of humour," and "gay in his clothing even among negroes," Hall ranged as far as the Gambia and Cape Verde, trading in textiles and other goods as well as in human beings. In fact, he was very likely the same Hall who, along with Captains Ellery and Ruff, engaged in retaliatory panyarring along the Gambia River earlier in the year (see chapter three). In mid-1755, Hall built a new trading compound on York Island amid the ruins of the old Royal African Company fort. In September 1755, Hall abandoned his operation when his landlord, the King of Sherbro, ruled against him in a dispute with another trader. Hall's employee, Nicholas Owen, took over the business, and, while at Bance Island in March 1756, received a visit from "Capt. Godfrey," who brought news of the British victory over the French at Crown Point on Lake Champlain. Whether Godfrey bought any captives from Owen on that voyage, his second aboard the *Hare*, is unknown.[44]

In exchange for 306⅔ gallons of rum, 102 pounds of tobacco, 57 bottles of snuff, 40 feet of boards, and some flour, Godfrey received one man, two girls, and a boy from William Norie, also of Sherbro. Like so many of the traders, Norie was probably originally a sailor. The 1770 membership roster for the Company of Merchants Trading to Africa listed him as a mariner now resident on the "Windward Coast of Africa," a geographic catchall that encompassed Sierra Leone and Sherbro. Norie had married into the powerful Anglo-African Caulker family. There is no record of Norie after 1770, but his daughter was well known throughout the region as "Miss Norie." Educated in England, Miss Norie returned to Sherbro for reasons unknown, but perhaps the fact that she had to work in England as a lady's maid for a "genteel family" influenced her decision. Back in Africa, she lived a life of wealth and style. One traveler described her as a "sensible and intelligent Woman" who "continued to dress in the English Fashion" and "maintained the Address of the European." The visitor also hinted that a life in Sherbro may not have been Miss Norie's first choice, observing that "She lives as the Natives do; but that I believe is the Effect of Necessity, not Choice."[45]

The *Hare* called just north of Sherbro, where a dangerous reef and the lack of a harbor made it necessary to anchor offshore. Here, Godfrey made the largest single purchase of the voyage: four men, three women, three girls, and one boy from William Skinner, to whom he delivered 799⅓ gallons of rum, 1 gallon of wine, 36 bottles of snuff, 180 pounds of tobacco, 1 barrel of tar, some beef, pork, flour, ham, brown sugar, some ship stores, and the *Hare*'s longboat. (Exactly why Godfrey was willing to part with the longboat is a mystery; perhaps his earlier judgment that it was poorly constructed was correct, or perhaps he had no more need for it.) Little is known about Skinner. Charts of the era show "Skinner's Place" south of Yawry Bay. He seems to have been from an Anglo-African family of fairly long standing: the records of Bence Island (as it was earlier known) contain references to debts owed by several Skinners going back at least to the early eighteenth century, which suggests that the original Skinner was a former company employee or a fugitive sailor.[46]

Eight more sellers furnished a total of fifteen captives to the *Hare*; a ninth appears on Godfrey's account but seems not to have sold any slaves. None of them can be traced in the surviving documents. Some were likely private traders, while others may have been ships' officers trading on their own accounts. Three of them—Padre Levis, Andr (possibly for "Andres") Gomar, and "Pistue a Black"—were probably Luso-African. The latter may have been a rendering of "Pissoe" or "Pissoa," a common surname in the region throughout the eighteenth century.[47] Most of the untraceable sellers appear toward the bottom of Godfrey's account among the southernmost traders, which suggests that they resided on the Bananas, on the Plantains, or near Sherbro. With the approximate point of sale known for about three-quarters of the *Hare*'s captives, it appears that just less than half were purchased in the Northern Rivers, between two and five at Sierra Leone proper (though likely not at Bance Island), and slightly more than half at points south of Sierra Leone Bay. It is through this knowledge that we can develop a portrait of the captives themselves.

As the *Hare* and its longboat shuttled between the Isles de Los and the ports of the Northern Rivers, some captives may have remained on their traders' compounds. A visitor described the scene at the younger Holman's compound. The seventy or so captives, of whom about forty were children, were kept outside, chained together in small groups. Some of the women were threshing and winnowing rice, demonstrating once again the dual economic nature of the slave through both use and exchange value.[48] Eventually, the captives were taken aboard the *Hare*. Although there is no record of it, it is possible that the captives were branded with a hot iron. The practice was a common one, intended to allow merchants to identify the captives aboard vessels with multiple consignees. We know that branding did occur on Vernon-owned vessels from a legal dispute over a privilege slave that occurred several years after the *Hare* sailed.[49] When there were only a few captives onboard and the weather was good, captains often allowed them to remain on deck during the daytime, where they might get fresh air and exercise beneath an awning. With such a small crew, however, Godfrey almost certainly erred on the side of caution and kept the captives in manacles below, allowing only a few at a time on deck. The rains added an additional layer of misery to the already-unspeakable conditions in the hold. With temperatures above ninety degrees above decks and humidity approaching 100 percent, to say nothing of the putrid smells, the air in the hold would have been almost unbreathable. During storms, crews usually stretched a tarp over the hold to prevent flooding, but the tarp blocked the circulation of fresh air. When the tarp was removed, noted one observer, "there is a steam then [*sic*] has come up between the gratings, but which means the air was communicated to them below, and has relieved them when they have been panting for breath."[50]

THE WORDS "SIERRA LEONE" meant little or nothing to the *Hare* captives. To the British they signified, in a narrow sense, the eponymous river and peninsula. In a still broader sense, they designated a stretch of coastline of uncertain boundaries, roughly the area between Cacheu and Cape Mount. At the time of the *Hare*'s voyage, Europeans' knowledge of Africa ended within a few leagues of the coast. Their geographic names grew out of maritime utility (the "Serra Lyoa" highlands made a good navigational reference) or were boundaries drawn in competition with European rivals. Europeans also tended to project their own categories of identity onto Africans, whether they applied or not. In Europe, older categories, such as religion and lineage, were giving way to newer ones rooted in language and the "nation." It would still be at least a half century before the transition to national consciousness would be complete (if indeed it ever was completed), and for the moment the various ways of sorting self from other coexisted in a knot of contradictory categories of nation, religion, and rank. Nevertheless, with the idea of "nation" rising in their own consciousness, Europeans tended to sort Africans into "nations" according to their political systems and languages. In Africa, however, even more than in Europe, politics and language did not necessarily coincide and often bore little resemblance to Africans' self-perceptions. Later, Europeans would drop "nations" and sort Africans into even more problematic "tribes." To say that the *Hare* purchased captives in "Sierra Leone," then, says little about the backgrounds of those men and women. For most, it was a place they passed through, not the place they came from. Learning something about them—in the absence of any documents that might allow for individual biography—requires us to delve into the region's history.[51]

Most historians today prefer terms like "Upper Guinea" or "Western Africa" to "Sierra Leone," at least when speaking of the area beyond the bay. Upper Guinea speaks to a history shared by the people from approximately present-day Senegal to northern Liberia, and inland as far as the western border of present-day Mali. This area features a wide variety of ecological zones, from the arid savannahs of present-day Senegal to the kola forests of Sierra Leone, and from the coastal mangrove swamps of Guinea-Bissau to the drier uplands of the Futa Jallon, in the present-day Republic of Guinea. This ecological diversity spawned a wide variety of agricultural and husbandry practices. Much of the region was rice-growing territory, which would become significant as residents crossed the Atlantic and carried rice knowledge with them. In other places, millet and sorghum prevailed. Goats and fowl existed throughout the region, but horses and cattle thrived best in the drier areas, away from the tsetse fly and other parasites.

Then as now, the area was linguistically diverse; over a dozen major indigenous languages are still spoken today.[52] Two language families dominate: Mande, spoken for the most part in inland areas, and the Atlantic (formerly called the "Mel") languages, most of which, with the exception of Fulfulde, are spoken along the coast. The very existence of so many languages and cultures has led many historians to suppose that the people taken from this area to the Americas had little in common, and therefore had little choice but to abandon many of the trappings of their earlier lives. But that diversity must be put into perspective. Several of the languages are closely related and even mutually intelligible. The Mande languages were and are widespread and broadly related. Some of them serve as linguae francae over a broad swath of West Africa. Speakers of one language can, to varying degrees, often understand speakers of another, depending on the specific languages and dialects involved.[53]

Lexical similarity, a tool used by linguists to measure the relationship between languages and dialects, offers some insight into the level of communication experienced by the *Hare* captives. The lexical similarity for two languages is derived by comparing lists of common, everyday words, such as numbers and parts of the body. A lexical similarity of 85 percent or higher indicates that the two speech variants are close enough to be considered dialects of the same language. While lexical similarity is far from a perfect indicator of mutual intelligibility, it provides a rudimentary basis for comparison. Spanish has a lexical similarity of 89 percent with Portuguese, 82 percent with Italian, and 75 percent with French. English has a lexical similarity of 27 percent with French and 60 percent with German (a figure that surely demonstrates the limitations of lexical similarity as a measure of intelligibility). Bamana and Vai, two Mande languages separated by hundreds of miles, have a lexical similarity of between 57 and 78 percent, depending on the word list. Many of the other northern Mande languages (especially from the Manding subdivision, which includes Mandinka, Maninka, Bamana, and Juula) score far higher, often over 90 percent. Bamana and Maninka, for example, have a lexical similarity of 94 percent, with some combinations of dialects reaching 98 percent. Mande speakers living up to eight hundred miles from one another can enjoy "a high degree of mutual intelligibility."[54] Mungo Park, who traveled hundreds of miles across West Africa speaking Mandinka, provides a qualitative perspective. Bamana, another Manding language, was simply "corrupted" Mandinka, while Yalunka, a Mande language that shared a "great affinity" with Mandinka, was still a separate tongue.[55] The Atlantic languages, of which Temne, Bullom, Limba, Landuma, Baga, Gola, and Kissi are probably most relevant here, share less with the Mande languages, apart from some borrowed words. And except for Bullom and Temne, they share relatively little vocabulary with each other and are not, for the most part, mutually intelligible.

Despite this linguistic diversity, residents of Upper Guinea shared a common history. Two major historical events, one in the distant past and the other in the recent past, can help us understand who the *Hare* captives were. Both events point to the cultural integration, rather than the isolation, of Upper Guinea. The first is the rise of the Mali Empire. Originally an inland polity on the upper Niger valley, by the fourteenth century Mali's forces had extended its influence to the Atlantic Ocean at the Senegal and Gambia Rivers. The expansion had two important repercussions. It introduced Mande languages and culture to the region and brought Islam to the coast. Neither, however, supplanted local languages or religions. Instead, Muslim merchants, administrators, and religious teachers dwelled among the coastal peoples, gradually becoming part of society's fabric. The area around Sierra Leone did not fall within the Mali Empire, but eventually it, too, was affected by it. In the mid-sixteenth century, with the empire in decline, an offshoot force known as the Mane swept toward the coast south of Sierra Leone, then northward toward the Northern Rivers. The Mane never achieved territorial dominion, but the end result was similar to what happened in Senegambia. Mane merchants, marabouts, and traders took up residence among the Baga, Temne, Bullom, and other coastal peoples. Culturally and linguistically speaking, by the early eighteenth century, Upper Guinea had been transformed by the extension of Mande religion, language, and trade, a process sometimes called "Mandingization." At the same time, Mande culture had been transformed, in turn, by contact with coastal peoples. Mande merchants and holy men could be found in enclaves ranging from modern-day Senegal to modern-day Liberia, trading, serving as rulers and administrators, and spreading the faith.[56]

The second event is known to historians as the Futa Jallon Jihad, which, as the name implies, was a campaign to spread an orthodox brand of Islam through the establishment of a theocratic state. It began in 1725 or 1726 in the Futa Jallon, the highland area that was the source of three of West Africa's major rivers, the Senegal, Gambia, and Niger, as well as numerous smaller rivers, including the Kissy, Scarcies, Dembia, and Rio Pongo. Before the jihad, the Futa Jallon had been home to Yalunka speakers (from which "Jallon" was derived), mostly agriculturalists who spoke a Mande tongue. In the sixteenth century, Muslim Fula pastoralists moved onto the plateau, where they faced high taxes and clashed with Yalunka agriculturalists over land use. Long-standing class and religious tensions came to a head when a committee of twenty-two Fula and Yalunka marabouts inaugurated a war to establish an Islamic state. Their fortunes fluctuated over the course of the eighteenth century, generating thousands of prisoners who would eventually be sold as slaves. In fact, one thing that attracted converts was the protection from enslavement that Islamic law afforded Muslims.

By 1747 the jihad had succeeded, but the security of the new Futa Jallon state was still precarious. It faced external threats and was overpopulated with potentially rebellious slaves. Its leadership grew fractious, and in 1751 the movement's religious leader, Karamoko Alfa, died. He was succeeded by the military leader Ibrahima Sori, who, as "Sori the Great" (Sori Mawdo), inaugurated a series of offensives designed to strengthen and expand his power.[57] Observing Islamic injunctions against the enslavement of Muslims, Futa Jallon raided for captives far and wide, relying on an army of at least twelve thousand, including a cadre of privileged royal slaves. The region to the north and east of Sierra Leone was the site of several military campaigns around the time of the *Hare*'s voyage. In 1753, Sori's army and its

Sulima allies attacked near the Labé section of the Futa Jallon, razing settlements to the ground and seizing captives, probably Yalunkas. In 1754 (and
again in 1755), Futa Jallon and Sulima laid siege to the "populous town" of
Farrabana but were forced to abandon the effort after three months of fighting. At approximately the same time, a jihad was being waged nearer the
coast in the Northern Rivers, on the eastern edge of Sierra Leone Bay, and in
the Sherbro hinterlands. Prisoners taken in these campaigns, which almost
certainly included some of the *Hare* captives, belonged to the various prov-
inces that made up the Futa Jallon confederation. Much of the slave trade
on the Upper Guinea coast, in other words, was either directly or indirectly
connected to the Futa Jallon state.[58]

It would be a mistake, however, to suppose that the Futa Jallon Jihad
introduced slavery to the region. Slavery had a long history throughout
Africa, as it did in Europe, Asia, and the Americas. Before the arrival of the
Portuguese, Upper Guinea not only employed slaves in a variety of capacities, but also sold them to Arab and Moorish traders who carried them
across the Sahara to Mediterranean markets. Still, the Atlantic trade brought
both quantitative and qualitative change, as African elites and their clients
demanded increasing amounts of European goods. As the American plantations matured and the demand for African laborers soared, many African
elites reorganized their polities to take advantage. It amounted to a complete retooling of state and society. To provide large numbers of slaves, they
needed a regular supply, which they obtained by raiding their neighbors.
Raiding, in turn, required armies, which were also needed to defend against
inevitable retaliation. The armies consisted largely of military slaves, sustained by agricultural slaves and supplied by the proceeds of the slave trade.
Slavery went from being what one prominent historian called a "marginal
feature" of society to a fully consolidated mode of production, a social formation in which the system of enslavement, the sale of captives, and the
domestic employment of slaves were integral and institutionalized.[59]

The Futa Jallon under Sori Mawdo was such a society, with slavery eventually pervading every aspect of life. As one of the leaders confided to James
Watt in 1794, "the sole object of their wars was to get slaves, as they could
not get any European articles they were in want of without slaves and they
could not get slaves without fighting for them." Over the course of the eighteenth century, slavery had come to dominate domestic production as well.
The precise proportion of slaves in Futa Jallon in 1754 is difficult to estimate,
but it may have been over half the population. On his 1794 visit, James Watt
concluded that slaves outnumbered free people in the Futa Jallon by five

to one. Of course, Watt visited forty years after the *Hare*'s voyage, so he was observing the apex of a trend that had just begun at midcentury. Slaves in the Futa Jallon generally fell into two categories: those born into slavery locally, and those captured in raids and wars. The former generally worked as domestic servants and enjoyed comparatively favorable treatment. Some of them managed to acquire land, and over generations they acquired many of the trappings of freedom, if not formal manumission. Many more were non-Muslim outsiders, working in agriculture and crafts. These slaves were kept in segregated slave villages known as *runde* and worked five days a week under the harsh supervision of an intendant, who himself was a trusted slave. The other two days, they worked for their own sustenance. Most of the grain they produced went to the aristocracy, which consumed it, dispensed it to the armies, or sent it to the coast to be sold as slave-ship provisions. Futa Jallon's plunge into the slave trade brought with it serious dangers. Not only did the constant raids and wars provoke retaliatory actions that resulted in the enslavement of many of its own residents, the heavy reliance on slave labor at home carried the risk of rebellion. In fact, Futa Jallon's slaves staged a rebellion in 1756, around the time of the *Hare*'s second voyage. The largest uprising, however, would not occur until the late eighteenth century in the Northern Rivers. Violence raged on a near-continuous basis from 1783 to 1796, when it was crushed.[60]

Traditionally, the victors in any battle had several decisions to make regarding their captives. First, they weighed whether to kill or enslave them. In wartime, these were seen as two sides of the same coin. It was commonly understood that a captive owed his captor a lifetime of service in exchange for being spared his life. Often, the decision of whether to execute was governed by the risk the person posed if kept alive. Soldiers, who might rebel or escape to fight again, were often put to death. The elderly were also often executed: they were unable to work, there was no external market for them, and they would have drained resources if kept as domestic slaves.[61] Young women were seen as less threatening and were more likely to be spared and put to work domestically. Those not needed locally could be sold to the trans-Sahara caravans for shipment to North Africa and the Arab world, where they were in particular demand, and some could even be sold to the Europeans on the coast. Most important of all, the rise of a transatlantic market offered another possibility for the disposal of male captives, who might otherwise constitute a threat. They could now be sold without fear that they might eventually return to cause harm. This was made possible by the fact that Europeans preferred adult men for plantation work. It was the rise of that market that bent the initial religious intent of the jihad increasingly in the direction of slave raiding. Most of the Futa Jallon captives were exported to the coast.

A network of Muslim merchants known as the Juula connected suppliers in the Futa Jallon with the coastal traders who sold to ship captains. Though the Europeans often referred to these as "Fula" caravans, they were actually still operated by Juula merchants, who were mostly Mande speakers. These Juula networks channeled metropolitan credit, in the form of European goods, hundreds of miles into the African interior, and in exchange carried captives down to the Northern Rivers, to Sierra Leone, and, eventually, to Sherbro.[62] The method of distributing captives of the Futa Jallon state to the various Juula leaders was probably similar to the method used in Segu, another slave-exporting state in Upper Guinea, as related by Mungo Park. First, the *mansa* (roughly, "king") distributed the captives in small groups to favored merchants in several villages. He did so for security's sake, to prevent a dangerous aggregation of captives in the capital city. From the merchants, he probably received goods, some on credit, others in payment for previous deals. The merchants then moved the captives to larger provincial marketing centers, usually located on the main water and land transportation routes, where they were bought by other Juula and prepared for their journey to the coast. Closer to the coast, they sold the captives to local traders, who might be African, Eurafrican, or European, and the traders in turn sold them to the ship captains. Individual captives, then, might undergo multiple transfers between their initial seizure and their sale to a slave ship.[63]

Four main routes connected the Futa Jallon with the coast near Sierra Leone. The first originated in the Bamana city of Segu and ran through the Futa Jallon capital of Timbo, then down through Susu territory to the trading towns on the Scarcies Rivers. The journey, undertaken during the dry season, would have been on foot; both Scarcies Rivers feature miles of boulder-strewn rapids above the coastal plain. Near the coast, some captives on this route would have been turned northward toward Wonkopong, where they were sold to local notables like Mongo Dandi and private traders like William Ord. In 1750, this area was controlled by non-Muslim Susus, who had migrated there with the commencement of the Futa Jallon Jihad and married into, and to a great extent displaced, many of the local Baga communities.[64] If his prodigious alcohol consumption is any guide, Mongo Dandi was a non-Muslim Baga-Bullom who acted as a landlord to English, African, and Eurafrican traders. During the coastal jihad of the 1750s, however, Futa Jallon tightened its control over the Northern Rivers, so it is quite possible that Mongo Dandi was deposed at about the time of the *Hare*'s visit. Yet another route connecting the Futa Jallon and the Northern Rivers ran down the Rio Nuñez to Kakundy, and another still ran down the Forecariah River, which ran parallel to the Scarcies a few miles north of it. It was some combination of these routes that a young Muslim boy named Sitiki traveled shortly after 1800. Taken in a wartime raid, Sitiki passed through Segu, where he was purchased by a governing official to tend sheep, noting that "their language differ[ed] only a little from that I spoke." After some time, he was sold to Fula long-distance traders and descended from the highlands where "water came in rivulets & fell in cascades." Reaching the coast at the Rio Pongo, he was shipped to Charleston and eventually brought to Spanish Florida.[65]

The Juula similarly linked the Sierra Leone River with the Futa Jallon through the market town of Port Loko. Situated up the Sierra Leone River, with a palaver house and a small marketplace overlooking a narrow river that was served by a small jetty, Port Loko came under the control of Buri Lahi Sankoh, a member of a Juula family, who in turn owed fealty to Futa Jallon.[66] Captives taken to Port Loko could reach Bance Island by canoe in just a day. Yet another route sent captives from the Upper Niger down the Jong and Bum Rivers toward Sherbro. Until the late 1750s, a non-Muslim Bullom elite controlled the Sherbro trade. In 1758, the Bullom traders found themselves subordinated to the Toure family of Juula traders, who enjoyed the political support of Futa Jallon and controlled trade in the Melikouri area of the Northern Rivers. The *Hare*, however, seems to have arrived a few years before this occurred. It is probable that most of the captives purchased at Sherbro traveled the southern route, while those purchased to the north of Sierra Leone Bay traveled northern routes. However, traders in all parts of greater Sierra Leone tended to travel scores or even hundreds of miles up and down the coast in search of captives, so the routes traveled to the eventual point of embarkation were not always direct.[67]

The Juula merchants who connected the Futa Jallon with the coast were savvy in the ways of the slave trade. Mungo Park, who traveled with them along the Gambia, noted the attention paid to preventing the captives from fleeing as they were led to the coast in caravans known as "coffles." Park's coffle included thirteen captives, eleven of whom had already been living as slaves. The right leg of one was chained to the left leg of another, and so on, to create a line. Each captive kept his or her chain from dragging on the ground by holding it up with a string. In addition, the captives were tied to each other at the neck in groups of four and, as an extra precaution, had their

FIGURE 4.1. *A Fula caravan near Sierra Leone in 1794. Caravans like this one delivered most of the* Hare *captives from the interior highlands to coastal middlemen, who in turn sold them to ship captains. Although Europeans referred to these coffles as "Fula" caravans, after the ethnic group in power in the Futa Jallon, most of the people running them were probably Mande-speaking Juula merchants. (National Maritime Museum, Greenwich, U.K.)*

hands tied and an extra chain looped around their necks at night. Those who exhibited "marks of discontent" had their feet secured to a three-foot notched board. Bearers of nonhuman commodities carried their burdens in a "long basket, from five to seven feet in length and from 9 inches to a foot broad," extending from well below the waist to three or four feet above their heads. Many polities demanded that coffles pay in order to pass through their territory. The caravans from Futa Jallon, however, sometimes consisted of over three hundred people, which allowed them to avoid these charges. Like merchants everywhere, the Juula depended on good market information and used their networks to gain it. When the leaders of Park's coffle received intelligence several hundred miles inland that there were few ships on the Gambia, they immediately reassessed their plans. One group, reckoning the cost of maintaining the captives too great if they had to wait for ships, immediately headed toward another market. Park's coffle continued toward the Gambia despite hearing of low prices, but stopped short when it became clear that the market really was poor. The leader then rented some land and houses and put the captives to work raising provisions.[68]

The ability to deploy a captive as a laborer or as a commodity gave merchants flexibility in their dealings. Ship captains, more so than private traders, were disadvantaged by the practice of using captives as laborers, for they had no parallel option: to them captives could only be deployed as commodities, and perishable, resource-consuming commodities at that. The longer a captain had to wait to assemble a full cargo of slaves, the more he stood to lose. For the Juula and other dealers, however, it was common practice to use captives for agricultural labor during the rainy season, when travel was difficult. Young Sitiki, mentioned earlier, tended sheep, but many more captives spent the rainy season working on rice plantations and other enterprises that were devoted to provisioning the same slave ships that would carry them to America. The Northern Rivers produced several such commodities, as did the area surrounding Sherbro. Captives who were not bought might be sent back up-country to work another season in one of the slave villages.[69] The dry season was the time both for slave sales and for raiding and military campaigns, which meant that one year's captives departed just as the next year's were assembled. In the area around Sierra Leone, this meant that captives would be available in the greatest numbers in the fall and would be most scarce during the spring. This seasonality helps explain why Godfrey found it so difficult to purchase captives at acceptable prices. Whether he intended at the outset to arrive before the dry season to get first crack at purchasing captives, or whether he did so out of ignorance is impossible to say. If it was intentional, the presence of so many similar-minded captains rendered his strategy too clever by half.[70]

Once they reached the traders near the coast, the merchants set up a camp of tree-branch huts to shelter slaves and bearers. At that point, a highly ritualized trading process began. The leader of the party lodged with the factor, who was expected to offer him a "boonyar," or a modest gift of kola nuts, Malaguetta peppers, tobacco, rice, and palm oil. Once the caravan leader ate a kola nut, he was considered to have committed himself to trading with his host. At that point the caravan leader launched into a lengthy oration recounting the many hardships of the journey, after which all rice and salt trades were negotiated. Following that, and following another boonyar and an oration extolling the hospitality of the host, they moved on to the more difficult goods: ivory, cattle, firearms, textiles, kola nuts, and slaves. Europeans found the whole process of negotiation—considered a type of palaver in itself—to be extremely slow and tedious and frequently let their impatience cost them money. "Foolas have no idea of the value of time," lamented one visitor to the Northern Rivers, "they would sit a whole day with inexhaustible patience to gain half a bar more." Another European agreed, noting, "They waste the time in this dealing and protract it so that what could be done in one hour, they spend several days at, wasting the time in talking." Coastal factors were additionally frustrated at the common practice of selling captives in lots, which forced them to accept the elderly and lame in order to acquire prime slaves. The entire process was prolonged due to the lack of written accounts. Merchants kept track of smaller amounts using a sophisticated finger-counting system and larger amounts using stone or gunflint counters. Negotiating for a dozen captives could easily take a day or more. Once that was done, all that remained was to sustain the captives until a willing buyer like Godfrey arrived.[71]

As we have seen, the majority of the captives sold in the Northern Rivers and Sierra Leone, as well as many at Sherbro and the islands, began their journeys in the Futa Jallon and neighboring areas. As such, it is possible to deduce several things about the *Hare* captives, or at least about a majority of them. First, most were probably not Muslims. Islam forbade the enslavement of Muslims, and Futa Jallon generally respected that stricture. In fact, the Muslim-gentile divide was the most important in Futa Jallon society, largely coinciding with that of free and slave. Second, most of the *Hare* captives probably spoke Mande languages, among them Yalunka, Mandinka, Maninka, Bamana, Koranko, and Susu. It is possible that some non-Muslim Fulas were among them as well, but as we have seen, the peoples of Upper Guinea were used to interacting with each other and many were multilingual. Third, most of the captives coming from the Futa Jallon were probably men, both because Europeans paid higher prices for them and because the local aristocracy wanted to make sure they could never return. Finally, many had already been living as slaves. Armies, such as those involved in the siege of Farrabana earlier in the year, included many slaves, and so many of the captives taken in those conflicts were slaves.[72]

But not all of the *Hare* captives came from the Futa Jallon. A probable minority came from areas closer to the coast; they were people of non-Mande background, like the Bullom, Temne, Limba, Baga, and Landuma peoples, as well as coastal Mande-speakers, especially Susus. The avenues of enslavement were many, including debt, punishment for crime, and self-enslavement as a result of famine. Precisely how large this minority was is impossible to say, but there are several reasons to believe it was more than just a few. To start, the *Hare* captives' sex ratio was much more balanced than was the norm for Muslim traders, who were more likely to retain women for both domestic work and the trans-Sahara trade. Godfrey actually purchased more females than males, thirty-seven to thirty-five, respectively.[73] There is also evidence that some of the *Hare* captives were older than the usual fifteen- to thirty-year-old demographic that characterized the slave trade. In one of the only descriptions of the *Hare* captives, the merchant who handled their sale in South Carolina lamented that some of them were "not young." As we have seen, Futa Jallon sent few elderly slaves to market, and few would have survived the journey if they had been sent. Finally, the *Hare*'s visit partly overlapped with a coastal jihad in the Northern Rivers and Sherbro hinterland. The dynamic of this conflict would have been similar to the one in the Futa Jallon, in that the principal victims would have been non-Muslim. Their linguistic and cultural background, however, would have been different, with fewer Mande speakers and more speakers of the coastal Atlantic languages. Nonetheless, captives from coastal areas would still have been quite familiar with Mande-speakers and their culture from two centuries of interaction and "Mandingization" dating to the Mane invasions and the more recent migration of non-Muslim Mande-speakers, especially Susus, from the highlands at the onset of the jihad. In sum, even the coastal people among the *Hare* captives would have been familiar with Mande ways, perhaps with some language ability and, in some cases, may have been native speakers of Mande languages. All of these factors would come into play once the captives reached South Carolina.

Exactly what the *Hare* captives thought of their captivity is likewise unknown, but some idea can be gleaned from other sources. Most of the captives probably knew of people being sold to white men from across the sea, and the common assumption that they were to be eaten is confirmed in numerous sources. The captives Mungo Park accompanied on their long march to the coast asked him repeatedly if his countrymen were cannibals and were incredulous when he told them they were being shipped overseas to work the land. One skeptic, who apparently believed Europeans lived on the ocean itself, touched his hand to the earth and asked, "Have you really got such ground as this, to set your feet upon?" The fear of being eaten, documented in many different regions at many different times, is significant both for its literal meaning and for what it says about how the men and women who were caught in the slave trade processed their captivity. Their fear of a fate far worse than slavery was the most extreme expression of dread and despair. In many captives' minds, only supernatural beings could engage in such unspeakable behavior. Not surprisingly, historians have noted that many Africans associated enslavement and slave traders with witches and evil magic.

It was not for nothing that ship captains and Juula merchants watched their charges closely for indications of suicidal intent. Godfrey noted that two of the *Hare* captives "Drowned on the Coast," perhaps in an effort to end their lives, though that is not certain. A woman named Nealee, who was part of Mungo Park's coffle, attempted suicide by refusing food. After several days she had trouble keeping up, and when a swarm of bees attacked the party, she was too debilitated to run away. Instead, she crawled into a small stream to escape, where she was "stung in the most dreadful manner." When she refused to proceed any farther, a "few strokes" from a whip got her going again. After an escape attempt a few days later, Nealee simply lay down on the ground. Not willing to lose a valuable captive, the Juula traders carried her on a litter and later tied her onto a donkey, which promptly threw her off. The other captives, afraid of becoming trapped in the wilderness, asked the caravan's leader to slit her throat. Nealee's captors ultimately acceded to her desire to end her life and left her by the side of the path to die.[74]

AS HE MADE his purchases, Godfrey confronted a host of other problems. First among them was the ongoing feud with members of his crew. In September, Godfrey had clashed with his ordinary seamen. In October, apparently while at the Isles de Los, he feuded with his officers. Trouble started when Godfrey came on deck in the early morning and discovered the entire watch (not including the helmsman) asleep because the men had taken "too many Drams" from some bitters they had stowed in their chests. The bitters had apparently come from the *Hare*'s stores, which Godfrey soon secured with a padlock. Later that morning, first mate John Arnold Hammond went looking for the bitters, only to find the case locked. Hammond confronted Godfrey, "so angry that he threatened to break [the case] open." Taken aback, Godfrey decided that it was "time to Take him in hand" and gave Hammond "a few blows." When Hammond "made a faint return"—which we must assume would have resulted in a beating for Godfrey, given that Hammond was twenty-four years younger—Godfrey sicced the dog on him. The dog promptly locked its jaws onto Hammond's breast, "end[ing] the fray." Godfrey also clashed with second mate and cooper Richard Cole over his drinking, telling the Vernons that Cole was "the Goodfornothingest fellow." The acrimony continued at the Scarcies. Godfrey accused Cole of paying debts—probably incurred through private trading—out of the *Hare*'s accounts. In response, the crew took to referring to Godfrey as "Old Son of a Bitch," saying, every time Godfrey left the vessel, "Dam his old Blood I hope he'l never Come aboard no more," and employing more foul language than the captain could tolerate. Godfrey's final gambit was to expel his officers from his table, refusing to eat or drink with them. The move quieted matters, at least for a while.[75]

These clashes cut Godfrey to the quick. On October 16, he spilled his frustrations in a letter to the Vernons, a rambling rumination on his relationship with his men. This letter, and to a lesser degree several others, reveals Godfrey's thin skin and his tendency to blame others for his problems, quite a handicap for a ship captain. He took the disputes, which were an inevitable outgrowth of maritime life, as personal affronts. The constant grumbling and name-calling wounded him the most. Hammond, especially, had "Treated me as tho I had bin very much Inferiour" and "Spoak as Short and unmannerdly as could be." None of the Vernons' other captains complained quite as much as Godfrey, and pouring out his troubles could hardly have increased his employers' esteem for him. At some level he seems to have understood this, because he felt the need to frame his complaints as explanations for why things were going poorly. Godfrey even estimated that Hammond's and Cole's shenanigans cost the equivalent of a slave, which is difficult to imagine. Pilferage of spirits, drinking to excess, grumbling behind the captain's back, and use of salty language occurred on every vessel. Perhaps Godfrey had grown touchy with age, no longer able to handle these frustrations with skill. Whatever the reason, after a maritime career of almost four decades, Godfrey seems to have grown strangely unsuited to commanding an oceangoing vessel.[76]

As Godfrey dealt with these problems in the Northern Rivers, another issue emerged. Over a year earlier, in early October 1753, the snow *Race Horse*, out of London and commanded by Captain William Canfield, had been "cut off" by a contingent of Bulloms somewhere to the north of Sierra Leone, with five crew members, including the captain, "Barbarously Murdered," in Godfrey's words. The specific origin of the attack is unknown, but it was likely precipitated by the same sort of conflicts that attended the slave trade all along the coast. Although Godfrey had nothing to do with the original dispute, he got involved when the European traders at Quia managed to purchase the leader of the attack. The traders then "Delivered" the man to Godfrey—who, at the time, was not aboard the *Hare*, but at Quia—"to make an Example" of the Bullom leader. Why Godfrey was chosen for this duty is unclear, although his status as a sojourner, as opposed to a resident, may have played a role—he may have been seen by the Quia traders as insulation against further retaliation. Nevertheless, Godfrey did not disappoint. He imprisoned the man aboard the *Hare* on October 5 and scheduled a public execution for October 7, so that the traders could attend. The prisoner, however, did not heed Godfrey's schedule and died on the morning of October 6, so Godfrey cut off the man's head and hands and displayed them aboard the *Hare* for "Several days."[77]

Godfrey's willingness to perform these duties was likely motivated by several factors, not the least of which was a desire to terrorize the local population. Accustomed to a world in which black people were thoroughly subordinated to whites, he may have found the situation on the coast, where Africans enjoyed a great deal more power, threatening. He noted with obvious satisfaction that the gromettos in the area all approved of the execution of this "Great Rogue," and they assured him that the act would deter future aggression. Another target audience for Godfrey's terrible display may have been his own crew, since it came at a moment of particularly tense relations. He had already struck and set the dog on one crew member; this latest act served notice that he could commit the most heinous acts in the name of maintaining proper order and hierarchy.

But this incident also represented another turn of the wheel in the ongoing game of retaliation that structured the slave trade, with Godfrey demonstrating convincingly that he was an experienced player. The incident seems to have had a connection to local political conflicts that were only partly related to the slave trade. In his letter to the Vernons, Godfrey noted specifically that the executed man was a Bullom; that is to say, he was of non-Mande background and was almost certainly a non-Muslim. He further notes that the Susu population "Commend[ed]" his actions, which in turn suggests that the original Bullom attack on the *Race Horse* may have stemmed from a dispute over local control of the slave trade. Not only would the profit from selling captives have been at stake, but so also would the income in the form of customs, payments for provisions, and wood and watering rights. The incident occurred in the Northern Rivers at a time of jihad, which raises the possibility that there may have been a religious dimension to it as well, with non-Muslim Bulloms under pressure from Muslim Susus backed by Futa Jallon. If one or more of these factors were in play, Godfrey was an unwitting accomplice to a local political power play, rather than simply "mak[ing] an Example" of the man.[78]

Godfrey's turn as executioner took place against a backdrop of minor frustrations, mundane sorts of things that happened on every voyage. Mice ate a keg of ship's bread, and over five hundred pounds of tobacco was ruined in shipping. Godfrey gave the tobacco to the captives. At some point the *Hare*'s stove went "bad" and caused a fire that consumed eight barrels of flour and eight water casks. There were numerous expenditures as well. Godfrey made no fewer than fourteen separate food purchases while on the coast: limes, peppers, fowl, palm oil, manioc (cassava), goats, plantains, and—most important of all, because it would be the main nourishment for the captives—immense quantities of rice. There were nonfood expenditures as well, with goods purchased at Bance Island and traded for with other ships: "old Junk" for oakum to caulk the *Hare*; a buccaneer gun; four gallons of brandy "for Slaves"; gunpowder; and eight iron bars, three of which were used to shore up the hatch.[79]

After making all its necessary purchases and preparations along the African coast, the *Hare* set sail for Barbados on January 9, 1755.

CHAPTER FIVE

Passages

Nobody associated with the *Hare* left a full narrative of its transatlantic cross-ing. The shards of evidence that do survive provide a glimpse of conditions, but most of the specifics remain forever lost. We do have some idea of the sort of food the captives ate. The accounts reveal that Godfrey exchanged 357½ gallons of rum for provisions on the African coast, at least ninety-six of which went toward rice, along with flour, four gallons of brandy, and smaller amounts of manioc, palm oil, fish, plantains, fowl, peppers, limes, and cala-bashes (which Godfrey called "pumpkins").[1] Precisely which foods went to the captives and which were consumed by the crew is unknown, but the fact that the *Hare* arrived in the New World quickly and with provisions to spare suggests that the captives had full rations for the entire voyage, which did not always happen. We also know that the Atlantic crossing was extremely rough. Arriving in Barbados, Godfrey wrote to the Vernons that a persistent and cold northeast wind had made for a "Tumbleing passage," which left the deck "Continualy Wet for Sixteen days" and the captives "Pintch[ed]" with cold and in precarious health.[2]

If many of the details of the *Hare*'s crossing are unrecoverable, we can fill in some of the blanks by examining other voyages. Illness was common to all slave ships, with "fluxes," or gastrointestinal diseases, the most pro-lific killers, aggravated by a host of other ailments ranging from "dropsy" (edema) to yaws, a bacterial infection that causes wartlike lesions. One observer described a lower deck "so covered with the blood and mucus which had proceeded from [the captives] in consequence of the flux, that it resembled a slaughterhouse."[3] Smallpox ravaged a number of slave ships in the 1750s, affecting crews and passengers alike. While British vessels gener-ally carried a surgeon, North American ones almost never did. The captives' medical care was delegated to a crew member who administered remedies—consisting mostly of shots of alcohol—according to a "Book of Directions."[4] That book may have been a 1729 treatise on diseases common to the slave trade written by a British surgeon. Tellingly, the author devoted more space to the health of crew members than to that of the captives. And the treatments were crude: in case of fever, for example, the surgeon was advised to "bleed immediately and purge him gently the Day following. . . . Whenever Pustles begin to appear, never bleed [rather], administer Cardiacs, and Diaphoretics in a moderate way." Eighteenth-century medicine being what it was, the captives may have been better off with just the rum shots.[5]

Rape by crew members was another very frequent occurrence. No evidence survives to say that this occurred aboard the *Hare*, but that means little, since reports of rape were generally rare in the type of commercial records that survive from the *Hare*'s voyage. Mention of rape and sexual violation aboard slave ships is common in other sources, however, to the extent that some historians suggest that it would have been unusual for such assaults not to occur on a voyage. Some rapists physically overpowered their victims, many of whom were probably weak from captivity. Others employed a different sort of coercion, rooted in the power dynamic of the slave ship, offering special treatment—perhaps more food or even passage in the officers' quarters—in exchange for performing sexual services. In either case, sexual abuse and the threat of it gave the captain and crew an additional weapon with which to control the captives.[6] Nonsexual violence was even more common, though there is also no explicit reference to it in the records of the *Hare*. Still, it does not take much imagination to see why Godfrey thought it advisable to bring an attack dog on the voyage.

Rebellion was a very real possibility on any slaving voyage. In the annals of the transatlantic slave trade, there are 451 recorded instances of shipboard rebellion. Undoubtedly, many times that figure went unrecorded, with perhaps one voyage in ten experiencing a serious revolt.[7] Foiled plots were even more common than insurrections. Several former captives recalled shipmates laying plans for rebellion, as did former ship captains and crew. John Newton discovered a plot aboard his vessel when a crew member "Surprized 2 of them attempting to get off their irons." Other plots were betrayed by fellow captives, or, as with one witnessed by Boyrereau Brinch, by a vessel's "linguist," or interpreter.[8] Captives were most likely to attempt seizure of a vessel while still in sight of land, where escape and return to neighbors and kin was still possible. Because almost no Africans knew how to navigate large sailing vessels, rebellions were far less common on the open ocean, although they did happen. Revolts were also more likely to occur on some stretches of the African coast than others, with Upper Guinea, including Sierra Leone, seeing the greatest number of revolts per voyage.[9] The reasons for this are unclear but may have to do with the region's geography. Unlike some stretches of coast, where vessels had to anchor miles offshore beyond a deadly surf, those calling at Upper Guinea ports often traveled up the rivers, where land and freedom remained tantalizingly within reach for months on end while a cargo was assembled. Godfrey and his crew would have recognized that their lives depended on keeping a close eye on their prisoners, whatever their animosities toward each other.

Typically, captives remained shackled while in sight of land. Once at sea, most captains released the women and children. Men might be freed for part of the day so they could exercise, though they were almost always kept separate from the women. The purpose of the physical exercise was commercial rather than humanitarian: it was seen as essential to the captives' health, and consequently to the price they would fetch at market. Sometimes, when captives were too ill or unwilling to exercise, crew members coerced them with whips, a practice known as "dancing the slaves." All of this was contingent on fair weather. When the weather turned foul, the captives remained chained in the hold, sometimes for weeks on end.[10] While these were the practices aboard most British slave ships, at least one observer charged that on smaller North American vessels, with their correspondingly smaller crews, captives spent more time shackled below than did those aboard British vessels. He may have been correct, with the likely result of the increased confinement being a more rigid discipline and greater illness.[11]

It was the job of the crew to prepare food for the captives in the ship's stove, which was then served in wooden tubs. The fare varied regionally. Vessels calling at Sierra Leone relied on rice, the regional staple, while ships visiting other parts of Africa stocked the local produce, with yams, corn, and beans most common. The *Hare* would also have filled its casks, probably at the "Watering Place" on Sierra Leone Bay, which boasted some of the best water on the African coast. After a time, the quality of the water mattered little, since the longer it sat in wooden casks, the more putrid it became. But at least the captives and crew of the *Hare* had enough water. The annals of the slave trade are replete with examples of vessels running low on water, adding to the already-unspeakable misery of the Middle Passage.

The cold northeast wind that drenched and sickened so many of the *Hare* captives had one saving grace: it made for a short voyage. The *Hare* sailed from Sierra Leone to Barbados in a remarkable twenty days. When taking into account an apparent quick stop at the Isles de Los, the *Hare*'s timing was even more impressive. By Godfrey's own report, it took a mere eighteen days to cover 3,121 miles, which translates into slightly more than

173 miles per day.[12] Although the *Hare* seems to have had an unusually fair wind, the Sierra Leone–Barbados passage was one of the quicker in transatlantic shipping, averaging just shy of forty-three days. By comparison, the average eighteenth-century slave ship took seventy days to cross, with passages of over a hundred days not uncommon.[13] With no surviving logbook, it is difficult to know the *Hare*'s precise course, but a logbook from another New England sloop that made a very similar passage less than three years later gives a fairly good idea. The *Good Hope*, skippered by Alexander Urquhart, set sail from the Isles de Los on April 28, 1757. Urquhart enjoyed "fresh breezes" for most of the voyage, encountering contrary winds in only the first few days before picking up the same easterly trade winds that propelled Columbus and other Europeans toward the Caribbean. The *Good Hope* arrived at St. Christopher's, approximately two hundred miles farther from the Isles de Los than Barbados, on May 25, a voyage of twenty-eight days. The two voyages are therefore quite comparable, so we can be fairly certain that Godfrey sailed essentially the same course.[14]

Despite the quick passage, four captives perished and several others arrived at Barbados seriously ill and near death. The precise mortality rate for the *Hare*'s voyage is difficult to calculate, since the records are inconsistent. Godfrey purchased seventy-two captives on the coast, but in a letter to the Vernons written shortly after arriving in Bridgetown, he reported that he had purchased sixty-five. The discrepancy may represent the difference between the number of captives purchased on the Vernons' account and the number of privilege slaves purchased on Godfrey's account, which was either six or seven. Two captives drowned while still in Africa, a result of possible suicides, and a third seems to have perished in the same manner on the Middle Passage. It is uncertain if this one was among the four that Godfrey reported losing on the crossing.

We cannot know for certain how the *Hare* captives responded to their ordeal. Nobody ever considered recording their thoughts; indeed, to Godfrey and the others, soliciting the thoughts of a captive contradicted the very essence of his mission to trade in commodified human beings. While many more Africans than previously thought survived to tell their stories— the number is well into the hundreds—most chose to say very little about the passage itself, as if it was too painful to recall or impossible to describe.[15] Ottobah Cugoano was typical in his reticence when he said, "But it would be needless to give a description of all the horrible scenes which we saw." Gustavus Vassa, who recorded his experiences for the express purpose of dramatizing the evil of the trade, left one of the most extensive descriptions of crossing the Atlantic in the hold of a slaver. But he devoted only 2,000 words to the experience, concluding, "In this manner we continued to undergo more hardships than I can now relate."[16]

It is possible to conjecture what the captives' experiences probably were like belowdecks. Historians' accounts of the Middle Passage tend to make heavy usage of modal verbs—the captives "must have" felt or experienced something. Given the cold northeast winds and the continual drenching of the *Hare*'s deck with spray and seawater, it is safe to assume that the captives were kept below for almost the entire crossing. Even conditions below, according to Godfrey's report, were far from dry. The captives spent the voyage seasick and shivering from the cold as the small vessel pitched and rolled through heavy seas. If they had not appeared already, intestinal ailments—diarrhea and dysentery—would have begun to spread, further weakening the captives. The decks, platforms, and bulkheads would have been slick with vomit and feces, mixed with brackish water, spreading infection through open sores caused by the captives' manacles. Amid the despair, some undoubtedly experienced some order of psychological trauma. Yet whatever feelings of disorientation the captives may have had were mitigated by the fact that, contrary to popular image, most captives in the holds of Upper Guinean slave ships could communicate with at least some, if not most, of their fellow captives. One slaver observed that speakers of coastal languages could translate for their inland neighbors, who in turn could communicate with those from farther inland than them. Boyrereau Brinch apparently knew several of his fellow captives by name, as did others.[17]

Perhaps one of the most important things to occur in the hold of a slave ship was the creation of "shipmate" relationships. A phenomenon familiar everywhere the slave trade deposited its victims, the shipmate relationship was a strong bond between those who experienced the Atlantic crossing together. Africans in the New World viewed the relationship through the prism of kinship, and ties could outlive the immigrants themselves. Historians tend to regard shipmate relationships in one of two ways. For some, they indicate a rupture with the captives' former lives in Africa, a separation from kin and country. For these historians, this relationship represents the moment when captives, forced to leave behind the old, embraced the new. It follows, then, that the communities built by these shipmates were entirely the result of a process originating on the ship itself and elaborated in the New World. Another approach to the shipmate relationship is quite different. Rather than emphasizing the isolation and randomness of the collection of individuals aboard the vessel, it stresses the many structuring factors that gave the captives something in common. Given the process of enslavement, some aboard the *Hare* and other vessels were likely related to one another, came from the same villages or regions, or served in the same military forces. But even if, as is likely, most of the captives were personal strangers, they still shared a great deal of language and culture. In all probability, the *Hare* captives conversed, quarreled, strategized, prayed, and lamented—if not all together, then at least in pairs, threes, and fours. The shipmate relationship would certainly be significant in the New World as a building block for the future that was firmly rooted in cultural and historical experience, rather than as a total break with the past.[18]

THE *HARE* REACHED BRIDGETOWN, the capital of Barbados, on January 26, 1755. Barbados lies approximately 130 miles off the coast of Venezuela and measures twenty-one by fourteen miles at its widest point. As the easternmost of the Antilles, it enjoyed the favor of slave-ship captains, who often used it to restock water and provisions. Its location to windward of the entire Caribbean made it a good dispatch point for incoming marine traffic. Ship owners frequently lodged instructions with their correspondents in Bridgetown, directing vessels on toward the Lesser Antilles, Jamaica, or North America. But the island's low silhouette made Barbados a notoriously difficult place to locate, "like sixpence throwne downe uponn newmarkett heath," as one seventeenth-century visitor said.[19] Mariners occasionally missed the island altogether, a very costly error since once leeward of Barbados it was extremely difficult and time consuming to beat back to it.[20] Approached from the Atlantic, Barbados appeared slightly elevated toward the northern end, sloping gradually toward the south. As a vessel drew nearer, a series of coral cliffs came into view, followed by the sugar estates, distinguishable by their mill buildings' boiling-house stacks. "It appeared wonderfully inhabited," wrote one traveler, "dotted with houses as thick as on the declivities in the neighborhood of London or Bristol, but with no woods, and with very few trees, even on the summits of the hills."[21]

This denuded landscape, where "two or three straggling cocoas [coconut palms] near each dwelling-house were all the trees to be seen," was a relatively recent development, entirely the work of human beings. When the British first occupied Barbados in 1627, it had been covered with lush, tropical forest. Within a few decades, most of the trees had been cleared and burned for fuel, as sugar estates enveloped the island. The result was the first slave-based plantation society in English America. For over a half century, Barbados was the leading English importer of African labor, having

FIGURE 5.1. *Bridgetown, ca. 1695. When this image was made, Bridgetown was the main port for England's most valuable colony. When the* Hare *arrived sixty years later, Barbados had been far surpassed by Jamaica, though it was still a significant producer of sugar. Bridgetown was important not only as the outlet for Barbadian sugar, but also as a provisioning port and a site for the exchange of mercantile intelligence. Godfrey landed the* Hare *captives here for almost four weeks before continuing on to South Carolina. He left five ailing captives behind to die. (Library of Congress)*

consumed slightly over half of all slaves imported to the colonies before 1701. By the time of the *Hare*'s voyage, its share had dropped to 17 percent, but this decline was relative, not absolute. Barbados was still an important plantation colony, importing more Africans in the third quarter of the eighteenth century than at any other time in its history. Its reduced share had less to do with a decline in sugar planting and more to do with the emergence of Jamaica, an island twenty-five times its size, as a slave-based plantation society toward the end of the seventeenth century. In the years since its founding, Barbados had earned a reputation as a place of misery. Few migrated there voluntarily, and the population consisted of penurious bookkeepers running absentee-owned estates, cruel overseers, and brutally exploited slaves.[22] It was perhaps out of an awareness of having been overtaken by Jamaica that a poet wrote:

> Tho' small this Spot, Important is its Worth;
> What mighty Sums dost thou still Yearly yield?
> Incredible to tell! No County sure,
> However large, in all Britainnia's Realm
> Can rival Thee in Worth. Great is thy Trade,
> And by thy Produce still increasing more.[23]

As the *Hare* rounded the southern end of the island, the capital of Bridgetown came into view. Situated on the island's leeside and originally called "the Indian Bridge," the town got its permanent name from the spans that had been built over a low-lying swamp fed by the Constitution River.[24] Bridgetown possessed the largest harbor on the island, Carlisle Bay, with a reputed capacity of five hundred vessels, though with a rocky bottom that was notorious for fouling anchors. With a population of about eleven thousand housed in approximately fifteen hundred buildings (not including the huts and outbuildings that were home to most of the slave population), Bridgetown was, in the words of a traveler who visited one year after the *Hare*, "very extensive and well built, and the merchant's [sic] houses elegant."[25] Beyond the harbor, Godfrey would have noticed the spire of St. Michael's Church, with its "curious clock," as he sailed past the guns of Needham's Fort, Willoughby's Fort, and James's Fort, which protected the harbor.[26] Once at anchor, the captives would have been able to observe at a distance the port's bustling wharves, the "men on horseback, carts moving in different directions, the shipping in the bay, and immense numbers of people wearing different dresses, as fancy or convenience suggested." Most vessels at the time did not tie up at the wharves, but rather anchored in Carlisle Bay, lightering cargoes, provisions, and people to and from the quayside.[27]

Godfrey's first action was to call upon Charles Bolton, a merchant and correspondent of the Vernons', to see if any new directions had arrived for him since receiving his initial instructions six months earlier. Strolling Bridgetown's narrow streets, which were fronted by two- and three-story buildings featuring ground-level shutters and upper-floor galleries, he hoped to find letters directing him to Jamaica, where the winter weather was healthier, the voyage shorter, and the prices likely higher than in South Carolina. When he arrived at Bolton's countinghouse, probably located in Cheapside, Bridgetown's fashionable commercial center one block off the harbor, he had no way of knowing that the Vernons had already sent instructions to Bolton on January 10 confirming his orders for South Carolina. When the instructions arrived on February 5, Godfrey promptly told his employers, "I fear you'l [sic] repent my Going to Carrolina at this Season of Year." In saying so he was thinking of the late spring cold that killed many captives. Conventional wisdom held that April or May was the earliest that a cargo of slaves should be landed in North America. In the end, however, Godfrey had no choice but to follow his employers' instructions, but he made sure to register his objection in order to escape culpability for an unprofitable voyage.[28]

The captives' health was an even more pressing matter than his destination. Ailing slaves would fetch low prices in any market. Four had already perished, and Godfrey feared that three more might never recover. While they would all benefit from some recovery time ashore, "breaking bulk," or unlading his vessel, would make him liable for the colony's five shillings per slave import duty. To avoid paying, Godfrey had to declare the number of captives he was temporarily landing before the island's treasurer, and upon departure would have to swear that he had not contracted with any Barbados resident for their future purchase.[29] Doing so, he received permission to land his captives for up to three weeks, but the colony's treasurer required him to "Walk them so that I take them aboard again," to stay in compliance with the law. Exactly where he took them is not certain, but he probably housed them at Charles Bolton's, since most merchants had yards where they housed slaves and conducted sales.

The walk through town (for those who could walk) would have been the *Hare* captives' first contact with dry land in many weeks, indeed for some their first in many months. It was also their introduction to the New World. Gustavus Vassa, who was housed in a merchant's yard in Barbados only a few years after the *Hare*'s voyage in a similar manner, recalled of his walk through town that "every object was new to me, every thing I saw filled me with surprise." He was struck first by the multistory buildings that lined Bridgetown's principal streets and was even more "astonished" by the men mounted on horseback, though he noted that for some of his fellow captives who came from areas with horses, this was nothing new. Once at the merchant's yard, he and his fellow captives were "pent up like so many sheep in a fold, without regard to sex or age." Boyrereau Brinch recalled the three months he spent imprisoned by a Bridgetown merchant in what he described as a "house of subjection." Captives over twelve years old spent their days in a large room chained together, picking oakum in a circle, at the center of which stood a driver brandishing a whip. One girl of noble birth, he recalled, who had been commiserating with her younger brother, attracted the attention of the driver, who promptly bludgeoned her to death with the butt of the whip. And from time to time, he reported, "the common sailors were allowed to come into the house and ravish the women in presence of all the assembly," having apparently bribed the jailors. Each day, the captives were led to "filthy brooks" to drink and wash themselves. After about two months, the shackles produced sores, which in turn attracted maggots that burrowed beneath the captives' skin, at which point the driver finally removed the chains. Eventually, Brinch was sold off to a Connecticut ship captain.[30]

As Godfrey negotiated with the colony's treasurer, trouble flared on another front. Crew members had begun to leave his vessel, undoubtedly motivated by the animosities that had built up since their arrival in Africa. Francis Welch, who had signed on in October while the *Hare* was still on the African coast, left the very day the *Hare* landed in Barbados. Barnt Hartwick and William Baggott ran two days later. Deserting a merchant vessel was illegal, punishable by up to thirty days' hard labor, but it was quite common. Slave ships and West Indiamen had the highest desertion rates of all, with one in eight sailors leaving. Captains and local authorities, however, did not always mete out the maximum punishments. Some shipmasters were quite willing to let mariners go, since fewer crew members amounted to a savings through the forfeiture of wages. Those who hoped to regain a crew member's labor generally understood that their cause was not helped by imprisonment or the lash, at least while the ship was still in port.[31] In fact, a bigger problem than desertion by sailors was the practice of captains discharging sailors in the Americas in order to save on wages and to rid themselves of their most troublesome crew members. But that only happened once the captives had been sold, not before they had been transported to their final destination, because the larger crew was still needed to discourage revolts. Right now Godfrey still needed his men.[32]

Legally speaking, the sailors who left the *Hare* in Barbados did not actually desert. Godfrey reported that three of them, William Baggott, Barnt Hartwick, and Francis Welch, had joined the British sloop-of-war *Tryal*. By law, sailors leaving a merchantman for a naval vessel could not be charged with "running" and were entitled to their wages.[33] As it turns out, only Hartwick and Baggott appear in the records of the *Tryal*, having signed on as supernumeraries, extra hands who received victuals but no pay, and the two deserted again six weeks later at Antigua. Welch may have told Godfrey he was signing on to the *Tryal* in order to keep from being hauled back to the *Hare*, but his name was never entered into the vessel's records. Lacking cash, Godfrey had to get an advance from Charles Bolton in order to pay the three men off.[34]

Second mate Richard Cole did not sign on to the *Tryal* either. After yet another tiff with Godfrey, the exact nature of which is obscure, he decided to discharge himself. Godfrey was incensed, insisting that the prerogative to discharge was solely his and ordering mate John Arnold Hammond to withhold Cole's sea chest. Cole then consulted with an attorney about pleading his case before a court in Bridgetown.[35] Cole apparently planned to argue that since he had not signed "Ye Act of Parliment," by which he probably meant the standard printed form of ship's articles that made specific reference to the 1729 act regulating seamen's wages and working conditions, he was free to discharge himself and collect wages. He may also have intended to argue that Godfrey violated his contract in going to South Carolina rather than Jamaica. Godfrey feared that Cole might win his case, since he considered the Bridgetown courts to be particularly favorable to sailors. The attorney refused to take the case, but Godfrey nevertheless found it expedient to pay off Cole and deliver up his sea chest. "I hope from his Extrodnary Conduct you'l [sic] be able to Save his wages," he told the Vernons, holding out the possibility that they might initiate proceedings against him back in Rhode Island.[36]

The *Hare*'s crew now consisted of Godfrey, mate John Hammond, and seamen William Burling, John Battey, and William Ball, and on February 17, Godfrey managed to hire another seaman, William Morony.[37] There was plenty of work to do—flushing out the hold, mending and re-rigging the sails, loading provisions, fixing leaks—but with at least three weeks in port and with the captives housed elsewhere, there was almost certainly opportunity for the men to take advantage of the town's many entertainments. A major entrepôt that saw some two to three thousand sailors pass through each year, Bridgetown boasted an array of taverns and ale houses, where a working man might enjoy a dram or a pint (or both many times over), along with local delicacies like avocado pears.[38] A small but growing number of tavern keepers were free people of color, and many doubled as crimps, or procurers of seamen to shipmasters. In the typical scenario, the seaman would avail himself of the easy credit offered by a tavern owner, only to find himself in debt. The proprietor would then inform the sailor that he had to choose between jail and working off the debt with a shipmaster designated by the crimp. The practice caused so many problems for ship captains whose crew members were detained either by rival captains, by crimps, or by local officials that Barbados passed a law allowing the town constables to seize any seaman found in a tavern after 8 P.M. without a pass. The sailor would then appear the following day before a justice of the peace, who had the option of placing him in jail, putting him in the stocks, or releasing him outright. The act also declared any debts contracted by a seaman without a pass from his master to be uncollectable in court. The effectiveness of this law is uncertain, but its very existence underscores the many snares awaiting sailors in Bridgetown.[39]

Bridgetown had other attractions. Roebuck Street on the edge of town was the principal gambling district, with cockpits and skittle alleys.[40] There were also houses of prostitution, or "hotels," as they were called locally. Most of Bridgetown's bagnios were owned by women, often "coloured" (as people of mixed-race ancestry were called in the West Indies) or black, and most of the prostitutes were enslaved, giving most or all of their earnings to their masters or mistresses. A common practice in these "hotels" was for a visitor to rent a room, then tip a female attendant to "draw the curtains." Alternately, a tar might bargain with a market woman or "huckster," whose master allowed her to "work out" on the streets of Bridgetown. The number of these women increased when the island's sugar economy was poor, as planters sent female slaves into the city to earn their keep. When sailors could not leave the vessel, the prostitutes came to them. Ship captains might opt to "lease" a woman from her master and keep her onboard for the entire time in port. Ordinary seamen could buy a few minutes' dalliance from one of the many prostitutes who greeted incoming ships in wherries and pinnaces. A clear hierarchy of color operated, with the lightest-skinned women fetching higher prices from wealthier clients and darker-skinned women reserved for poorer clients, like common sailors. While some enslaved prostitutes were able to parlay their affairs into self-purchase or manumission, most were probably not.[41]

Whatever the crew's escapades, work continued aboard the *Hare*. Godfrey took on some passengers, Francis Mountain and his four slaves at five pounds sterling per head, saying "[I] hope it will Defray [a] Great part of my Charges."[42] However, after more than two weeks ashore, the captives were still not doing well. The Vernons' agent in Barbados, Charles Bolton, told Godfrey in mid-February that at least five of the captives would probably not survive a voyage to South Carolina. Bolton proposed to sell them in Barbados, a scheme Godfrey endorsed, saying that any money received would be a "Clear gain." A few days later, one man had died and two girls were "so low" that Godfrey mused "that I had as Good Knock them in ye head as Pretend to carry them away."[43] In other words, rather than bear the continued expense for medical care (such as it was) or pay import duty in the event that he should need to land them permanently, Godfrey thought it perhaps better simply to murder two young girls. In its starkness, his comment, even if not entirely serious (since there is no evidence that Godfrey actually killed the girls), distilled his conception of the voyage to its very essence: the voyage was about making money from the commodification of human beings. Any other consideration was an afterthought at most.

Meanwhile, letters continued to cross the Atlantic as part of the extensive network of merchant capital that orchestrated the *Hare* captives' enslavement and transportation. In October, the Vernons had instructed Thomlinson, Trecothick, & Co. of London to insure the *Hare* for two hundred pounds and the captives for four hundred pounds. In January, as the *Hare* crossed the ocean, they had informed their correspondent Gabriel Manigault of Charles Town, South Carolina, that Godfrey would arrive with slaves sometime in March. A day later they had sent, care of Charles Bolton, the instructions that had so disappointed Godfrey, ordering him to South Carolina. On February 24, Gabriel Manigault wrote the Vernons to say that he would handle the *Hare*'s cargo and that the market was good. Mundane as this correspondence may seem, it would be no exaggeration to say that the transatlantic slave trade could not have functioned on the scale it did without this type of paper infrastructure.

The *Hare* sailed for South Carolina on about February 20, 1755, without seaman William Ball, who jumped ship on February 16.[44] After setting sail, Godfrey abruptly sent five captives back to Bridgetown, convinced that they would not survive the voyage. Why he waited until after departure is unknown. Most likely, their condition worsened significantly in a very short time, perhaps as a result of bad weather or a sudden outbreak of sickness. A total of six *Hare* captives, then, did not make the voyage to South Carolina, these five and the one who died at Bridgetown. The five were received by Charles Bolton, who put them up for auction "sometime after his departure," probably in March. It appears, moreover, that Bolton attempted to engage in shill bidding and purchased one or more of the captives himself. "I never intended to purchase any of them, but only by bidding to Raise the Sales, but however I must be Content," he said, informing Godfrey that he had paid twenty-six pounds, fifteen shillings, and sixpence. By the end of the month, however, the older of the two girls (likely the same girls that Godfrey had considered murdering) died. A physician hired by Bolton informed him that one of the men and the other girl would soon die, too. She died in mid-April, by which time Bolton believed that only one of the five captives left at Barbados stood a chance of survival.[45] With no sales record to trace the captives, their trail goes cold there, but given their delicate health, the fact that four of the five apparently did not survive two months, and the very high first-year mortality rates throughout the island, it is quite possible that all five were dead within a year.

CHAPTER SIX

The Sale

The first few months of 1755 had been blustery along the Carolina coast. In February, powerful gales had blown several entering vessels away from Charles Town harbor. The normally fearless flotilla of bar pilots that greeted every inbound vessel had been reduced to a mere two pinnaces. Gusts nearly capsized one of the two, stripping it of its foresail and anchor and setting it adrift on its side for several hours. Rough seas swept the pilot overboard, but he managed to return to shore unharmed. A few weeks later, another Charles Town–bound vessel was dismasted on an attempt to enter the harbor and put in 150 miles north at Cape Fear, North Carolina. Rebellion Road, as Charles Town Harbor was known locally, had other navigational hazards aside from the choppy spring weather. The Ashley and Cooper Rivers, which, as later generations would boast, "come together at Charleston to form the Atlantic Ocean," normally churn up a series of shallow sandbars. Just a month before the *Hare*'s arrival, a pilot ran a British man-of-war onto No Man's Land breaker. A second pilot had to bring the vessel off at high tide. Approaching Rebellion Road, Godfrey could do nothing about the foul weather, which was surely weakening his captives, but he paid a pilot to steer his vessel in, which was required by law.[1]

"Flat and woody" is how Governor James Glen described South Carolina in the middle of the eighteenth century. The coastal plain that stretches from North Carolina to Florida slopes so imperceptibly to the Atlantic Ocean that early settlers judged it a waste of time to build water-powered mills—the region's streams simply did not flow swiftly enough to power them. In Glen's time, more than four-fifths of the province was covered in Spanish moss–shrouded pines, with ferns and creepers tangled at the base of their trunks. The remaining areas consisted of occasional "savannahs," or "wide extended Plains . . . natural Lawns," and river swamps rich in "black greasy Mould," their waters once darkened by a canopy of cypress and live oak, now drained, cleared, and circumscribed by dikes to create rice fields.[2]

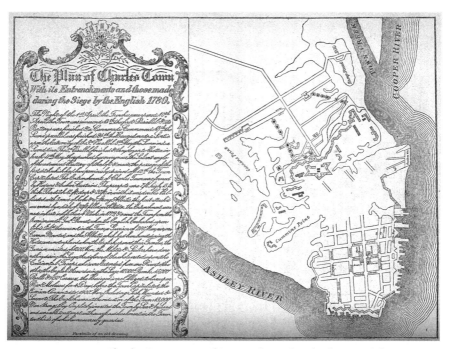

FIGURE 6.1. *Charles Town, 1780. This map shows the Charles Town's basic grid. In September 1752, the city was devastated by a hurricane. When the* Hare *arrived in March 1755, the residents were still rebuilding. Both the State House and St. Michael's Church were under construction, and the Watch House would not be complete until 1767. The sale of the* Hare *captives probably took place at one of Gabriel Manigault's storehouses on Tradd Street. (Courtesy of the University of Texas Libraries, University of Texas at Austin)*

    The capital, Charles Town, occupied the southern tip of a long, flat peninsula that sat between the Ashley and Cooper Rivers. It was the fourth-largest port in North America, after Philadelphia, New York, and Boston, and ahead of Newport. Six main thoroughfares inscribed a crooked grid upon the city: King Street, Meeting Street, and the Bay running north–south, while Queen, Broad, and Tradd Streets sliced east–west, creating sixteen large blocks. These large blocks were cut in all directions by narrower streets and alleys. One anonymous traveler estimated that there were 1,100 dwelling houses, although it is doubtful that he counted the many smaller slave-quarter structures that lay at the rear of most lots, and this figure did not include the many warehouses and public buildings.[3]

    At the time of the *Hare*'s arrival, Charles Town's residents were rebuilding following a devastating hurricane in 1752. One of the more extensive projects involved the creation of a new civic square at the intersection of Broad and Meeting Streets. On the northwest corner, less than a year after the storm, workers laid the cornerstone of a new state house, a meeting place for the colony's legislature, the Commons House of Assembly. A two-story brick building featuring a triangular pediment atop four slender pillars, the State House's Georgian style invoked the power and authority of the Crown, as channeled through the provincial government. In 1755, however, this edifice was still under construction. On the southeast corner, workers had recently laid the foundation of the new St. Michael's Anglican Church. Eventually, its whitewashed spire would be the highest point in the city, visible for miles out to sea, but at the moment it was five years from completion. To the northeast sat the market, an avenue of covered stalls stretching eastward for two long blocks toward the Bay, which one anonymous guide described as "well regulated and plentifully supplied with Provisions." Another, perhaps more reliable observation characterized it as "a low and dirty . . . market house." In 1767, the colonial-era power center would be complete with the construction of a Watch House on the southwestern corner. Here, runaway slaves taken up by the town patrol were held for their masters. It would also feature a public pillory for whippings, brandings, and ear croppings. At the time of the *Hare* captives' arrival, however, most activity of this sort took place in the workhouse in the town's northwest corner. Whether any structure sat on that spot in March 1755 is uncertain, but with the hurricane hitting only two and a half years earlier, it is entirely possible that the lot was vacant.[4]

The economic center of the city—and indeed, of the entire Low Country— lay two blocks east on an avenue known as "the Bay," which ran north–south along the Cooper River. Hugging land on the western edge was a row of two-story buildings nearly a mile long, with mercantile establishments on the ground floor and residences above. In 1751, Governor Glen reported one hundred buildings on the quayside, including forty-seven mercantile houses, seven taverns or "dram shops," two goldsmiths, a lodging house, a dancing school, and assorted blacksmiths, bricklayers, attorneys, and ship's carpenters. Opposite these and running along the river was the town's main wharf, with eight separate piers, or "bridges," as they were known locally. Upon the bridges sat merchants' warehouses, where laborers, both free and bound, received, weighed, stored, and shipped produce of the country. In January, when the previous year's harvest was ready for shipment, scores of vessels landed and took on cargoes at these bridges, creating, in Glen's words, "a kind of floating market." Slightly north of the Bay's midpoint sat a

FIGURE 6.2. *A View of Charles Town, 1776. The Charles Town waterfront as seen from across the Cooper River, with St. Michael's Church to the left and St. Phillip's to the right. The* Hare *would have moored at one of these "bridges," as docks were called locally. The Exchange, at center, was not built until the 1760s. The low buildings to the left are on the Bay, the town's main commercial thoroughfare. (Yale University Art Gallery)*

gun emplacement known as the Half Moon Battery. The site of the customs house, it served as the principal point of entry from the sea. It also functioned as Charles Town's unofficial common, where official proclamations were read, laws posted, and in decades past, pirates hanged.[5]

At the time of the *Hare*'s arrival in 1755, more than four-fifths of the colony's nonindigenous population of seventy-six thousand lived within sixty miles of the coast in the area known as the Low Country. Over 60 percent of the residents were enslaved. As the only mainland colony with an enslaved majority, South Carolina's demography was halfway between that of a West Indian sugar island and the mainland plantation colony of Virginia. The Caribbean resemblance was most pronounced in the Low Country; by 1760, fifteen of eighteen parishes had black majorities of 70 percent or higher. Less than a quarter of the South Carolina population lived in the area known as the backcountry, which had far fewer slaves. The backcountry population was growing, with the largest surge to come in the 1760s with a British victory in the French and Indian War and a Carolinian victory over the Cherokees.[6]

South Carolina was first and foremost a rice-growing colony, but it had not always been so. Deerskins, dried meat, and Indian slaves had been the colony's principal exports during the seventeenth century. However, with the successful introduction of commercial rice culture in the 1690s (or, technically, the reintroduction—experimental plantings had been done in the 1670s) and the military defeat of the Yamasee and Tuscarora peoples in the 1710s, Carolina became the Atlantic World's premier rice exporter. By midcentury, rice accounted for almost 55 percent of the value of the produce shipped out of the colony. The primary market for Carolina rice was Britain, which usually imported half of the total product, though all but a small portion of this was soon re-exported to Germany, France, Belgium, and the Netherlands. The British West Indies was another market, although its share fluctuated greatly between a low of about 1.5 percent in 1737 and a high of about 25 percent in 1762. The third major rice market emerged after 1730, when Parliament repealed earlier restrictions and allowed direct exports to continental Europe south of Cape Finisterre, the point where northwestern Spain juts into the Atlantic. Exports to Portugal (Spain itself was not a major buyer) rose and fell, peaking at 29 percent of total output in 1766.[7]

Rice was a labor-intensive crop, requiring not only traditional agricultural work, like planting and harvesting, but also constant attention to its elaborate infrastructure. Since the colony's founding, enslaved labor played a significant role. Most of Carolina's first slaves, as well as its first free European settlers, came from the Caribbean, Barbados specifically. They traded for deerskins and raised livestock, sometimes living on their own for extended periods of time on isolated ranches, known as "cow pens." This way of life, however, declined around 1700, as rice planting took hold. Suddenly in need of more laborers than could be reliably and affordably obtained from the West Indies, Carolina planters began to import them directly from Africa. As early as 1708, the colony had a black majority. Captive importations from Africa followed the fortunes of the rice economy, slowing during the depressed 1720s, then dramatically increasing in the 1730s. A large majority of the Africans who arrived in these years, perhaps seven in ten, came from Central Africa and probably shared a great deal of linguistic and cultural matériel. After 1739, when a group of these Central Africans drew upon that shared culture to rebel against and execute a score of whites—an event known as the Stono Rebellion—colonial legislators sought to reduce the numbers of Africans in hopes of preventing future revolts. They placed a prohibitively high duty on slave importations in 1740, which, along with a nine-year war, drove captive importations to near-negligible levels (see table 4 in appendix 3).[8]

The Commons House repealed the duty in 1744, and with the conclusion of the war in 1748, the colony resumed importations of captives. The twenty-five years from 1751 to 1775 saw the number of African arrivals increase at twice the rate of the previous quarter century. South Carolina, while never importing as many captives as the West Indian colonies, nevertheless became a regular market for British slave traders. The present wave of Africans was, moreover, different from the one that had preceded it in the 1730s. Whereas 70 percent of those entering in the 1730s had come from Central Africa, approximately 58 percent of the Africans arriving in 1751–75 came from Upper Guinea, that is, from Senegambia, Sierra Leone, and the Windward Coast. A closer look reveals that over that twenty-five-year period, the proportion rose from about half in the 1750s to about six in ten during the 1760s, so Upper Guineans actually increased in significance over the years immediately prior to the American Revolution (see table 5 in appendix 3). As we have seen, Upper Guinea encompassed a variety of linguistic, ethnic, religious, and political groups. At the same time, however, trade, multilingualism, intermarriage, and a long history of living beside people of different backgrounds meant that, for all of their differences, Upper Guineans were accustomed to diversity of a particular type. Moreover, most of these captives were Mande speakers enslaved through the process of war and jihad.

The Vernons' letter of January 9 reached Gabriel Manigault at his counting house on Tradd Street in Charles Town, South Carolina, on February 24, 1755. William Vernon was a longtime acquaintance. The two men had done business for years, and on at least one occasion Vernon had visited Manigault in Charles Town. Their previous dealings had involved goods such as rice, turpentine, and cloth. Vernon had even once sent a load of potatoes, which Manigault praised as "the largest I ever saw," though he regretted that some had spoiled on the trip. This time, however, Vernon asked Manigault to handle a cargo of another sort. "This advises you that we have a Sloop upon the Coast of Africa, Caleb Godfrey Comdr," Vernon wrote, "who have [been] ordered to your Place with his Slaves." The letter then casually instructed Manigault on how to sell the cargo and remit the proceeds. Manigault, though a very prominent merchant, had not built his fortune through slave trading. From time to time he handled small shipments of slaves from the British West Indies, but he seldom handled ships coming directly from Africa. Nonetheless, he was a merchant, and if a valued correspondent shipped him slaves, he would handle the slaves. The local market was good, he informed Vernon in his response, though he hoped the ship would arrive in April rather than March, when the cold weather killed

FIGURE 6.3. *Gabriel Manigault, 1757. The son of a Huguenot cooper,
Gabriel Manigault became one of the wealthiest merchants in Charles Town.
Although he handled the sale of the* Hare *captives, he was not a major slave
factor. His ten-year business relationship with the Vernon brothers ended in
a dispute over the commission due to Captain Godfrey. (Art Resource)*

many captives and jeopardized profits. He then turned to other business and
awaited news of the vessel's arrival.[9]

Much like the Vernons, Manigault was born to the countinghouse. Like
the Vernons, too, his father was an artisan—in this case, a cooper. A native
of France and a Huguenot, Pierre Manigault had immigrated to South Carolina after Louis XIV revoked the Edict of Nantes in 1685, ending eighty-seven

years of toleration and heralding a crackdown on all Protestants. Once in the New World, his work as a cooper led him into rum distilling, which then grew into an import-export business. Son Gabriel entered the world of commerce at the age of twenty-one and quickly prospered. As time passed, he cultivated the image of a gentleman, serving in the Commons House of Assembly and becoming a patron of the South Carolina Library Society and the South Carolina Society, a fraternal organization that began in the colony's Huguenot community but soon became a major fixture of Charles Town's embryonic civic culture. He remained a member of Charles Town's Huguenot Church but for political and business more than spiritual reasons hedged his bets by attending St. Phillip's Anglican Church as well. What little we know of his personality suggests that he was a classic patriarch, emphasizing the duties of his dependents and maintaining an appropriate distance from them. His son Peter, who was studying law at London's Inner Temple, addressed his father in a letter (without apparent irony) as "Hon[ore]d Sir" and referred to "The frequent opportunities I have lately taken at expressing my Duty to you," before gingerly rebutting his father's accusation that he had neglected his studies.[10] Latter-day eulogists would portray Manigault as a slaveholding humanitarian, citing his reluctance to engage in the slave trade. And indeed, Manigault was well aware of the hardships associated with transatlantic crossings, though in truth he was concerned more with the safety and comfort of whites. When he learned his son was contemplating returning home aboard a man-of-war that was carrying a new governor, he cautioned that "such ships are commonly very much crowded with passingers when Governors comes out in them, with some other Inconveniencys I could mention, it is my Opinion you will be as safe & better accommodated on board a good merchants ship, with a good com[mande]r." Slaves, soldiers, and other rabble could travel aboard crowded naval vessels, but not the scion of a prominent Carolina family.[11]

In many respects, Gabriel Manigault embodied the South Carolina economy of the eighteenth century. His main line, the exchange of rice, pitch, tar, and other Carolinian products for northern flour, West Indian rum, Portuguese wines, and British textiles, often in his own vessels, had made him one of the wealthiest men in the colony. The owner of several rural estates, he was also a major producer, once bringing to market 1,639 barrels of rice, an output equivalent to about five ordinary plantations. Having pledged himself as security for a colonial treasurer whose finances were wiped out in the 1752 hurricane, he covered an entire year's worth of tax certificates, some seven thousand pounds sterling. One year later, he lent the colony £3,500 in South Carolina money at 6 percent interest. But none of this would have been remotely possible without the colony's enslaved labor force. Manigault, like the colony as a whole, grew rich from the value of rice, indigo, and naval stores. Their food was grown, their houses built, their children nursed, and their graves dug by enslaved laborers. South Carolina, like all of the plantation colonies of the mid-eighteenth century, consumed laborers.

The *Hare* reached Charles Town on the evening of March 4, 1755. For those captives who were lucky enough to be on deck, the first glimpse of the place where they were to spend the rest of their lives would have been the large, dry palmetto at the southwestern tip of Sullivan's Island, which mariners used to locate the entrance to the harbor. As they continued their approach, a low, treeless headland known as Cummin's Point would have materialized to the southwest, followed eventually by two church spires that seemed to rise out of the water between the two spits of land, at last followed by the outline of a sizable town. The first person they saw would have been the pilot, who may well have been black. In fact, given the boat-handling skills possessed by some Africans, there is a chance the pilot came from Upper Guinea. In order to prevent the spread of disease, all pilots were required to ask shipmasters whether they had "plague, malignant fever, small pox, or any other contagious distemper" aboard. No other person would be allowed aboard, and no crew member, not even the captain, would be allowed to disembark in the town before performing ten days' quarantine. Pilots who discovered sickness aboard after having received assurances would have to perform quarantine as well, though they would receive compensation from the captain.[12]

The following day, Gabriel Manigault learned of the *Hare*'s arrival from the pilot, who also informed him that there were seventy captives, all in good health, though this information was erroneous. Manigault immediately wrote the Vernons of the vessel's safe arrival and dispatched a doctor to examine the captives at Sullivan's Island, a narrow, hook-shaped island of sand near the harbor's entrance. At the tip of the island near the palmetto that had guided them into the harbor stood a pest house. The structure was brand new. The earlier building had been entirely destroyed in the 1752 hurricane. There had been only fifteen people there the night the storm hit. Winds and water collapsed the structure and ripped it from its foundation, sweeping the occupants into the water. The nine survivors had ridden the rafters for several hours before finally floating to safety.[13] The colony soon erected a new structure, which visitors described as "a large house" capable of holding several hundred people and featuring "pretty good conveniences."[14]

So, with the spires of Charles Town visible only four miles away, the *Hare* captives awaited their fate. The quarantine law envisioned captives being housed onshore at the pest house for the entire ten days. However, it did allow captains to keep them aboard ship for part of that time, as long as they spent six hours per day on shore in the summer (five hours in the winter) over a five-day period. Whether Godfrey took advantage of this provision is unknown. In the meantime, it was expected that the crew should spend its time "purifying and cleansing the said slaves from any infectious distemper." This was likely done with the advice of the doctor sent out by Manigault, although it was technically illegal for anyone other than the pilot to come aboard the vessel. Records of other slave sales reveal that dispatching a doctor was a very common practice, and within a few years of the *Hare*'s voyage the law was amended to require examination by an official port physician, suggesting that the assembly may have recognized the wisdom of an ongoing extralegal practice.[15]

While the captives were at Sullivan's Island, Gabriel Manigault prepared for their sale. In this he was aided by William Banbury, a nephew and fellow merchant, whose usual business involved the importation of such wares as flour, rum, hams, and Madeira.[16] Manigault's reasons for bringing Banbury into the deal are obscure: perhaps he wanted to provide advantageous work for his nephew, or perhaps he truly had qualms about dealing in slaves. Also obscure are the terms of the agreement between Manigault and Banbury. The account with the Vernons mentions only Manigault, so whatever Banbury's share was, it came out of Manigault's commission. Among their first tasks was to place an advertisement in the *South Carolina Gazette*, the colony's sole newspaper, which was done in Banbury's name. It was of course desirable that the sale attract as many buyers as possible, and with so many potential purchasers living in rural precincts, it was vital that notice go out as early as possible. Manigault chose Wednesday, March 19, 1755, for the sale, the first day of the new court session, a time when many planters would be in town for business. In addition to placing the newspaper ad, Manigault ordered the printing of several handbills and hired a postboy to distribute them throughout the countryside.[17]

The advertisement, which ran in the March 6 and March 13 editions of the *Gazette*, was rather curious. It featured a crude engraving of two identical dark, savage-type figures in headdresses and skirts and read in its entirety, "To be sold on Wednesday the 19th Instant, a choice cargo of *Windward* and *Gold Coast* negroes, Just imported in the *Hare*, *Caleb Godfrey*, Master, in a Passage of about *Five* Weeks, by William Banbury."

In addition to listing Banbury rather than the better-known Manigault as the seller, the notice understated the duration of the *Hare*'s voyage by about a week, not including the stay at Barbados. But even more interesting is the claim that some of the *Hare* captives hailed from the Gold Coast. It was not unusual for slave ships to purchase captives on the Windward Coast (which in the nomenclature of the era included Sierra Leone) en route to the Gold Coast, but nowhere in the surviving documents, including those of the Gold Coast forts, is there any hint that the *Hare* visited the region on this voyage. Moreover, the extremely short passage from the Isles de Los to Barbados makes it all but certain that it never visited the Gold Coast—no vessel could have made such a voyage in less than three weeks.

There are two plausible explanations for mentioning the Gold Coast in the advertisement. The first is that Banbury or Manigault simply misunderstood Godfrey or were mistaken in their geography. But that is doubtful, since South Carolina merchants were quite knowledgeable about Africa, at least in regard to the slave trade. More likely, the statement was inserted deliberately—that is, it was a lie. South Carolina slave dealers and consumers had well-developed ideas about the capabilities of Africans of different backgrounds. They observed a hierarchy of ethnicities that translated into very real price differences, with certain ethnicities fetching an additional thirty pounds or more for otherwise-comparable captives. Most prized were captives from Senegambia, who were believed to be familiar with rice culture, and the Gold Coast, who were viewed as strong, hearty workers, if perhaps slightly dangerous and prone to rebellion. Those from the "Windward Coast," including Sierra Leone, ranked second in the Carolinians' favor, apparently for their familiarity with rice. Those from Central Africa, called "Angolas" by the Carolinians, were deemed acceptable but not as desirable as the others. Lowest in the esteem of the planters were the so-called Calabars, mostly Igbos from the Bight of Biafra, who were universally disparaged as slight, sickly, and prone to suicide. Thus in suggesting that some of the *Hare* captives came from the Gold Coast, Banbury and Manigault were playing to a set of planter stereotypes that had very real market implications.[18]

The captives completed their quarantine on March 14, 1755, but before Godfrey could take them to Charles Town, he needed to attend once more to the imperial bureaucracy and pay the gunpowder tax to the colony's Powder Receiver. Since the previous century, all vessels trading in South Carolina were required to pay a duty based on the size of the vessel. The tax was designed to ensure that the colony had a sufficient supply of gunpowder in case of war, and all that was collected was stored in the powder magazine, a stout one-story, multigabled building located two blocks from the water-front. Before landing their goods, entering captains were required to pay either a half pound of "good, cleane and serviceable" powder for each meas-ured ton of vessel, or two shillings per ton in the local currency, which added up to nine pounds for the *Hare*.[19] In addition to the Powder Receiver, Godfrey was required to pay the comptroller, who received his manifest as well as the fees of the Naval Office, the Customs Office, the treasurer, and the secretary, as well as various additional fees, totaling thirty-six pounds and fifteen shil-lings. These fees were more bothersome than burdensome, and the main duties—on the captives themselves—were yet to be paid.[20]

Godfrey and Manigault ferried the captives from the pest house to Charles Town at the first opportunity, which would have been either March 14 or 15. South Carolina prohibited shipboard sales, so the *Hare* captives would have been housed in a merchant's yard. Manigault owned several commercial properties in Charles Town, as did Banbury. The precise address at which the *Hare* captives were kept is not known. The most likely candidates are the two storehouses with cellars owned by Manigault, both located on Tradd Street.[21] There the *Hare* captives sat for five or six days being prepared for sale. We do not know exactly what Manigault, Banbury, and Godfrey did to make them appear healthy for buyers, but we can be certain that they tried. They do appear to have fed the captives well. Expenses included two quarters of beef weighing a total of 251 pounds, one and one-quarter bush-els of peas, and one pound and five shillings for "greens @ sundry times."[22] Afraid that the spring weather would sicken the captives, Godfrey spent an additional nine pounds on four blankets—most of the captives, presumably, went without. It was also a common practice in the slave trade to shave and oil the bodies of the captives, which gave them what one observer described as a "sleek appearance."[23] The *Hare*'s accounts include an entry for "grinding 2 razors" at Charles Town, as well as some "Palm Oyle" purchased at Sierra Leone, so it seems probable that Godfrey did prepare the captives in this way. The tendency to view the captives as nonhuman pieces of merchandise led some sellers to adopt extreme methods. At least one Jamaican merchant reportedly managed to hide the fact that some of his captives had dysentery by stuffing oakum in their anuses, but this was probably not a common prac-tice since it would likely work only once (if that).[24]

By the day of sale, March 19, the captives were ready. Slave sales in colo-nial South Carolina were conducted in a variety of ways. Domestic sales were conducted either privately or by public auction, in the case of estate sales and the like, which entailed some sort of fiduciary responsibility on the part of the seller. Sales of newly arrived captives, however, were usually conducted differently. Instead of auctioning them one at a time, factors grouped them by type—the strongest men, for example—and, at the signal of a gunshot or drumbeat, loosed buyers into the yard. When labor was in great demand, buyers might actually come to blows, as each purchaser attempted to grab as many of the best-looking captives as possible. George Baillie, who worked as a merchant in South Carolina and Georgia during the 1750s and 1760s, recalled that buyers "rushed into the yard with great violence, and laid hold of the most healthy and good looking Slaves, which parcels they afterwards picked and culled to their mind," sometimes even working in teams to maximize the number of captives they could purchase. Once they had what they wanted, the captives were "immediately purchased, and hurried out of the yard."[25] Gustavus Vassa, who provided the only surviving description from a captive's point of view, recalled that "The noise and clamour with which this is attended, and the eagerness visible in the countenances of the buyers . . . increase the apprehensions of the terrified Africans, [as] relations and friends [are] separated, most of them never to see each other again."[26] Once the sale of the first group of captives was finished, the process was repeated for each successive classification of captives. Only those who never sold, labeled "refuse slaves," were dispensed of at public auction. A representative of the colonial government known as the Publick Waiter attended all sales to ensure payment of the import duty.[27]

This method of sale, known in the British Caribbean as "the scramble," probably emerged in the early eighteenth century at a time when captive importations increased dramatically. From the seller's point of view, the scramble held several advantages over the auction method. The first of these was control of information. Auctions were usually conducted by a public vendue master, who was required to allow purchasers to inspect the merchandise. In contrast, factors running scrambles seem to have minimized the amount of time that buyers had to examine the captives. Baillie suggested that buyers had no opportunity to examine the captives before a scramble, while Vassa wrote that purchasers had the chance to examine captives aboard ship but not at the sale itself. Limiting access in this way induced some buyers to overlook illnesses and injuries. The second advantage of a scramble over an auction was its efficiency. Loosing buyers en masse upon a group of captives disposed of the captives more quickly than auctioning them off one at a time. The faster the sale, the lower the risk of loss through death or illness.[28]

Not all sales, however, saw the sort of frenzy described by Baillie and Vassa. In fact, the sale of the *Hare* captives seems to have gone much more quietly. With the market reportedly good and with the sale scheduled to coincide with court day, Manigault hoped for a quick conclusion. To encourage attendance and perhaps to loosen the buyers' purses, he served wine and punch. The captives, however, were still not entirely recovered from their journey. When they entered the yard, the captives appeared "to great disadvantage, much Owing to cold weather," and purchasers worried that they might not survive the several remaining damp and blustery weeks of the Carolina spring. Other buyers were put off when they saw that a large proportion of the captives were "not young," while still others complained that there were "much to [sic] many Women among them."[29] In all, twenty-five captives sold on March 19 for a total of £5,760, an average price of just over £230. Of these, fifteen were men, five were women, four were boys, and one was a girl. Manigault did know his customers—they wanted male laborers. The twenty-five captives were purchased by twelve individuals; seven bought a single captive, while four others bought two. The single largest parcel consisted of nine captives. The sales record suggests that the adult male captives were divided into two or three groups, since captives in an individual scramble all had to have the same price. Only two of the men rated the highest price of £280; most of the rest seem to have been priced at £245. The terms of sale varied widely. Some bought for cash, others on credit. Some paid in full, while others put in down payments. Some pledged payment in a few weeks, others in a year. Later, Manigault revealed that he had felt compelled to be flexible in order to spur sales.

Disappointed in the first day's sales, Manigault decided to handle the sale of the remaining captives differently. The following day he tried a private sale, which is to say he invited select gentlemen to make an offer on whichever captives they wanted. This brought in several buyers of notably elite standing. They purchased eighteen more captives—eleven men and seven women—at an average price of over £296, which was actually higher than the average price of the preceding day. Most sales saw higher prices toward the beginning and not the end, but Manigault essentially subsidized the second day's sales by selling most of the captives interest-free. But not even these terms could induce his customers to purchase all of the remaining captives, so he placed them up for sale by auction, hiring a professional vendue master to run the proceedings. The remaining thirteen captives (plus one very small child who was sold with his or her mother but not counted in the total) sold at an average price of £193, almost all at no interest. All of these "refuse slave" purchasers bought one captive each, except for the one who purchased the woman and child.

THE *HARE* PURCHASERS were a diverse group. There were planters, merchants, artisans, and tavern keepers. They included old and young, men and women, longtime residents and recent arrivals. They resided in Charles Town, in the well-developed plantation districts near the capital, in more distant developing plantation areas, and in the backcountry. For some, the purchase added to an already sizable portfolio of human property, while for others it represented a tentative foray into the ranks of the slaveholders. In short, the men and women who purchased captives were about as diverse as any group of free South Carolinians could be. Within this diversity, however, it is possible to notice a number of subgroups and patterns. Understanding what these patterns were, and who the buyers were, is a necessary first step toward understanding the New World experiences of the *Hare* captives.

Most of the *Hare* purchasers came from the upper reaches of South Carolina society. This is hardly surprising, since all had to possess enough money to buy a slave or at least convince Gabriel Manigault that they would be able to come up with the funds. Estate inventories, which provide a snapshot of an individual's personal property (which included slaves but not real estate), survive for nine of the purchasers. The wealthiest, all planters or merchants, had twenty thousand pounds or more in personal property (see table 6 in appendix 3). A second tier of solid but hardly elite planters possessed five to ten thousand pounds in personalty. For all of these men, purchasing a slave was quite easy, especially given the credit relationships they enjoyed with the town's merchants. But there were several purchasers of decidedly more modest means. At least two (and likely several more for whom inventories do not exist) owned less than two thousand pounds in personal property. Among these were the shipwright and bar pilot George Ducatt and the self-described "planter" William Bready, whose £1,922 in personalty included nine bondpeople—a respectable, but hardly distinguished, number.[30] The captive from the *Hare* who fetched the least was purchased for £130 in local currency, slightly less than £19 sterling. For people like Ducatt and Bready, this was hardly a negligible sum. For each, the purchase would require a careful weighing of the risk that the slave might fall ill, die, or flee against the possibility of increased future earnings. In this instance, their calculations told them to buy.

Ducatt and Bready were far from the bottom tier of South Carolina slave owners. Slave ownership was widespread in South Carolina, and almost universal among those with over one hundred pounds in personal property. "Refuse slaves" could be had for as low as thirteen pounds, perhaps even less, allowing whites of modest means to enter the ranks of the slaveholders, though the gambit often failed. One shoemaker who bought a captive from a different ship hoped that the application of "Proper Remedys & kitchin Physick" might bolster a captive he purchased, described as "very Mauger [sic] & full of sores." The man turned out to have an intellectual disability, which was not readily apparent at the sale. The owners of the vessel refused to take the captive back, and the shoemaker was compelled to maintain his slave while likely receiving no labor at all from him—if indeed the man survived.[31] The risks inherent in purchasing refuse slaves undoubtedly scared many buyers off. Speculators, who could better absorb a loss, and physicians, who could rely on their professional skills to nurse a captive to health, were frequent buyers of refuse slaves.[32]

The purchase of a captive represented much more than the ability to control and enjoy the fruits of someone else's labor. Slave ownership denoted a certain stability. Mastery also conveyed social enfranchisement, if not always elite status. Wealth in South Carolina, as in most slave societies, was distributed quite unevenly, with the richest 10 percent controlling 40 percent of the wealth. Slave ownership was the norm for all but the poorest whites. Nine of every ten white rural families owned slaves. Even in urban Charles Town, seven in ten whites were members of the slave-owning class, though the holdings were much smaller than in rural areas. With slaveholding so widespread, it is no wonder that white South Carolinians sorted one another not so much according to whether one owned bondpeople, but rather according to how many. "If a man has not as many slaves as they," observed one traveler, "he is esteemed by them an inferior." Another noted that one of the worst insults that could be delivered to a planter was to say that he was "in the grass," meaning that his plantation was weedy, which in turn implied that he did not possess enough slaves to run it properly.[33]

Examining the ethnic and geographic origins of the *Hare* purchasers is akin to reading geological strata, in this case for the European settlement of South Carolina rather than of the earth. At least one of the purchasers, Thomas Mell, descended from the Barbadians who helped found the colony in the 1670s.[34] Four more were descendants of the Huguenot refugees, who, like the Manigaults, arrived at the end of the seventeenth century. Together, the Barbadian- and Huguenot-descended purchasers were among the wealthier, more established groups in the colony, with many owning both Charles Town residences and rural plantations. English merchants, an ever-present if peripatetic group, were another identifiable cohort among the *Hare* purchasers. Men such as William Lloyd and William Stone probably came as the New World agents or correspondents of larger firms. Some entered the ranks of the planters and remained in the colony; others sought to return to England at the first opportunity. In the next layer were the migrants from Ireland and, to an even greater extent, Scotland, who began arriving in the 1710s and whose numbers increased as time passed. Some of these, such as the Irish-born lawyer and planter James Parsons, were wealthy to begin with and grew more so in the colonies. Others were of modest background, such as Scots Hance McCulloch and Thomas Bell, who was a Presbyterian minister. Finally, representing the stream of migrants from continental Europe was Swiss-born Christian Minnick, who had settled with a number of his countrymen. These migrants had begun arriving in the 1730s as part of a deliberate effort to populate backcountry areas with white Protestants.

The purchasers shared a few other ties of little consequence to the lives of the *Hare* captives. Some of the buyers were related to each other, which may have allowed a few shipmates to stay together, perpetuating and strengthening ties of language and culture on individual plantations. Indeed, related and neighboring planter families often attended slave sales together. When the *Hare* sold the captives from its second voyage in 1756, it seems fairly clear that a group of planters from St. John's Berkeley consisting of blood relatives and in-laws all attended together. Between them, the group purchased ten, which means that almost one-sixth of the captives on the vessel ended up living within walking distance of one another.[35] No similar cluster of relatives seems to have attended the 1755 sale, although two of the buyers, Charles Lorimer and Susannah Wedderburn, married very shortly after the sale took place. The six captives they purchased likely remained together, at least in the near term. Coincidentally, twenty years later Lorimer married the daughter of another *Hare* purchaser, Alexander Fraser, raising the possibility that those captives may have been reunited—if they survived that long.[36] Several other *Hare* purchasers were fellow members of fraternal and civic organizations. No fewer than five were or would become members of the St. Andrew's Society, which catered to the colony's Scottish population.[37] In fact, given the relatively small white population of the colony and the status of Charles Town as the only town of consequence, many of the purchasers probably knew each other. But these ties were largely incidental and likely did not influence the distribution of captives in any significant way.

The purchasers were furthermore geographically scattered, hailing from almost every part of the colony, as well as from Georgia, where the legalization of slavery in 1751 had spurred a wave of migration. None of this is surprising given Charles Town's role as the principal entrepôt from Virginia to Spanish Florida. One purchaser, Peter Peguine, left no local trace at all, raising the possibility that he was a mariner, soldier, or other transient who happened to buy a captive while passing through Charles Town. He and the woman he bought could have landed anywhere in the Atlantic World.

Even so, the *Hare* captives found themselves clustered in particular localities. This clustering owed not so much to connections among the purchasers as it did to the state of the plantation economy at the moment of the *Hare*'s arrival, with certain regions importing labor faster than others. For the first four decades of the century, South Carolina's rice-planting economy had been concentrated in a central core surrounding Charles Town, corresponding roughly to the Low Country portions of Berkeley and Colleton Counties. These parishes, which included St. John's Berkeley, St. Thomas & St. Denis, Christ Church, St. James Goose Creek, St. George Dorchester, St. Andrew's, St. John's Colleton, and St. Bartholomew's, were home to many of the colony's largest plantations. In 1755, with the slave trade newly reopened following a decade of negligible importations, many of these planters were looking to expand their labor forces. Twenty, or about 36 percent, of the *Hare* captives initially went to the rural sections of this central core region, where they were put to work on rice and indigo plantations. This figure does not include the nine captives purchased by Henry Laurens; they may have spent their first year on his partner's plantation in St. John's Berkeley before removing to his new plantation in St. James Santee the next year. Not counting the Laurens captives, these twenty all resided on holdings within thirty miles of Charles Town, and at least sixteen *Hare* captives lived within a twenty-mile radius. If we include the eleven captives who went on to reside in Charles Town itself, it appears that more than half of the *Hare* captives were living within twenty miles of the capital, with about half of those residing within ten miles.

The next-largest destination for the *Hare* captives was Craven County, to the northeast of Charles Town and Berkeley County, a region outside the central core. The county's coastal parishes were blossoming as a rice-planting region. The transformation began in the 1730s. A 1734 visitor to Georgetown, the area's most significant town, found "a great many more houses than inhabitants" but added that he did "believe it will not be long ere it is thoroughly settled."[38] He was half right: Craven County did become a planting region, but war and the slave importation ban arrested the process. These two obstacles were removed in 1748, and with the price of staples rising,

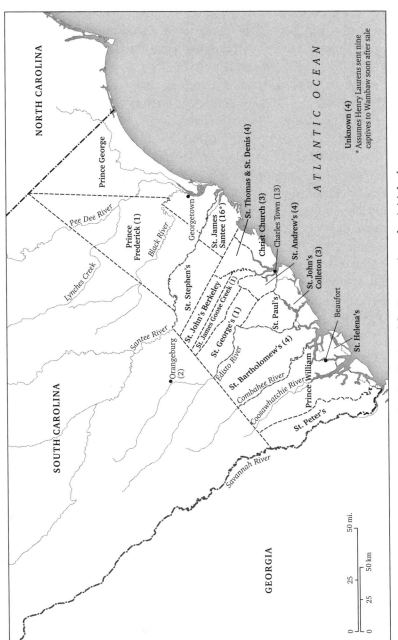

NORTH CAROLINA

SOUTH CAROLINA

GEORGIA

ATLANTIC OCEAN

Prince George

Pee Dee River

Lynches Creek

Black River

Prince
Frederick (1)

Georgetown

Santee River

St. Stephen's

St. James
Santee (16*)

St. Thomas & St. Denis (4)

Christ Church (3)

Orangeburg
(2)

St. John's Berkeley

St. James Goose Creek (1)

St. George's (1)

Edisto River

St. Paul's

Charles Town (13)

St. Andrew's (4)

St. John's
Colleton (3)

St. Bartholomew's (4)

Combahee River

Beaufort

St. Helena's

Coosawhatchie River

Prince William

St. Peter's

Savannah River

Unknown (4)

* Assumes Henry Laurens sent nine
captives to Wambaw soon after sale

MAP 6.1. *Geographic distribution of the Hare captives after initial sale*

0   25   50 mi.

0   25   50 km

the local planters craved laborers. Many of these planters were of Huguenot descent. In fact, part of the parish of St. James Santee became known as "French Santee," where even the Anglican Church found it expedient to offer French-language services. Only two *Hare* purchasers, Elias Horry and Daniel Lessesne, owned significant property in this part of the colony. In 1756, Henry Laurens would join them, and circa 1758 Paul Douxsaint would begin planting in the area. Between them they had purchased sixteen *Hare* captives, or almost 30 percent of the total. However, many of these captives likely moved to other areas within a few years. In the spring of 1755, Horry and Lessesne, purchasers of seven captives, were apparently operating as partners. Their partnership appears to have lasted only for a few months. The only trace of the firm, apart from the *Hare* sales record, is an advertisement taken out in the *Gazette* a few weeks earlier announcing that the two, along with a Thomas Cordes, would be handling the estate sale of planter Daniel Horry. The seemingly short duration of the partnership raises the question of the captives' fate. What did Horry and Lessesne do with the captives once they went their separate ways, as they apparently did almost immediately after the purchase? It is quite possible that they were distributed among the plantations of one or both partners, located in St. James Santee and Prince George Parishes, respectively. Or the partners may have simply sold the captives off.

The last, smallest group of purchasers lived in the backcountry, or perhaps more accurately, the "Middle Country." The area inland from the Low Country, still under Indian control, was just beginning to receive European settlers in the 1750s. In the 1730s, the colony had initiated a "township scheme," the goal of which was to attract white immigrants to settle in areas outside the Low Country, approximately sixty miles inland. In 1751, the assembly decreed that three-fifths of all duties on imported captives subsidize the settlement of Protestant immigrants. In addition to mitigating the perceived danger of racial imbalance, proponents saw the townships as a bulwark against Indian raids. Christian Minnick was a native of Switzerland who settled with a number of his countrymen near one of these settlements in Orangeburg. William Bready was another who had responded to the colony's township settlement plan; in this case he settled in Fredericksburg Township, which was in Craven County, inland from the rice-growing areas of Georgetown and French Santee. Bready apparently did well, since five years later he moved to the more central and more expensive St. John's Berkeley.[39]

The sheer pervasiveness of slaveholding in South Carolina raises the question of what the *Hare* purchasers actually thought about slavery. On one

FIGURE 6.4. *Henry Laurens, 1782. Henry Laurens bought nine captives from the* Hare, *more than any other purchaser. One of South Carolina's wealthiest merchants, he handled the sale of several thousand African slaves. In 1755, he was still one year away from purchasing his first plantation, so he probably sent his nine* Hare *captives to live with his partner and brother-in-law, John Coming Ball, before sending the slaves to their jointly operated Wambaw estate in 1756. (Yale University Art Gallery)*

level, the question is almost impossible to answer. Twenty-six different men and women purchased at least one captive from the *Hare*. Each undoubtedly had his or her own individual perspective on slave owning, but few of them left any statements behind that might allow access to their thought processes. A notable exception is Henry Laurens, who spent most of his life as either a slave trader or a planter. More reflective than most, he once wrote to his son John, "I abhor slavery." That, however, was written more than twenty years later, in 1776, well after he had established himself as one of the wealthiest men in the colony. It is quite telling that in all of the years prior to 1776, when Laurens was amassing his fortune by trading in slaves (among other commodities) and running plantations, he never once expressed misgivings about enslaving another human being.[40]

If knowing the attitudes of each individual purchaser is impossible, it is possible to discern the shared ideology that justified slavery in society at large, called "patriarchy" or "patriarchalism" by historians. Patriarchalism was, at root, a political ethos that envisioned a world ordered by a divinely ordained organic hierarchy, sometimes called the "great chain of being." According to this vision, every living being had its proper place and rank. God sat at the top, kings and nobility below him, and on down through the various ranks of commoners, animals, and so on. In addition to ordering the world, this hierarchy ordered individual households, each envisioned as a miniature kingdom functioning according to the same principles, with the father at the head and other members, including women, children, servants, and slaves, coming under his authority and protection.[41] Peter Taylor, who purchased two *Hare* captives, typified the ideal. A wealthy planter, he was surprisingly candid about the source of his wealth. "The Thriving circumstances of The Inhabitants of this province," he wrote, "are in a Great Degree owing to the Labour of the slaves employed therein." But this did not mean that slavery was in any way wrong, merely that in the divinely ordered hierarchy, masters should show their "Gratitude" for faithful service by "promoting the Eternal Felicity of so usefull a Body of reasonable Creatures."[42] That is, slave owners had a responsibility to repay their laborers by bringing them to Christ. This was the essence of the patriarchal ideal: reciprocal obligations within an unapologetically hierarchical and unequal context.

On the other hand, of course, patriarchalism justified severe punishment for anything deemed refractory, and planters fully expected resistance. Unlike their more paternalistic descendants, colonial-era slaveholders expected masters and bondmen to be heirs to the state of war that had justified the initial act of enslavement. One Carolinian quoted the radical Whig essayist John Trenchard to warn his fellow slaveholders against allowing slaves to carry their masters' weapons home after militia muster. "What a ridiculous Imagionation [it is]," he commented, "to conceive Men will be Servants when they can be Masters."[43] The law therefore granted masters extremely broad power over the enslaved, and in practice there were almost no limits at all. Violence was an everyday feature of plantation life. One traveler to the Low Country observed field laborers "governed by an overseer, armed with a broad sword, and under him a black driver who always carries a whip." During the slave-trade hearings of the 1790s, a former South Carolina planter tried to tell Parliament that drivers "seldom or never" whipped slaves in the field, then conceded that whippings at the close of the day were every bit as frequent and violent as in the notoriously brutal West Indies.[44] Yet another master "disciplined" a woman in his household with thumbscrews and pressed the tongue of a boy "into a small reed."[45] And while South Carolina law expressly forbade the wanton murder of a slave, the crime was defined as only a misdemeanor punishable by a fine, effectively ceding masters the power of life and death over their bondpeople. And they exercised that power. As one visitor summarized, "a man will shoot a negro with as little emotion as he shoots a Hare."[46]

While it is certain that most of the "discipline" was meted out privately by masters and overseers, it was also done publicly, with individual acts of violence serving to dramatize the collective dominance of the white minority. In the wake of the Stono Rebellion, fifteen years before the *Hare*'s arrival, legislators passed a new, comprehensive set of laws known as the Negro Act. The act gave every white resident of the colony the right to whip any slave encountered off a plantation who could not produce a "ticket" or pass signed by the master. Cases involving slaves with different masters were generally given over to special slave courts. These ad hoc tribunals consisted of three white freeholders and were presided over by a local justice of the peace. By design, slave courts worked quickly, as bystanders and onlookers weighed in freely on matters of guilt, innocence, and punishment. The rate of conviction is unknown, but it seems clear that slave courts had few qualms about sentencing offenders to death. During the 1750s, the courts condemned some thirty-eight slaves for offenses ranging from murder and poisoning to arson and burglary.[47] One of the *Hare* purchasers, George Ducatt, once served on a panel that sentenced a young man named Quash to hang for burglary. After that particular execution, Quash's head was "sever'd from his Body, and fixed upon the Gallows" to terrorize other would-be thieves into obeying their masters and the rule of law. Most of the other *Hare* purchasers would have done the same.[48]

Following the sale, the evidentiary trail for the *Hare* captives as individuals goes cold. It is possible, in most cases, to know where and on what types of slaveholdings they found themselves, but surviving records do not provide the material needed to trace any of them as individuals. Once again, not knowing their names proves an insurmountable obstacle. Yet if individual biography is out of the question, it is still quite possible to sketch the communities into which the *Hare* captives entered in the spring of 1755, and in that sense to arrive at some idea of the contours of their New World existence.

CHAPTER SEVEN

Town and Country

By examining the types of work done on the slaveholdings of the *Hare* purchasers, it is possible to develop a reasonable portrait of the captives' lives. For the able-bodied, work occupied most of the daytime hours every day except Sunday. Labor also exerted a strong influence beyond the actual time during which it was performed. Work routines not only delineated masters' time from slaves' time, they influenced laborers' material conditions and imposed broad, if permeable, parameters on community and cultural life. However, any inferences drawn here must be understood to be suggestive, not conclusive. Work regimes did not determine an individual's destiny; many other things shaped how their lives turned out, and most of these experiences are unrecoverable. One other point deserves emphasis. While it is possible in most cases to know where the purchaser lived, and therefore where the captive lived, it is not always possible to know how long the captive stayed in that location. Some slaveholders moved. Others owned multiple properties and shifted slaves among them. Still others may have sold their captives. And if they conformed to statistical norms, eighteen of the fifty-six *Hare* captives who reached South Carolina were dead within one year.[1]

Fourteen *Hare* captives were purchased by masters who lived in or near Charles Town. Of these, nine were women, four were men, and one was a child of unrecorded sex. This total includes the three women purchased by William Lloyd, who resided just across the Cooper River on Wando Neck, but excludes the nine purchased by Henry Laurens. At the time of purchase, Laurens lived in Charles Town but very likely shipped most or all of his *Hare* captives out of the city. Wealthy urbanites like Laurens sometimes deployed up to thirty men, women, and children to work in a variety of household- and commerce-related tasks.[2] While many Africans lived in Charles Town, most slave owners favored Creole or acculturated slaves for their town houses. In this case, since Laurens was on the verge of purchasing a share of a rural plantation from his brother-in-law, John Coming Ball, it seems probable that Laurens would have dispatched the nine Africans to Ball's place rather than house several travel-weakened, non-English-speaking slaves at his Charles Town residence.[3] The single man purchased by Lachlan McIntosh may have spent a year in Charles Town, where his master worked as a clerk for Henry Laurens and conducted additional business on his own account. McIntosh, a Scot who came to South Carolina from Georgia in 1750, was in the process of accumulating slaves for a move back to Georgia, which he undertook in late 1756. Though separated from his shipmates by hundreds of miles, McIntosh's captive may well have found himself among people of similar background. Of twenty-three captives known to have been purchased by McIntosh between 1754 and 1758, twelve had sailed from the "Windward Coast" and undoubtedly included many from Sierra Leone. In 1763, McIntosh wrote Laurens to say that he was in financial trouble but would try to avoid selling off his slaves. Laurens guaranteed McIntosh's debt, but whether that kept his slaves together is unknown.[4] Also uncertain is the fate of the captives purchased by merchant and sometime factor William Stone. In July 1754, he announced that he would be selling all of his stock and departing the colony. The sale took time, and in the meantime he purchased three women from the *Hare*. Three years later Stone was apparently still in town, but by 1760 he again announced his intention to leave, auctioning off all of his property, including "such of his negroes as may not be engaged before."[5]

Those captives who remained in the city lived in smaller households than those residing in rural areas. During the 1750s, about four-fifths of all urban masters kept fewer than twenty slaves, and the *Hare* purchasers were no exception.[6] The three women purchased by merchant William Lloyd lived alongside approximately seven other slaves at his residence on the Bay. His 1761 estate inventory shows four "Negro Wenches," Phillis, Anna, Cloie, and Sue. If the groupings in the inventory are indicative, the latter two had spouses but the former two were the only ones with children. Ducatt's household on Tradd Street was smaller, with only three slaves, one of whom, a woman identified as "Sary," may have been from the *Hare*. There is no mention of the child that Ducatt purchased along with the woman. In all probability, the child perished within a few years, as many children did.[7]

The *Hare* captives who performed domestic labor would have spent much of their time not in the residence itself, but in one of the city's many enclosed yards. Charles Town's merchants and tradesmen often lived in two-room apartments above their shops. Most of these buildings hid several structures at the rear, usually a kitchen with slave quarters on the second floor, privies, and perhaps a stable or carriage house.[8] The most typical urban slave dwelling of the mid-eighteenth century was a two-story building situated toward the back of a fifty-foot lot with a kitchen and washhouse on the ground floor and living quarters above. A passageway allowed for access to and from the street, and a large yard in between provided a work space. Other outbuildings, including privies, stables, and carriage houses lined the edges of the yard, and some residences included a well and a kitchen garden. This arrangement allowed white householders to view most of the daily goings-on from the second-story rear window of the main residence.[9]

In Charles Town at large, nearly half of all enslaved men practiced a skilled trade like carpentry or silversmithing.[10] But since most of the *Hare* captives who remained in Charles Town did not work for tradesmen, it is not likely that they joined the ranks of the skilled laborers. The only purchaser who practiced a trade was the shipwright George Ducatt, but he purchased a woman, and we can assume that he did not train her to that trade. Slaves who lived in merchants' households were very likely put to work at the myriad chores associated with maintaining a respectable Georgian household. Most of these tasks were given to women—it is no accident that two-thirds of the *Hare* captives who remained in Charles Town were female. Domestic labor ranged from laundry to cooking to home manufactures to waiting at the table. We can gain a sense of what some of the work involved by looking at the master's possessions. William Lloyd, who lived on the Bay, owned a variety of items, all of which projected an aura of refinement, and all of which required care. His mahogany tables needed waxing; his silver shoe buckles and gold sleeve buttons needed polishing; his thirty pounds' worth of china and glass needed dusting; when he entertained, somebody had to pass his sauce boat and wield his punch ladles. George Ducatt's Tradd Street house was more modest, but the labor would have been similar. His silver needed polishing, his mirror needed dusting, and his pewter knives needed washing.[11]

Not all domestic work, however, involved merely cleaning, cooking, and washing. At least three *Hare* captives were purchased by proprietors of one of the many public eating and drinking establishments—one in thirteen Charles Town residences had a liquor license. The man purchased by Alexander Chisholme probably performed a variety of tasks at his master's coffee house on the Bay. The establishment included an "orange garden," which gave the proprietor a sideline retailing citrus trees and seeds. The license held by Paul Smyser, who lived on Broad Street very close to the State House, suggests that he also ran a tippling shop of some sort. However, like many Charles Town shopkeepers and tradesmen, Chisholme and Smyser both aspired to acquire plantations outside the city. Smyser began buying land in 1759 in several different parishes, securing additional laborers, including at least three boys, and eventually settled on a small plantation near Goose Creek, approximately ten miles from town. He nevertheless continued to operate his Charles Town tavern throughout the 1760s. Whether the man and woman he purchased remained in town or were dispatched to his plantation is unknown. It is quite possible that the African woman named Molly, who fled his Goose Creek plantation in 1759 wearing a plain white wrapper and osnaburg coat, was the woman he purchased from the *Hare*. Chisholme proved less successful than Smyser in his quest for squiredom. An intended move to Pon Pon in 1750 apparently fell through, and another move announced only days after he made his purchase from the *Hare* seems likewise to have come to naught. Eight years later, in 1763, he was still at the same address on the Bay. The man he purchased, if still alive, probably performed a wide range of tasks for the coffee house and residence.[12]

Despite the small size of the urban households, which suggests the *Hare* captives lived in isolation, Charles Town featured the greatest concentration of Africans in North America. At the time of the *Hare*'s voyage, a large and growing proportion of Africans entering North America—eventually more than half—were from Upper Guinea. Thus, in many respects, Africans in Charles Town had significant opportunity to connect with people of similar linguistic and cultural backgrounds. Unlike the Iberian American cities of the era, where Africans of similar backgrounds created fraternal organizations and lay brotherhoods in the Catholic Church, those living in and near Charles Town would have congregated in less formal settings. But the opportunities were many. Masters frequently hired out laborers in slack times. Others allowed their slaves to hire out for cash wages on the condition that they remit a fixed sum every week. Some slaves even lived on their own. Most of these were men who practiced a skilled trade, but women did so as well, earning money, for example, as itinerant washerwomen. Those who did not have these privileges could escape the confines of the back courts while marketing or running errands.[13]

Merely by going about their daily business, the former *Hare* captives would have found ample opportunity to chat and gossip. The streets were filled with people, and the wharves teemed with longshoremen, draymen, and hucksters. Marketers and hawkers were particularly numerous and visible. Renowned for their tenacity in haggling, many marketers were women who had cut their teeth in the fiercely competitive marketplaces of

West Africa and the Caribbean. The largest purely social assemblies were usually reserved for Sundays. One traveler reported people meeting at church "in great numbers" to talk and gamble at pawpaw, huzzle-cap, and pitch penny.[14] Larger gatherings could only be held outside of the city. One commentator observed a dance held on the Charles Town peninsula, five miles from town. About sixty people attended, well supplied with "Rum, Tongues, Hams, Beef, Geese, Turkies and Fowls, both drest and raw, with many luxuries of the table, as sweatmeats, pickles," which they carried over their shoulders in bags and baskets suspended from poles. In addition to the dancing, cards, and dice, participants took turns mocking their masters and mistresses. Gatherings of up to two hundred as near as one mile from town were reportedly quite common.[15] The *Hare* captives in Charles Town may have lived with few or no countrymen, but they would have had many chances to connect with them on a regular basis.

THE RURAL PLANTATIONS, where about three-quarters of the *Hare* captives lived, presented a very different environment. The typical plantation quarter was several times larger than the typical urban household, which meant that virtually every large estate had at least some laborers from Upper Guinea who potentially shared something in common with the *Hare* captives. As time passed, the proportion of Upper Guineans would only increase. Rural laborers did not have the same mobility as their urban counterparts, and therefore did not have the same chance to enlarge their sphere of acquaintances. That is not to suggest that they lacked mobility entirely. Rural slaves could and did range throughout neighborhoods, sometimes even beyond. But plantation life was in most respects far more circumscribed. Given the choice between urban and rural life, most slaves would have opted for the city.

At least twenty *Hare* captives were purchased by rice planters, though this does not necessarily mean that all twenty worked rice. Several of these planters engaged in other activities to which they might have deployed slave labor, and most owned houses in Charles Town where they may have sent a *Hare* captive (although as mentioned earlier, large slaveholders would have preferred Creole and acculturated laborers for their town residences). Specific information on the type of crop grown is absent for nine purchasers, but many of these were surely rice planters. Rice planting probably shaped the lives of more *Hare* captives than any other economic activity.

The confirmed rice planters among the *Hare* purchasers were quite wealthy. That is hardly surprising, given capital requirements of the typical rice plantation. Estimates for the amount of startup capital needed ranged from £1,000 sterling in 1710 to £2,476 in 1772, and conventional wisdom held that at least thirty or forty hands were necessary for profitability. But smaller operations were possible. Samuel Simons, who purchased one woman and two boys from the *Hare* for his new rice operation on Seewee Bay, owned twenty-three slaves and £5,638 in personal property upon his death in 1761. Thomas Mell planted rice with the ostensible minimum of thirty slaves, but not all were able-bodied adults. Alexander Fraser and Peter Taylor better fit the image of the wealthy rice planter. Taylor owned multiple plantations, making it impossible to know for sure to which holding the *Hare* captives were dispatched. Fraser would acquire two additional plantations in the coming years. James Parsons and Henry Laurens were what might be considered "rice planters-in-waiting." At the time they purchased captives from the *Hare* (one woman by Parsons, eight men and one woman by Laurens), they were preparing to make the transition from urban professional to country gentleman. Within a year, Laurens had purchased his first plantation, Wambaw in St. James Santee, and the following year Parsons completed his purchase in St. Bartholomew's. Both men's holdings grew prodigiously, and within a few years each had acquired additional estates.[16]

Rice plantations demanded a great deal of labor, so those captives who landed on them were thrust into sizable communities of bondpeople. But while the total number of slaves owned by some rice planters was very large, they generally kept the number on any individual plantation below one hundred. Parsons, for example, owned 336 slaves at the time of his death but scattered them across eight different holdings, which ranged in size from seventeen to seventy-three residents. Taylor similarly divided his 123 people between his holdings in St. James Goose Creek and St. Paul's. With numbers like that, rice-planting areas had extremely large black majorities, in some instances approaching 90 percent. On top of that, most wealthy planters liked to spend large amounts of time at their Charles Town residences, especially during the winter–spring social "season." Some, including Peter Taylor, occasionally left their plantations without any white supervision at all, a violation of the colony's residency law. As a result, captives in rural quarters experienced a great deal of autonomy, though with whites enjoying the right to interfere at will, that point should not be taken too far.[17]

Absenteeism forced most planters to rely on overseers, but the practice only aided the cause of black autonomy. For one thing, the colonial statute mandating the presence of at least one white person for every ten slaves was seldom followed to the letter. Overseers, moreover, occupied a very precarious place in the rural power structure. Torn between conflicting directives, one to produce the best possible crop, the other to maintain the health and morale of the plantation's laborers, overseers inevitably found their jobs frustrating. Armed with swords and pistols, they cajoled, threatened, beat, and raped their way toward meeting their employers' demands. The more they drove their charges, the more their labor force succumbed to the Low Country's seemingly limitless array of ailments. Attuned to the overseer's dilemma, laborers routinely undermined those they found overly harsh by going to the master with charges of neglect or abuse, sometimes winning concessions. When these tactics failed, some slaves attacked their overseers. Actions of this sort struck at the heart of the plantation hierarchy, and whites responded with the most brutal of punishments. One such rebel was placed in a cage and suspended from a tree in the woods, to die of thirst as he was pecked by a flock of birds.[18]

If the widespread absenteeism and the use of overseers gave laborers a great deal of discretion in running their affairs, the extensive use of subordinate black managers, known as "drivers," widened the space for self-directed action. Compared with overseers, drivers occupied an even more tenuous position in the plantation hierarchy. Unlike the overseers, who were free, white wage-earners with the right to quit, drivers were black and enslaved. They owed their positions to the planters, and some laborers viewed them as too close to whites. Drivers gave tasks to laborers, enjoyed special privileges, and meted out punishments, often with the same brutality as any white overseer. In order to function, however, they needed some level of compliance from the laborers. And in many cases they enjoyed genuine respect, for while masters had the power to anoint whomever they desired, they were aware that the natural leaders in their quarters would probably make the most effective managers. Most drivers, therefore, were probably Creoles, if for no other reason than linguistic and cultural familiarity, but there is no doubt that some were African-born. Muslims, of whom there were many in the Low Country, were particularly conspicuous among them. Historian Michael Gomez has suggested that whites may have viewed Muslims (particularly groups like the Fulas, whose physiognomy was often seen to be more European) as more intelligent than other Africans. By the same token, religious faith may have prompted some Muslims to separate themselves from non-Muslims in the quarters, creating a sense of aloofness that appealed to plantation owners. Whatever the case, a large black majority, planter absenteeism, and a reliance on overseers and black drivers to manage the plantations all combined to maximize Low Country slaves' opportunities for self-directed action.[19]

Rice plantations required a host of skilled workers in addition to the management provided by drivers. Most of these skilled laborers were enslaved, accounting for approximately 12 percent of all male rice plantation workers in the 1750s. Women were largely excluded from the ranks of the skilled laborers: only 2 percent practiced a skill that was recognized by whites. The most common occupations, probably found on virtually all rice plantations of any size, involved working with lumber: coopers, carpenters, and sawyers. Boatmen were also common, given that most plantation produce reached Charles Town by water. Bricklayers, blacksmiths, and leather workers were also present in smaller though growing numbers. For reasons of language alone, most of these positions probably went to Creole or African-born slaves who had been in the colony for a number of years. But Africans who arrived in possession of a skill sometimes caught the attention of whites. African-born watermen appear to have had the greatest recognition, with the skills of smiths and other tradesmen more likely to be dismissed in favor of European craftsmanship. The best information on this question in the case of the *Hare* captives comes from Charles Lorimer, though he cultivated indigo rather than rice. Among his twenty slaves were a cooper, a bricklayer, sawyers, boatmen, and "girls that can sew, wash, and iron well." The odds are good that at least some of the four men he and wife Susannah Wedderburn purchased from the *Hare* were among these.[20]

Perhaps the most important factor that made the Low Country into North America's most fertile incubator of African culture was the method of organizing plantation labor. Unlike most other colonies, where slaves worked from dawn to sundown under the constant direction of a master or a deputy, an arrangement known as the "gang system," Low Country planters employed a "task system" in which workers were given specific and standardized duties to perform, after which their time was their own. Tasks were designed to occupy an entire day, but laborers were often able to finish them early, leaving them time to engage in self-directed activities, which ranged from cultivating their own gardens to visiting other plantations. Whether the system represented a European innovation or whether it represented African agricultural practice adapted to plantation slavery, or some combination of the two, is a matter of historical debate. Whatever its origins, the system was well established by the time of the *Hare* captives' arrival.[21]

Overseers were nominally responsible for assigning the day's tasks, which were calibrated to the ability of the laborer, but in practice, drivers handled much of the day-to-day apportioning. Rice required an extensive network of ditches and sluices, which allowed for the flooding and draining of individual fields as needed. The tasks themselves varied with the agricultural calendar: sowing in the spring; flooding and weeding during the summer months; harvesting in the fall; and "mud work," which included ditching and the maintenance and clearing of new fields, during the winter months. Through a long process of tacit negotiation over the preceding six decades, the tasks involved had been standardized throughout the region. According to one observer, the usual mid-eighteenth-century task for planting corn was one-half acre; for furrowing rice, one-quarter acre; for sowing rice, one-half acre; for the first cleaning (weeding) of corn, one-half acre, "unless the ground is too full of roots"; for the second cleaning the task was raised to one acre; for the first hoeing of rice, one-quarter acre; for the second it varied according to the quality of the land. To ensure consistency, overseers and drivers used a special pole to measure the rows in delineating tasks.

For the many *Hare* captives who had grown rice back home, much of the routine was familiar. The similarities throughout the entire production process, from sowing to harvest to cooking, are so many that one scholar has proposed that an entire "rice complex" had been moved from Africa to America. And the similarities are indeed striking. All fieldwork was done with a hoe, as in Africa. Women sowed the seeds, as in Africa, and they did so in precisely the same manner, by dropping rice into the ground and using a bare foot to cover it with dirt. The ditches and sluices used to control water in the Low Country were virtually identical to those employed along the coast near Sierra Leone. The method of processing the grains was entirely African. As they had an ocean away, women winnowed the grain by tossing it in the breeze and catching it in specially designed fanner baskets of their own manufacture. They then separated the outer husk from the inner kernel by pounding the grain with a long wooden pestle in a mortar made from the trunk of a tree. The dull, rhythmic pounding of wood on wood, the same sound as heard every morning throughout Upper Guinea, prompted one observer to dub South Carolina a "rice thumping country."[22]

However similar the processes were, there was one fundamental difference. Carolina rice was grown for sale on a global market using primarily enslaved labor. Low Country rice fields were vast when compared to those cultivated for subsistence by free Africans. To produce as much as possible, planters drove their laborers to the breaking point. As one observer noted, cultivation involved "standing . . . ancle, and even mid-leg deep in water, which flouts an ouzy mud . . . in a furnace of stinking putrid effluvia," and he offered that "a more horrible employment can hardly be imagined."[23] Processing, undertaken during the coldest months, exhausted and broke down the women who did it. As planter and horticulturist Alexander Garden noted, pounding rice was "a very hard & Severe operation." Those who overworked their bondpeople, he admonished, "often pay dear for their Barbarity by the loss of many valuable Negros. And how can it well be otherwise, the poor wretches being obliged to labour hard to compleat their task & often overheat themselves then Exposing themselves to the Cool air or drinking Cold Water, are immediately seized with Dangrous Pleurisies & Peripneumonies."[24]

The garden plots that slaves cultivated in their time off not only gave laborers a significant role in their own provisioning, but also allowed many slaves to sell surplus produce in town markets and to the various peddlers who plied the Low Country's roads and waterways. This in turn allowed the slaves to accumulate small sums of cash, which they used to purchase livestock, pipes, textiles and clothing, guns, and—in one rare and remarkable case—the use of another slave for a period of fifty years.[25] The task system also afforded slaves a comparatively large amount of community time outside the view of the master. It was common for more able workers to complete the tasks of slower workers, which says a great deal about the importance of community time, as well as the role of the task system in facilitating it. None of this, however, suggests that task labor was easy. Workers who could not complete their tasks during daylight hours worked by torchlight into the night. Nor was task labor free from violence. When George Baillie told Parliament that Low Country planter drivers "seldom" whipped slaves in the field, he nevertheless conceded that was only because drivers knew there was "time enough to punish them" at the end of the day for any uncompleted tasks. Tasking may have been preferable to gang labor, but it was still plantation slavery in the service of merchant capital.[26]

We can glimpse the Low Country slaves' relative autonomy through the testimony of Tom, who was examined by the Governor's Council in 1748 in connection with a suspected rebel conspiracy. Tom lived on the Ball plantation in St. John's Berkeley Parish, where several Upper Guineans from the *Hare*'s second voyage would find themselves only six years later. On the evening in question, Tom testified that he saw a group of slaves passing in a boat. It was not at all unusual to see slaves piloting boats without any whites aboard—many slaves, known as "patroons," did so as their primary occupation. Recalling that someone at the Akins plantation owed him money (suggestive once more of the economic viability of many Carolina slaves) Tom asked the people in the boat to take him there. Once at the Akins estate he saw no whites, but "a good many Negroes," who "Eate and drank together" and "played and Laughed." Though Tom had never visited the Akins place before, he knew at least two of the men who were there. In all, his evening's experience reveals the existence of a vibrant, independent, and geographically extensive network of the enslaved.[27]

IN ADDITION TO RICE, several of the *Hare* captives produced indigo. The deep blue dye, made from the leaves of a tropical bush, fetched high prices on European markets for textile production, which was on the rise. The best indigo came from the Caribbean, and the French islands dominated the market. During the 1740s, Carolina planters began to experiment with the crop as a hedge against falling rice prices. Indigo returns soared as business picked up after King George's War, when Parliament instituted a bounty. Carolina planters responded by increasing production, though their dyes were of notoriously poor quality. Grown in all parts of the Low Country, indigo was particularly important in the newer plantation regions away from the Charles Town core, such as those on the Santee and around Port Royal, and in some of the Middle Country immigrant settlements, on lands poorly suited to rice.[28] Only months before the *Hare* arrived in South Carolina, indigo planters were flush with cash and "mad for more Negroes." Prices had been such that several planters converted rice acreage to indigo production, and the redoubtable Henry Laurens opined that indigo planters would be driving the demand for slaves for the foreseeable future. His forecast proved optimistic: the indigo market cooled just before the *Hare* arrived, but would-be dye makers were still looking for labor.[29]

No fewer than twenty-two *Hare* captives went to indigo planters. The true number may have been higher than that, though not all of their slaves would have worked in indigo. Many indigo planters also planted rice—the seasonal work requirements of the two crops complemented each other—which meant that those plantations that grew both had particularly grueling work routines. Of the twenty-two *Hare* captives who wound up on indigo plantations, thirteen went to four planters who cultivated both staples. These four, Peter Taylor, Alexander Fraser, Paul Douxsaint, and Henry Laurens, were all extremely wealthy and owned multiple holdings, not all of which produced indigo, so some of the captives who did land with indigo planters probably did not cultivate the staple. Two smaller planters who produced primarily indigo purchased the other nine captives. One of these, Charles Lorimer of John's Island, had purchased two men and one woman. It is also probable, given Lorimer's marriage to fellow *Hare* purchaser Susannah Wedderburn, that the two men and one boy she purchased were merged with Lorimer's workforce and worked in indigo as well. Merchant William Lloyd, mentioned earlier, probably sent his three women to work his indigo plantation at Wando Neck, also across from Charles Town, although there is a chance he deployed one or more to his town residence.[30]

Indigo production demanded a great deal of skill. In their advertisements for overseers, planters specified that experience producing the crop was essential, and when they sold slaves with indigo expertise, they were sure to underscore the fact, as Charles Lorimer did when he advertised a driver "who understands planting very well, a fellow who is skilful in making the best of indico." Indigo was sown in the spring on drier lands unsuitable for rice. Once the plants had matured, indigo required relatively little attention, which allowed laborers to attend to the more exacting demands of Carolina gold. When the bushes matured, usually around midsummer, workers cut leaves off the upper branches. The bushes would yield two more cuttings, but these were often of poorer quality, and many dual rice-and-indigo planters forewent a second cutting so that their hands could concentrate on rice.[31]

The truly difficult part of indigo production came with the processing, which had to be done immediately after the cutting. Workers placed the cuttings into the largest of three vats, where the leaves "steeped" in water for up to twenty-four hours, by which time the dye had come off the plant and dissolved into the liquid. This fermentation process produced a withering stench that attracted clouds of insects, prompting many planters to exile their operations to the more remote reaches of their plantations. The water was moved to a second, smaller vat, where workers stirred it vigorously with long-handed paddles. This process, called "beating," along with the constant pumping of water, went on for hours and was as fatiguing as any other plantation work. Once the overseer or driver determined that the mixture was ready—this was one reason why planters needed experienced managers—he fixed the dye with a precisely calibrated dose of lime. The beater's contents were then transferred to the smallest vat, where the liquid slowly seeped out, leaving a muddy paste. Removing the paste to a tablelike trough, laborers kneaded the substance into rectangular cakes of deep blue and left them to dry, at which time they were ready for shipping.[32]

The *Hare* captives who worked exclusively in indigo had less autonomy than those who worked in rice. For one thing, lower startup costs (at least compared with rice) meant that indigo operations could be smaller than rice plantations. Fewer workers meant smaller quarters and fewer people of similar linguistic and cultural background, although as we have already seen, smaller operations could and often did house people from the same parts of Africa. In addition, work routines were less conducive to community autonomy. Indigo had burst onto the scene well after the negotiation of the task system on rice plantations. Because of this, and due to the quasi-industrial demands of indigo, planters organized work along the lines of the gang system. In season, laborers spent all day and part of the night toiling under the watch of the overseer. The loss of free time as a result of the employment of gang labor was mitigated in part by the dependence of indigo planters on skilled laborers. Drivers who knew exactly when to stop beating the dissolved dyestuff or precisely when to add lime to fix the process were granted greater privileges, though all understood that failure to perform would result in demotion to fieldwork. There is a good chance that some of the skilled slaves on indigo plantations were African-born. An Old World plant of probable Asian origin, indigo had been made into dye for centuries in Africa, including in Sierra Leone and other parts of Upper Guinea. Whether any of the *Hare* captives had experience manufacturing indigo dye is unknown, but Charles Lorimer's 1761 attempt to sell a driver "who is skilful in making the best of indico" certainly raises the possibility.[33]

Finally, four *Hare* captives wound up living outside the central plantation area. Hance McCulloch, purchaser of two men, had been working as an overseer near Jacksonborough, in Colleton County, to the south of Charles Town. Sometime after this, and perhaps around the time he made his purchase, he seems to have moved to the area known as "Indian Land" in the southern part of the colony near Georgia. A border region until 1732, the area was just beginning to develop a plantation economy. With relatively few slaves present, McCulloch's captives probably lived in relative isolation. We can say more about the man and woman who lived at Christian Minnick's in similar circumstances. Minnick had come to South Carolina in the 1730s and settled in Orangeburg, a backcountry community with a large German Lutheran population. Minnick, like most locals, was not a planter—he raised cattle. With only six slaves in the household and relatively few in the neighborhood, the *Hare* captives would have found it difficult to find residents with similar backgrounds. The pressure to learn German was probably great, but it is likely that his captives eventually learned to converse in English as well. The stock-raising economy, in many respects a throwback to the days before rice planting, would have offered some of Minnick's laborers a measure of day-to-day control over their lives. Cattle raising was common in parts of Upper Guinea, so Minnick's captives may have been able to draw on their prior experience. South Carolina was an open-range society, and enslaved cowboys spent a great deal of time wrangling cattle, so it is quite possible that the man Minnick purchased from the *Hare* roamed in solitude on distant savannahs. The woman he purchased, however, probably remained at the Minnick household and would not have had the same level of mobility.[34]

Though the South Carolina economy was unquestionably dominated by rice production, the *Hare* captives would have encountered a variety of different labor situations. Most of them certainly wound up working in rice, although a significant minority worked at urban pursuits, and still others found themselves employed making indigo or raising cattle. While each of these activities involved different ways of organizing work, each afforded the captives some space to engage in activity outside the control of whites. That point should not be exaggerated or universalized. Slave owners varied greatly in their strategies and management styles. But of all of the slave societies in North America, the Carolina Low Country afforded its plantation laborers the greatest amount of control over their own affairs and in the process maximized the potential for the continuation and elaboration of African cultural practices.

CHAPTER EIGHT

Shipmates and Countrymen

Whether on rice and indigo plantations, in Charles Town, or on the isolated savannahs of the backcountry, slavery imposed severe limitations on the *Hare* captives' lives in the New World. Yet enslavement did not determine all aspects of existence, and the contours of everyday life were largely in the hands of the Africans and Creoles of the Low Country's many communities. These communities, or neighborhoods, varied widely as a result of many factors: the particular crop regime or economic activity; the temperament and plantation practices of local whites; the geographic location; the density of the population; the proximity of other polities, such as the Spanish or native groups; and the state of development of the locality. But from the perspective of the *Hare* captives, no issue loomed larger than the presence of those who spoke the same language and who shared an understanding of the world. The proximity of "countrymen," in the terminology of the era, was a potential source of comfort at a time of extreme fear and uncertainty. In the first months of New World captivity, a more experienced countryman or countrywoman could explain plantation routines and perhaps even save a new arrival from punishment. A countryman could help with the all-important process of language acquisition. Lastly, someone of a similar background could help introduce the newcomer to the plantation community and to the wider neighborhood. For the newly arrived *Hare* captives, a great deal depended on the presence of people of similar backgrounds.

It is hard to know exactly how many of the *Hare* captives lived in clusters that permitted them contact with their countrymen and countrywomen. To start, we do know that forty-four of the fifty-six were purchased along with at least one other *Hare* captive, while eleven were purchased singly, but even being purchased together did not necessarily mean the captives would stay together. Africans throughout the Americas placed a special importance on the shipmate relationship. Shipmates treated one another as kin, and recognition of the bond might continue into subsequent generations. However, being purchased in company with another *Hare* captive did not guarantee an enduring, close shipmate relationship. As we have already seen, several purchasers owned multiple properties, and the possibility of separation onto different estates was certainly present, whether immediately or in later years. Horry and Lessesne, for example, bought seven captives between them but never operated a plantation together, which means they probably divided the captives between themselves or resold them immediately.

Separation through death was another distinct possibility. With captives arriving on the plantations weak from their ocean crossing, one in three perished in the first year. Even for those who survived the first year's "seasoning," the overall unhealthiness of the Low Country would have continued to claim victims. A smallpox epidemic in 1760, which killed one in ten Charles Town residents, likely boosted the already high mortality rate. The six children from the *Hare* would have faced the steepest odds of all. Half of all children born on rice plantations did not survive into adulthood, and the percentage was surely much higher for new arrivals. The death of an owner and the subsequent division of his estate could also separate shipmates. At least five purchasers died within ten years of the sale, and one of them, Presbyterian minister Thomas Bell of James Island, died just one year after buying a single man from the *Hare*. All things considered, it seems probable that more than half of the *Hare* captives found themselves living without a shipmate within five years of their arrival.[1]

For some of the *Hare* captives, language differences may have prevented close shipmate relationships. While there is good reason to believe that most of the *Hare* captives could communicate with each other on at least a basic level, there were certainly some who could not. The problem may have been mitigated while aboard ship, with the multilingual captives translating for the others, but once split into smaller groups on the plantations, those who could not converse in one of the Mande languages may have found themselves unable to speak with their own shipmates. Slaveholder mobility would also have wreaked havoc on the efforts of the *Hare* captives to form enduring relationships with fellow Upper Guineans. Eight purchasers relocated within five years of the *Hare*'s arrival. Since these moves involved entire households, including all slaves, they may not have broken relationships within the plantation community, but they would have severed relationships with neighbors, which for many were probably at least as important. In rare instances, a move might have the effect of reuniting shipmates. The eight men and one woman Laurens sent to Wambaw Plantation in 1756 were probably pleased when the man purchased by Paul Douxsaint arrived in the neighborhood a year or two later. And we have already seen that the marriage of Charles Lorimer and Susannah Wedderburn brought their six *Hare* captives back together (if indeed they had ever been separated). But even so, Lorimer moved to England in 1764, so slaveholder mobility once more put asunder what it had earlier joined together. The structure of captive purchases, geographic mobility, and high mortality rates therefore posed great challenges to the endurance of shipmate relationships. The relationships, while certainly important for those who were fortunate to have them, were fragile, enjoyed over the long term by only a minority of the *Hare* captives. For many, the only real constant in life was instability.[2]

Yet perhaps the most important thing to know is that 58 percent of all Africans entering the colony between 1751 and 1775 came from Upper Guinea, making it statistically probable that the *Hare* captives would have encountered not merely the odd countryman here and there, but many individuals from the same part of the continent.[3] The thin documentary record makes it impossible to recover the African origins of all the captives on the plantations where the *Hare* captives lived, but a few sources afford a glimpse. The most suggestive information comes from the slave-sale records of the firm of Austin & Laurens, which can be supplemented by information from other sources, like runaway advertisements. Henry Laurens and George Austin were the era's most prolific slave factors, handling over three thousand captive sales between 1753 and 1758, approximately 20 percent of all of the Africans imported into South Carolina over that five-year period. Of the twenty-six purchasers (twenty-four if the two partnerships are merged together), thirteen purchased additional captives from ships handled by Austin & Laurens. It should be emphasized that an appearance in the Austin & Laurens records does not mean that the person never purchased captives from another dealer. The firm handled only 20 percent of incoming captives, so many planters bought additional captives from other factors. To get a rough estimate of the actual numbers, it would be necessary to multiply the Austin & Laurens totals by five. In short, the Austin & Laurens records are the best surviving source on who purchased captives from which part of Africa, but they are far from complete and therefore present an extreme worst-case scenario for the existence of cultural and linguistic clusters.

Of the thirteen *Hare* purchasers who also bought from Austin & Laurens, eight purchased captives from the Upper Guinea regions of Senegambia, Sierra Leone, and the Windward Coast (see table 7 in appendix 3). In other words, the documentary record reveals that no fewer than twenty-one of the fifty-six *Hare* captives went to masters who bought other Upper Guineans at roughly the same time. All of the caveats mentioned earlier apply: not all people from Upper Guinea shared linguistic ties, one in three probably died within a year, and there is no way to know whether the captives were separated onto scattered holdings or simply sold off at a later date. On the other hand, the figures in the table inevitably understate the number of captives from Upper Guinea present on the purchasers' slaveholdings, especially in the case of the larger planters, such as James Parsons, Alexander Fraser, and Elias Horry, who almost certainly had Upper Guineans on their plantations. In some instances, it is quite clear that the *Hare* captives entered plantation communities with many people of similar backgrounds. The man purchased by Lachlan McIntosh, for example, would have found himself among quite a few people from the Windward Coast, the slave trade for which drew for the most part on the same routes as did that of Sierra Leone.[4] In other cases, the *Hare* captives would have been culturally and linguistically isolated within a small household; this was likely so for the man who worked with at least two Central Africans at Alexander Chisholme's coffee house. The individual slaveholdings on which the *Hare* captives found themselves housed widely varying proportions of Creoles and Africans of all backgrounds, but there is good reason to suppose that many, perhaps even a sizable majority, lived among others from Upper Guinea.

Neither rural plantations nor urban households were isolated entities. Any meaningful definition of "community" must take into account the fact that relationships among the enslaved could encompass multiple slaveholdings.[5] These larger neighborhoods were the most important units of African culture in South Carolina, all the more so given the insecure nature of the shipmate relationships in the New World and the small pool of "countrymen" on the lesser slaveholdings. South Carolina's slaves were, in the words of Philip D. Morgan, "remarkably mobile." Whether exercising their customary right to Sunday visits, running errands, going into town to sell produce in the market, or running away to visit friends and kin, Low Country slaves could journey fifteen miles or more in a single day.[6] Not all were equally mobile, of course. Boatmen, carters, and artisans traveled the most, while women and children were far less likely to. With the sparse documentary record precluding the reconstruction of the ethnic makeup of individual plantations, doing so for entire neighborhoods is, to say the least, a bridge too far. However, an incomplete set of records for one neighborhood, one in which a large number of *Hare* captives eventually came to reside, suggests that the chances for the formation of enclaves of Mande speakers from Upper Guinea were quite good.

Henry Laurens was the largest purchaser of captives from the *Hare*. At the time of the sale, he was a partner with George Austin in one of Charles Town's largest mercantile houses. Sometime in the mid-1750s, around the time that the *Hare* arrived, Laurens began planning his transformation from a man of commerce to country gentleman. It is impossible to know for certain what he did with the nine captives he purchased from the *Hare*, but the fact that he purchased eight adult men and one woman strongly implies that he was assembling a labor force for a rural plantation rather than a staff for his town residence. But as yet, Laurens did not own a plantation. He would not until almost a year later, when he purchased a half share in Wambaw Plantation in St. James Santee Parish from his brother-in-law, now partner, John Coming Ball. In the intervening year, Laurens most likely sent his captives straight to Wambaw in anticipation that he would eventually become part owner. He could have also sent them to Ball's Hyde Park Plantation, located on the east branch of the Cooper River, about twenty-three miles from Charles Town, for safekeeping until he could acquire land of his own.[7]

John Coming Ball also owned several slaves from Upper Guinea. The 1750s were clearly a time of expansion for him, and he had been active in the slave market. Sales records reveal that Ball purchased at least twenty-eight captives during the period 1751 to 1758. Ten of them came from Upper Guinea; of the others, the single largest group consisted of ten women and three men from the Bight of Benin, a region that supplied relatively few captives to South Carolina. The existence of the ten captives from Upper Guinea, along with the nineteen Upper Guineans that we know were purchased by Henry Laurens over the same time period, means that the two partners bought no fewer than twenty-nine people—and probably many more—from that part of Africa. The Upper Guinean captives they purchased were relatively balanced in terms of sex and age, at least by the standard of the slave trade: eleven men, eight women, six boys, and five girls. Assuming one-third succumbed to disease in the first year, no fewer than twenty Upper Guineans resided on their holdings. Over the same period, Ball and Laurens purchased thirty-one captives from other parts of Africa, with the Lower Guinean regions of the Gold Coast and the Bight of Benin accounting for all but five. The surviving documents, then, suggest that Upper Guineans were a significant presence on the Laurens and Ball slave quarters.

It is unclear how Laurens and Ball distributed their captives over their holdings, whether the captives stayed at Hyde Park before going to Wambaw, went directly to Wambaw, or were split between the two. Subsequent developments suggest that Laurens's *Hare* captives moved around. In 1762, seven years after their arrival and six years after Laurens purchased his share of Wambaw, he bought a second plantation, this one located on the east branch of the Cooper River in St. John's Berkeley, a neighborhood that included several Ball plantations, including one owned by John Coming Ball. The acquisition of a new plantation often led to a reshuffling of the labor force, with selected slaves transferred to the new holding. Whether Laurens shifted any *Hare* captives from Wambaw to Mepkin, as the new place was called, is unknown but certainly possible, since Ball, Laurens's partner, shipped Wambaw captives to his own Cooper River plantation. The 1765 probate inventory of John Coming Ball's Cooper River holdings includes six slaves with the prefix "Wambaw" affixed to their names (e.g., "Wambaw Hercules"), indicating that they had once lived on the French Santee property he owned jointly with Laurens.[8]

Those who did move from Wambaw to Mepkin or to one of the other nearby Ball plantations would have found themselves in one of the colony's wealthiest plantation neighborhoods. The families there—the Balls, the Harlestons, and the Laurenses—were all related to one another by blood or marriage. In 1753, with slave importations picking up after a long hiatus, Elias Ball took it upon himself to tally his adult male slaves by place of birth. He listed seventeen "country born," or Creoles; fourteen Upper Guinean captives, whom he labeled "Gambias"; and three "Angolas." Over the next five years, these planters bought a large number of African slaves, including not only many from Upper Guinea, but also several from the *Hare*'s 1755–56 voyage to Sierra Leone. Along with the ten Upper Guinean captives known to have been purchased by John Coming Ball, members of the neighboring (and allied) Harleston family purchased at least thirteen Upper Guineans (including nine from Sierra Leone), and members of the nearby Akin family purchased two Sierra Leonians. In all, neighbors purchased forty-four captives from Austin & Laurens in 1753–58, thirty-five of whom came from Upper Guinea and seventeen of whom embarked at Sierra Leone. No records of their post-1758 purchases survive, but with their neighbor and relative Laurens acting as factor for no fewer than twenty-four voyages, including three that came directly from Bance Island, it is probable that a significant number of captives from Sierra Leone and Upper Guinea found themselves living within an hour's walk of each other.[9]

Comparable records do not exist for other neighborhoods. However, other records can help fill the void at the parish level. We know how many Africans entered the colony every year, we know the proportion that came from Upper Guinea, and we know the total slave population of each parish starting in 1761. Using the Austin & Laurens records to estimate the geographic distribution of newly arrived Africans, it is possible to derive rough estimates of the number of captives from Upper Guinea for individual parishes (see table 8 in appendix 3). Not surprisingly, the data in table 8 suggest that newly arrived Upper Guineans (those entering the colony between 1753 and 1761) were not evenly distributed within the colony. Instead, they were more numerous in those parishes that were experiencing a rapid expansion in the plantation economy, especially in those northeast and southwest of Charles Town, where growth had been retarded during the 1740s by slave-import duties and war. While the older plantation parishes, such as St. John's Berkeley and St. James Goose Creek, all imported their share of captives, the newcomers there had a smaller demographic impact because populations were already high. For example, the approximately 220 Upper Guineans who came to St. John's Berkeley in 1753–61 and survived their first year constituted about 6 percent of the 1761 population. Conversely, Upper Guineans comprised a larger share of the population in quickly developing outlying parishes, such as St. Bartholomew's and St. James Santee, where rice culture was expanding, and Prince Frederick, where indigo spurred a demand for labor. These parishes had relatively small slave populations at the start of the decade, so an influx of a few hundred Africans within a few years, over half from Upper Guinea, would have had a more noticeable effect than in the older plantation regions. Three in ten slaves in some parishes were recent arrivals from Upper Guinea, and in Prince Frederick the proportion approached one-half.

The experiences of the *Hare* captives certainly varied, so some likely lived in enclaves of people of a similar background, and some likely did not. The nine captives on Henry Laurens's Wambaw Plantation in St. James Santee would have witnessed a large and continuous influx of people from Upper Guinea, who undoubtedly had a strong influence in the region's quarters. They almost certainly lived with others of similar backgrounds. On the other hand, the man purchased by Thomas Mell was one of approximately 230 Upper Guineans to arrive in St. James Goose Creek during 1753–61, so while he almost certainly found countrymen with whom to socialize, the area's slave neighborhoods would have been dominated by "country born" slaves and earlier arrivals, probably Central Africans. The pressure to adapt was undoubtedly stronger for him and for others in his situation than it was for those in areas where Upper Guineans constituted a larger proportion of the population. In almost none of these cases, however, is it likely that the *Hare* captives were totally isolated. To the contrary, most of them would have had dozens of people of similar backgrounds in the immediate neighborhood, and hundreds within the same parish. The number and concentration varied, but in purely demographic terms it seems conditions were good for the elaboration of Upper Guinean cultures in South Carolina.

THE GROUP WE HAVE CALLED "Upper Guineans" lived in close contact with one another on individual plantations and in the wider neighborhoods and parishes. Yet while perhaps useful as a stand-in to differentiate the people of one part of Africa from another, "Upper Guinean" is not an identity. There is no language by that name, and nobody, then or now, would ever declare himself or herself to be an "Upper Guinean," the region being too linguistically, religiously, and culturally diverse. It is reasonable, therefore, to ask what good it does to discover that "Upper Guineans" composed a majority of the Africans entering South Carolina from 1751 to 1775, or that they lived in close proximity with one another, or that they enjoyed a great deal of control over their daily lives, if it turns out they were a haphazardly assembled "crowd" rather than a people with some consciousness of itself as a distinct group.

The answer in part, as we saw in chapter 4, is that the cultural diversity of Upper Guinea does not necessarily mean the peoples of the region lived in small, insular polities. On the contrary, the region's diversity necessitated communication and accommodation. People were accustomed to dealing with difference, with many being multilingual. Linguists estimate that half of the population of modern Africa is multilingual, and while that percentage is probably higher than in past centuries, it is hardly a new phenomenon.[10] Upper Guineans also shared a common history. In this case, the salient development was the expansion of Mali, which spread Mande languages and culture throughout the region in the process known as "Mandingization." Finally, it must be recognized that the slave trade did not draw randomly on Upper Guinea or any other part of Africa. Using the standard tools of historical analysis, it is possible to identify the regions and polities that supplied captives at specific moments in time. During the *Hare*'s period, the jihad in the Futa Jallon was the major catalyst for enslavement. Indeed, without that, Upper Guinea would have remained a minor contributor to the diaspora, as it had been before 1726. From that, and knowing precisely from where the *Hare* purchased its captives, the suggestion here has been that most of the *Hare* captives were non-Muslim Mande speakers from the interior of Upper Guinea, along with a minority of coastal speakers of Atlantic languages. So how did all of this play out in South Carolina?

Specific documentation for these issues in eighteenth-century South Carolina as a whole is extremely thin. Virtually no detailed, firsthand descriptions of eighteenth-century cultural practices survive, in contrast to the nineteenth and twentieth centuries, which produced the traveler, missionary, and ethnographic accounts that have allowed historians to analyze what came to be known as Gullah (in Georgia, Geechee) culture. In this case, reading nineteenth- and twentieth-century sources backward (a method sometimes known as "upstreaming") must be undertaken very carefully, for the simple reason that (to paraphrase historian John K. Thornton), in the eighteenth century, African cultures were still "arriving," whereas in the nineteenth they were "surviving." The more or less coherent Gullah culture of the antebellum period would have looked very different during the period of heavy African in-migration a century earlier. Perhaps the best way to approach the eighteenth century is by posing two different, though related, questions. The first has to do with how the *Hare* captives and the many others from the same region of Africa drew the boundaries of self and other in South Carolina: Did they actually see themselves as sharing a common identity? The second speaks to the issue of expressive culture: to what extent did the *Hare* captives and their contemporaries perpetuate Mande or Upper Guinean practices?

On those occasions when eighteenth-century white Carolinians actually distinguished African from Creole slaves, they generally did not distinguish among the different African groups, employing all-encompassing terms like "New Negro." The major exceptions to this rule are merchant correspondence, shipping data, scattered references in plantation records and estate inventories, and runaway notices in the newspapers. These sources have allowed historians to discern, albeit to different degrees, the existence of ties among Africans of similar backgrounds.[11]

The difficulty is that all of these sources present African background from the perspective of whites. Runaway notices, which are far and away the most plentiful source identifying differences among Africans and the foundation for much of what we know, are a case in point. By their very nature, runaway notices appeared only when the person in question was not present to identify himself or herself. Moreover, the vast majority of runaway advertisements did not supply ethnonyms. Instead, they employed generic terms like "New Negro" or the toponyms favored by European slave traders, such as "Gambia" (a river), "Sierra Leone" (a river and a mountain range), "Windward Coast" (a nautical term), "Guinea" (a catchall for West Africa), "Calabar" (a name for two different slaving ports), and "Angola" (a Portuguese colony). Some slaveholders, including several *Hare* purchasers, did have some sense of their bondmen's backgrounds and made certain to use ethnonyms, likely gleaned from the captives themselves or from slaves who spoke the same language. They occasionally inserted these ethnonyms into their advertisements to increase the chance of capture. Henry Laurens once advertised for a "Mindinga" named Footabea, and James Parsons took out several notices for runaways, including "two tall likely young new Banbara fellows," a "lad of the Pappa country," and a "new Surago negro." But these notices were exceptions to the rule. Only about 3 percent of all runaway advertisements for Africans supplied an ethnonym. Most slave owners reported only the African coastal area from which the fugitive embarked, which they had probably learned from the slave factors at the time of purchase, not from the captive.[12]

Another set of sources relies more consistently upon self-identifications: workhouse advertisements. Unlike runaway advertisements, in which slaveholders described the fugitives, notices for the Charles Town workhouse were far more likely to be based on self-identification by the captives themselves. Though often lumped together with runaway notices, workhouse advertisements were the product of a very different process. Whereas runaway notices were authored by planters in reference to slaves who were no longer present, workhouse notices were taken out for fugitives who were in the possession of the workhouse warden. The fugitive's owner was in most cases unknown, so one of the first tasks of the workhouse warden was to question new inmates for the purposes of placing a notice in the colony's newspapers, which meant they had to ask the inmate some variation on the question, "Who are you?" Some wardens showed more interest in identifying inmates' "countries," no doubt in hopes that the information would lead to the prompt reclamation of the fugitive and payment of the requisite fees. Christopher Holson, warden in the early 1750s, rarely bothered to ascertain their backgrounds, terming most Africans "new negroes," with the exception of a few "Eboes," suggesting some familiarity with them. The wardens of the 1760s and 1770s, such as John Brown and especially Michael Kalteisen, displayed more interest in ascertaining inmates' origins, with a correspondingly wider variety of ethnonyms appearing in their advertisements.

Inmates' responses to the warden's questioning varied. Some volunteered the names of their masters and plantations; others pretended not to know or understand. For many, however, language really did constitute a barrier. In these cases, wardens relied on interpreters, either other inmates or their own slaves. One Central African who spoke no English was questioned by "another negro who understands his language," while "Peter, a Mandingo," was questioned by "the workhouse negro." On still another occasion, the warden's bondman translated for a mixed group of captives, consisting of one "Bambare" and three "Mandingos."[13] Some workhouse advertisements identified captives using a mixture of toponyms, ethnonyms, and generic terms, suggesting that the warden managed to identify or find interpreters for some, but not all of the inmates. For example, one 1767 notice mentioned a "Mandingo" and two "new negroes." Another from 1772 listed five "Mandingos," one "Timene," one "Koshey" [Kissi], one "Ebo," five "Angolas," and nine from the "Guiney Country," a generic term that suggests he was unsuccessful at eliciting a statement of origin from them.[14] The nature of workhouse notices, with fugitives present and undergoing some sort of questioning, means that they contain many more self-identifications than do the runaway notices. That is certainly not true in all cases, but it is worth noting that the workhouse notices contain many more ethnonyms, and a much more extensive variety of them, than the runaway advertisements, which is consistent with a situation in which the inmates themselves, rather than the slave owner, supplied the information. Slave-trading toponyms like "Gambia" and "Windward Coast," then, appeared almost exclusively in runaway advertisements, while ethnonyms like "Mandingo," "Bambara," and "Kishee" appeared almost exclusively in workhouse notices.[15]

Of the Upper Guinean ethnonyms appearing in workhouse notices before 1776, "Mandingo" accounted for just under half of the total (see table 9 in appendix 3). Together, three Mande-speaking groups (Mandinka, Bamana, and Yalunka) accounted for 56 percent of all Upper Guineans for whom some ethnic identifier is given. The dominance of the "Mandingos" and other Mande speakers is even more striking in the years prior to 1769. That year marked the first appearance of the ethnonym "Kishee," for the Kissi people of present-day Sierra Leone and Guinea. Kissis, whose language is of the non-Mande Atlantic family, constituted the second-largest Upper Guinean group in the workhouse notices. Although there were probably Kissi speakers present in South Carolina before 1769, their sudden appearance in large numbers at the workhouse after that date suggests that there was a real influx around that time, likely due to a shift in the geography of warfare in the Futa Jallon and adjacent areas. Prior to 1769, Mande groups accounted for some 63 percent of all Upper Guinean ethnonyms in workhouse notices.[16]

Workhouse notices are only one measure of Mande dominance, and an imperfect one at that. But other sources support the notion that most Upper Guinean captives in the region were of Mande background. While the South Carolina government never asked slave importers to identify the "nation" or ethnic group of the captives they brought in, officials in Spanish Florida during the 1750s and 1760s did. Prior to 1770, Florida planters did not import most of their captives directly from Africa, instead purchasing most of their laborers in South Carolina and Georgia. So while the Florida records hardly constitute a scientific sample of the Carolina population, they do corroborate the notion that Mande speakers predominated among Upper Guinean captives. In all, over three-quarters of all Upper Guineans entering Florida between 1752 and 1763 were of Mande background (see table 10 in appendix 3). And as in South Carolina, the single largest group by far was identified as "Mandinga." The wide array of ethnonyms and the small proportion of toponyms in the record suggests, as in the case of the workhouse notices, that these identifications were provided by the captives themselves.[17]

The prominence of "Mandingo" as an identifier in the Charles Town workhouse notices offers an important clue to the *Hare* captives' probable self-perceptions. There are two possibilities. The first is that most of the people identified as "Mandingos" in workhouse notices had indeed considered themselves to be Mandinkas while in Africa, a relatively direct transfer of ethnic identity to South Carolina. The second is that the term "Mandingo," as used in eighteenth-century South Carolina, may have included a larger community of speakers of Mande languages, especially speakers of the closely related Manding languages (which include Mandinka, Maninka, Bamana, and Juula), one that had taken on new meanings as it was transplanted in New World soil. It may be that some Mande speakers accepted or even embraced a designation of "Mandingo" rather than attempting to educate the workhouse warden in the finer points of Upper Guinean identity. It is therefore conceivable that sometimes an identification of "Mandingo" in a workhouse advertisement was the product of an exchange between the inmate, an interpreter, and the warden. In such cases, it is impossible to know the dynamic that led to the assignment. The identification of a "Mandingo" man named Peter in 1760 relied to an unknown extent on "the workhouse negro, who can talk with him." Whether Peter said he was a Mandingo or whether an African-born interpreter assigned him that category because he spoke a related Mande language is impossible to say. He may even have been identified as a Mandingo because he spoke a Mande tongue as a second language. Similarly, it is possible that some workhouse ethnonyms were assigned by the warden through pure misunderstanding. One warden confessed difficulty in communicating with three inmates, noting that "what I can understand they all belong to one man," raising questions about his identification of the men as Mandingos.[18]

Of course, these scenarios are not mutually exclusive. In fact, the most likely possibility is some combination of them, involving a large population of self-identified Mandinkas, mostly from Senegambia, alongside other speakers of Mande languages. "Mandingo" may even have encompassed smaller numbers of Atlantic-language speakers, especially those who were bilingual in one of the Mande languages or whose homelands had experienced some degree of Mandingization. In South Carolina, then, the ethnonym "Mandingo" probably represented a New World elaboration on a transformative process that had begun with the expansion of the Mali Empire in the Middle Ages, continued through the Mane invasions of the sixteenth century, and strengthened through the extension of Mande trade networks and political leadership in the eighteenth century. It is even possible, given the vast extent of the Juula trading networks, that "Mandingo" attracted Africans who came from the hinterlands of the Gold Coast and the Bight of Benin. In sum, "Mandingo" may have functioned as a cultural and linguistic common denominator not just for Mande speakers but for other captives from Upper Guinea who sought some measure of familiarity in an environment that included Europeans, black Creoles, and Africans of totally unrelated backgrounds.[19] Clearly not all Mande speakers embraced "Mandingo" identity, and certainly many speakers of the Atlantic languages chose not to do so. But the overwhelming dominance of "Mandingo" as a category in workhouse notices strongly suggests some combination of two trends: an influx of Mandinka speakers from Senegambia and (to a lesser extent) the Sierra Leone hinterland numbering in the tens of thousands, and an embrace of Mandingo identity by at least some Africans of other backgrounds. It would be a mistake, however, to conclude that the "Mandingos" of colonial South Carolina were somehow inauthentic. In Africa as in South Carolina, Mandinka identity could not be essentialized. It derived its meaning from its historical, political, and indeed, cultural contexts. "Mandingo" identity in South Carolina was therefore a capacious one, rooted in African culture and history but adapted to local circumstances.

If the hypothesis that "Mandingo" identity in the mid-eighteenth-century Low Country was fed by two streams, one consisting of people who thought of themselves as such before arriving and a second comprised of other Mande speakers attracted by some sense of the familiar, most *Hare* captives probably fell into the latter group. The fact that they embarked from ports near Sierra Leone, rather than farther north at the Gambia, suggests that there were probably more Yalunka, Kuranko, and Susu speakers, along with a sizable minority of Atlantic-language speakers, such as Fulas, Temnes, and Kissis. In other words, while the Mande-speaking *Hare* captives certainly would have shared some common ground with Senegambian Mandinkas, and even would have been able to communicate at a more-than-rudimentary level, they still would have found it necessary to make accommodations— this on top of the adaptations they were already making to enslavement and to those Africans with whom they had no basis for communication.

Those *Hare* captives who spoke Mandinka, then, would have had little trouble forming speech communities. Those who spoke another Mande language, probably at least a plurality of the *Hare* captives, would have had little problem communicating with many of the residents of their slave quarters and neighborhoods but would have been forced to cope in varying degrees with different vocabulary and pronunciation. Those who spoke a Mande language as a second tongue would have found their ability to communicate governed by their proficiency in that language. Monolingual speakers of the Atlantic languages were the most likely candidates for isolation, with countrymen likely nearby (especially in Charles Town), but fewer and farther between than countrymen for Mande speakers, the major exception being the apparent influx of Kissis in the 1770s.

Workhouse advertisements reveal the existence of speech communities, with men and women often fleeing in groups of similar backgrounds. Of the twenty-four parties of Upper Guineans who fled in groups, two-thirds were comprised of people sharing the same ethnonym (see table 11 in appendix 3). To compute it slightly differently, over 70 percent of those individuals captured with one or more fellow fugitives chose to run with someone bearing the same ethnonym. The preponderance of these Upper Guinean partnerships strongly implies two things: first, that regional origin mattered to newly arrived Africans; and second, that it was quite possible, even very common, for them to form relationships based on language and background. In fact, given the level of trust involved in any collective plan to flee, the fact that nearly seven in ten chose someone of the same background underscores the significance of these ties.

The multiethnic fugitive groups are equally suggestive, with the evidence pointing in two directions at once. On the one hand, multiethnic cooperation implies an expanding solidarity in the plantation quarters, perhaps even the early erosion of ethnicity and language as organizing principles, something that would become more pronounced over time as Low Country slaves came to think of themselves as "black" rather than as Africans of different backgrounds. But the fact that three of the mixed groups were composed entirely of Mande speakers, in each instance a combination of "Bambaras" and "Mandingos," indicates that something else was happening at the same time, namely, the formation of bonds among Mande speakers. The case of the "Bambaras" is particularly intriguing. "Bambara" was an exoethnonym, meaning an ethnonym bestowed by a people other than the one described. In Upper Guinea, it was most often applied by Muslim slave traders to Mande people, especially Bamana speakers, from the middle Niger. Whether the "Bambaras" in the Charles Town workhouse identified themselves as such or whether they were identified as such by other Upper Guinean inmates is unknown. Either is possible, although if it were a self-identification, one would expect them to provide a term other than "Bambara." Regardless, the "Bambaras" were clearly distinct from the "Mandingos," which suggests some level of difference. Still, the act of running away with "Mandingos" reveals a level of trust and an ability to communicate (the Manding languages have a lexical similarity of over 80 percent) that appears to have transcended other differences.[20]

Taken together, the workhouse data suggest that identity among Upper Guineans in the Carolina Low Country was developing simultaneously along three tracks. The first of these involved the firm establishment of a "Mandingo" identity among Mandinka speakers, primarily from Senegambia, of whom there were many. The second involved the Mandingization of other Upper Guineans, encompassing other Mande speakers and possibly some Atlantic-language speakers, especially those who were bilingual. Finally, the cooperation between Upper Guineans and people from other parts of Africa, along with Creoles, points to an eventual decline in the significance of language and ethnic identity. For the *Hare* captives, language and background still held tremendous importance.

The *Hare* captives' linguistic backgrounds probably broke down once more by sex. Unlike most slave ships, which carried three men for every two women, the *Hare* initially took on more women than men. By the time of the sale, however, mortality had pushed the sex ratio to a more typical three men for every two women. With the Futa Jallon Jihad driving most slave trading at Sierra Leone, it is probable that most of those enslaved as a result of the war and shipped from the interior were men. They were also more likely to be speakers of Mande languages. The women aboard the *Hare*, in contrast, were, as a group, more likely to have been enslaved closer to the coast, and therefore more likely to be speakers of Atlantic languages. They were also less likely to be bilingual, since the activities that led to the acquisition of a second language, such as long-distance trade, more often fell to men. In the aggregate, then, the women of the *Hare* were probably more linguistically isolated in South Carolina, especially those who lived in rural areas. The lack of mobility for female speakers of the Atlantic languages, at least relative to men, would have complicated any effort to break down the isolation through visits.

Another important nonethnolinguistic category of identity was religion. Most of the *Hare* captives were probably Mande speakers of non-Muslim backgrounds. However, it is virtually certain that some of the *Hare* captives, possibly even a sizable minority, were Mande- or Fula-speaking Muslims. For Muslim captives, religion would have been as important a category of identity as language or ethnicity, perhaps an even more important one. Muslims in Africa and elsewhere generally divided the world into dar al-Islam (literally, "House of Islam"), to signify those areas under Muslim control, and dar al-Harb (literally, "House of War"), for those areas dominated by nonbelievers. Low Country Muslims would have perceived themselves as residing in the latter, on plantations owned by Christians. Omar Ibn Said, a Fula who arrived at Charleston in about 1807, consistently referred to English as the "Christian language."[21] How Muslims on Low Country plantations regarded their non-Muslim fellow slaves is difficult to know. On the one hand, non-Muslims may well have harbored animosity toward those they associated with war and enslavement. On the other hand, the long and largely peaceful history of Muslim administration and trade may have blunted any hostile feelings, especially toward those with no direct connection to the war.

ALMOST ALL OF WHAT historians know of the Low Country's African-derived cultural practices dates to observations made in the nineteenth and twentieth centuries, several decades after the end of the slave trade. Although these sources can never reveal what contemporary sources might, they nevertheless can contribute to our understanding of earlier practices.[22] Most important is a recognition that no stable or unified "slave culture" existed in the mid-eighteenth century, with an average of 1,700 Africans arriving every year. Though Africans recognized their common legal status and certainly felt the need to build bridges with other slaves, they sought out the familiar and formed their closest relationships (whenever possible) with people of similar backgrounds. They were therefore engaged in two simultaneous cultural projects: the building of a common black or slave culture, and the transformation of specific African practices to suit the new environment.

Upstreaming from nineteenth- and twentieth-century sources offers some insight into the former process, but much less into the latter.

An understanding of the mid-eighteenth-century world of the *Hare* captives requires, methodologically speaking, a disentangling of the Upper Guinean from the Central African and other strands that eventually became Gullah culture. Reverse engineering antebellum Gullah culture is, needless to say, a fraught endeavor. Identifying specific Upper Guinean contributions is problematic, especially as they combined with European and other African practices and mutated over time. Nevertheless, it is possible to identify several Gullah practices of probable Upper Guinean origin, which in turn offer a glimpse, however imperfect and incomplete, of expressive culture in Low Country plantation quarters as practiced in the 1750s.

Working backwards from the nineteenth century sheds no light whatsoever on earlier Upper Guinean practices that never became part of the later Creole culture. Why certain practices were taken up while others were not is impossible to say for certain. Historians and anthropologists have conjectured that a given practice was more likely to persist if it fell outside the purview of the master (as defined by local custom) and squarely within the purview of the enslaved. The more interest taken by the slave owner, the more pressure (to the point of force) Africans came under to accommodate his demands. Work routines provide both an example of this process and a sense of its limitations. Masters took a strong interest in rice production and spent a great deal of energy devising ways to extract as much labor as they could from their bondpeople. Even so, the task system and the toleration (if not outright embrace) of many African production techniques suggests that even such things as coerced labor regimes might be the subject of cultural negotiation. At the other end of the spectrum, the religious life of their workers was a matter of scant interest to most Low Country planters, who generally allowed slaves to practice without interference. It should not be surprising, then, that the most visible Upper Guinean contributions to Gullah cultural practice fall in the area of sacred and spiritual cosmology. An examination offers not only some sense of the *Hare* captives' probable practices but also valuable clues to their interactions with Africans of different backgrounds.

The construction and use of amulets and charms is one of the more readily identifiable Upper Guinean practices in the Low Country. Travelers to Upper Guinea in the eighteenth century rarely failed to mention charms, so widespread was their use. Upper Guineans, like many Africans, envisioned a universe overseen by a powerful, yet distant entity. Day-to-day occurrences, such as illness or a beating from an overseer, were the result of actions taken by local spirits, either on their own or at the behest of ritual specialists who knew how to influence them. A person could therefore combat illness or address a personal conflict by contacting these lesser deities, again with the aid of a specialist. The most common method involved the creation of a ritual object, called a "greegree" by Mande speakers or a "fetish" by Europeans, which could take a variety of forms. One greegree constructed by slaves at Bance Island to bring about the death of anyone who divulged the location of a runaway consisted of "a few Splinters of Bamboo, in a Bundle, and then about five or six peices [sic] of Old Iron and Nails, all Tyed up with Tarred Twine, then Greased all over & put into a Canvas Bagg, like a Tobacco Pouch, this wrapt up and so put under Ground." Often, the greegree was positioned at a strategic location to combat evil or witchcraft. One greegree designed to deter theft from a rice field consisted of cloth placed on a nearby orange tree. Still other charms consisted of pieces of cloth tied to the end of a pole, an axe attached to a tree, a pot placed upon a stake, and a pewter dish set on the ground. Greegrees were also placed in a pouch or bag to make an amulet that could be worn around the neck or carried elsewhere on the body. Upper Guineans regarded amulets constructed by Mande Muslim marabouts as especially potent. Consisting of a leather bag with Koranic verses inside, they protected against misfortunes ranging from drowning to snakebites to shark attacks, all of which were understood to be caused by malevolent magic.[23]

Greegree construction was one of the more distinctive Upper Guinean arts to arrive in the Americas, whether known as "gris-gris," "zin-zin," or "ouanga" in the French colonies, "Mandinga bags" in Brazil, or "conjure bags" in the Low Country.[24] No description of an eighteenth-century Low Country conjure bag survives, but in its nineteenth- and twentieth-century incarnation, a typical amulet might contain hair or fingernails from the target of the charm, graveyard dirt, and pieces of cloth and string, which might be used to bind the materials together.[25] North American conjure bags contained three basic types of ingredients: items from the land of the dead, such as graveyard dust; objects, such as hair, that represented the person to be affected by the magic; and materials that bore some linguistic resemblance to the target and might serve as the basis for a play on words. Historian Sharla Fett describes conjure bags as "a stunning array of mutually referential materials combined to embody and direct spiritual force."[26]

But the fact that these later American conjure bags contained different ingredients from the eighteenth-century Upper Guinean greegree not only suggests that the art itself may have been different in the eighteenth century, but also points to a specific set of transformations that likely took place in the years after the slave trade. The Mande greegrees of the eighteenth century contained a wide array of objects, but no contemporary source mentions the inclusion of hair, fingernails, or graveyard dirt, all of which were staples of American conjure bags in later eras. These items, however, were common in similar amulets used in Central Africa, where they were used to summon the power of local spirits known as *minkisi*. Accounting for almost 30 percent of all Africans taken to the Low Country, Central Africa was the second-most prolific source of African labor in the Low Country after Upper Guinea. More linguistically and culturally unified than the Upper Guineans, Central Africans exerted a strong influence on Low Country cultural life.[27]

The most probable scenario for the development of the conjure bag involves the initial transfer of separate and distinct Upper Guinean and Central African practices in the mid-eighteenth century. This period was followed by a time, perhaps in the late eighteenth or early nineteenth century, during which the two traditions mingled with one another, a consequence of sustained contact between the two groups in Low Country quarters. But with the slave trade still active, the influx of ritual experts from both regions would have ensured that the convergence was gradual. Examples from other colonies support the notion that a distinctly Upper Guinean version of the practice continued in the Americas. Absalom, the son of a "Mandingo" marabout who lived on the Danish island of St. Thomas, confessed as part of his conversion to Christianity that he made charms and "got well paid for the most unmeaning and foolish tricks." In Brazil, *bolsas de Mandinga* containing Muslim and Christian inscriptions circulated among Africans of many backgrounds.[28] Eventually, with the closing of the slave trade and resulting decline in the number of specialists from Africa, the two traditions likely merged. Because Mande greegrees depended so heavily on the availability of Muslim marabouts who were literate in Arabic, a group whose numbers fell after 1808 with each passing year, it is reasonable to suppose that Central African practices, which depended on more readily available ingredients like graveyard dirt, eventually overshadowed Mande practices. As well, the inclusion of slips of paper inscribed with biblical verses in some nineteenth-century charms likely emerged as the population of literate Muslims declined.[29]

Societies, or culture circles, dedicated to ushering children into adulthood and training specialists were another hallmark of Upper Guinean culture. Membership and rituals often secret, the societies were organized by sex.

The most famous of these was the Poro Society, along with Sande, its female counterpart, which prevailed in the area stretching from just north of Sierra Leone Bay southward along the Atlantic coast. Secretive culture circles of this sort appear to have been less common in the interior highlands, where most of the *Hare* captives were probably raised. Residents of these areas did, however, observe formal age grades and mark passage from one to another. Mande society was further organized corporately into nobles, commoners, and slaves, alongside special occupational "castes" that included Juula traders, leather workers, blacksmiths, and poet-musicians.[30] Historians have proposed that while it was not possible to replicate the formal political function of these societies under the constraints of New World slavery, Africans nevertheless managed to reestablish their local regulatory function. Black churches of the antebellum period were invested with an authority to govern and discipline members that was both strong and quite regular. One missionary of the 1830s described a plantation world of "societies organized among themselves" and recounted an incident in which a member charged with divulging the "secret of stealing" was punished by being forced to sit on the lowest of three levels of seats, reminiscent of the high-low seats of Poro-Sande. The removal of cadets from regular life to a sacred and often isolated space for formal instruction was another hallmark of Upper Guinean culture circles that became a feature of later Low Country Christianity.[31]

Christianity among Low Country slaves was at an embryonic stage in the 1750s, but there were some formal organizations already that the *Hare* captives might have encountered or participated in. A petition to the South Carolina legislature dating to the year 1800 offers a rare glimpse of institutionalized instruction of adolescents in South Carolina slave quarters. The petition was initiated by a slave owner named Leroy Beuford, who was dismayed that his slave John had been executed for poisoning Beuford's brother. Several slaves who knew John not only testified to his activities as a conjurer but alluded to his formal training as one. According to one witness, John said "that he went to a free School to Learn to Conjure Sixteen years," while a second witness testified that John had only gone to the "free School" for three years. The inherent secrecy means that there is no way to know what the nature or extent of these schools was, but the existence of a formal protocol for training ritual specialists, modeled perhaps along the lines of Poro-Sande, seems more than a mere possibility. The fact that both of the words "Poro" and "Sande" survived into the twentieth century as Gullah names points to the same conclusion.[32]

A final issue, Islam, needs special attention. There can be no doubt that the number of Muslims in South Carolina reached well into the thousands in the decades after 1750. If we make the plausible, perhaps even conservative, assumption that 10 percent of all Upper Guineans entering South Carolina and Georgia were Muslims, that figure would surpass ten thousand.[33] Several documents refer to the Muslim population. Perhaps the most explicit dates to 1823, fifteen years after the close of the legal slave trade. Written in the wake of the Denmark Vesey conspiracy, in which a group of slaves associated with Charleston's African Church plotted to seize control of the city and sail to Haiti, the tract urged slave owners to oversee their bondmen's religious instruction more carefully. "Most of our imported Negroes are Muhammedans," warned the author, "and that they may teach what they know of the Koran to their children, unless Christians take the trouble to instruct them in the religion of the Gospel."[34] In this case the author surely overstated the proportion, likely out of a Vesey-inspired sense of crisis. But other observations suggest that the percentage was far from negligible. Returning from the Gambia in 1797 onboard a slave ship bound for South Carolina, Mungo Park estimated that 25 out of the 130 captives aboard had been free Muslims in Africa (he did not offer an estimate of the number of Muslims present who had been living as slaves), and that most of the twenty-five could write Arabic.[35] Readily identifiable Muslim names, such as Marmadow (Mamadou, the regional version of Mohammed), Bocarrey (Bocari), and Almanser (Al-Mansur), appear in numerous other documents, and it is likely that many of the Old Testament names appearing in estate inventories and other sources, such as Abraham, Jacob, and Sarah, are Anglicized versions of Arabic originals.[36] Charles Ball, who lived in South Carolina in the first decade of the nineteenth century, knew "several" Muslims and recounted the story of the capture and enslavement of one of them in great detail.[37] And the Georgia Sea Islands were home to what seems to have been a particularly vibrant Muslim community in the early nineteenth century, led by Bilali Mohammed and Salih Bilali.[38]

Given its widespread and varied nature in Africa, Islam likely took two forms on the plantations of South Carolina. On the one hand were devout Muslims, some with formal schooling and literacy in Arabic, who were lifelong believers and, as much as was possible under the conditions of slavery, practiced a relatively orthodox form of Islam. Bilali Mohammed and Salih Bilali represent this population. Given the dynamic of the time and place, however, with non-Muslims bearing the brunt of capture and enslavement, not to mention the fact that most of the Upper Guinea population was non-Muslim to begin with, these orthodox practitioners were probably a minority. Indeed, their distinctiveness and aloofness, noted by Michael Gomez, is a likely reflection of their small numbers. On the other hand, a majority of Upper Guinea captives—and perhaps a majority of all Africans entering the colony in the 1760s and 1770s—consisted of non-Muslims who were nonetheless quite familiar with Islam, and who very possibly employed Muslim marabouts as diviners and charm-makers. For non-Muslims from Upper Guinea, Islam was not so much a set of rigid doctrines and prescriptions as a flexible set of practices that might be employed and adopted as long as they were useful, and combined with others as dictated by circumstance. Thus scholars who have argued that Islam, rooted in the Abrahamic Tradition, paved the way for Christianity, are probably correct, in the sense that many non-Muslims would have noted the parallels without feeling any particular need to uphold orthodoxy. At the same time, those scholars who have argued that Islam did not serve as an easy conduit to Christianity and that Muslims in the Americas preserved and even passed on their faith are also correct, at least in reference to those who did consider themselves practicing Muslims.[39]

There is no way to know which or how many of the *Hare* captives were Muslims. There were probably at least a few. Whether the Muslims from the *Hare* continued to practice Islam in South Carolina is even more difficult to say. It is probably safe to assume that the older and more devout Muslims made some attempt to maintain their faith. There are many examples of African Muslims performing the duties of their faith, such as the *shahada* (profession of faith), *salah* (daily prayers), and the observance of Ramadan. It would have come as a comfort to observant Muslims that those pillars of the faith that were difficult or impossible to uphold under slavery, such as the *haj* (pilgrimage to Mecca) and the *zakah* (the giving of alms) were not required of those who could not afford them. But the possibility that some of the *Hare* captives worshipped as a part of a larger community should not be dismissed. It is a matter of record that Muslims in Brazil and the Caribbean formed quite extensive religious associations, so the Muslim community of Bilali Mohammed and Salih Bilali in the Georgia Sea Islands at the turn of the century was probably not unique.[40]

All of the *Hare* captives, whatever their backgrounds, unknowingly participated in the making of Gullah and African American culture at large through their everyday focus on making their way on a new continent, in a new social and economic system, and with a new set of neighbors and peers.

CHAPTER NINE

Remittances

All things considered, Gabriel Manigault thought the sale had gone well. In the context of the larger market, the *Hare* captives were "poor quality," with too many women and too many of them "not young." And Manigault did have to deal with a small postsale hitch: one of the purchasers demanded a rebate after discovering that one of his captives was "wanting a finger." He remedied the problem by granting a small "abatement" in the price. But timing is everything, and the Vernons' risky decision to send captives to the South Carolina market in the early springtime had paid off. The first ship of the year in a hot (or at least warm) market, the *Hare* did better than it might have if it had arrived only a few months later. As Manigault told the Vernons, "I think them exceedingly well sold."[1]

As a part of the commission he earned as factor, it was Manigault's job to find a return cargo to pay for the captives. Over the course of his career, Manigault had seen significant changes in the handling of remittances, as the payments for slaves were called. In the early eighteenth century, factors were intermediaries, responsible for collecting payments from purchasers and forwarding them on to traders, most of whom were in England. The factor loaded the vessel with as much produce and cash as he could assemble and forwarded the balance when payments from the purchasers rolled in. Under this arrangement, slave-ship owners assumed the risk for any bad debts. The system began to change in the boom decade of the 1730s, as British merchants began insisting that Charles Town factors assume responsibility for bad debts incurred by purchasers. And when the Carolina slave trade resumed after 1748, rather than make remittances as credit payments rolled in, factors had taken to making payment all at once, filling the vessel with as much produce as possible and forwarding the remainder in bills of exchange. This method, known as "bills in the bottom," is how Manigault planned to forward the proceeds to the Vernons.[2]

There were things to do, however. The platforms that had been constructed in the hold to house the captives needed to be dismantled. The hold itself needed to be scoured to rid it of the stench of incarceration. Godfrey's account for the weeks following the sale shows expenditures for brooms, tar brushes, and a "scrubin" brush. Short of crew, he spent two shillings and sixpence to hire "a Negro for Labour," probably one of the many Charles Town slaves who "worked out" and paid a weekly amount to his master.[3] The Carolina gold that would constitute a portion of the payment for the *Hare* captives was delivered by slaves. Rice generally arrived in Charles Town on boats skippered by white or black patroons, who carried it to the "bridge," or wharf, of the planter's commission merchant. The merchant's clerk would then record the arrival in a "wharf book," then, perhaps a few days later, weigh the rice and seal it into barrels, recording the number of pounds contained in each sealed barrel in a separate "seal book." The rice then awaited shipment in a warehouse, guarded by slaves. These watchmen were known to warm themselves by firelight, with wayward sparks sending the occasional wharf or two up in flames.[4]

On April 10, the lading of the *Hare* was complete. In the place of fifty-six people were now 129 barrels holding about 600 pounds each, and 25 half barrels (which were easier to fit into the small spaces aboard the *Hare*) of rice of about 300 pounds each, for a total of 75,260 pounds of neat rice, which at 42s.6d. per hundred pounds worked out to £1599.5s.6d. Expenses for rice casks, the loss of 45 pounds of rice in repacking from barrels to half barrels, fees for wharfage and porterage, and Manigault's 5 percent commission totaled £85.12s. Cash advances to Godfrey had come to £240.3s.9d., including Manigault's commission. Rounding out the remittance was £6,125 in bills of exchange (£875 sterling), also subject to a 5 percent commission. The return cargo of rice, therefore, accounted for about one-fifth of the value of the *Hare* captives. This should not be too surprising. Rice was far bulkier than captives, with several shiploads of rice necessary to equal the value of one shipload of commodified human beings. This was in fact a common feature of the slave trade, and it helped sustain an entire branch of trade dedicated to carrying plantation produce to market. Even so, the rice and bills did not quite square all accounts. On board the *Hare* were still seven captives, the children Godfrey and Manigault judged too young to bother selling in Charles Town. The Vernons had told Godfrey that he might, at his discretion, bring a few young captives back to Rhode Island, so their odyssey was still not over.

On the day of the sale, the crew of the *Hare* was down to six, including Godfrey. William Burling then left the vessel on March 24. To replace him,

Godfrey hired three more men, Robert and William Harvey, apparently brothers, and John Bloodworth, a cook. There was no shortage of seamen in Charles Town. Slavers frequently discharged crew after delivering captives. Often done against the wishes of the sailors and in violation of prior contracts, discharging crew allowed masters to save on wages for the final leg of the voyage, when there were no captives to oversee. The practice caused quite a bit of distress for the town's better sort, resulting in streets and alleyways crawling (sometimes literally) with tars in various gradations of health, with "squalid countenances, and ulcerated limbs." One seaman recalled two of his comrades leaving the vessel hoping to sign on to a man-of-war, only to die on the streets of Charles Town. Those with money found lodgings with people like Daniel Matheny, who was indicted in 1756 for keeping a "disorderly house for soldiers, sailors, &c.," or at the "old rotton Punch Houses," cited by the rector of St. Phillip's Church as incubators of yellow fever. Those with still more cash might have patronized one of the doxies who worked the alleyways. Many of these prostitutes were enslaved, although there is no evidence of the institutionalized pimping that prevailed at Barbados. Some sailors drifted into crime, such as the four who robbed Samuel Palmarin at knifepoint two miles outside of Charles Town. Colonial officials tried to address these issues by requiring all shipmasters to submit a crew list and pay for any sailor left behind, but the measure failed.[5]

Godfrey probably spent much of his time preparing the vessel, finding crew, and attending to the imperial and colonial bureaucracy. But he surely had time for more. Charles Town offered better accommodations to shipmasters than it did to common seamen, with merchants sometimes inviting them to their houses. Pelatiah Webster, who visited in 1765, encountered a group of slave-ship masters in the library of one of Charles Town's better sort. He found the "Guinea captains" to be a "rough set of people, but somewhat carressd by the merchts on acco[unt] of the g[rea]t profits of their commissions." Whether Godfrey enjoyed that sort of relationship with Manigault is not recorded, but it seems improbable. As accounts were being reckoned, the merchant and the shipmaster had a falling out. The issue was the "coast commission" of 5 percent on the purchase of the captives in Africa that Rhode Island slave captains were accustomed to receiving. Normally, the commission merchant who handled the sale paid half. It cut into profits, to be sure, but merchants in the Caribbean found it advisable to pay in order to keep the consignments coming. Godfrey clearly expected it—most of the instructions given to Rhode Island slavers specified as much in writing— but Manigault refused to pay. The dispute over Godfrey's coast commission would go on for over a year. Henry Laurens even weighed in on Godfrey's behalf, but Manigault never bent, and the Vernons never offered to cover it either. If Godfrey ever did dine at Manigault's, it was probably not a pleasant evening.[6]

On April 5, Manigault wrote the Vernons to say the *Hare* would sail within the next four days. His prediction proved overly optimistic. Heavy spring winds still lashed the port, and the *Hare*, along with several other vessels, remained "wind-bound" for over a week. The *Hare* finally left Rebellion Road on April 13, probably soon after high tide at 8:24 A.M. The fact that several other vessels remained windbound suggests that the foul weather continued for a good portion of the trip up the coast.[7]

The precise date of the *Hare*'s return to Newport is unknown. The only announcement appeared in the *South Carolina Gazette* on May 15, so the *Hare* probably arrived at Malbone's Wharf at the very end of April after less than two weeks at sea.[8] Manigault had notified the Vernons of Godfrey's impending departure, so they would have been expecting him. In all likelihood the reunion was a cordial one. After all, Godfrey had turned a profit. The Vernons had laid out approximately £1,090 sterling for the voyage, including rum, wages, and the cost of the vessel. With the *Hare* captives selling in South Carolina for £9,251.15s.6d. (after deducting for the cash discounts offered by Manigault), and if we assume Godfrey took the seven young captives back to Rhode Island and sold them for £21 sterling each, the Vernons received a total of £1,281 sterling, which works out to a return of about 17.5 percent on their investment. Given the incomplete nature of the documentary record, this figure is certainly high, perhaps by a few percentage points. Even so, in a business for which the average rate of return was about 10 percent, the voyage had unquestionably met expectations. Pleased at the outcome, the Vernons immediately began planning a reprise.[9]

IN THE YEARS after the *Hare*'s voyage, the slave trade engulfed Sierra Leone and the rest of the Upper Guinea coast. During the period prior to the *Hare*'s voyage, from 1726 to 1750, Europeans carried off an average of 665 captives per year from Sierra Leone. In the quarter century after 1750, that number increased by a factor of five, to 3,362 people per year. These figures almost certainly understate the true total, since many of those taken from the Windward Coast likely came from ports close to Sierra Leone. The region was not unique—the slave trade was on the rise all along the African coast. But Sierra Leone, along with Senegambia and the Windward Coast, the other two regions of Upper Guinea, rose from the least prolific regional supplier of plantation slave labor to the second-largest supplier, behind only West Central Africa. Although it would recede in importance after 1800, Upper Guinea remained a significant source of captive labor until the end of the slave trade in the mid-nineteenth century.[10]

Two factors accounted for the rise. The first was the ever-increasing demand for labor in the Americas. Historians know that demand (as opposed to an increase in the availability of captives) drove the expansion, because prices on the African coast more than doubled between 1760 and 1775, and were six to seven times higher at the conclusion of the legal trade in 1807.[11] African merchants and states responded to the demand by supplying more captives. The numbers of captives eventually reached unsustainable heights, inflicting lasting demographic, social, and economic damage across much of the continent.[12] In Upper Guinea, the most common mechanism for enslavement was the continuing series of Muslim holy wars. The jihad in the Futa Jallon, which had likely been the catalyst for the enslavement of most of the *Hare* captives, was responsible for the major surge in exports in the 1760s and 1770s; the Futa Jallon sent an ever-growing number of coffles to traders on the Gambia, the Isles de Los, and the Scarcies and in Sierra Leone. The triumph of Ibrahima Sori over his most potent enemy in 1776 brought some relief from the constant strife in the Futa Jallon itself, but the newly stable state continued its slave raids, with Islam providing a justification. A controversy over succession following the death of Sori in 1791 weakened Futa Jallon, but slave raiding and the state monopoly on the trade continued into the new century. A second jihad in the Senegambia region of Futa Toro, which began in 1776 and ran for several decades, had much the same effect.[13]

Following the voyage of the *Hare*, the Vernons continued to profit from the demand for African labor in the New World colonies. As one of their earlier slave-trading ventures, the *Hare*'s 1754–55 voyage demonstrated that the brothers had what it took to turn a profit in the slave trade, and that Sierra Leone could become a viable alternative to the Gold Coast as a source for captives. Godfrey had initiated commercial contacts that, if cultivated, would ease future ventures. Now the brothers could distribute risk by sending out two or more vessels to different parts of the coast. Poor trading conditions at one location might be offset by better conditions at the other. That is essentially what the Vernons did, dispatching Godfrey and the *Hare* on a repeat voyage from Sierra Leone to South Carolina in November 1755, followed a few months later by the sloop *Titt Bitt*, bound for the Gold Coast.[14]

The chance of repeating the success of the previous year was dimmed by the outbreak of war between Britain and France, which had already been brewing shortly before the *Hare*'s first voyage. A few days before the *Hare* had sailed, Lieutenant-Colonel George Washington was forced to abandon Fort Necessity, the base he had constructed to oust the French from the forks of the Ohio. While the *Hare* was at sea, tensions had only increased. In February 1755, while the *Hare* was at Barbados, the London-based Company of Merchants Trading to Africa instructed the commanders of their trading forts to be "in the best posture of defence you possibly can, in order to prevent the bad consequence of a surprise," noting that the "attempts of the French at the back of our Settlements in North America" would probably result in war. That same month the Rhode Island General Assembly voted to raise a force of three hundred men to be placed at the disposal of the king in the event of war with France. And in March 1755, while the *Hare* was quarantined at Sullivan's Island, the *South Carolina Gazette* notified readers that General Edward Braddock had arrived in Virginia to oust the French from the Ohio country. The march, of course, would prove disastrous for him and the British. For North Americans, the declaration of war that came on May 18, 1756, was a formality; they had already been fighting for two years.[15]

Godfrey set sail again for Sierra Leone in November 1755, after a turnaround time of seven months. The second voyage of the *Hare*, lasting from 1755 to 1756, is not as well documented as the first, but the basic contours are clear. The *Hare* reached Africa in early March. Exactly where and from whom Godfrey purchased his captives is unrecorded, but he appears to have retraced his earlier steps as much as possible. Post-voyage litigation would reveal that he once again patronized George Dowdall at the Isles de Los, which suggests that he traded once more to the north of Sierra Leone Bay between the Scarcies and the Dembia. It is more likely that Godfrey purchased captives at Bance Island on this voyage than on the first. The proprietors sold no captives to private traders in 1755, but sold 276 in 1756. We know that Godfrey called at Bance Island because Sherbro-area trader Nicholas Owen was at the fort when he arrived on March 8, 1756, with word of the British expedition to Crown Point, New York.[16]

The *Hare* set sail for South Carolina in April after a very short time of one month on the African coast, during which Godfrey managed to purchase eighty captives and, therefore, had no reason to linger. However, as would become clear later, the captives he bought were in very bad shape. Whether they were in poor health when Godfrey purchased them or whether their condition was a result of the voyage is unknown. It may be that Godfrey accepted unhealthy captives so that he could sail as soon as possible. With a declaration of war all but inevitable, he may have feared capture by French naval vessels or privateers. His instructions this time sent him straight from Africa to South Carolina, bypassing Barbados, on the assumption that the Caribbean would see more French patrols. The fears proved well placed: around the time Godfrey sailed from Africa, French warships began searching the African coast and the West Indies, netting at least fifteen British slave ships, including several Newport vessels, but the *Hare* was not among them.[17]

The captives on the second voyage spent sixty-nine days at sea, more than twice as long as did the captives the previous winter. And unlike the first voyage, the 1755–56 passage was unbroken by a stop in Barbados. It is hardly surprising that the sixty-three captives who arrived in Charles Town in June 1756 were, in the words of consignee Henry Laurens, "the most shocking Cargo we ever beheld." Initially hopeful that the captives would fetch a high price, Laurens had advertised them as "Likely and Healthy slaves" and expected a good crowd of buyers. And indeed the mob of potential buyers outnumbered the captives by three to one, with many having traveled eighty or ninety miles for the sale. But as word leaked out that the captives were nothing but "refuse slaves," the crowd grew restless. Only twenty-three sold on the first day. Laurens described the remaining captives as "a most scabby Flock," suffering from yaws and eye infections, with three "very puny" children and six to eight suffering from what he considered "the worst infirmity of all": old age. It took Laurens a full two weeks to dispose of all of them, the final thirteen at public vendue.[18]

Among this second set of *Hare* captives were six children, four boys and two girls between six and ten years old, purchased by Elias Ball, the brother of John Coming Ball, Henry Laurens's partner. Unlike any of the purchasers from the previous year's voyage, Elias Ball actually wrote down the names he gave the captives. Ball's decision to record the names of his new captives has allowed historians to document the lives of several slaves from their purchase along the African coast to their lives in South Carolina. One, whom Ball named "Mandingo Peter," offers support for the notion that most of the Upper Guinean captives entering the colony were Mande speakers. Peter fathered children with a woman named Monemia and eventually moved from the Balls' Comingtee Plantation to Kensington Plantation. He died sometime before 1816. Sancho was another captive from the *Hare*'s second voyage. He worked as a field hand, fathered children with a woman named Affie, and fled the plantation during the American Revolution, only to be returned. He lived to see his wife and children sold away from him and died in 1833, at approximately eighty-six years old. The girl Ball called Priscilla

proved to be the most remarkable of the 1755–56 *Hare* captives. She gave
birth to ten children, most of whom survived to have children of their own.
Edward Ball, historian and descendant of the same Ball family that owned
Comingtee, managed to document Priscilla's descendants down to the present. To this day Priscilla's family tree is probably the best-documented African American lineage in the United States.[19]

These matters aside, the *Hare*'s second voyage had been a money loser
for the Vernons. Laurens anticipated that the brothers would blame Godfrey
and him for the poor sale (which they apparently did), so he preemptively
argued that Godfrey had purchased the best captives he could find and that
the sale would have gone better with a healthier cargo. In addition to suspecting that Godfrey's and Laurens's incompetence had killed the second
voyage's profits, the Vernons also seem to have soured on Sierra Leone as
a source of captives. Henceforth, for most of their slave-trading career, they
would favor the Gold Coast. Sixteen years would pass before the Vernons
would be involved with another Sierra Leone voyage, and over the course
of fifty years and forty-five slaving voyages, they would dispatch only three
more vessels there.[20]

A dispute over some ivory and beeswax widened the rift between Godfrey and the Vernons. Godfrey claimed that he purchased the items on his
own account at the Isles de Los, while the Vernons contended they were part
of the *Hare*'s cargo and therefore belonged to them. As the *Hare* was being
unloaded in Newport, the Vernons ordered that a tusk be placed in their
warehouse and later told the mate to retrieve the cake of wax. When Godfrey
sent a slave to retrieve the items, he was rebuffed. Godfrey sued the Vernons
and won, but the appeal dragged on for years and the case was eventually
arbitrated. The final outcome is unknown.[21]

The American Revolution disrupted the Vernons' activities, including slave
trading. Taking the Whig side, they, along with many others, were forced to
evacuate Newport during the British occupation of 1776–79, losing a significant portion of their fortune. William Vernon served on the Eastern Navy
Board, and when the war was over, the two brothers looked to resurrect their
trading career in Newport, which proved difficult. The occupation and ensu-
ing flight of so many merchants, first Whig, then Tory, weakened the town's
business community. Providence, once Rhode Island's second city, now
dominated. The brothers found reentry into the slave trade difficult. Prices
along the familiar Gold Coast were much higher than before, with traders demanding gold instead of rum. Political independence left American
merchants legally barred from their customary markets in the British

Caribbean (not that they had much regard for the law). In 1785, a Vernon ship carried captives to South Carolina, the first since the *Hare*'s second voyage in 1756. In 1793, William Vernon partnered with Boston merchants to outfit a "voyage of speculation" to Mozambique. The first voyage failed, but subsequent voyages were profitable. Four more would follow. They sold their captives in disparate markets: Trinidad, Cuba, St. Eustatius, and the French Indian Ocean colony of Mauritius. Samuel Vernon died in 1792, and William in 1806. The last Vernon-backed vessel delivered captives to South Carolina in 1807, the final year of the legal slave trade in the United States. Over a half century of slave trading, the Vernons were involved, either as principal organizers or as investors, in the removal of over 5,600 Africans.[22]

Gabriel Manigault lived for twenty-seven more years after handling the sale of the *Hare* captives. Despite telling the Vernons that he was retiring to his plantation, he remained in trade for more than ten years. Manigault family lore long held that Gabriel never blotted the family escutcheon by trading in slaves. The voyage of the *Hare* obviously demonstrates otherwise, as do customs records that show him paying duties on captives imported from the Caribbean. Still, the *Hare* is his only known commission on slaves imported directly from Africa, and he turned down the Vernons' request that he handle the *Hare* on its second voyage. In his later years he supported Charles Town's merchant community in its battles with the king's customs collectors, and when independence came, he loaned $220,000 to the new state of South Carolina. For over a century after his death in 1781, the Manigault family would rank among the wealthiest in the region.[23]

The *Hare* purchasers lived out lives as diverse as their origins. Though there was some shifting among them, the majority remained in South Carolina. Most survived for at least ten years after the *Hare* arrived, their deaths fairly evenly distributed throughout each decade from the 1760s to 1800s. The last surviving purchaser, Lachlan McIntosh, died in 1806, having removed (for the second time) to Georgia shortly after the sale. He would eventually become a supporter of Georgia's independence movement and a leader of one of its political factions, which eventually led him to slay a rival patriot leader in a duel. Revolutionary chaos would later cost him most of his wealth, including his plantation.[24]

The later life of the single largest purchaser, Henry Laurens, took many unexpected turns. The most prolific seller of African captives in all of North America, Laurens, perhaps like Manigault, expressed distaste for the slave trade. Unlike Manigault, however, for Laurens the Guinea trade was directly responsible for a significant share of his fortune. After purchasing Mepkin

Plantation in 1762, he withdrew from the factorage business. Directing his considerable talents toward planting, he built a far-flung and integrated empire in South Carolina, Georgia, and Florida. After experiencing frustration with Crown customs officials, Laurens became increasingly involved in the Whig opposition to ministerial policy. He eventually, and rather reluctantly, supported independence and presided for a time over the Continental Congress. His son John, born only seven months after his father purchased nine captives from the *Hare*, became a member of George Washington's staff. In 1778, John proposed arming and freeing American slaves to fight against the British, arguing that Southerners "cannot contend with a good Grace, for Liberty, until we shall have enfranchised our Slaves." The plan died in the South Carolina legislature, and John Laurens died soon afterward in a minor skirmish near Beaufort. It is entirely possible that John Laurens knew some of the *Hare* captives. Could any of them have inspired his belief in what he called the "rights of mankind"? We can only wonder.[25]

During the American Revolution, Laurens—who as a slave factor had imprisoned thousands of Africans in his Charles Town warehouse yard—was made a captive himself. Appointed emissary to the Netherlands, Laurens's ship was seized by the Royal Navy en route to Amsterdam, and Laurens was locked up in the Tower of London. While there, erstwhile business correspondent Richard Oswald, one of the proprietors of Bance Island, worked for his parole—one slaver laboring to free another from captivity. Laurens had done business with Oswald on many occasions, acting as his factor on several shipments of captives from his installation at Sierra Leone and as his correspondent in his effort to establish a plantation colony in British Florida. Amid suspicion that the old slave trader was "too much the prisoner's friend," Laurens was eventually paroled, with Oswald and his successor as Bance Island proprietor, Alexander Anderson, respectively posting bonds of two thousand and four thousand pounds as bail. Exchanged for Lord Cornwallis after his defeat at Yorktown, Laurens was named one of the American peace commissioners at Paris. Among other things, Laurens and Oswald appear to be responsible for an article in the treaty prohibiting evacuating British soldiers from "carrying away any Negroes." There is, it would appear, honor among thieves.[26]

Caleb Godfrey endured a miserable few years in Newport battling the Vernons in court before finally leaving town. Cheated out of his coast commission by Gabriel Manigault, he failed to make enough money from his two voyages aboard the *Hare* to retire from the sea. In 1758, he was forced to mortgage his property but was able to pay it off two years later. He apparently accomplished this by skippering West India vessels. He appears in a 1761 list of "Captains of Vessels in Newport," though because his son by the same name became a shipmaster, it is impossible to know for certain which specific voyages were his. In 1762, he took out a strange advertisement in the *Newport Mercury*. With characteristic touchiness, the notice alluded to his having "high differences with several of the principal Traders of this Town" (perhaps a reference to his ongoing legal battle with the Vernons) and asked "those Persons who has wronged me in my Reputation to desist for the future." He then went on to advertise sugar, coffee, and tea for sale. He followed up a few weeks later by announcing that he would be moving to New York or Philadelphia and asking his debtors to settle all outstanding obligations, before advertising the same commodities for sale, along with butter and "genteel cut WIGS." And indeed, he seems to have made good on his word. In 1763, a Philadelphia newspaper carried an offer of forty shillings' reward for the return of a lost watch with a built-in compass to "Capt. Godfrey" of Chestnut Street.[27]

Godfrey's sojourn in Philadelphia appears to have been a short one. In 1765, a Captain Godfrey skippered another Rhode Island sloop in the Honduran logwood trade. While the vessel was in Central America, a maroon colony consisting of seventy fugitive slaves began attacking logwood traders and vessels venturing up the region's rivers, killing at least seven sailors and capturing at least eleven more. The Baymen, as the traders were called, were forced to evacuate parts of the colony. It was not recorded whether Godfrey was directly involved in any of the violence. In 1766, a Caleb Godfrey was listed as captain of the sloop *Sally*, taking on cargo at Taylor's Wharf in Newport. It is impossible to know for certain whether these were references to Caleb Godfrey the elder or younger. If they did refer to Caleb senior, he would have been about sixty years old. By that time he was ailing, as a 1765 payment of one pound, eighteen shillings, and sixpence to Dr. William Hunter of Newport for visits and emetics attests. The Godfrey name appears in the maritime record into the mid-1770s, for example, in a customs entry recording Godfrey as arriving from Hispaniola in 1775 as master of the *Hope*, but this almost certainly refers to his son. For reasons unknown, between 1772 and 1775 his name dropped from the list of Newport taxpayers. He may have lost his property or he may have moved, although that would seem unlikely. Caleb Godfrey died in 1782 at the age of seventy-eight.[28]

John Arnold Hammond, the mate, spent the rest of his life in Newport's maritime trade. A few years after accompanying Godfrey to Sierra Leone, Hammond skippered the sloop *Union* on a voyage to Edenton, North

Carolina. After his signal to take on a pilot was ignored, a sudden gale buffeted the *Union* for four days, eventually tossing the sloop ashore at Cape Hatteras, to be pounded to pieces in the surf. Hammond survived to sail aboard a privateer during the Seven Years' War, after which he skippered vessels in the Caribbean and coastwise trades.[29] Richard Cole, second mate, cooper, and Godfrey's perpetual tormentor, seems to have followed a similar path, with numerous records showing him employed in the coastwise trade. In 1756, a sloop on which he was sailing as mate lost a cargo of wheat and flour in a gale off Maryland, but the incident did not hamper his maritime career. Between 1756 and 1759 he captained at least two different vessels on numerous runs, after which he vanished from the maritime record. He may have died or relocated, or simply tired of the sea: in 1761 a Richard Cole served in the French and Indian War. After that, all traces of him disappear.[30]

Much less is known about the ordinary seamen. William White, William Jones, William Ball, Robert and William Harvey, and John Bloodworth are impossible to distinguish from contemporaries bearing the same names. They could have wound up virtually anywhere in the Atlantic World. John Battey, a native Rhode Islander and one of only two ordinary seamen to make the entire voyage, seems to have continued his maritime career into the 1760s. Notices for held mail appeared in newspapers in Newport and New London, Connecticut, suggestive of an itinerant life. Little is known beyond that, but with so many Batteys in the area, including shipmasters, it seems probable that he followed that line in some capacity.[31] William Moroney, who signed on at Barbados, traveled a similar path, though based in Philadelphia. Unlike Battey, he appears to have advanced to shipmaster by the mid-1760s, working in the West Indies trade.[32] Francis Welch, who signed on at Sierra Leone and left the *Hare* at Barbados, had mail held in New York one year later, once more indicative of a life spent at sea.[33]

As for the vessel itself, it appears that after the 1755–56 voyage the Vernons decided to redeploy the "Sloop Hair" in the Honduran logwood trade under the command of a new captain. The outcome of that voyage is unknown, but two years later the *Hare* received a commission from Rhode Island governor Stephen Hopkins to exchange French prisoners of war at Hispaniola for English prisoners. Twelve leagues north of Hispaniola, the New York privateer *Hawk* seized the *Hare* and carried it to an Admiralty Court in Jamaica. The reason for the seizure is unknown, but since Rhode Islanders often used prisoner exchange as a cover for trading with the enemy, that was quite possibly the cause. The privateer's agents at Jamaica thought it "imprudent" to proceed against the *Hare*, so captain, crew, and vessel were released. The *Hare* immediately made for Port au Prince, where, finding there were no prisoners, it took on a cargo of sugar and molasses. Five days later, a French privateer seized the *Hare*, carried it to Cuba, and deposited the crew onshore, miles from any settlement. The crew members made their way to Havana and eventually took passage to Rhode Island, arriving on May 1, 1759. After that date, the *Hare* disappears from the historical record.[34]

Historical circumstance forces us to address the fate of the *Hare* captives not as individuals, but collectively. For most, we can safely assume that their lives were comparatively short and filled with toil. The death or insolvency of a planter could bring great disruption to the slave quarters, resulting in sales and separations. Overseers could inject violence and misery into their lives, suddenly and capriciously. Still, the power of the master was not total. Slaves had resources, and they deployed them in a never-ending campaign of strategic advance and tactical retreat. The net result of their efforts was the opening of scattered spaces for individual action and community autonomy. As we have seen, the *Hare* captives likely filled these spaces with cultural practices rooted in the Mande world they had been forced to leave behind. And they were surely not alone, as thousands of men, women, and children streamed onto the plantations of the Low Country, speaking Mande languages in their everyday lives.

That world was disrupted in 1778, when, in the midst of a rebellion led by the planter elite, the king's troops invaded the Low Country. Starting in Georgia and moving up through the Carolinas to Virginia, British forces shattered the status quo on Low Country plantations. Rebelling in the name of liberty, the revolutionary movement's leaders (who included Gabriel Manigault and *Hare* captive purchasers Henry Laurens and Lachlan McIntosh) worked hard to limit the application of that principle to their bondmen: liberty belonged to whites only. Slaves, however, possessed a clearer sense of the moment's potential. When it became apparent that a peaceful emancipation would not be theirs (if indeed they ever harbored such fantasies), they took full advantage of the chaos sown by the invasion, fleeing to British lines and fighting their former masters when they had to. When the British evacuated Charles Town almost four years later, as many as one-quarter of all Low Country slaves had either perished or left forever.[35]

Many of the *Hare* captives did not live to see this moment. Twenty-four years had passed between their arrival and the coming of the king's troops (who landed first in Georgia and did not succeed in taking Charles Town for two more years). Those who had been adults in 1755 would now have been well into what we consider middle age, but for eighteenth-century slaves, with bodies broken by decades of hard labor, old age is probably a more accurate description. Physical infirmities would have made resistance and self-liberation difficult, though some surely tried. The five who had arrived as children would have had to beat the odds to survive into adulthood. Now in their thirties, they would have been in a position to flee, though doing so often meant leaving kin and friends behind.

There is a very slight chance that one or more of the *Hare* captives returned to Sierra Leone. When the British evacuated Charleston (as it was now called), they carried an unknown number of slaves with them. Stopping first at New York, they were eventually taken to Nova Scotia, where they, along with others from Virginia and other parts of America, established a settlement of over three thousand. Nova Scotia's climate, both natural and social, proved inhospitable, so in 1792 they removed to the new British colony of Sierra Leone, founded five years earlier as a refuge for England's "Black Poor." The names of these voyagers were entered into a "Book of Negroes," copies of which exist today in the National Archives of the United Kingdom and the United States. Most of the "Nova Scotians" provided the names of their former masters, but none of the *Hare* purchasers are among them. It is of course possible that a *Hare* captive who changed masters after 1755 had his or her name entered into the record, but—once again—we do not know their names.

In September 1754, as Godfrey was purchasing captives in the Northern Rivers, the annual meeting of the Society of Friends in Philadelphia, inspired by the publication earlier in the year of a small pamphlet titled *Some Considerations on the Keeping of Negroes*, approved an "Epistle of Caution and Advice" condemning slave keeping and, by implication, slave trading. The time had come, the Quakers declared, to "earnestly exhort all to avoid, in any manner encouraging that Practice of making Slaves of our Fellow Creatures." The event would prove to be the beginning of a decades-long, multinational, multiracial movement against slavery and the slave trade. Criticism of slavery had swirled through Quaker discourse for decades before Godfrey set sail, but no movement to end the trade or the institution had ever resulted until this moment. What began as an intradenominational effort to persuade Friends to renounce slaveholding merged with Enlightenment ideas, giving rise to a sustained effort to destroy an institution that had existed for millennia.[36]

The author of the tract that so moved the 1754 meeting was a tailor from New Jersey named John Woolman. Several years earlier, while working for a shopkeeper, he had been called upon to make out a bill of sale for a woman who belonged to his employer. Taken by surprise, Woolman did as he was told, but not before informing the buyer, a fellow Quaker, that he considered it to be inconsistent with the tenets of Christianity. Later, when another Friend asked Woolman to write out a conveyance for a slave, he demurred. The experience shook him deeply, and he began traveling about the colonies to persuade his coreligionists to end their involvement with slavery. In 1747, his travels took him to Newport, where he gained little headway. With slave trading and slaveholding Friends like Abraham Redwood and Thomas Richardson setting the tone, Newport had long proven resistant to antislavery appeals. The ground began to shift with the coming of the French and Indian War. With the peace testimony as one of their defining beliefs, the Friends found the call to arms, even the drive to provision armies, extremely troubling. Ultimately, the Quakers' turmoil and soul-searching provided an opening for Woolman and his antislavery message. In 1758, the Philadelphia Yearly Meeting approved a resolution calling for the disciplining of any Friend who bought, sold, or kept slaves, though it fell short of actually calling for disownment.[37]

In 1760, five years after the *Hare* returned from its first voyage, Woolman decided to try again. After a rough thirty-mile crossing in an open boat from Long Island to New London, Connecticut, he worked his way across southern New England, arranging as always to "conference with [slaveholders] in private concerning their slaves." Arriving in Newport, he immediately arranged for further meetings, but this town was clearly different from the others. "The great number of slaves in these parts, and the continuance of that trade from thence to Guinea," he wrote, "made a deep impression on me." Overcome at the colossal task facing him, he prayed for help in his labors. After touring the Boston area, he returned to Newport just as a slave-trading Friend was about to auction off "a large number" of Africans, a sight that literally sickened him.[38] Employing his considerable gifts of persuasion, he convinced the Newport Friends to adopt a new query forbidding the buying or selling of slaves and requiring good treatment of those already there. The Yearly Meeting would not enjoin members from owning slaves until 1770, and evasion was common, but it did represent the first stirrings of an antislavery movement. The slave trade remained legal in Rhode Island until 1787, though traders would violate the law for at least two more decades. A 1784 gradual emancipation law put slavery itself on the road to extinction, but people continued to live in slavery and other forms of unfreedom into the early nineteenth century. Not that it mattered to the *Hare* captives, however, whose fates had long been sealed.

Ethnonyms, Linguistic Terms, and Geographic Place Names

Scholars generally agree that the names for the languages and peoples of Africa are in many ways a relic of a colonial past in which Europeans imagined Africans as belonging to discrete "tribes," each with its own distinct language or dialect. In reality, many African languages and dialects, especially those that are closely related, form a continuum that defies simple categorization. A similar point can be made regarding the concept of discrete "ethnicities." In much of Africa, a person's identity hinges on multiple factors, including locality, religion, age grade, gender, and other categories. The question of identity is even more problematic for the time period covered here. That said, the list below provides a quick reference to some of the ethnonyms, linguistic terms, and place names used in the text. Many of them have variant spellings, depending on whether the place or group in question has a history of British, French, or Portuguese rule. Some, especially the Mande words, can be spelled in the N'Ko alphabet. For this text I have adopted the spellings as rendered in Heine and Nurse, eds., *African Languages*; Dalby, "Mel Languages in the Polyglotta Africana"; Vydrine, "Who Speaks 'Mandekan'?"; and *Ethnologue*, the website maintained by SIL International at https://www.ethnologue.com/.

TABLE A.I: Ethnonyms, Linguonyms, and Toponyms Used in the Text

Term	Variations	Notes
Almami	Almamy	Title of the ruler of the Futa Jallon state
Balanta		Ethnonym and Atlantic language spoken in Guinea-Bissau
Bamana	Bambara, Bamanankan	Mande language spoken in Mali, closely related to the other languages of the Manding subdivision
Bijago	Bijogo, Bidyogo	Ethnonym and Atlantic language spoken in Guinea-Bissau
Bullom		Ethnonym and Atlantic language historically spoken near Sierra Leone Bay and Sherbro, close to and largely subsumed by Temne
Diola	Jola	Atlantic language spoken in Senegambia and Guinea-Bissau (not to be confused with Juula)
Fulfulde	Fula, Pholey, Fulbe, Fulani, Peul	Atlantic language spoken by Fula people
Fula	Pholey, Fulbe, Fulani, Peul, Pullo	Ethnonym for a people spread over a wide area of Upper Guinea
Futa Jallon	Jallonkadu, Fuuta Jallon, Futa Djallon, Fuuta Jaloo	Region in the Guinea highlands; also the name of an Islamic state
Gola		Atlantic language spoken in southern Sierra Leone and Liberia
Juula	Djula, Joola	Mande language and term for members of long-distance trading networks. It eventually acquired quasi-ethnic status. The Jakhanke are a specific clan of Juula operating in Upper Guinea. Not to be confused with Diola or Jola.
Karamoko		Muslim scholar and leader in Upper Guinea
Kissi	Kishee, Gizi, Kisi	Ethnonym and Atlantic language spoken in Sierra Leone and Guinea
Kissy	Kissi	A river in the Northern Rivers region. Susu and Baga are the languages spoken there, not Kissi.
Koranko	Kuranko	Ethnonym and Mande language spoken in northern Sierra Leone
Labe		City and province of the Futa Jallon state
Landuma	Landoma, Tiapi, Cocoli	Ethnonym and Atlantic language spoken in Guinea and Guinea-Bissau

Term	Variations	Notes
Limba		Ethnonym and Atlantic language spoken in northern Sierra Leone
Mande	Mandekan	Division of the Niger-Congo language phylum. Mande languages are spoken throughout much of the Upper Guinea hinterland.
Manding		Subdivision of the western Mande languages that includes Mandinka, Maninka, Bamana, and Juula
Mandinka	Mandingo	Ethnonym and Mande language spoken in Senegal, Gambia, and Guinea-Bissau, closely related to the other languages of the Manding subdivision
Maninka	Malinke	Ethnonym and Mande language spoken in Senegal and Gambia, closely related to the other languages of the Manding subdivision
Mane		Group of Mande speakers that invaded coastal Sierra Leone in the 16th century
Marabout		Muslim teacher in Upper Guinea
Mende		Ethnonym and Mande language spoken in southeastern Sierra Leone
Nalu		Ethnonym and Atlantic language spoken in Guinea and Guinea-Bissau
Northern Rivers	Rivers of Guinea	Coastal region between Senegambia and Sierra Leone that features numerous streams flowing westward into the Atlantic
Runde		Slave villages in the Futa Jallon
Segu	Segou	Non-Muslim Bamana state on the upper Senegal River that was deeply involved in the transatlantic slave trade
Sherbro	Shebro	Ethnonym, the name of a region, and an Atlantic language spoken in southern Sierra Leone
Sulima	Soolima	Yalunka region and onetime polity located between modern Sierra Leone and Guinea, not to be confused with location of the same name near the Gallinas estuary
Susu	Soso, Soosoo	Ethnonym and Mande language spoken in northern Sierra Leone and Guinea, closely related to Yalunka

Term	Variations	Notes
Temne	Timmany	Ethnonym and language of the Atlantic division of the Niger-Congo phylum. It is spoken in and around Sierra Leone Bay.
Timbo		Capital city of the Futa Jallon
Vai		Ethnonym and Mande language spoken in southern Sierra Leone
Windward Coast		Geographical designation for the area between Senegambia and the Gold Coast, which included Sierra Leone. It also referred to the area south of Sierra Leone including Liberia and Ivory Coast
Wolof		Ethnonym and Atlantic language spoken in Senegambia
Yalunka	Jallonké, Dialonké, Jalunga	Ethnonym and Mande language spoken in northern Sierra Leone and Guinea, closely related to Susu

Reconstructing the Route of the *Hare*

Because no logbook for the *Hare* survives, there is some question regarding the route it took, especially after it left Sierra Leone for Barbados. There are two sources of uncertainty, though in both cases the discrepancies are easily explained, making it very probable that the route outlined in the text was the correct one. The first source of uncertainty is a series of paper slips in the Vernon Papers that appear to show the *Hare* purchasing provisions down the African coast as far as the Bight of Benin, about 1,400 miles from Sierra Leone by ship.[1] In this case it is fairly easy to dismiss the possibility that the *Hare* traveled this route in 1754–55, since Godfrey's letters clearly establish that he sailed from the Isles de Los around January 11, 1755, and arrived in Barbados only eighteen days later on January 29, 1755. It was an exceptionally fast crossing, one that precludes the possibility of a multistop detour down the African coast. These slips therefore almost certainly date to the 1755–56 voyage or a different voyage.

The second source in question regarding the *Hare*'s route comes from the sale advertisement placed by William Banbury in the *South Carolina Gazette* on March 6 and March 13, 1755, which claims that the captives came from the "Windward Coast" and the "Gold Coast." As we have seen, "Windward Coast" was a term that encompassed Sierra Leone. The claim that the *Hare* visited the Gold Coast can be easily dismissed on the same grounds as the slips of paper mentioned above: it was simply impossible to sail from Sierra Leone to Barbados in eighteen days by way of the Gold Coast. It is also not plausible that the *Hare* could have traveled to the Gold Coast and back to Sierra Leone before sailing for Barbados. Contrary winds made this a difficult, though not impossible trip. Slave ships almost never traveled in that direction, and the time frame for the entire voyage once again would have made it impossible. As discussed in the text, the simplest explanation for the Gold Coast claim in the advertisement is that Manigault and Banbury either made a mistake or misrepresented the origin of the captives so that they could charge a higher price.

A final issue worth mentioning involves the *Hare*'s stop at Cape Verde. If the conclusion is that the undated slips of paper date to the 1755–56 voyage, then no solid evidence exists to say that the *Hare* stopped at Cape Verde. However, in the narrative offered here I do suggest that Godfrey stopped there. First, if the *Hare* did indeed stop there on the second voyage, it is not unreasonable to infer that Cape Verde was a familiar way station for Godfrey. For obvious reasons, shipmasters favored the known over the unknown, and he probably knew the winds, harbors, currents, and markets and may even have had contacts there. Many New England vessels visited Cape Verde, especially those intending to slave along the Upper Guinea coast. A second reason has to do with the *Hare*'s cargo of rum. As mentioned in the text, New England captains often sought to improve the ship's "assortment" of trade goods before attempting to purchase captives. Cape Verde was a popular place to acquire other goods, not to mention take on provisions and make repairs. In sum, while we cannot be completely certain that the *Hare* stopped at Cape Verde in 1754, the chances are very good that it did.

Tables

TABLE I. Average Annual Value and Destinations of Commodity Exports from New England and Slaves Carried on New England Ships, 1768–1772

Commodity	Value, Pounds Sterling
Fish	£152,155
Livestock, Beef, Pork	89,953
Wood Products	65,271
Whale Products	62,103
Potash	22,399
Grains, Grain Products	19,902
Rum	18,776
Other Products	8,552
Slaves	63,575–89,000
Total	£501,686–527,111

Sources: McCusker and Menard, *Economy of British America*, 108; TSTD2, http://slavevoyages.org/tast/database/search.faces?yearFrom=1768&yearTo=1772&ptdepimp=20100.20200.20300.20400.20500.

Note: For my estimate on slave prices, see chap. 1, n. 20.

TABLE 2. Captive Embarkations between Cacheu and Cape Mount, 1768

Embarkation Point	Total	Percentage
Between Cacheu & Sierra Leone		
Private Trade	3,000	22.6
French Contract	1,200	9.0
Sierra Leone		
French Contract	1,200	9.0
Bance Island	1,500	11.3
Private Trade	2,100	15.8
Between Sierra Leone & Gallinas	2,000	15.0
Between Gallinas & Cape Mount	2,300	17.3
Total	13,300	

Source: "An Account of the Number of Negroes Bartered for on the Coast of Africa in 1768, from Cape Blanco to Rio Congo," Eg. 1162A, British Library.

Note: The table does not include Cacheu itself, which was controlled by the Portuguese.

TABLE 3. Traders Who Sold Captives to the *Hare*, 1754

Name	Number	Location
Alexander Ross	1	unknown
William Harriss	1	Isles de Los?
Andrew Morrison	3	Bance Island
John Holman	5	Dembia, Pongo
Robert Simpson	1	unknown
George Dowdall	5	Isles de Los
William Ord	4	Wonkopong
James Tweed	3	Scarcies
William Norie	4	Sherbro
Baillie and Key	7	Banana Islands?
John Langton	2	Kissy/SL
William Skinner	11	Sherbro/Plantains
John Wallace	3	Scarcies
Padre Levis	2	unknown
Andr Gomar	2	unknown
George Thompson	1	unknown
James Potter	1	unknown
George Hall	3	unknown
Capt. Millitring	1	unknown
Richard Hall	1	Sherbro River
Robert Wright	2	Banana Islands
Patrick Clow	8	Plantains
James Ordrich	1	unknown
Richard Boardwell	4	unknown

Source: Slavery Collection, New-York Historical Society

TABLE 4. Captive Importations from Africa to South Carolina and Georgia, 1701–1775

Years	Captives Imported
1701–1725	5,470
1726–1750	35,674
1751–1775	75,527
Total	116,671

Source: TSTD2, http://slavevoyages.org/tast/assessment/estimates.faces?yearFrom=1501&
yearTo=1866, accessed June 11, 2015.

TABLE 5. African Embarkation Regions for Captives Entering South Carolina
and Georgia, 1751–1775

Senegambia	Sierra Leone	Windward Coast	Gold Coast	Bight of Benin	Bight of Biafra	West Central Africa	Other	Total
22,347	12,435	9,264	10,900	2,345	6,351	11,575	311	75,528

Source: TSTD2, http://slavevoyages.org/tast/assessment/estimates.faces?yearFrom=1751&
yearTo=1775, accessed June 4, 2015. TSTD2 gives the total figure as 75,527.

TABLE 6. Summary of the *Hare* Captive Purchasers

Purchaser	Purchase Date and Phase of Sale	Number of Captives	Value of Real Property in S.C. Currency, with Date of Valuation
Alexander Chisholme	March 19 (initial)	1	
Lachlan McIntosh	March 19 (initial)	1	
Susannah Wedderburn	March 19 (initial)	3	
Samuel Simons	March 19 (initial)	3	£5,638 (1761)
(Elias) Horry	March 19 (initial)	7	
(Daniel) Lessesne	March 19 (initial)		
John Williams	March 19 (initial)	1	
Mrs. David	March 19 (initial)	1	
Thomas Mell	March 19 (initial)	1	£7,874 (1760)
Charles Lorimer	March 19 (initial)	2	
Thomas Bell	March 19 (initial)	1	
Christian Minnick	March 19 (initial)	2	
Hance McCulloch	March 19 (initial)	2	£6,337 (1769)
Peter Taylor	March 20 (private)	2	£49,957 (1765)
Peter Peguine	March 20 (private)	1	
William Lloyd	March 20 (private)	2	£20,275 (1761)
James Parsons	March 20 (vendue)	1	>£300,000 (1779)ᶜ
William Bready	March 20 (private)	1	£1,922 (1768)
Francis Smith	March 20 (private)	2	
Henry Laurens	March 20 (private)	9	
James Moore	March 20 (vendue)	1	
Alexander Chisholme	March 20 (vendue)	1	
Paul Smyser	March 20 (vendue)	2	
William Stone	March 20 (vendue)	3	
Charles Lorimer	March 20 (vendue)	1	
George Ducatt	March 20 (vendue)	2ᶠ	£1,327 (1760)
William Lloyd	March 20 (vendue)	1	£20,275 (1761)
Paul Douxsaint	March 20 (vendue)	1	£531,788 (1779)ᵈ
Alexander Fraser	March 20 (vendue)	1	

Sources: See individual references.

ᵃIndicates purchaser owned a Charles Town residence in addition to a rural plantation.

ᵇParsons owned seven plantations in different parishes.

ᶜThe value of Parsons's estate is illegible in the original but appears to be considerably over £300,000.

ᵈEstate is valued in inflated Revolutionary currency and is therefore not comparable to colonial valuations.

ᵉLaurens purchased Wambaw Plantation in 1756 but left the management of it to his partner and brother-in-law John Coming Ball, and continued to reside primarily in Charles Town.

ᶠDucatt is listed as having purchased one woman "and child," but the sales record only counts the mother in the totals.

1755 Residence	Later Residence
Charles Town	
Charles Town	Georgia (1756)
St. Andrew's	Christ Church (1757)
Christ Church	
St. James Santee	
Prince George	St. Thomas/St. Denis (1757)
unknown	
unknown	
St. James Goose Creek	
John's Island	Christ Church (1757)
James Island	
Orangeburg	
Jacksonborough	
St. James Goose Creek[a]	
unknown	
Wando Neck[a]	
Multiple[ab]	
Fredericksburg Township	St. John's Berkeley (1758)
Chehaw River, St. Bartholomew's	
Charles Town	St. James Santee (1756)[e]
St. George Dorchester	St. Peter (1767)
Charles Town	
Charles Town	St. James Goose Creek (1759)[a]
Charles Town	England (ca. 1760)
John's Island	Christ Church (1757)
Charles Town	
Wando Neck[a]	
Charles Town	St. James Santee (1758)
St. James Goose Creek[a]	

TABLE 7. Documented Ownership of Other African Slaves by *Hare* Purchasers

Name	*Hare* Captives	Total Austin & Laurens Captives	Origins of Austin & Laurens Captives
Chisholme, Alexander	2	2	WCAf (2)
Douxsaint, Paul	1	2	WindC (2)
Ducatt, George	2	1	WindC (1)
Fraser, Alexander	1	8	WCAf (8)
Horry, Elias	7	11	WCAf (5); GC (6)
Laurens, Henry	9	32	Sen (12); SL(2); WindC (5); GC (11); Benin (1); Biafra (1)
Lessesne, Daniel	7	2	SL (2)
Lloyd, William	3	1	Biafra (1)
McIntosh, Lachlan	1	23	WindC (12); GC (6); WCAf (5)
Moore, James	1	2	Sen (2)
Parsons, James	1	1	Sen (1)
Stone, William	3	4	WCAf (4)
Smyser, Paul	2	3	WindC (2)

Sources: Austin & Laurens Account Book, Beinecke Rare Books Library; *South Carolina Gazette*.

Notes

Partner of Lessesne

Partner of Horry

Runaway Ads for 2 "Banbaras";
2 "Angolas"; 1 "Pappa"; 1 "Surago"

TABLE 8. Captives from Upper Guinea in the *Hare* Purchasers' Parishes, 1753–61

Parish	Purchaser	No. in Austin & Laurens Records	Percentage in A&L Records	Est. Total Africans Arriving 1753–61
Christ Church		29	1.5	364
	Samuel Simons			
	Susannah Wedderburn (1757)			
	Charles Lorimer (1757)			
Orangeburg Twp.		9	0.5	113
	Christian Minnick			
Prince Frederick		229	12.1	2,877
	William Bready (1755)			
Prince George		117	6.2	1,470
	Daniel Lessesne			
St. Andrew's		51	2.7	641
	Susannah Wedderburn (1755)			
	Thomas Bell			
St. Bartholomew's		103	5.5	1,294
	Francis Smith			
	Hance McCulloch			
St. George Dorchester		43	2.3	540
	James Moore			
St. James Goose Creek		46	2.4	578
	Thomas Mell			
	Alexander Fraser			
	Paul Smyser (1759)			
St. John's Berkeley		44	2.3	553
	William Bready (1758)			
	Henry Laurens (1762)			
St. John's Colleton		74	3.9	930
	Charles Lorimer (1757)			
St. James Santee		94	5.0	1,181
	Elias Horry			
	Henry Laurens (1756)			
St. Thomas & St. Denis		60	3.2	754
	Daniel Lessesne (1757)			
	William Lloyd			

Source: Austin & Laurens Account Book, Beinecke Rare Books Library.

Note: Table 8 uses the locations of the purchasers in the Austin & Laurens accounts to gain an idea of which parishes were importing the most captives in the years surrounding the *Hare* captives' arrival. To derive an estimate of how many captives arrived in individual parishes, each parish's share of the Austin & Laurens accounts was multiplied by 23,709, the total number of Africans entering the colony from 1753 to 1761. (See TSTD2, http://slavevoyages.org/tast/assessment/estimates.faces?yearFrom=1753&yearTo=1761, accessed June 11, 2015.) The percentage of 1-year survivors was calculated assuming a 67 percent survival rate. The number of Upper Guineans was

Est. 1-year Survivors, 1753–61	Est. Upper Guinea, 1753–61	Total Slaves, 1761	Percentage of Total Slave Populations Consisting of Upper Guineans Arriving 1753–61
244	145	1,647	8.8
76	45	285	15.8
1,928	1,143	2,543	45.0
985	584	3,265	17.9
429	255	2,644	9.6
867	514	1,374	37.4
362	215	1,606	13.4
387	230	2,494	9.2
370	220	3,419	6.4
623	369	1,870	19.8
791	469	1,254	37.4
505	300	2,128	14.1

calculated by multiplying the total number of surviving captives by 59.3 percent, their proportion of all importations from 1753 to 1761 (see TSTD2, http://slavevoyages.org/tast/assessment/esti-mates.faces?yearFrom=1753&yearTo=1761, accessed June 11, 2015). The percentage of newly arrived (1753–61) Upper Guineans in the individual parishes was then calculated using total slave population figures from the 1761 parish tax returns, which constitute the best data for the period. See Public Treasurer of South Carolina, General Tax Receipts and Payments, 1761–69 (1771), South Carolina Department of Archives and History.

TABLE 9. Upper Guinean Ethnonyms in South Carolina Workhouse
Advertisements, 1750–1775

Ethnonym	Frequency	Percentage
Mandingo	86	43.7
Jahlonke	6	3.0
Bambara	20	10.2
Bonda	2	1.0
Fula	10	5.1
Araba	1	0.5
Limba	4	2.0
Bola	1	0.5
Temne	4	2.0
Kissi	63	32.0
Total	197	

Sources: Littlefield, *Rice and Slaves*; *South Carolina Gazette*; *South Carolina Gazette and Country Journal*; *South Carolina and American General Gazette*.

Note: Advertisements for slaves taken to the Camden Goal are included, as are those taken up by private parties. Mande-speaking groups are in boldface. While my distribution largely mirrors Littlefield's, I have found 11 more "Mandingo" notices than he lists.

TABLE 10. Upper Guinean Captives in Spanish Florida, 1752–1763

Nation	Frequency	Percentage
Bambara	1	2.1
Fai (Vai)	1	2.1
Fula/Pul	3	6.4
Ganga	2	4.3
Guisi (Kissi)	1	2.1
Guolofo (Wolof)	2	4.3
Limba	1	2.1
Mandinga	27	57.4
Meni (Mende)	1	2.1
Susu	2	4.3
Timini (Temne)	2	4.3
Yalongo (Yalunka)	4	8.5
Total Upper Guinea	47	
Unidentified and Other African Regions	176	

Source: Landers, *Black Society in Spanish Florida*, 269–75.

Note: Mande ethnonyms are in boldface.

TABLE 11. Runaway Groups at the Charles Town Workhouse, 1750–1775

Single Ethnonym	Number of Groups	Avg. Size	Multiple Ethnonyms	No. of Groups	Avg. Size
Bambara	2	2.5	All Mande	3	2.3
Fula	2	3.5	Mande + Other	3	2.3
Kissi	6	2.5	Other	2	
Mandingo	5	3.4			
Koranko	1	2.0			

Sources: South Carolina Gazette; South Carolina Gazette and Country Journal; South Carolina and American General Gazette.

Note: Advertisements for slaves taken to the Camden Goal are included, as are those taken up by private parties. Mande-speaking groups are in boldface.

NOTES

Abbreviations

AAS	American Antiquarian Society, Worcester, Mass.
BL	British Library, London, England
BNA	British National Archives, Kew, England
BRBL	Beinecke Rare Books Library, Yale University, New Haven, Conn.
CSL	Connecticut State Library, Hartford, Conn.
LNR	Land and Notarial Records, Rhode Island State Archives, Providence, R.I.
NAS	National Archives of Scotland, Edinburgh, Scotland
NCH	Newport City Hall, Newport, R.I.
NHS	Newport Historical Society, Newport, R.I.
NYHS	Samuel and William Vernon Papers, Slavery Collection, New-York Historical Society, New York, N.Y.
NYPL	New York Public Library, New York, N.Y.
NYSHA	New York State Historical Association Library, Cooperstown, N.Y.
PAST	*Papers of the American Slave Trade,* ed. Coughtry
PHL	*Papers of Henry Laurens,* 10 vols., ed. Hamer et al.
RIHS	Rhode Island Historical Society, Providence, R.I.
RISA	Rhode Island State Archives, Providence, R.I.
RISCJA	Rhode Island State Supreme Court Judicial Archives, Pawtucket, R.I.
RLA	Redwood Library and Athenæum, Newport, R.I.
SCAGG	*South Carolina and American General Gazette*
SCDAH	South Carolina Department of Archives and History, Columbia, S.C.
SCG	*South Carolina Gazette*
SCGCJ	*South Carolina Gazette and Country Journal*
SCHS	South Carolina Historical Society, Charleston, S.C.
SCL	South Caroliniana Library, University of South Carolina, Columbia, S.C.
TSTD1	*The Trans-Atlantic Slave Trade: A Database on CD-Rom,* ed. Eltis et. al.
TSTD2	*Voyages: The Trans-Atlantic Slave Trade Database,* Version 2, ed. Eltis and Halbert, online at www.slavevoyages.org

Introduction

1. On slavery and natal alienation, see Finley, *Ancient Slavery and Modern Ideology,* 75–77; Patterson, *Slavery and Social Death,* 5–7, 54–58; Meillassoux, *The Anthropology of Slavery,* 33–35. On the use of African names as sources in historical research, see Nwokeji and Eltis,

"Roots of the African Diaspora," 365–79. For a discussion of names in South Carolina, see Cody, "There Was No 'Absalom' on the Ball Plantations," 563–96.

2. The number of Africans arriving in North America before 1776 (279,943) is taken from TSTD2 at http://slavevoyages.org/tast/assessment/estimates.faces?yearFrom= 1501&yearTo=1775 (accessed May 18, 2015). The number of English migrants who arrived during the Great Migration (20,000) comes from Meinig, *Atlantic America, 1492–1800*, 92. The number of migrants to British America (921,500) comes from Bailyn, *Voyagers to the West*, 25, 26. Diouf, *Servants of Allah*, 48, puts the Muslim share of the African Diaspora at 15–20 percent. Even a more conservative estimate of 10 percent puts the total number of African Muslims arriving in North America at 39,000.

3. Mintz and Price, *The Birth of African-American Culture*, quotations on 18, 66, 53, 19. Mintz and Price did not use the word "creolization" in their initial work, preferring the term "encounter model." The literature on creolization is vast. For an updated statement, see Price, "The Concept of Creolization." For an overview of the concept and its history, see Cohen and Toninato, *The Creolization Reader*. For a critique, see Palmié, "Creolization and Its Discontents"; Palmié, "Is There a Model in the Muddle?," 178–200. Both E. Franklin Frazier and Melville J. Herskovits stated their positions in multiple publications. For a good summary of Frazier's views, see *The Negro in the United States*, 3–21. For a summary of Herskovits's views, see *The Myth of the Negro Past*.

4. Brathwaite introduced the term "creolization" before Mintz and Price wrote. See *The Development of Creole Society in Jamaica*. A few other authors came to similar conclusions before Mintz and Price's essay appeared. See for example Mullin, *Flight and Rebellion*; Wood, *Black Majority*. A partial list of major works on North America that employ some variant of creolization, either explicitly or implicitly, would include Joyner, *Down by the Riverside*; Sobel, *The World They Made Together*; Stuckey, *Slave Culture*; Ferguson, *Uncommon Ground*; Mullin, *Africa in America*; Morgan, *Slave Counterpoint*; Morgan, "The Cultural Implications of the Atlantic Slave Trade"; Frey and Wood, *Come Shouting to Zion*; Berlin, *Many Thousands Gone*.

5. The debates between the "Creolization" and the "Revisionist" schools of interpretation have been well covered elsewhere. Important Revisionist statements include Thornton, *Africa and Africans*, and Lovejoy, "The African Diaspora." For overviews of the debate, see Sidbury, "Globalization, Creolization, and the Not-So-Peculiar Institution"; Frey, "The Visible Church"; Sidbury and Cañizares-Esguerra, "Mapping Ethnogenesis." See also Palmié, "Is There a Model in the Muddle?" It should be noted that later explorations of creolization incorporated a much higher quotient of archival material. See, for example, Price, *Alabi's World*.

6. For an early summary of the TSTD1 findings, see Eltis, "The Volume and Structure of the Transatlantic Slave Trade." Summaries for TSTD2 may be found in Eltis and Richardson, *Extending the Frontiers*, and in Eltis and Richardson, *Atlas of the Transatlantic Slave Trade*. For a response that stresses the viability of the Creolization model, see Morgan, "The Cultural Implications of the Atlantic Slave Trade." Works that used existing slave trade data to examine specific African groups before the publication of TSTD1 include Littlefield, *Rice and Slaves*; Creel, *"A Peculiar People"*; Thornton, "African Dimensions of the Stono Rebellion"; Hall, *Africans in Colonial Louisiana*; Chambers, "'My Own Nation'"; Gomez, *Exchanging Our Country Marks*.

7. A partial list of works informed in some measure by TSTD would include Heywood, *Central Africans and Cultural Transformations*; Lovejoy and Trotman, *Trans-Atlantic Dimensions of*

Ethnicity; Sweet, *Recreating Africa*; Falola and Childs, *The Yoruba Diaspora in the Atlantic World*; Chambers, *Murder at Montpelier*; Hall, *Slavery and African Ethnicities*; Childs, *The 1812 Aponte Rebellion*; Rucker, *The River Flows On*; Young, *Rituals of Resistance*; Byrd, *Captives and Voyagers*; Diptee, *From Africa to Jamaica*; Konadu, *The Akan Diaspora in the Americas*. Of course, these works do not all reach the same conclusions. For recent works stressing the transformation of specific African identities and cultural forms in the Americas, see Sweet, *Domingos Alvares*; Hawthorne, *From Africa to Brazil*; Graham, "Being Yoruba in Nineteenth-Century Rio de Janeiro."

8. See Berlin, "From Creole to African"; Berlin, *Many Thousands Gone*; Mark, *"Portuguese" Style and Luso-African Identity*; Heywood and Thornton, *Central Africans, Atlantic Creoles, and the Foundation of the Americas*.

9. Sidbury and Cañizares-Esguerra, "Mapping Ethnogenesis," 182, 184.

10. In addition to the works mentioned above, major examples of work on North America include Woodson, *The African Background Outlined*; Creel, *"A Peculiar People"*; Walsh, *From Calabar to Carter's Grove*; Walsh, "The Chesapeake Slave Trade"; Young, *Rituals of Resistance*; Brown, *African-Atlantic Cultures and the South Carolina Lowcountry*. Gwendolyn Midlo Hall's work on colonial Louisiana and Jane Landers's work on Spanish Florida are two examples of North American studies that have benefitted from ecclesiastical and other sources common to Catholic colonies. See Hall, *Africans in Colonial Louisiana,* and Landers, *Black Society in Spanish Florida*.

11. Harms, *The* Diligent, sets the standard for voyage studies, but the lack of a sales document made it impossible to investigate the captives' lives in Martinique. See also Vignols, "La Campagne Négrière de *La Perle*"; Wax, "The Browns of Providence and the Slaving Voyage of the Brig 'Sally,' 1764–1765"; Tattersfield, *The Forgotten Trade*; Mouser, *A Slaving Voyage to Africa and Jamaica*; Sharafi, "The Slave Ship Manuscripts of Captain Joseph B. Cook"; Newson and Minchin, *From Capture to Sale*; Walvin, *The Zong*. Diouf, *Dreams of Africa in Alabama*, does explore the captives' New World lives, though in a very different setting from the present work. For a more skeptical view of voyage studies, see Eltis, "Tales from the Ships."

12. Some, though not all, of the documents pertaining to the *Hare* have been published in Donnan, *Documents*, 3:146–57. One merchant who did apparently collect logbooks was Aaron Lopez, whose papers include logs for several voyages.

13. Some effort has been made to gauge the geographic distribution of Africans in Virginia. See Walsh, "The Chesapeake Slave Trade," 139–70; Chambers, *Murder at Montpelier*, 83.

14. Well-known composite studies include Huggins, *Black Odyssey*; Rediker, *Slave Ship*; Smallwood, *Saltwater Slavery*.

15. Eltis and Richardson, *Atlas of the Transatlantic Slave Trade*, 13–15. Interestingly, the cited figure refers to the number of captives, not the number of voyages. TSTD2 records more voyages originating from Great Britain (10,066) than from Brazil (9,145), but since more of the missing 20 percent of all voyages likely came from Brazil, it seems almost certain that Brazil sent out more ships. See http://slavevoyages.org/tast/database/search.faces?yearFrom=1514&yearTo= 1866 (accessed June 12, 2015).

16. TSTD2, http://slavevoyages.org/tast/database/search.faces?yearFrom=1514&yearTo= 1866&ptdepimp=20000 (accessed May 18, 2015). See also Eltis, "The U.S. Transatlantic Slave Trade."

17. Turner, *Africanisms in the Gullah Dialect*; Joyner, *Down by the Riverside*; Creel, *"A Peculiar People."* See also Young, *Rituals of Resistance*, and Palmié, "Is There a Model in the Muddle?"

18. For the Black Rice debate, see Wood, *Black Majority*; Littlefield, *Rice and Slaves*; Carney, *Black Rice*; Edelson, *Plantation Enterprise*; Eltis, Morgan, and Richardson, "Agency and Diaspora in Atlantic History"; Fields-Black, *Deep Roots*; Hawthorne, *From Africa to Brazil*; and Edelson et al., "AHR Exchange: The Question of Black Rice."

19. http://slavevoyages.org/tast/assessment/estimates.faces?yearFrom=1501&yearTo=1866 (accessed June 3, 2015).

20. O'Malley, *Final Passages*; O'Malley, "Beyond the Middle Passage"; Richardson, "The British Slave Trade to Colonial South Carolina"; Littlefield, "The Slave Trade to Colonial South Carolina"; McMillin, *The Final Victims*. On the influence of Upper Guinea, see Creel, *"A Peculiar People,"* 37–44, 45–63; Gomez, *Exchanging Our Country Marks*, 88–105; Schaffer, "Bound to Africa."

21. Berlin, *Many Thousands Gone*; Melish, *Disowning Slavery*; Sweet, *Bodies Politic*.

22. Interpretations that stress the marginality of the slave trade to the New England economy include McCusker, "The Rum Trade and the Balance of Payments of the Thirteen Continental Colonies"; McCusker, *Rum and the American Revolution*; Richardson, "Slavery, Trade, and Economic Growth in Eighteenth-Century New England"; Ostrander, "The Colonial Molasses Trade"; Ostrander, "The Making of the Triangular Trade Myth"; Platt, "Triangles and Tramping"; James, "Of Slaves and Rum"; Deutsch, "The Elusive Guineaman."

23. For comparability's sake, I have used the 1770 population for the colonies and the 1771 population of England. I have included New York in these calculations, though its omission has little effect on the totals. For the population of the American colonies, see U.S. Census Bureau, *Historical Statistics of the United States*, 1168. For the population of England see Porter, *English Society*, 361. For the number of voyages, see TSTD2, http://slavevoyages.org/tast/database/search.faces?yearFrom=1730&yearTo=1775&ptdepimp=10300.10400.10500.10600.20100.20200.20300.20400.20500.20600 (accessed November 28, 2014).

24. Curtin, *Atlantic Slave Trade*, 127–30.

25. Rodney, *Upper Guinea Coast*, 1–38; Jones and Johnson, "Slaves from the Windward Coast"; Thornton, *Africa and Africans*; Barry, *Senegambia*, xi–xvi; Brooks, *Eurafricans in Western Africa*; Hall, *Slavery and African Ethnicities*; Eltis and Richardson, *Atlas of the Transatlantic Slave Trade*, 94–97; Fields-Black, *Deep Roots*; Hawthorne, *From Africa to Brazil*; Green, *The Rise of the Trans-Atlantic Slave Trade*.

26. The linguistic classifications are taken from Heine and Nurse, *African Languages*, 18–22.

27. Shaw, *Memories of the Slave Trade*; Bailey, *African Voices of the Atlantic Slave Trade*; Hartman, *Lose Your Mother*.

28. See Phillips, *Cambridge*; Unsworth, *Sacred Hunger*; Condé, *Segu*.

Chapter One

1. Account of William Vernon, 1751–66, Godfrey Malbone Account Book, RIHS; "A Portage [*sic*] Bill of Men's Names[,] Quality[,] Time of Entry[,] Wages pr Month & When Discharged,"

box 2, folder 4, NYHS (hereafter cited as "Portage Bill," NYHS). For examples of the customs paperwork, see CO 388/46, fol. 38, BNA.

2. Samuel and William Vernon to Thomlinson, Trecothick, & Co., June 1, 1754, William Vernon Letterbook, no.3, 1751–1775, NHS.

3. For a similar argument in connection with Liverpool, see Behrendt, "Human Capital in the British Slave Trade."

4. "Itinerarium of Dr. Alexander Hamilton," in Martin, *Colonial American Travel Narratives*, 252. See also Birket, *Some Cursory Remarks Made by James Birket*, 27–29.

5. Taylor, *A Voyage to North America*, 58.

6. Dexter, *Extracts from the Itineraries*, 23. Exactly how Stiles derived his measurement is something of a mystery since maps of the time do not show anything close to thirty miles of wharfage. Stiles may have counted portions of coastline outside of central Newport.

7. Rhode Island Historical Preservation Commission, *The Southern Thames Street Neighborhood*, 6, 40.

8. Rudolph, "Eighteenth Century Newport," 26.

9. Crane, *A Dependent People*, 24, 54. For the Vernons' rankings, see Rate Assessment List, Newport, 1760, RISA.

10. On Newport's tradesmen, see Rudolph, "Eighteenth Century Newport," 26. For a glimpse of a Newport distillery, see the *Pennsylvania Gazette*, March 12, 1772, 2. On ropewalks, see Champlin, "The Art, Trade, or Mystery of the Ropemaker," 81–94. On the nearby truck farms, see Taylor, *A Voyage to North America*, 56–57. On the alms and workhouses, see Withey, *Urban Growth*, 15, and Herndon, *Unwelcome Americans*, 1, 14. Locations have been taken from Ezra Stiles, "Map of the City and Harbor of Newport," 1758, RLA, and Charles Blaskowitz, "A Plan of the Town of Newport in Rhode Island."

11. For Newport's slave population, see Crane, *A Dependent People*, 76. On the arrival of slave ships during the 1750s, see TSTD2, http://slavevoyages.org/tast/database/search.faces?yearFrom=1750&yearTo=1759&mjslptimp=20100 (accessed August 27, 2009).

12. *Boston News-Letter*, March 5, 1772, 3, gives Primus's wife's master's name as Ebenezer Malbone, but this is probably an error. For a more detailed account that gives the name as Evan Malbone, see the *Pennsylvania Gazette*, March 12, 1772, 2. On African Americans in Rhode Island, see Sweet, *Bodies Politic*, 58–101.

13. Rees, "Mercantilism and the Colonies," 563, and McCusker and Menard, *The Economy of British America*, 35–50. Scholars debate the extent to which a coherent "mercantilist" ideology actually existed. See Pincus et al., "Forum: Rethinking Mercantilism," 3–70.

14. On the New England economy, see McCusker and Menard, *The Economy of British America*, 91–111; Newell, *From Dependency to Independence*; Newell, "The Birth of New England in the Atlantic Economy," 11–68.

15. On the value of the carrying trade, see Shepherd and Walton, *Maritime Trade*, 116. Roughly half of all Rhode Island rum was exported, and about half of all rum exports went overseas, mostly to Africa. See McCusker, *Rum and the American Revolution*, 475.

16. Breen, "Baubles of Britain."

17. James, *Colonial Rhode Island*, 160–63, 169–70.

18. Davies, *Calendar of State Papers*, 45:95; *Journal of the Commissioners for Trade and Plantations*, 9:128–32. For a general overview, see Pares, *Yankees and Creoles*.

19. Historians who have argued that the slave trade was of secondary significance include Platt, "'And Don't Forget the Guinea Voyage'"; Deutsch, "The Elusive Guineaman"; McCusker, *Rum and the American Revolution*, 492–97. Arguments for the economic importance of the slave trade include Crane, *A Dependent People*, 16–37; Crane, "The First Wheel of Commerce"; Coughtry, *Notorious Triangle*. Those who have argued for its relative unimportance tend to emphasize that Rhode Island sent many more vessels to the Caribbean than to Africa. Those who argue for its importance tend to emphasize the greater value of slave cargoes. In his overview of the U.S.-based slave trade, David Eltis argues that it was of "peripheral" importance both in comparison with other slave-trading powers and with the national economy, despite a surge between 1785 and 1808. See Eltis, "The U.S. Transatlantic Slave Trade," 360–66.

20. This calculation is based on the assumption that New England ships sold 12,715 captives in the New World. The number of slaves comes from TSTD2, http://slavevoyages.org/tast/database/search.faces?yearFrom=1768&yearTo=1772&ptdepimp=20100.20200.20300.20400.20500 (accessed March 14, 2013). In devising the price estimate I follow Eltis and Richardson, "Prices of African Slaves," 200–201. Their figures, however, give only the mean price of a prime male slave, which was £42.6 in 1766–70 and £46.1 in 1771–75. I have adjusted the price downward to reflect the fact that not all captives were prime male hands. Shepherd and Walton, *Maritime Trade*, 144, estimate the value at £80,000 per year. While the figure is not unreasonable, it is based on old data.

21. Here I differ with McCusker, *Rum and the American Revolution*, 492–97. On the value-to-weight ratio of gold, slaves, and plantation produce, see Eltis, *The Rise of African Slavery*, 114–15. On the value of shipping and "invisible" earnings (interest, insurance, and mercantile profits), see Shepherd and Walton, *Maritime Trade*, 116–36.

22. For an argument stressing the importance of slave-produced commodities, though not the slave trade itself, to the New England economy, see Bailyn, "Slavery and Population Growth," 253–59; Bailey, "The Slave(ry) Trade," 373–414.

23. Mason, *Reminiscences of Newport*, 31, 35, 179; "Itinerarium of Dr. Alexander Hamilton," in Martin, *Colonial American Travel Narratives*, 289–90. On coffee houses and social clubs, see Bridenbaugh, *Cities in Revolt*, 161–64.

24. Ellery and Vernon, "The Vernon Family and Arms," 128–38.

25. Ibid., 130.

26. Dexter, *Literary Diary of Ezra Stiles*, 1:13, 328, 430.

27. Coughtry, *Notorious Triangle*, 242; Rudolph, "Eighteenth Century Newport," 47. William Vernon to Samuel Vernon, Aug. 1, 1746, Roderick Terry, Jr., Autograph Collection, RLA. On the Vernons' privateering, see Robert Morris to Godfrey Malbone and Samuel Vernon, March 18, 1744, and Mathias Jones to William Vernon, April 4, 1748, in Adams et al., *Commerce of Rhode Island*, 49–50, 56–57. See also Admiralty Papers, 4:139, 6:76–78, RISA.

28. William Vernon to Samuel Vernon, March 13, 1745, William Vernon Letters, SCL. For more on the Vernon-Manigault relationship, see Gabriel Manigault to William Vernon, November 7, 1747, and February 12, 1747/8, and Samuel and William Vernon to Gabriel Manigault,

January 9, 1755, and January 10, 1755, Manigault Family Papers, SCHS; Gabriel Manigault to William Vernon, February 24, 1755, March 5, 1755, March 21, 1755, and April 5, 1755, NYHS.

29. Protest of Captain Joseph Tripp, 399, LNR.

30. Bill of Lading for Sloop Hair [sic], March 7, 1757, Vernon Papers, box 49, folder 2, NHS.

31. Crane, *A Dependent People*, 87.

32. Samuel and William Vernon to Nathaniel Hammond, June 6, 1770, in Adams et al., *Commerce of Rhode Island*, 333.

33. See note 28, above.

34. Coughtry, *Notorious Triangle*, 92.

35. For Thomlinson, Trecothick, & Co., see Samuel and William Vernon to Thomlinson, Trecothick, and Company, June 28, 1753, June 1, 1754, and July 22, 1754, William Vernon Letterbook, NHS. For Michael Bland, see Samuel and William Vernon to Michael Bland, August 8, 1751 and October 10, 1751, William Vernon Letterbook, NHS. On the Ireland venture, see Samuel and William Vernon to Thomlinson, Trecothick, and Company, June 1, 1754, William Vernon Letterbook, NHS. On shipping, see Registers of Passes, ADM7/87, ADM7/88, ADM7/89, and ADM7/90, BNA.

36. Samuel and William Vernon to Broom and Barrows, February 25, 1754, William Vernon Letterbook, NHS.

37. Protest of Peter Dordin and Edward Taylor, February 2, 1761, 7:154, LNR; Record of Bill of Exchange, July 1, 1766, 7:651, LNR; Sailing Instructions to Captain Nathaniel Hammond in Adams et al., *Commerce of Rhode Island*, 332–33.

38. Michael Herries to Richard Oswald, January 15, 1767, Letters to Richard Oswald, 1764–69, BRBL.

39. Samuel and William Vernon to Nathaniel Hammond, June 6, 1770, in Adams et al., *Commerce of Rhode Island*, 332–33.

40. TSTD2; Instructions to Thomas Teakle Taylor, May 12, 1759, NYHS.

41. For most British ships, it is possible to find basic information in Admiralty pass logs, large bound volumes that recorded the "nature," or rig, of every outbound vessel; the name; the home port; tons burthen; the number of guns; the present location of the vessel; the master's name; the size of the crew, subdivided into British and foreign sailors; the place where the ship was built; and the intended destination. The volume that covers the period of the *Hare*'s voyage is ADM 7/89, BNA. Several other vessels named *Hare* appear in Admiralty records, but none was described as a sloop, which our vessel certainly was. Colonial shipping generally did not appear in these records unless the vessel touched in Britain, which, of course, the *Hare* did not. Unfortunately, any comparable records that may have existed for Rhode Island, South Carolina, or Barbados do not survive for the relevant years.

42. For a contemporary definition of a sloop, see Falconer, *Universal Dictionary of the Marine*. To complicate matters, the term "sloop" was often applied to small square-rigged naval vessels with two or more masts, as in "sloop-of-war." But in this case, it is virtually certain that the *Hare* indeed was a single-masted, fore-and-aft rigged vessel. On sloops, see Chapelle, *History of American Sailing Ships*, 11, 19–28; Baker, *Sloops and Shallops*; Goldenberg, *Shipbuilding*, 46–47, 77; Millar, *Early American Ships*; Jarvis, "'The Fastest Vessels in the

World,'" 31–50. For an example of a Rhode Island slave-trading sloop with a topmast and a topgallant, see Mouser, "The Voyage of the Good Sloop 'Dolphin,'" 251.

43. Protest of Captain Ebenezer Tyler, May 1, 1759, 7:118–19, LNR. This was almost certainly the same vessel. A search through British admiralty records for the 1750s reveals no other sloops with the same name, and it was highly unlikely that two vessels of the same rig and same name would have been based in the same colony.

44. Goldenberg, *Shipbuilding*, 77. On the tonnage of English ships, which tended to be larger than colonial vessels, see Davis, *The Rise of the English Shipping Industry*, 76–80. For the data on Rhode Island slaving vessels, see TSTD2, http://slavevoyages.org/tast/database/search.faces?yearFrom=1700&yearTo=1799&ptdepimp=20100&slaximpFrom=70&slaximpTo=80&rig=27 and http://slavevoyages.org/tast/database/search.faces?yearFrom=1700&yearTo=1799&rig=27&ptdepimp=20100&tonmodFrom=50&tonmodTo=70 (accessed August 19, 2015). The tonnage per hogshead ratio comes from Coughtry, *Notorious Triangle*, 84. Coughtry emphasizes that there was significant variation, with some vessels carrying as few as 0.6 hogsheads per ton, while others carried as many as 1.8.

45. On the *Hare*'s hull, see William Vernon to Thomlinson and Trecothick, June 1, 1754, William Vernon Letterbook, no. 3, NHS. For an example of a Rhode Island vessel that was condemned in Africa due to a leaky hull, see Mouser, "The Voyage of the Good Sloop 'Dolphin,'" 258. Copper sheathing did not come into widespread use until the late eighteenth century.

46. On the general features of slave ships, see Rediker, *Slave Ship*, 41–72. On sloops in the slave trade, see Rediker, *Slave Ship*, 64–65. Estimates for the *Hare*'s dimensions come from the measurements given for fourteen American sloops built in the eighteenth century, as described in Millar, *Early American Ships*. See also Baker, *Sloops and Shallops*, 119. Data on the number of guns carried by Rhode Island slave ships is mostly absent, but several vessels are listed in records as lacking them altogether. In some cases it is possible that swivel guns were not counted as part of a vessel's armament. On the deck plan and placement of the longboat, see Chapelle, *History of American Sailing Ships*, 25–26. For an example of carriage guns in a longboat, see Donnan, *Documents*, 3:137. On shipboard insurrections, see Behrendt, Eltis, and Richardson, "The Costs of Coercion"; Taylor, *If We Must Die*.

47. Chapelle, *History of American Sailing Ships*, 25–26.

48. Baker, *Sloops and Shallops*, 110–19.

49. McCusker, *Rum and the American Revolution*, 474.

50. "Capt Godfrey Acct of rum on board Sloop *Hare*," box 2, folder 4, NYHS. The discussion that follows is based on this list.

51. On partnerships in the Rhode Island slave trade, see Lin, "The Rhode Island Slave-Traders." It should be noted that Lin's study is largely based on investor, tax, and inventory data from the postrevolutionary period. Similar documentation for the colonial period is extremely hard to come by (see below), so a comparable analysis for the colonial period is not feasible, all of which leaves open the possibility that participation in slave trade was not as democratic in the colonial period as it was after independence. For the relative wealth of the *Hare*'s rum provisioners, see Rate Assessment List, Newport, 1760, RISA. Note that Rhode Island's tax lists generally did not give an individual's actual wealth but rather his share of the town's total levy as determined by the General Assembly. Rate assessors in the individual

towns were responsible for calculating the overall rate and tax responsibility of each individual property owner. Neither the declarations of wealth nor the actual rates survive. On Rhode Island's taxation process, see "An Act for Proportioning a Rate," in Bartlett, ed., *Records of the Colony of Rhode Island*, 6:62–64; *Charter, Granted by His Majesty, King Charles II*, 219–21.

52. Rate Assessment List, Newport, 1760, RISA; Roberts, *Genealogies of Rhode Island Families*, 1:281–82; Mason, *Annals of Trinity Church*, 117; Dexter, *Extracts from the Itineraries*, 15. On Cranston's maritime career, see Protest of the Crew of the Brig *Success*, May 19, 1741, 4:36, LNR; Crew list, 5:221, LNR; *American Weekly Mercury* (Philadelphia), June 14, 1744, 2; *Boston Post Boy*, August 20, 1744, 3; *American Weekly Mercury*, September 27, 1744, 2. For the 1765 slaving voyage, see voyage #36313, TSTD2. For his distilling activities, see John Banister Daybook, 331, 380, RIHS.

53. See Newport Tax Books for 1772, 1775, NHS. See also the 1746 account of Jonathan Thurston in the John Chaloner Account Book, AAS, which he paid in rum.

54. On the career(s) of the mariner Jonathan Thurston see Bill of Exchange, April 20, 1731, 4:244, LNR; see also Protest, 4:245, LNR; Insurance document, 5:486–87, LNR; Chapin, *Rhode Island in the Colonial Wars*, 33; Protest dated October 17, 1749, 5:625–26, LNR; Bill of Exchange, April 21, 1753, 6:25, LNR; Will and Inventory of Jonathan Thurston, Newport Probate Record, 1:93, 264, NCH; *Boston Evening Post*, December 7, 1761, 3. See also John Chaloner Account Book, AAS; Letter of Marque, 4:445–46, LNR; Indenture, July 2, 1744, 5:294–95, LNR; Will of Jonathan Thurston, Records of the Newport Town Council, 1743–51, 10:198–200, NCH; *Newport Mercury*, November 25, 1765, 4; Rate Assessment List, Newport, 1760, RISA.

55. Rate Assessment List, 1760, RISA; Newport Tax Book, 1772 and 1775, NHS.

56. For the Coggeshall genealogy, see Coggeshall and Coggeshall, *The Coggeshalls in America*, 37. See also the *Boston Weekly News Letter*, September 25, 1740, 1; Receipt of Sarah Coggeshall, May 23, 1739, 4:406, LNR; Bill of Lading, August 12, 1749, 5:660, LNR; Will of Nathaniel Coggeshall, Sr., Newport Probate Record, 1:231–32, NCH; Bartlett, *Records of the Colony of Rhode Island*, 5:326. Both Nathaniel Coggeshalls also appear in the Rate Assessment List, Newport, 1760, RISA, and in the Newport Tax Book, 1772, NHS, but without mention of their occupations or activities. Nathaniel Jr. appears in the John Chaloner Account Book, AAS, but with no occupational identification. On John Colman, see Newell, *From Dependency to Independence*, 135–39.

57. John Chaloner Account Book, AAS. On the career of Thomas Richardson Sr. see "Thomas Richardson," in Garraty and Carnes, *American National Biography*, 18:456–57; James, *Colonial Rhode Island*, 169–70; Withey, *Urban Growth*, 20. For an overview of his mercantile activities, see Thomas Richardson Account Book, NHS. For his 1749 will, see Records of the Newport Town Council, 1743–51, 10:198–200, NCH. See also Rate Assessment List, Newport, 1760, RISA.

58. Rate Assessment List, Newport, 1760, RISA; *Newport Mercury*, May 16, 1774, 3; Bartlett, *Records of the Colony of Rhode Island*, 5:82.

59. *Newport Mercury*, February 18, 1765, 3; *Boston Evening Post*, June 11, 1750, 2. For his mercantile and distilling activities, see Thomas Richardson Account Book, 623, 634, NHS; Entry for June 16, 1752, in William Vernon Account Book, 1751–59, Vernon Papers, NHS. For his membership in the Baptist Church, see Dexter, *Extracts from the Itineraries*, 14. In 1758 the

colony put him in charge of military stores on Block Island. See Bartlett, *Records of the Colony of Rhode Island*, 6:163.

60. "Accounts of the Cargo on board the Sloop Hare Caleb Godfrey Mastr for ye Coast of [*sic*] Affrica," box 2, folder 4, NYHS. In calculating the value of the rum, I used the price series for New England rum at Boston as given in McCusker, *Rum and the American Revolution*, 1080. Currency conversions from Massachusetts money are based on McCusker, *Money and Exchange*, 149. Calculating the value of the non-rum cargo was far more difficult. No prices current exist for Rhode Island or Boston in this period. I relied instead on those published in the *New York Mercury* during the month of June 1754. Problems also arose from ambiguities in the original document and the use of measurements like "caggs," sugar loaves, and tierces, which do not conform to the standard measurements quoted in the New York price current. Using the New York prices and those actually recorded in the document, which I presumed to be in Rhode Island currency, I calculated the approximate value of the *Hare's* non-rum cargo in pounds sterling as follows (figures rounded to nearest pound): beef, £41; Carolina beef, £8; pork, £16; flour, £13; bread, £6; tar, £2; for a total of more than £85. I was not able to devise reliable estimates for the value of the *Hare's* Irish corn, hams, sugar, tobacco, or wine, but together they were almost certainly worth significantly less than £100 sterling. For insurance, see William Vernon to Thomlinson, Trecothick, and Co., June 1, 1754, William Vernon Letterbook, no. 3, 1751–75, NHS. For an example of a Rhode Island slave ship with sheep aboard, see the Log of the Ship *Sally*, entry for August 13, 1767, series A, part 2, reel 10, *PAST*.

Chapter Two

1. *New England Historical and Genealogical Register*, 63:158–60.

2. Newport Town Records, Land Evidence, 2:293–94, 3:190–91, 8:1910–11, 10:224–26, 16:226, NHS.

3. Macgunnigle, *Rhode Island Freemen*, 5, 25.

4. See John Banister Daybook, 324, RIHS; Deposition of Gilbert Phillips, November 15, 1757, *Godfrey v. Vernon*, case no. 14,159, RISCJA.

5. MacSparran, *Letter Book*, 140; Quincy, *Twenty Sermons*.

6. *Boston Weekly News Letter*, September 25, 1740, 1; Admiralty Papers, vol. 5, folder 50, RISA.

7. William Vernon to George Austin, April 14, 1756, William Vernon Letterbook, no. 3, 1751–75, NHS.

8. Vickers and Walsh, *Young Men and the Sea*, 106–9.

9. Affidavit of Caleb Godfrey, ca. 1724, CO 388/27, p. 39, BNA. In the affidavit, Godfrey's age is given as "about 20 Years." Petition of William Wanton, June 4, 1728, in Davies, *Calendar of State Papers*, 36:109. Although Wanton's petition dates to 1728, the events took place in 1724.

10. Petition of Richard Partridge in Stock, *Proceedings and Debates of the British Parliaments*, 5:216. Whether this was the same *Little George* that experienced a shipboard slave revolt in 1737 is unknown. Godfrey was not on that particular voyage.

11. Godfrey Malbone Account Book, 1728–1738, Malbone Family Collection, 15, 36, 43, RIHS.

12. *American Weekly Mercury*, May 4, 1732, 4, and May 11, 1732, 4; *Boston Gazette*, April 28, 1740, 3; John Banister Daybook, 1746–1750, 173, 243, 308, 330, 441, 488, RIHS.

13. John Harris to Governor William Mathews, September 25, 1736, in Davies, *Calendar of State Papers*, 43:65.

14. Coughtry, *Notorious Triangle*, 241–43, 245. See also Donnan, *Documents*, 3:121, 142.

15. Donnan, *Documents*, 3:131.

16. John Banister to Philip Houghton, January 28, 1748, in Donnan, *Documents*, 3:142. Houghton only refers to "Capt Godfrey," but since Banister employed Caleb Godfrey for so many years, he almost certainly meant Caleb rather than John Godfrey. See above.

17. William Vernon to Thomlinson, Trecothick, and Company, June 1, 1754, William Vernon Letterbook, no. 3, 1751–1775, NHS.

18. Caleb Godfrey to Isaac Winslow, February 9, 1749, Roderick Terry, Jr., Autograph Collection, RLA.

19. Rediker, *Slave Ship*, 57–60.

20. Coughtry, *Notorious Triangle*, 56–57.

21. Ibid., 67; Christopher, *Slave Ship Sailors*, 35–36.

22. This discussion is based on the *Hare*'s "Portage [Portledge] Bill," NYHS. All Rhode Island currency conversions are based on McCusker, *Money and Exchange*, 153–54.

23. Instructions to Captain Caleb Godfrey, November 8, 1755, box 1, folder 14, NYHS. First mates were usually allowed anywhere between one and three privilege slaves. See Instructions from Isaac Elizer and Samuel Moses to Capt. John Peck, October 9, 1762, in Coughtry, *Notorious Triangle*, 68; Adams et al., *Commerce of Rhode Island*, 96.

24. Protest of John Arnold Hammond, 6:384, LNR. For his birth and marriage, see Rhode Island Births and Christenings and Rhode Island Marriages, online at FamilySearch.org, https://familysearch.org/search/record/results#count=20&query=%2Bgivenname%3A%-22john%20arnold%22~%20%2Bsurname%3Ahammond~%20%2Bbirth_place%3A%22new-port%2C%20ori%22~%20%2Bbirth_year%3A1730–1730~ (accessed March 9, 2013).

25. "Portage Bill," NYHS; Instructions to Captain Caleb Godfrey, November 8, 1755, NYHS. Once more I have assumed that the Vernons issued similar instructions for both of the *Hare*'s voyages.

26. Protest of Peter Franklin, April 19, 1751, 5:663, LNR; *SCG*, March 13, 1755, 2; *New York Mercury*, May 31, 1756, 2, and January 1, 1759, 3.

27. Rediker, *Between the Devil and the Deep Blue Sea*. See esp. chaps. 2 and 5.

28. On the binding out of young, poor men to Rhode Island ships, see Herndon, "Domestic Cost of Seafaring," 61.

29. Christopher, *Slave Ship Sailors*. On mortality, see Behrendt, "Crew Mortality," 55; Rediker, *Slave Ship*, 244–47.

30. Hoxse, *Yankee Tar*, 9.

31. Rediker, *Between the Devil and the Deep Blue Sea*, 80–81; Nash, *Urban Crucible*, 64; Roland, Bolster, and Keyssar, *Way of the Ship*, 83–86.

32. Colman, "The Insolvent Debtor in Rhode Island," 422; Herndon, "Domestic Cost of Seafaring."

33. Pares, *Yankees and Creoles*, 18.

34. Cremer, *Ramblin' Jack*, 87; Martin, *Journal of a Slave Dealer*, 37; Rediker, *Between the Devil and the Deep Blue Sea*, 136.

35. Mason, *Reminiscences of Newport*, 180.

36. *Boston Post Boy*, February 11, 1754, 2.

37. Preston, *Rhode Island and the Sea*, 35.

38. "Portage Bill," NYHS.

39. Nash, *Urban Crucible*, 179, 183.

40. "Portage Bill," NYHS.

41. Caleb Godfrey to Samuel and William Vernon, September 7, 1754, NYHS.

42. Birth, marriage, and death information is cited in Church of Jesus Christ and the Latter Day Saints, Endowments for the Dead, 1877–1970; Heir Indexes, 1870–1956; and Baptisms for the Dead, 1943–1970, on FamilySearch.org (accessed August 18, 2009). For Batty's admission to freeman status, see Macgunnigle, *Rhode Island Freemen*, 14. For service on a privateer, see Chapin, *Rhode Island in the Colonial Wars*, 6. See also *Boston Post Boy*, June 11, 1750, 1; *New York Mercury*, May 21, 1755, 3; *Newport Mercury*, September 14, 1762, 3; *New London Gazette*, May 4, 1764, 3. On the Batty family, and for another John Batty who was a large landowner and almost certainly did not sail on the *Hare*, see Battey, *Samson Battey of Rhode Island*, 20.

43. Chapin, *Rhode Island in the Colonial Wars*, 21, 36, 149.

44. Emma Christopher finds that only 5 percent of all seamen working out of Britain were black and suggests that the number working on slave ships was smaller still. For Rhode Island, she suggests that the percentage "does not appear to be very substantial." See Christopher, *Slave Ship Sailors*, 80, 83.

45. Coughtry, *Notorious Triangle*, 58–59.

46. Vickers and Walsh, "Young Men and the Sea," 23–24; Vickers and Walsh, *Young Men and the Sea*, 105–6.

47. Crew breakdowns for Rhode Island ships that called at ports in Britain during 1750s may be found in the Registers of Passes, ADM7/87, ADM7/88, ADM7/89, and ADM7/90, BNA. Each vessel was required to report the number of British (including North American) and non-British crew members.

48. Roland, Bolster, and Keyssar, *Way of the Ship*, 84–85.

49. On the anational or antinational consciousness of seamen, see Rediker, *Between the Devil and the Deep Blue Sea*, 79–80; Rediker, *Villains of All Nations*, 7–8, 164, 176.

50. On astrology in England, see Thomas, *Religion and the Decline of Magic*, 308–10; Hunter and Gregory, *An Astrological Diary*; Curry, *Prophecy and Power*.

51. Mason, "The African Slave Trade in Colonial Times," 319; Leventhal, *In the Shadow of the Enlightenment*, 14–20, 57–58.

52. John Sherman Horoscope Book, NHS. See also Potvin, "John Sherman's Book of Horoscopes," 185–93.

53. Voyage #36251, TSTD2.

54. Hall, *Worlds of Wonder, Days of Judgment*, 15.

55. Rediker, *Between the Devil and the Deep Blue Sea*, 173–85.

56. Ibid., 185.

57. Hunter and Gregory, *An Astrological Diary*, 12.

58. Instructions to Caleb Godfrey, November 8, 1755, NYHS. For comparison, see William Vernon to Thomas Teakle Taylor, May 12, 1759, box 1, NYHS; Instructions to Nathaniel Hammond, June 6, 1770, in Adams et al., *Commerce of Rhode Island*, 332–33.

59. Instructions to Caleb Godfrey, November 8, 1755, NYHS; William Vernon to Messrs. Thomlinson and Trecothick, June 1, 1754, Vernon Papers, NHS.

60. The term "Windward Coast" was used by the British to refer to the stretch to the windward of the Gold Coast, where the Royal African Company had kept its African headquarters. It was sometimes restricted to the area south of Cape Mount but more often included Sierra Leone and even Senegambia. For more discussion, see Jones and Johnson, "Slaves from the Windward Coast."

61. Instructions to Caleb Godfrey, November 8, 1755, NYHS. The first mention of the attacks at Portudal in a North American paper was in the *South Carolina Gazette*, July 11, 1754, 2. Given their strong connection with South Carolina, it is plausible that the Vernons received a copy of the *Gazette*, or they may have learned of the attacks from the *New York Mercury*, August 12, 1754, 2.

62. *Boston Post Boy*, July 8, 1754, 2. The *Boston Post Boy* was the only newspaper that carried Rhode Island shipping notices, but it did not do so consistently. The previous issue, for July 1, 1754, made no mention of Rhode Island departures. TSTD2 gives the *Hare*'s sailing date as July 5, 1754, but the *Boston Post Boy* makes clear that July 5 was the date of the report from Rhode Island, which included the previous two weeks' outbound clearances. The *Hare*'s portage bill shows that the last crew member signed on June 29. Thus, the *Hare* would have sailed between June 29 and July 5, 1754.

63. *The English Pilot*, 5:19. On the Beaver's Tail lighthouse, see Bartlett, *Records of the Colony of Rhode Island*, 5:384. On Fort George, see Bartlett, 5:387.

64. *Boston Post Boy*, July 2, 1754, 1–2; *Boston Gazette*, July 4, 1754, 1–2. "Mr. Whitefield" was the evangelist George Whitefield, who was on his fifth trip to the American colonies. "Major Washington" was actually Lieutenant Colonel George Washington. For a complete account of the battle, see Anderson, *Crucible of War*, 50–65.

Chapter Three

1. This discussion is based upon the following logbooks: Logbook of Slave Traders, CSL; Isaac Carr Nautical Logbook, 1773–1775, NYSHA; Logs of the *Sally, Hanna, Cleopatra,* and *Affrica*, series A, part 2, reel 11, PAST; Log of the *Louisa*, NYPL.

2. Bruyns and Mörzer, "Techniques and Methods of Navigation before 1740," 60.

3. Ibid.; Bruyns and Mörzer, "Development of Navigational Methods," 98–99; Bruyns and Mörzer, "Sources of Knowledge: Charts and Rutters," 70.

4. Bruyns and Mörzer, "Development of Navigational Methods," 90.

5. Falconer, *Universal Dictionary of the Marine.*

6. Logbook of Slave Traders, CSL; Falconer, *Universal Dictionary of the Marine.*

7. It is probable, but not entirely certain, that the *Hare* called at Cape Verde on this voyage. Fragmentary accounts in the ship's papers reveal that the *Hare* made several purchases at Cape Verde, but these appear to date to the 1755–56 voyage. Coughtry, *Notorious Triangle,*

100, suggests that it was very common for Rhode Island vessels to stop at Cape Verde, and the fact that Godfrey called there on one of the voyages strongly suggests he did so routinely. For more discussion, see appendix 2.

8. On the visibility of Fogo, see Martin, *Journal of a Slave Dealer*, 36.

9. Duncan, *Atlantic Islands*, 18–22, 168–72, 215–22; Martin, *Journal of a Slave Dealer*, 35–36.

10. Entry for March 13, 1757, Logbook of Slave Traders, CSL.

11. Accounts of the *Hare*, box 2, folder 18, NYHS. By law, during the seventeenth century, the seat of government alternated between Ribeira Grande and Praia. Almost all officials, however, preferred and remained in Ribeira Grande. In 1770, with Ribeira Grande in decline, the seat of government was officially moved to Praia. See Duncan, *Atlantic Islands*, 176–79. It appears also that "St. Jago" was used by British sailors for both the island and the town, while "Porto Praya" was used consistently for the town of Praia.

12. Duncan, *Atlantic Islands*, 174.

13. Accounts of the *Hare*, NYHS.

14. Harms, *The* Diligent, 112–13.

15. Duncan, *Atlantic Islands*, 184–90; Dampier, *A Voyage to New Holland*, 16, 27; Accounts of the *Hare*, NYHS.

16. Clarke, *Sierra Leone*, 2.

17. Anonymous, West Africa 1, Add Ms 59777 A, p. 17, BL.

18. Mouser, "Iles de Los as a Bulking Center," 77–90.

19. Kup, *History of Sierra Leone*, 5.

20. *The English Pilot*, 5:19.

21. http://www.bbc.com/weather/features/18037255 (accessed September 4, 2015); http://www.bbc.com/weather/2409306 (accessed September 4, 2015).

22. Clarke, *Sierra Leone*, 20.

23. Caleb Godfrey to Samuel and William Vernon, August 22, 1754, NYHS.

24. On the voyage of the *Sierra Leone*, see Mason, "The African Slave Trade," 340–42; Donnan, *Documents*, 3:147–49. The documents appear identical, except for the fact that Mason lists the *Sierra Leone*'s owner as William Johnston and Co., while Donnan lists them as Wilkinson and Ayrault. I cannot explain the discrepancy.

25. Accounts of the *Hare*, NYHS; Caleb Godfrey to Samuel and William Vernon, August 22, 1754, NYHS.

26. Rodney, *Upper Guinea Coast*, 194; Anonymous, West Africa 1, Add. Ms. 59777A, BL. On the seasonality of the slave trade and merchants' efforts to "sort" their cargoes to suit African consumer tastes, see Behrendt, "Markets, Transaction Cycles, and Profits."

27. Robert Heatley to Samuel and William Vernon, October 19, 1774, NYHS.

28. Caleb Godfrey to Samuel and William Vernon, August 22, 1754, and September 7, 1754, ibid.

29. Caleb Godfrey to Samuel and William Vernon, August 22, 1754, and September 7, 1754, ibid.

30. At the time of the *Hare*'s visit, the installation was known as "Bance Island." Previously, it had been known as "Bence" or "Bense" Island, and during the 1750s it was occasionally referred to as "George Island." The current name is "Bunce Island." For consistency's sake I will use the 1750s name, "Bance Island," throughout.

31. On the general history of Bance Island, see Davies, *Royal African Company*, 219; Kup, *History of Sierra Leone*, 54–55, 96–97, 108–13; Fyfe, *History of Sierra Leone*, 4–7; Hancock, *Citizens of the World*, 172–220. On the attack by José Lopez, see Rodney, *Upper Guinea Coast*, 213–14, and T70/1465, pp. 58–66, BNA. On Lopez's indebtedness to the Royal African Company, see T70/654, 92, T70/655, 36, T70/363, entry for June 9, 1724, BNA.

32. *Journals of the House of Commons*, 26:247–48, 258; Hancock, *Citizens of the World*, 177–89. In his testimony before Parliament, Oswald called his landlord "Ba Samma." The proper title, "Bai," is often imperfectly translated as "king." On the ethnicity of Bai Samma, see Kup, *History of Sierra Leone*, 190–91.

33. See Samuel Staple to the Board of Trade, August 9, 1751, Co388/45, p. 69, BNA; Report on George [Bance] Island, January 2, 1751, Co388/45, p. 71, BNA; Report on Bance Island, "State and Condition of Bance Island," August 14, 1756, Co388/47, BNA.

34. "A Plan of the Fort & Factory on George Island in the River Sierraleon," CO 700 Sierra Leone 1a, BNA; "West Side of George Island on the River Sierraleone," 1b, BNA. For the elephant attack, see Sierraleon Journal, 1723–1724, T70/363, p. 39, BNA.

35. "A Plan of the Fort & Factory on George Island in the River Sierraleon" and "West Side of George Island on the River Sierraleone," CO 700 Sierra Leone 1a and 1b, BNA.

36. Ibid. On negotiations at the palaver house, see James Low to Sir Archibald Grant, January 30, 1762, GD345/1180/1762, NAS.

37. "State and Condition of the Fort and Factory on George Island," Co388/45, "State and Condition of the Fort at Bance Island," Co388/47, "State and Condition of the Fort at Bance Island," May 26, 1763, CO 388/51, BNA; Anonymous, West Africa 1, Add Ms 59777 A, BL. Thomas Knight and Alex McIntosh to Richard Oswald, August 5, 1774, Letters to Richard Oswald, BRBL; Lambert, *House of Commons Sessional Papers*, 68:262. In 1757, Nicholas Owen referred to grometto sailors as "free people who volonterely went with us . . . for a small demand of wages." See Martin, *Journal of a Slave Dealer*, 39. On the distinction between factory slaves and gromettos at Bance Island during the 1720s, see T70/363, pp. 4, 18, BNA. Historians who have examined other slave-trading regions have suggested that nearly all African laborers at the forts were enslaved, though they note that castle slaves were generally treated differently from the sale slaves. See Law, *Ouidah*, 39; St. Clair, *Door of No Return*, 132–43; Shumway, "Castle Slaves of the Eighteenth-Century Gold Coast (Ghana)," 84–98.

38. For Godfrey's use of gromettos, see "Sundry Disbursements of the Sloop *Hare*, Caleb Godfrey, Master, on the Coast of Affrica," box 2, folder 18, NYHS.

39. James Low to Sir Archibald Grant, May 10, 1762, GD345/1180/1762, NAS. Bance Island had long operated out-factories for the purchase of slaves. See for example T70/654 and T70/655, BNA.

40. For a list of out-factories in 1763, see "State and Condition of the Fort of Bance Island in the River Sierra Leone, Africa," CO 388/51, BNA.

41. James Low to Sir Archibald Grant, April 2, 1762, GD345/1180/1762, NAS.

42. James Low to Sir Archibald Grant, February 10, 1762, GD345/1180/1762, NAS.

43. On the out-factories in general, see James Low to Sir Archibald Grant, February 10, 1762, February 22, 1762, and May 10, 1762, GD345/1180/1762, NAS.

44. "State and Condition of the Fort and Factory," and "State and Condition of Bance Island," CO 388/47, BNA.

45. Hancock, *Citizens of the World*, 204–14.

46. "Sundry Disbursements," NYHS.

47. Godfrey recounted the story in two different letters to the Vernons. See Caleb Godfrey to Samuel and William Vernon, September 4, 1754, and September 7, 1754, NYHS.

48. Caleb Godfrey to Samuel and William Vernon, August 22, 1754, September 4, 1754, and September 7, 1754, NYHS.

49. "Portage Bill," NYHS. Elizabeth Donnan transcribed the name as "Barnb [i.e., Barnabas or Barnaby] Harlwick." See Donnan, *Documents*, 3:146. A close examination of the original suggests "Barnt Hartwick" is correct. "Barnt" is likely a rendering of the German/Scandinavian name "Bernt," and "Hartwick" is both an English and a German surname.

50. Caleb Godfrey to Samuel and William Vernon, September 7, 1754, NYHS.

51. Christopher, *Slave Ship Sailors*, 125–42; Martin, *Journal of a Slave Dealer*, 24–29.

52. Martin and Spurrell, *Journal of a Slave Trader*, 88.

53. Christopher, *Slave Ship Sailors*, 29, 184.

54. Richard Oswald to the Board of Trade, July 6, 1752, CO 388/45, p. 80, BNA.

55. For an overview, see Diouf, *Fighting the Slave Trade*, introduction.

56. Donnan, *Documents*, 3:52–65.

57. "Mr. Parfitts Information respecting Trade between Sierra Leone & Cape Lopaz [*sic*], including the Islands St. Thomas &c," Add Ms 12,131, pp. 1–3, BL.

58. Newton, *Thoughts upon the African Slave Trade*, 24.

59. Ibid.

60. Kelley, "The Dirty Business of Panyarring and Palaver."

61. Ibid.

62. Dorjahn and Fyfe, "Landlord and Stranger," 391–97; Mouser, "Landlords-Strangers," 425–40; Brooks, *Landlords and Strangers*.

63. Kelley, "The Dirty Business of Panyarring and Palaver"; Corry, *Observations*, 59.

64. Mathews, *Voyage to the River Sierra Leone*, 79.

65. For descriptions of palavers at Sierra Leone, see Atkins, *Voyage to Guinea*, 52–53; Smith, *New Voyage to Guinea*, 32; Falconbridge, *Two Voyages to Sierra Leone*, 29, 54–57, 81–82, 172–73, 198–99; Winterbottom, *An Account of the Native Africans*, 1:127–33; Corry, *Observations*, 43; Lambert, *House of Commons Sessional Papers*, 69:11.

66. Atkins, *Voyage to Guinea,* 53.

67. Lovejoy and Richardson, "Trust, Pawnship, and Atlantic History," 333–55.

68. Afzelius, *Sierra Leone Journal*, 128–29.

69. "Account of Slaves Purchased," Trade Book, 1772, 1773, Paul Cross Papers, SCL; Kelley, "The Dirty Business of Panyarring and Palaver."

70. Newton, *Thoughts upon the African Slave Trade*, 24.

71. Mathews, *Voyage to the River Sierra Leone*, 80.

72. Add Ms 12,131, BL.

73. Martin, *Journal of a Slave Dealer*, 37–38.

74. Copy of a Letter from James Skinner and Robert Lewis to the Committee of the Company of Merchants Trading to Africa, June 5, 1754, CO 388/46, pp. 121–22, BNA.

Chapter Four

1. Hancock, *Citizens of the World*, 204–14. See also "An Account of the Number of Negroes Bartered for on the Coast of Africa in 1768, from Cape Blanco to Rio Congo," Eg. 1162A, BL. The author was Jonathan Roberts, who commanded at Cape Coast Castle on the Gold Coast, but his estimates for other regions, including Sierra Leone, are probably accurate in terms of percentages. Raw numbers during the 1750s, however, were likely lower. To my knowledge, no comparable subregional breakdown exists for the 1750s.

2. Kup, *History of Sierra Leone*, 149–50; Fyfe, *Sierra Leone Inheritance*, 62–76; Rodney, *Upper Guinea Coast*, 216–22; Mouser, "Trade, Coasters, and Conflict," 45–64; Brooks, *Eurafricans in Western Africa*, 177–78, 298. For more and for the quotation, see Lambert, *House of Commons Sessional Papers*, 69:85.

3. Martin, *Journal of a Slave Dealer*, 57, 59, 85.

4. Paul Cross to Unknown, n.d. (ca. 1781), Paul Cross Papers, SCL.

5. Benjamin Hore to Paul Cross, October 15, 1778, Paul Cross Papers, SCL.

6. For goods advanced to private traders, see "Invoice of Goods Delivered to Mr. Paul Cross," "List of Goods from Peter Brancker, 1781," Capt. Mercer to Paul Cross, October 24, 17??, and "List of Goods from Capt. Harrison," Paul Cross Papers, SCL. For advances from private traders to African merchants, see "List of Goods to Moses Aaron Momadue," Paul Cross Papers, SCL.

7. "Account of Slaves Purchased," Trade Book, 1773, Paul Cross Papers, SCL.

8. Martin, *Journal of a Slave Dealer*, 45, 61 (quote), 73–74. William Harrison to Paul Cross, January 25, 1782, Paul Cross Papers, SCL.

9. Austin & Laurens Account Book, 12–13, BRBL. They earned £1908 and £1740 in South Carolina currency, respectively, which was worth £282 and £249 sterling. That would buy £38,800 and £34,200 in goods today, or $59,254 and $52,229 as of this writing. See Purchasing Power of British Pounds from 1264 to the Present, http://www.measuringworth.com/calculators/ppoweruk/ (accessed July 22, 2010).

10. Paul Cross to Unknown, n.d. (ca. 1781), Paul Cross Papers, SCL. For conversions, see above.

11. Martin, *Journal of a Slave Dealer*, 76; Newton, *Authentic Narrative*, 59.

12. For Nicholas Owen, see Martin, *Journal of a Slave Dealer*, 85. Marcus Rediker suggests, very plausibly, that John Newton also had an African wife. See Rediker, *Slave Ship*, 61.

13. Newton, *Authentic Narrative*, 75–76.

14. "An Acco't of Slaves Purchas'd of Whom and Cargo Disposed of from on Board the sloop *Hare* Caleb Godfrey master on the Coast of Affrica," NYHS. The document was published, with a slightly altered title, in Donnan, *Documents*, 3:151.

15. "Sundr. Disbursments on ye Sloop *Hare* Caleb Godfrey Mastr on ye Coast of Affrica," NYHS.

16. John Clarkson, Add Ms 12,131, folio 28, BL.

17. Hawkins, *History of a Voyage*, 150–59. The reliability of this narrative has been questioned, largely because the ethnic groups described by the author have never been identified. His description of the Northern Rivers, however, is generally considered accurate. For a discussion of enmity among private traders, see Mouser, *American Colony*, 105–14.

18. Lambert, *House of Commons Sessional Papers*, 69:12; Rodney, *Upper Guinea Coast*, 229; Skinner, "Mande Settlement," 32–62. In the literature on Senegambia, this area is often called the "Southern Rivers." See Barry, *Senegambia*.

19. *Africa Pilot*, 195.

20. Martin and Spurrell, *Journal of a Slave Trader*, 13; Austin & Laurens Account Book, 1753–58, 12–13, BRBL. Godfrey spelled the name "Wallis."

21. Entry for April 5, 1757, Logbook of Slave Traders, CSL; Hancock, *Citizens of the World*, 186–87.

22. "Sundr. Disbursements . . . on ye Coast of Affrica," NYHS. "Masseboy King of Nunko" appears to have resided between the Isles de Los and the Scarcies. See the Entry for March 22, 1757, Logbook of Slave Traders, CSL. "Mongoyallaw" may have been a person, since "Mongo" was a Susu honorific that the Europeans analogized to "king." Godfrey and other Rhode Islanders apparently used it as a name for a river located near the Scarcies and Quia (also known as "Quiaport"). It may bear some connection to Yallaboi Island in the Scarcies estuary. See Log of the Ship *Sally* and Ship *Cleopatra*[,] Nathaniel Briggs, master, 1767–1783, series A, part 2, reel 11, p. 1, *PAST*.

23. Thompson, *Account of Two Missionary Voyages*, 30–32. On the progress of Islam in this area, see Rodney, *Upper Guinea Coast*, 234; Skinner, "Islam and Education," 3–4; Skinner, "Mande Settlement," 43. Special thanks to Bruce Mouser for identifying Mongo Dandi.

24. "Sundr. Disbursements. . . on ye Coast of Affrica," NYHS.

25. Thompson, *Account of Two Missionary Voyages*, 31–32.

26. Martin and Spurrell, *Journal of a Slave Trader*, 13–14; Austin & Laurens Account Book, 1753–58, 14–15, BRBL; voyage #27081, TSTD2; List of Freemen, T70/1510, BNA.

27. "An Acco't of Slaves Purchased," NYHS.

28. Henry Laurens to John Holman, September 8, 1770, 7:344, *PHL*; John Hopton to John Holman, September 8, 1772, in Donnan, *Documents*, 4:451.

29. Mouser, "Trade, Coasters, and Conflict," 52–53; Mouser, *American Colony*, 43–45; Donnan, *Documents*, 4:577, 586; Koger, *Black Slaveowners*, 110–18.

30. "An Acco't of Slaves Purchased," NYHS.

31. Testimony of Gilbert Phillips, November 15, 1757, *Godfrey v. Vernon*, RISCJA.

32. Entries for March 26, 28–31, April 1, and April 23, 1757, Logbook of Slave Traders, CSL.

33. William Harrison to Paul Cross, January 25, 1782, and Certificate of Payment, December 14, 1782, Paul Cross Papers, SCL.

34. "An Acco't of Slaves Purchased," NYHS.

35. Martin and Spurrell, *Journal of a Slave Trader*, 12, 67; Henry Laurens to Langton, Shepherd, & Co., August 19, 1756, in *PHL* 2:290–91.

36. Caleb Godfrey to Samuel and William Vernon, October 26, 1754, NYHS.

37. Two 1751 rosters can be found in CO 388/45, BNA. For Morrison's "sickly" condition, see 71.

38. *The English Pilot*, 5:19.

39. Martin, *Journal of a Slave Dealer*, 29.

40. Captain Daniel to the Board of Trade, March 1, 1752, CO 388/45, p. 76, BNA; Martin, *Journal of a Slave Dealer*, 29.

41. Golberry, *Travels in Africa*, 1:36.

42. "Capt. Caleb Godfrey to Sam. and Wm. Vernon for Deficiency on Sloop '*Hare*'s' Cargo to Africa," NYHS.

43. Newton, *Authentic Narrative*, 58–76. He identifies his master and mistress in Martin and Spurrell, *Journal of a Slave Trader*, 18.

44. Martin, *Journal of a Slave Dealer*, 38–39, 42–45, 57–58, 64–67, 69. Hall took passage to the West Indies aboard the Connecticut snow *Africa*. The *Africa* made a second voyage to Sierra Leone in 1757, and it is the journal of that voyage that has furnished so much information for this chapter.

45. "List of Freemen Commencing 15th May, 1750," Entry for June 29, 1770, T70/1510, BNA; Lambert, *House of Commons Sessional Papers*, 72:85.

46. Several maps give the location of "Skinner's Place." For an example, see *The English Pilot*, 5:20. John Newton also purchased slaves from Skinner. See Martin and Spurrell, *Journal of a Slave Trader*, 18. For the earlier Skinners in the area, see T70/363, p. 12, BNA.

47. See T70/363, p. 12, BNA; Lewis Pissoa to Paul Cross, August 12, 1779, William Harrison to Paul Cross, January 25, 1782, and Certificate of Payment, December 14, 1782, Paul Cross Papers, SCL. Other spellings include "Pasoe." The name may have been a rendering of "Pessoa," a Portuguese surname that also translates as "person."

48. Afzelius, *Sierra Leone Journal*, 106.

49. Fiske, *Gleanings from Newport Court Files*, entry no. 1068.

50. Lambert, *House of Commons Sessional Papers*, 73:104.

51. The highly problematic, if not outright destructive, nature of European categories like "nation" and "tribe" is a major theme in almost all scholarship on Africa. For a discussion of the issue, see Wright, "'What Do You Mean There Were No Tribes in Africa?'" For a discussion of the concept of nation and tribe in European thought, see Hudson, "From 'Nation' to 'Race,'" 247–64.

52. Williamson and Blench, "Niger-Congo," 18–20. On the stability of the coastal languages, see Hair, "Ethnolinguistic Continuity on the Upper Guinea Coast."

53. Wolff, "Language and Society," 324.

54. Vydrine, "Who Speaks 'Mandekan'?," 2n3; Bird, "Development of Mandekan," 148.

55. Park, *Travels*, 346, 502–3.

56. Rodney, *Upper Guinea Coast*, 39–70; Wylie, "The Influence of the Mande"; Skinner, "Mande Settlement," 499–520; Massing, "The Mane"; Howard, "Mande Identity Formation." The terms "Mande" and "Manding" refer to larger linguistic and cultural groups. Specific Mande languages include Mandinka, Malinke, Bamana, Juula, Susu, Koranko, Yalunka, Mende, and Vai. Mandinka, Malinke, Bamana, and Juula are Manding languages, a subdivision of the Mande languages.

57. Fyfe, *Sierra Leone Inheritance*, 78–84; Harris, "The Kingdom of Fouta-Diallon"; Levtzion, "Notes on the Origins of Islamic Militancy in the Futa Jallon," 1–4; Rodney, "Jihad and Social

Revolution"; Barry, *Senegambia*, 95–102; Gomez, *Pragmatism in the Age of Jihad*, 72–73; Thornton, *Warfare in Atlantic Africa*, 43.

58. Laing, *Travels*, 399–411. During the 1750s there was another jihad in the coastal region around the Scarcies Rivers, but it appears to have taken place after the *Hare*'s voyage. On the coastal jihad, see Rodney, *Upper Guinea Coast*, 234; Skinner, "Mande Settlement," 37, 43. Lofkranz and Lovejoy, "Maintaining Network Boundaries," have argued that West African Muslims generally observed strictures against enslaving fellow Muslims and against trading with non-Muslims, to the extent that West Africa sent far fewer captives across the Atlantic than it might otherwise have done. Despite this, there were many violations and ways to evade the strictures.

59. Lovejoy, *Transformations in Slavery*, 10.

60. Harris, "The Kingdom of Fouta-Diallon," chap. 2, sec. B; Barry, *Senegambia*, 113–17; Mouser, *Journal of James Watt*, 44, 51; Mouser, "Rebellion, Marronage, and Jihad," 27–44.

61. Mouser, *Journal of James Watt*, 44.

62. Mouser, "'Walking Caravans,'" 38; Perinbam, "Notes on Dyula Origins and Nomenclature," 676–90; Curtin, *Economic Change in Precolonial Africa*, 1:59–91; Barry, *Senegambia*, 76; Lovejoy, *Transformations*, 93–94. On the Juula and credit links between Futa Jallon and the Northern Rivers, see Park, *Journal of a Mission to the Interior of Africa*, 160. For accounts of "Fula" traders, see Rodney, *Upper Guinea Coast*, 224–29; Afzelius, *Sierra Leone Journal*, 103; Mouser, *Journal of James Watt*, 6, 8, 53, 89. On the Juula relationship with the Futa Jallon state, see Barry, *Senegambia*, 97.

63. Park, *Travels in the Interior Districts of Africa*, 382–83.

64. Skinner, "Mande Settlement," 37, 43.

65. Mouser, *Journal of James Watt*, maps A–F. For Sitiki's narrative, see Griffin, *The Odyssey of an African Slave*, 14–16.

66. Skinner, "Mande Settlement," 38, 43.

67. Misevich, "On the Frontier of 'Freedom,'" 43.

68. Park, *Travels*, 518–22, 530–31; Mouser, *Journal of James Watt*, 6, 8, 89; Winterbottom, *Account of the Native Africans*, 1:170; Mouser, "'Walking Caravans,'" 45. On Juula information networks, see Wright, "Darbo Jula," 41.

69. Afzelius, *Sierra Leone Journal*, 112.

70. Mathews, *Voyage to the River Sierra Leone*, 147–48; Barry, *Senegambia*, 117; Mouser, "'Walking Caravans,'" 47–48; Behrendt, "Markets, Transaction Cycles, and Profits," 187.

71. Winterbottom, *Account of the Native Africans*, 170–71, 176; Afzelius, *Sierra Leone Journal*, 103.

72. Rodney, *Upper Guinea Coast*, 237; Barry, *Senegambia*, 100.

73. "An Acco't of Slaves Purchas'd," NYHS.

74. Park, *Travels*, 493–98.

75. Caleb Godfrey to Samuel and William Vernon, October 16, 1754, and October 26, 1754, NYHS.

76. Caleb Godfrey to Samuel and William Vernon, October 16, 1754, NYHS. See also Caleb Godfrey to Samuel and William Vernon, October 26, 1754, NYHS.

77. Caleb Godfrey to Samuel and William Vernon, October 16, 1754, NYHS. Godfrey did not name the attacked vessel and gave the name of the executed captain as "Cofeald," but it seems clear he meant Captain William Canfield of the *Race Horse*. See voyage #77634, TSTD2.

78. Caleb Godfrey to Samuel and William Vernon, October 16, 1754, NYHS.

79. "Sundr. Disburstments," NYHS.

Chapter Five

1. "Sunds. Expended," and "Sundr. Disburstments," NYHS.

2. Caleb Godfrey to Samuel and William Vernon, January 29, 1755, and February 5, 1755, NYHS.

3. Falconbridge, *Account of the Slave Trade*, 32.

4. Lambert, *House of Commons Sessional Papers*, 69:116.

5. Aubrey, *The Sea-Surgeon*, 27.

6. Rediker, *Slave Ship*, 215; Christopher, *Slave Ship Sailors*, 189–91.

7. TSTD2, http://www.slavevoyages.org/tast/assessment/essays-intro-03.faces (accessed June 6, 2011); Eltis, "African Agency and Resistance."

8. Winter, *The Blind African Slave*, 127; Martin and Spurrell, *Journal of a Slave Trader*, 71.

9. Richardson, "Shipboard Revolts," 69–92; Taylor, *If We Must Die*.

10. Practices aboard American vessels were similar to those aboard British vessels in most details, except where noted below. See Mason, "The African Slave Trade in Colonial Times," 318. Mason, a descendant of a slave-trading family, noted that Rhode Island vessels also tried to disinfect the hold by swabbing it with vinegar. That may have occurred aboard the *Hare*, but the surviving accounts do not list vinegar as an expense.

11. Park, *Travels*, 539.

12. Caleb Godfrey to Samuel and William Vernon, January 29, 1755, NYHS. Assuming that Godfrey was accurate in his reporting, twenty days would constitute the fastest recorded time for the Sierra Leone–Barbados passage. The next fastest time was twenty-eight days. See TSTD2, http://slavevoyages.org/tast/database/search.faces?yearFrom=1700& yearTo=1799&mjbyptimp=60200&mjslptimp=34200 (accessed June 7, 2011).

13. TSTD2, http://slavevoyages.org/tast/database/search.faces?yearFrom= 1700&yearTo=1800 (accessed June 7, 2011). The standard deviation was 34.7 days.

14. Logbook of Slave Traders, CSL.

15. Handler, "Life Histories," 130. Hundreds more narratives and testimonies will be published in the next few years, courtesy of the Society for the History of the African Diaspora—Documents (SHADD) project, based at York University in Toronto.

16. Published narratives include Cugoano, "Narrative of the Enslavement of Ottobah Cugoano," 124–25; Carretta, *Olaudah Equiano*, 58–59. See also Law and Lovejoy, *Biography of Mahommah Gardo Baquaqua*; Smith, *Narrative of the Life and Adventures of Venture*; Curtin, *Africa Remembered*, 162, 213; Austin, *African Muslims in Antebellum America*; Handler, "Life Histories," 133–34; Blassingame, *Slave Testimony*, 198, 227, 308–20, 327, 687. Boyrereau Brinch (Jeffrey Brace), who devoted about seven hundred words to the Middle Passage and more to his confinement in Africa, is an exception to the rule. See Winter, *The Blind African Slave*, 126–28. It should be noted that not all of these narratives originated in circumstances that would have allowed for an extensive description (along with the implicit condemnation) of the slave trade and Middle Passage.

17. Lambert, *House of Commons Sessional Papers*, 68:179; Winter, *Blind African Slave*, 126–27. See also, for example, the testimony of Primus, who boarded the ship with his father and, it seems, others from his village, in Sigourney, *Sketch of Connecticut*, 81–90. It is interesting to note that four of the captives aboard the *Amistad*, which was not a transatlantic but a local Cuban slave vessel, appear to have known one other captive while in Africa. See Barber, *History of the* Amistad *Captives*, 11–12, 27.

18. Very little empirical research has been done on the shipmate relationship at sea. Most of what exists is entirely deductive in nature. For the classic statement of the view that the shipmate relationship represented the start of a new, creolized identity, see Mintz and Price, *Birth of African-American Culture*, 43–47. For one of the only empirical explorations of the phenomenon, and one that sees the hold of a slave ship as a "place of rebuilding—a place where the most intimate of human relationships were recreated in a *culturally specific* way" (emphasis mine), see Hawthorne, "'Being Now, as It Were, One Family,'" esp. at 72.

19. Quoted in Dunn, *Sugar and Slaves*, 5.

20. Steele, *English Atlantic*, 24.

21. Young, "A Tour through the Several Islands," 264.

22. Bernard Bailyn found that only 495 out of 9,364 British migrants to the colonies during 1773–76 went to the West Indies. Of these, 257 went to Jamaica, which means the remaining 2.5 percent were divided among eleven different colonies, including Barbados. See Bailyn, *Voyagers to the West*, 92.

23. Weekes, *Barbados: A Poem*, 15.

24. Welch, *Slave Society*, 36.

25. Ibid., 53; Thompson, *Sailor's Letters*, 112.

26. "Barbados," in *The North American and the West-Indian Gazetteer*.

27. Butterworth, *Three Years Adventures*, 128–29. Butterworth visited in 1787.

28. Caleb Godfrey to Samuel and William Vernon, February 5, 1755, NYHS. On the architecture and geography of Bridgetown, see Welch, *Slave Society*, 38–42; Challenger et al., "The Streets of Bridgetown Circa 1765," 76–87.

29. Hall, *Acts Passed in the Island of Barbados*, 163–65, 227, 282.

30. Carretta, *Olaudah Equiano*, 60; Winter, *Blind African Slave*, 128 (first quotation), 133 (second quotation), 136 (third quotation).

31. Earle, *Sailors*, 168, 172.

32. Christopher, *Slave Ship Sailors*, 202–5; Rediker, *Slave Ship,* 251–53.

33. On leaving a merchantman for a naval vessel, see Rediker, *Between the Devil and the Deep Blue Sea*, 103. Godfrey did deduct £5 from Hartwick's pay for loss or damage to a boat.

34. "List of Supernumeraries Borne for Victuals Only," Ship Muster for the Sloop *Tryall* [*sic*], ADM 36/585, BNA. Barnt Hartwick is listed as "Bornt Hotwick" and William Baggott appears as "William Beckett." On supernumeraries in the Royal Navy, see Rodger, *The Wooden World: An Anatomy of the Georgian Navy*, 28–29.

35. Normally such matters would fall under the jurisdiction of the Vice-Admiralty Courts. However, in Barbados the law also provided for the ad hoc creation of special courts to hear disputes between ship captains and sailors in the event that the Vice-Admiralty Courts could not convene in a timely fashion. It seems probable that Cole

contemplated taking his case before one of the latter. See Hall, *Acts Passed in the Island of Barbados*, 27.

36. Caleb Godfrey to Samuel and William Vernon, February 4, 1755, February 5, 1755, and February 19, 1755, NYHS. The surviving copy of the *Hare*'s 1754–55 portage bill is not the standard printed form of ship's articles, which included a reference to the 1729 act in the text and had the crew's signatures below. It is written entirely in Godfrey's hand and was probably his own working copy. For an example of the standard form ship's articles used on another Vernon vessel of the time, see the "Articles and Portage Bill of the Brigantine *Marygold*, 1758–59," NYHS. For a discussion of sailors suing for their discharge on the grounds that the voyage deviated from its initial plan, see Rediker, *Between the Devil and the Deep Blue Sea*, 141.

37. "Portage Bill," NYHS. In a letter dated February 4, 1755, Godfrey told the Vernons that he had only two seamen left, William Ball and John Battey. However, the "portage" bill clearly indicates that William Burling was paid off in Charles Town, South Carolina, on March 24, 1755. It may be that Burling left the *Hare* temporarily, either to enjoy himself in port or perhaps to investigate signing onto the *Tryal* with his shipmates.

38. Welch, *Slave Society*, 58.

39. Hall, *Acts Passed in the Island of Barbados*, 19.

40. Welch, *Slave Society,* 47.

41. Beckles, *Natural Rebels*, 141–50, quotation on 145. See also Welch, *Slave Society*, 88–93.

42. Caleb Godfrey to Samuel and William Vernon, February 19, 1755, NYHS. This may have been the Sgt. Francis Mountain who was stationed in Virginia in the 1740s. See the *Virginia Gazette*, September 12, 1745, 4.

43. Caleb Godfrey to Samuel and William Vernon, February 16, 1755, and February 19, 1755, NYHS.

44. Gabriel Manigault to Samuel and William Vernon, March 5, 1755, NYHS, says that Godfrey arrived on March 5 after a voyage of eighteen days, which puts his departure at February 16, 1755. He was almost certainly mistaken. In the same letter, Manigault gives the time of the *Hare*'s Atlantic crossing as sixteen days, which is at least two days too short. It seems probable that Manigault confused the length of the *Hare*'s passage from the Isles de Los to Barbados with the timing of its passage from Barbados to South Carolina. In Godfrey's final letter from Barbados, which is dated February 19, 1755, he clearly states that he intends to sail on February 20.

45. Charles Bolton to Caleb Godfrey, March 29, 1755, NYHS.

Chapter Six

1. *SCG*, February 6, 1755, 2, and March 13, 1755, 2; *The English Pilot*, 4:24–25.

2. Glen, "A Description of South Carolina," 4–6.

3. *Short Description of the Province of South Carolina*, 31.

4. Rogers, *Charleston in the Age of the Pinckneys*, 58; Olwell, *Masters, Slaves, and Subjects*, 18–19. For the date of the laying of the State House cornerstone, see *SCG*, July 2, 1753, 1. On the market, see *Short Description of the Province of South Carolina*, 35.

5. "Governor James Glen's Valuation, 1751," in Merrens, *The Colonial South Carolina Scene*, 181, 189–91. On the Half Moon Battery, see Shields, "Mean Streets, Mannered Streets," 3. The Exchange, which currently occupies the spot, was not built until the 1760s.

6. The figure for 1755 is an interpolation of the 1750 and 1760 population statistics as given in U.S. Census Bureau, *Historical Statistics of the United States*, 2:1168. On the population of the Low Country, see Morgan, *Slave Counterpoint*, 95–97.

7. U.S. Census Bureau, *Historical Statistics of the United States*, 2:1193. See also Coclanis, *Shadow of a Dream*, 81, 133–34; Morgan, "The Organization of the Colonial American Rice Trade."

8. On the Stono Rebellion, see Wood, *Black Majority*, 308–26; Thornton, "African Dimensions," 1101–3; Olwell, *Masters, Slaves, and Subjects*, 21–25; Smith, *Stono: Documenting and Interpreting a Southern Slave Revolt*; Rucker, *The River Flows On*; Hoffer, *Cry Liberty*. On slave importations, see Littlefield, "The Slave Trade to Colonial South Carolina"; Richardson, "The British Slave Trade to Colonial South Carolina." For current estimates, see TSTD2.

9. William Vernon to Gabriel Manigault, January 9, 1755, William Vernon Letterbook, no. 3, 1751–1775, NHS; Gabriel Manigault to William and Samuel Vernon, February 24, 1755, box 1, folder 9, NYHS. For Manigault's previous dealings with the Vernons, see William Vernon to Samuel Vernon, March 13, 1745, William Vernon Letters, SCL; Gabriel Manigault to William Vernon, November 7, 1747, and February 12, 1747/8, Vernon Letters, SCL. On Manigault's life and career, see Crouse, "Gabriel Manigault." Crouse, p. 98, says Manigault's countinghouse was on Tradd Street, but other evidence suggests that he had additional facilities on Church Street and Union Street. See *SCG*, January 22, 1752, 2, February 22, 1752, 4, and April 10, 1755, 3.

10. Peter Manigault to Gabriel Manigault, September 27, 1753, Manigault Family Papers, SCHS. See also Ramsay, *History of South Carolina*, 266–67; Crouse, "Gabriel Manigault," 98–99.

11. Gabriel Manigault to Peter Manigault, July 5, 1754, Manigault Family Papers, SCHS.

12. Cooper and McCord, *Statutes*, 3:771–74.

13. *SCG*, September 19, 1752, 2.

14. Jones, "The Journal of Alexander Chesney," 3; Harrison, "Journal of a Voyage to Charlestown," 143–44.

15. Cooper and McCord, *Statutes*, 3:773–74, 780.

16. On Banbury, see Crouse, "Gabriel Manigault," 106; Stumpf, "South Carolina Importers of General Merchandise," 3.

17. Gabriel Manigault to Samuel and William Vernon, March 21, 1755, NYHS; Draft on Samuel and William Vernon by Caleb Godfrey, April 1755, NYHS.

18. On planter perceptions of African ethnicity, see Littlefield, *Rice and Slaves*, esp. at 8–32. The notion that South Carolina planters prized Africans from rice-growing areas for their familiarity with rice culture has come under criticism by historians who note (among other things) that no direct references to rice appear before 1758, and that no statements claiming the captives were proficient in rice growing appeared before 1784. See Eltis, Morgan, and Richardson, "Agency and Diaspora in Atlantic History," 1348–49. However, even critics recognize that since later notices specifically touted the rice-growing capabilities of certain

Africans, it is possible that these notions circulated earlier without finding their way into advertisements.

19. Cooper and McCord, *Statutes*, 3:588. The payment of nine pounds indicates that the *Hare* was measured at ninety tons, considerably larger than the sixty-ton figure given in chap. 1. However, in the eighteenth century, "measured tonnage" was approximately one-third greater than the actual carrying capacity of a vessel ("tons burthen"). The two figures, then, are in essential agreement. For a discussion, see Davis, *The Rise of the English Shipping Industry*, 7, 74.

20. "The Sloop *Hare*, Caleb Godfrey Commander to Gabriel Manigault," NYHS.

21. See Manigault's advertisement in the *South Carolina Gazette*, April 10, 1755, 3. Other possible locations include Church Street and Union Street. See *SCG*, February 22, 1752, 4, and January 22, 1752, 2.

22. "Sund. Disburstments on Sloop *Hare* at Charlestown So. Carolina," Manigault Account with Caleb Godfrey, 1755, and "Sundr. Disburstments on ye Sloop *Hare* Caleb Godfrey Mastr on ye Coast of Affrica," NYHS.

23. Williamson, *Contrary Voices*, 137.

24. Falconbridge, *Account of the Slave Trade*, 46.

25. Lambert, *House of Commons Sessional Papers*, 73:184.

26. Carretta, *Olaudah Equiano*, 60.

27. Kelley, "Scrambling for Slaves"; Cooper and McCord, *Statutes*, 3:740.

28. Kelley, "Scrambling for Slaves."

29. Gabriel Manigault to Samuel and William Vernon, March 21, 1755, and April 12, 1755, NYHS.

30. See table 6 for individual amounts. The purchasers' inventories may be found in Books T–BB, SCDAH. Bready described himself as a planter in his will. See Charleston Wills, 12:358, SCDAH.

31. Henry Laurens to Robert and John Thompson, April 20, 1757, 523–24, *PHL*.

32. Kelley, "Scrambling for Slaves."

33. Olwell, *Masters, Slaves, and Subjects*, 44–45 (first quotation); *American Husbandry*, 392 (second quotation).

34. Mell, *Genealogy of the Mell Family*, 17–31.

35. Donnan, *Documents*, 3:161. The buyers were Henry Laurens, Elias Ball, and Nicholas Harleston. The sale was handled by Laurens, which probably helped to bring out the others. An examination of twenty more sales by Laurens between 1753 and 1758 reveals that many buyers shared a surname with at least one other purchaser at the sale, suggesting that it was common for kinsmen to attend sales together. See Austin & Laurens Account Book, BRBL.

36. On Charles Lorimer, see Howe, *History of the Presbyterian Church*, 251, 279, 321. On James Wedderburn, husband of Susannah, see Wedderburn, *The Wedderburn Book*, 1:376. On Alexander Fraser, see Edgar and Bailey, *Biographical Directory*, 2:254–55; Fraser Papers, SCHS.

37. The members were George Ducatt, Alexander Fraser, Charles Lorimer, Lachlan McIntosh, and James Parsons. See *Rules of the Society*.

38. "A Gentleman's Travels, 1733–34," in Merrens, *The Colonial South Carolina Scene*, 114.

39. On the townships, see Weir, *Colonial South Carolina*, 208–9.

40. Quoted in Harris, *Hanging of Thomas Jeremiah*, 157.

41. Morgan, *Slave Counterpoint*, 257–84; Olwell, *Masters, Slaves, and Subjects*, 191–200.

42. Will of Peter Taylor, Charleston Wills, 10:719, SCDAH.

43. *SCG*, October 17, 1754, 2. The quotation is from Trenchard's *An Argument Shewing, That a Standing Army Is Inconsistent with Free Government,* 10.

44. Lambert, *House of Commons Sessional Papers*, 73:185, 188.

45. Jones, *Detailed Reports*, 15:191.

46. Samuel West Memoirs, 266, AAS.

47. Olwell, *Masters, Slaves, and Subjects*, 71–79.

48. *SCG*, April 6, 1734, 2.

Chapter Seven

1. Morgan, *Slave Counterpoint*, 445.

2. For the size of Charles Town slaveholdings, see Morgan, "Black Life in Eighteenth-Century Charleston," 190.

3. On Laurens's planting activities, see Edelson, *Plantation Enterprise*, 200–54.

4. Jackson, *Lachlan Mcintosh*, ix, 5–9; *PHL*, 3:361–62, 390; Austin & Laurens Account Book, 1753–58, BRBL; *SCG*, November 7, 1754, 2.

5. *SCG*, May 11, 1752, 2, November 7, 1754, 2, October 27, 1758, 2, and May 3, 1760, 1.

6. Morgan, "Black Life in Eighteenth-Century Charleston," 190.

7. Inventory of William Lloyd, Book V, 73–74, and Inventory of George Ducatt, book T, 400–401, Probate Inventories, SCDAH.

8. Rogers, *Charleston in the Age of the Pinckneys*, 66–67; Poston, *Buildings of Charleston*, 37–41.

9. Herman, "Slave and Servant Housing in Charleston," 90.

10. Morgan, "Black Life in Eighteenth-Century Charleston," 199, 201.

11. Ibid.

12. On Smyser, see *SCG*, July 22, 1751, 4, August 1, 1761, 3, August 14, 1762, 2, April 28, 1767, 1, and November 1, 1770, 4. See also Plat for 250 Acres on Saltcatcher River, 1759, Plat for 300 Acres in Berkeley Co., 1765, Plat for 500 Acres in Granville Co., 1769, Colonial Plat Books, SCDAH; Will of Paul Smiser, Charleston Wills, 21:830–31, SCDAH; Austin & Laurens Account Book, BRBL. On Chisholme, see *SCG*, July 9, 1741, 3, February 27, 1744, 3, November 19, 1750, 2, December 17, 1753, 2, March 27, 1755, 3, and August 27, 1763, 2. On the rise of suburban provisioning farms after 1740, see Hart, *Building Charleston*, 113–14.

13. Morgan, "Black Life in Eighteenth-Century Charleston."

14. Quincy, "Journal of Josiah Quincy, Junior, 1773," 455.

15. *SCG*, September 17, 1772, 1.

16. On startup costs, see Morgan, *Slave Counterpoint*, 35. For Simons, see Charleston Wills, 8:376–77, and Probate Inventories, T:236–37, SCDAH. For Mell, see Charleston Wills, 8:406–10, and Probate Inventories, T:273–74, SCDAH. For Taylor, see Charleston Wills, 10:718–23, and Probate Inventories, X:91–94, SCDAH. For Fraser, see Edgar and Bailey, *Biographical Directory*, 2:254–55; Heitzler, *Goose Creek*, 173. For Parsons, see Charleston Wills, 18:344–55, and Probate Inventories, Y:190–201, SCDAH. For Laurens, see Wallace, *Life of Henry Laurens*, 203–6.

17. For Parsons, see Charleston Wills, 18:344–55, and Probate Inventories, Y:190–201, SCDAH. For Taylor, see Charleston Wills, 10:718–23, and Probate Inventories, X:91–94, SCDAH. For Taylor's violation of the residency law, see Wood, *Black Majority*, 325n67.

18. Morgan, *Slave Counterpoint*, 326–34; Olwell, *Masters, Slaves, and Subjects*, 211–18; Trinkley, Hacker, and Fick, "Investigation of an Eighteenth Century Overseer Site." For a description of an overseer carrying a sword, see Samuel West Memoirs, 263–64, AAS. On punishment by hanging in a cage, see Crèvecoeur, *Letters from an American Farmer*, 178.

19. Morgan, *Slave Counterpoint*, 343–46; Joyner, *Down by the Riverside*, 65–68. On Muslim drivers, see Gomez, *Exchanging Our Country Marks*, 82–86; Gomez, "Africans, Culture, and Islam in the Lowcountry," 107–8; Austin, *African Muslims in Antebellum America*, 65–113.

20. Morgan, *Slave Counterpoint*, 205–44. It should go without saying that Africans of both sexes possessed and practiced a great many skills that never received notice in plantation records. On Lorimer, see *SCG*, January 17, 1761, 2; *Supplement to the SCAGG*, April 18, 1764.

21. For an overview of the task system, see Morgan, *Slave Counterpoint*, 179–87. The debate over the origins of the task system is closely tied to the debate over the origins of Carolina rice culture. For a sampling of the debates, see Edelson et al., "AHR Exchange: The Question of Black Rice," 123–71.

22. Quoted in Morgan, *Slave Counterpoint*, 148. On the process and its links with Africa, see Carney, *Black Rice*.

23. *American Husbandry*, 393–94.

24. Alexander Garden to William Shipley, April 5, 1755, Henry Baker Correspondence, 1749–1770, Osborne Shelves, fc 109/II/159, BRBL. An exception would probably be the enslaved laborers who worked on the rice plantations that supplied slave ships. See chap. 4. On illness, see McCandless, *Slavery, Disease, and Suffering*, esp. chap. 3.

25. See for example Lambert, *House of Commons Sessional Papers*, 73:185, 191. On slave marketing in general, see Olwell, *Masters, Slaves, and Subjects*, 141–80; Morgan, *Slave Counterpoint*, 251–52, 358–74.

26. Edelson, *Plantation Enterprise*, 155–56; Lambert, *House of Commons Sessional Papers*, 73:185.

27. South Carolina Council Journal, no. 17, part 1, 1748–4, p. 80, SCDAH. The conspiracy itself seems to have been vastly exaggerated, if not entirely fabricated. See Morgan and Terry, "Slavery in Microcosm," 121–45.

28. On the geographical spread of indigo, see Rogers, *History of Georgetown County*, 88; Bridges and Williams, *St. James Santee Plantation Parish*, 49; Rowland, Moore, and Rogers, *History of Beaufort County*, 161–62; Johnson, *The Frontier in the Colonial South*, 39–40.

29. Henry Laurens to Smith & Clifton, May 26, 1755, 1:254–56, *PHL*.

30. For Taylor, see Probate Inventory of Peter Taylor, X:91–94, SCDAH; for Fraser, see *SCG*, December 17, 1753, 2; for Douxsaint, see Inventory of Paul Douxsaint, BB:154–57, SCDAH; for Lloyd, see *SCG*, December 16, 1754, 4; for Lorimer, see *SCG*, January 17, 1761, 2. Laurens, of course, was still a merchant but would acquire a plantation the next year. His early planting activities are somewhat murky. Biographer David Wallace notes that Laurens's first plantation was in "indigo country." See Wallace, *Life of Henry Laurens*, 130. It is confirmed that within a few years Laurens had devoted at least one of his plantations exclusively to indigo.

See Edelson, *Plantation Enterprise*, 203, 213. See also the Probate Inventory of John Coming Ball (Laurens's partner), W:198–202, SCDAH.

31. *SCG*, January 17, 1761, 2. On indigo production, see Chaplin, *Anxious Pursuit*, 190–208; Morgan, *Slave Counterpoint*, 159–64.

32. Chaplin, *Anxious Pursuit*, 190–208; Morgan, *Slave Counterpoint*, 159–64.

33. Edelson, *Plantation Enterprise*, 159–61. For Lorimer, see *SCG*, January 17, 1761, 2. Lorimer and wife Susannah Wedderburn bought four men from the *Hare* and owned "upwards of 20 valuable slaves," including women and children. If adult males comprised about one-third of his labor force, or seven out of twenty, then there was a real chance that a *Hare* captive was the one mentioned.

34. On Minnick, see Easterby, Olsberg, and Lipscomb, *Journal of the Commons House of Assembly* (1757–1761): 1109; Meriweather, *Expansion of South Carolina*, 48–50; *SCG*, November 26, 1763, 4.

Chapter Eight

1. On mortality among newly arrived Africans, see Morgan, *Slave Counterpoint*, 445. For mortality on the plantations and during the 1760 smallpox epidemic, see McCandless, *Slavery, Disease, and Suffering*, 128–29, 213–24.

2. For specific information on the mobility and mortality of the *Hare* purchasers, see table 6.

3. http://slavevoyages.org/tast/assessment/estimates.faces?yearFrom=1751&yearTo=1775 (accessed June 4, 2015).

4. For example, of the British vessels that purchased most of their captives on the "Windward Coast" between 1751 and 1776, and for which the specific ports of purchase are known, more than half bought their captives at Cape Mount and points north. Several of these "Windward Coast" vessels purchased their captives as far north as the Rio Pongo and Gambia. See TSTD2, http://slavevoyages.org/tast/database/search.faces?yearFrom=1751&yearTo=1775& mjbyptimp=60300&natinimp=7 (accessed June 11, 2012). See also Jones and Johnson, "Slaves from the Windward Coast."

5. Kaye, *Joining Places*, esp. at 4, 10. See also Walsh, *From Calabar to Carter's Grove*.

6. Morgan, *Slave Counterpoint*, 524. See also Morgan, "Colonial South Carolina Runaways," 78n59.

7. For the deed, see *PHL*, 2:180.

8. The names appear in the Probate Inventory of John C. Ball, X:1–18, SCDAH. One of them was simply named "Wambaw."

9. The totals are calculated from the Austin & Laurens Account Book, BRBL; "Henry Laurens Account Book" [wastebook] in Donnan, *Documents*, 4:305–8. Laurens handled a total of six Grant & Oswald vessels from Bance Island, Sierra Leone. Three arrived before 1758 and three afterward. On Laurens's career as a slave trader, see Rawley, *London, Metropolis of the Slave Trade*, 82–97; Higgins, "Charles Town Merchants and Factors," 205–17. On Grant & Oswald, see Hancock, *Citizens of the World*, esp. chap. 6.

10. Wolff, "Language and Society," 317.

11. For an argument that these ties gave way relatively quickly, see Morgan, *Slave Counterpoint*, 447–48. For an argument that the ties were more enduring, see Gomez, *Exchanging Our Country Marks*, 3–4.

12. For Laurens, see *SCG*, September 3, 1753, 4. For Parsons, see *SCG*, November 24, 1761, 4, and December 19, 1761, 4. See table 7 in Littlefield, *Rice and Slaves*, 129–31, and discussion below.

13. *SCG*, April 27, 1765, 3, October 30, 1762, 3, and January 1, 1759, 3. Bamana and Mandinka are closely related, so it is not surprising that one person can interpret for both. See below for further discussion.

14. *Supplement to the SCGCJ*, May 5, 1767, 5, and August 4, 1772, 3.

15. Compare the runaway and workhouse columns in table 7 in Littlefield, *Rice and Slaves*, 129–31.

16. Philip Misevich has demonstrated that recaptives labeled "Mandinga" in nineteenth-century Cuba were not, in fact, Mandingo. Rather, the word "Mandinga" was applied indiscriminately to captives embarking at the Rio Pongo. See Misevich, "The Origins of Slaves Leaving the Upper Guinea Coast in the Nineteenth Century," 162–64. The same point probably does not apply in this case. Misevich analyzed the Mixed Commission Registers of recaptives in Havana, where officials apparently used "Mandinga" as a geographic portmanteau. Work-house notices, as argued above, were generated through a very different process and were more likely to rely upon self-identification. See below for more discussion of the meaning of "Mandingo" in South Carolina.

17. Landers, *Black Society in Spanish Florida*, 269–75. The twenty-seven "Mandingas" in the Florida importation records were the third-largest group. The array of ethnonyms appearing in the registers is very broad, with over fifty different entries. Many, if not most, appear to be of Central African provenance. The most frequent category was Congo, with thirty-eight people, followed by Criollo (Creoles) with twenty-eight. "Ganga" was an identifier common in the Spanish colonies, denoting a person from Upper Guinea, but it had no apparent correspondence with any specific African ethnicity.

18. *SCG*, October 30, 1762, 3, and February 2, 1760, 2.

19. Sweet, *Domingos Alvares*, 16, 86, has termed a similar phenomenon in Brazil "meta-ethnicity."

20. *SCG*, November 1, 1759, 3, July 24, 1762, 2, and June 3, 1766, 4. The meaning of "Bambara" in the New World has been the subject of debate. See Hall, *Africans in Colonial Louisiana*; Hall, *Slavery and African Ethnicities*, 96–98; Caron, "'Of a Nation Which the Others Do Not Understand'"; Lofkranz and Lovejoy, "Maintaining Network Boundaries," 217. For the lexical similarity of Bamana and Mandinka, see Vydrine, "Who Speaks 'Mandekan'?," 2n3.

21. Alryyes, *A Muslim American Slave*, 63.

22. Young, *Rituals of Resistance*, 110. The best surviving eighteenth-century sources for African cultural practices in South Carolina are probably the eyewitness accounts of the Stono Rebellion. Historians who have read those accounts for clues about African practices include Thornton, "African Dimensions," and Smith, "Remembering Mary, Shaping Revolt."

23. Fisher, *Extracts from the Records of the Royal African Companies*, 50; Winterbottom, *Account of the Native Africans*, 1:255, 258–60.

24. Hall, *Africans in Colonial Louisiana*, 163–64; Sweet, *Recreating Africa*, 179–85.

25. *Drums and Shadows*, 125.

26. Fett, *Working Cures*, 102–4. See also Chireau, *Black Magic*, 46–48; Young, *Rituals of Resistance,* 112–13.

27. TSTD2, http://slavevoyages.org/tast/assessment/estimates.faces?yearFrom= 1501&yearTo=1866 (accessed July 31, 2012). On Central Africans in South Carolina, see Creel, *"A Peculiar People,"* 43–44; Thornton, "African Dimensions"; Gomez, *Exchanging Our Country Marks,* 150–51; Young, *Rituals of Resistance.*

28. *Periodical Accounts,* 168–69; Sweet, *Recreating Africa,* 185.

29. On the use of biblical verses in charms, see Chireau, *Black Magic,* 25.

30. Curtin, *Economic Change in Precolonial Africa,* 31–37; Roberts, "Production and Reproduction of Warrior States," 404–5.

31. Creel, *"A Peculiar People,"* 181–83, 288–90; Gomez, *Exchanging Our Country Marks,* 99–101.

32. Turner, *Africanisms in the Gullah Dialect,* 150, 156.

33. Figures for the slave trade as a whole are from TSTD2, http://slavevoyages.org/tast/assessment/estimates.faces?yearFrom=1501&yearTo=1866 (accessed August 2, 2012). This figure is probably closer to a minimum than a maximum. It does not take into account the probability that some captives from Lower Guinea were Muslim. Sylviane Diouf has suggested that 15–20 percent of all Africans taken to the New World were Muslims, but since Islam experienced significant growth in the nineteenth century, a lower figure is probably warranted for the earlier period. See Diouf, *Servants of Allah,* 48.

34. *Practical Considerations,* 30.

35. Park, *Travels,* 538.

36. For these names, see *SCGCJ,* December 28, 1773, 3; Gomez, *Exchanging Our Country Marks,* 70; Account and Blanket Book, 1720–1778, Ball Family Papers, SCHS.

37. Ball, *Fifty Years in Chains,* 101–13.

38. Curtin, *Africa Remembered,* 145–51; Austin, *African Muslims in Antebellum America: A Sourcebook*; Austin, *African Muslims in Antebellum America,* 85–113; Gomez, *Exchanging Our Country Marks,* 76–79; Gomez, "Africans, Culture, and Islam in the Lowcountry."

39. Diouf, *Servants of Allah,* 1–2. See also Addoun and Lovejoy, "Muhammad Kaba Saghanughu," 201–17.

40. Diouf, *Servants of Allah,* 58–59, 104; Reis, *Slave Rebellion*; Addoun and Lovejoy, "Muhammad Kaba Saghanughu."

Chapter Nine

1. Gabriel Manigault to Samuel and William Vernon, March 21, 1755, NYHS. On the drop in demand a few weeks later, see Henry Laurens to William Whaley, May 12, 1755, 1:245–46, *PHL.* Henry Laurens to Wells, Wharton, & Doran, May 27, 1755, 1:257, *PHL.*

2. Richardson, "The British Slave Trade to Colonial South Carolina," 151.

3. "Sund Disbursments on Sloop *Hare* at Charlstown So Carolina," NYHS.

4. On the shipping and storage of rice, see South Carolina Council Journal, no. 17, part 1, 1748–49, p. 78, SCDAH. On watchmen, see *SCG,* February 22, 1773, 1.

5. *SCG,* May 25, 1743, postscript; Lambert, *House of Commons Sessional Papers,* 184; Clarkson, *Substance of the Evidence,* 59; *SCG,* May 1, 1756, 1; Easterby, Olsberg, and Lipscomb, *Journal of the Commons House of Assembly,* 9:200. On prostitutes, see Morgan, "Black Life in Eighteenth-Century Charleston," 210–11; *SCG,* November 14, 1761, 2.

6. Harrison, "Journal of a Voyage to Charlestown," 144. On the dispute, see Henry Laurens to Samuel and William Vernon, June 12, 1756, 2:218, *PHL*.

7. *SCG*, April 10, 1755, 2, and April 17, 1755, 1.

8. *SCG*, May 15, 1755, 2.

9. These calculations are necessarily rough, given the incomplete nature of the documentation. On the overall profitability of the transatlantic slave trade, see Klein, *The Atlantic Slave Trade*, 98.

10. TSTD2, http://slavevoyages.org/tast/assessment/estimates.faces?yearFrom= 1501&yearTo=1866 (accessed August 19, 2015). I have calculated the total for Upper Guinea by combining the Senegambia, Sierra Leone, and Windward Coast totals.

11. Richardson, "Prices of Slaves," 33, 47.

12. Manning, *Slavery and African Life*, esp. chap. 4; Lovejoy, *Transformations in Slavery*.

13. Barry, *Senegambia*, 99–100. Barry's dates differ slightly from those given in Rodney, "Jihad and Social Revolution," 280.

14. A brief account of the voyage of the *Titt Bitt* can be found in Wax, "Thomas Rogers and the Rhode Island Slave Trade," 294–95.

15. Company of Merchants Trading to Africa to Thomas Melvil, February 12, 1755, CO 267/6, BNA; Bartlett, *Records of the Colony of Rhode Island*, 5:410–11; *SCG*, March 6, 1755, 1.

16. On Dowdall, see Testimony of Gilbert Phillips, November 15, 1757, *Godfrey v. Vernon*, case no. 14,159, RISCJA. For Godfrey's visit to Bance Island, see Martin, *Journal of a Slave Dealer*, 69; Hancock, *Citizens of the World*, 205.

17. The basic outline of the voyage can be found in Donnan, *Documents*, 3:159–64. For the capture of British vessels, see Donnan, *Documents*, 3:173–74. On the Vernons' strategy of avoiding the Caribbean, see William Vernon to Austin & Laurens, June 1, 1756, William Vernon Letterbook, no. 3, 1751–1775, NHS.

18. *PHL*, 2:236, 238–39.

19. Ball, *Slaves in the Family*, 193–94.

20. Henry Laurens to Samuel and William Vernon, July 5, 1756, 2:238–39, *PHL*. For the Vernons' slave-trading career, see TSTD2.

21. *Godfrey v. Vernon*, case no. 14,159, RISCJA.

22. Kelley, "People of Business: The Vernon Brothers and the Rhode Island Slave Trade."

23. Crouse, "Gabriel Manigault"; Ramsay, *History of South Carolina*, 266–67.

24. Jackson, *Lachlan Mcintosh*, 131–35.

25. Egerton, *Death or Liberty*, 81.

26. Wallace, *Life of Henry Laurens*, 371, 388.

27. Caleb Godfrey Mortgage Record, Newport Town Records, Land Evidence, 11:87, NHS; *Pennsylvania Gazette*, July 26, 1759, 2; Dexter, *Extracts from the Itineraries*, 103–4; *Newport Mercury*, December 20, 1762, 3, and January 3, 1763, 4; *Pennsylvania Gazette*, October 27, 1763, 1.

28. *Pennsylvania Gazette*, October 3, 1765, 2; *Newport Mercury*, December 15, 1766, 1; Dr. William Hunter Physician's Account Book, 53, NHS. See record for October 10, 1775, in RG 36, Records of the U.S. Customs Service, Records of the Customshouses, Newport, R.I., National Archives at Boston.

29. Dexter, *Extracts from the Itineraries*, 103–4; Chapin, *Rhode Island in the Colonial Wars*, 77; Protest of John Arnold Hammond, 6:384, LNR. In 1765, a John Hammond died in a slave insurrection aboard the Vernons' brig *Othello*. See Wax, "Thomas Rogers and the Rhode Island Slave Trade," 297. It is possible that this was the same person, but unlikely. There was more than one John Hammond in Newport, and locals seem to have used the middle name "Arnold" to distinguish among them. Later references to "John Arnold Hammond," or "Arnold Hammond," suggest that he was not the John Hammond killed aboard the *Othello*. See for example *Newport Mercury*, May 16, 1774, 3.

30. Protest of Peter Franklin, 5:663, LNR; *New York Mercury*, May 31, 1756, 2, and June 14, 1756, 3; *Pennsylvania Gazette*, July 29, 1756, 3; *New York Mercury*, January 1, 1759, 3, and May 7, 1759, 3; *Newport Mercury*, September 18, 1759, 3; Chapin, *Rhode Island in the Colonial Wars*, 54.

31. *Newport Mercury*, September 14, 1762, 3; *New London Gazette*, May 4, 1764, 3; Battey, *Samson Battey of Rhode Island*, 20.

32. *Pennsylvania Gazette*, September 11, 1755, 2; *New York Mercury*, November 16, 1766, 3, and July 6, 1767, 3.

33. *New York Mercury*, October 11, 1756, 3. Francis Welch was also the name of a missionary captured by a French vessel while en route to South Carolina. See *New York Gazette Revived in the Daily Post-Boy*, February 24, 1752, 2. It seems unlikely that the same Francis Welch would find himself stranded at Sierra Leone three years later and work his way to South Carolina as an ordinary seaman.

34. Bill of Lading for the Sloop Hair [*sic*], March 7, 1757, Vernon Papers, folder 2, box 29, NHS; "Protest of Captain Ebenezer Tyler of the sloop Hare," May 1, 1759, 7:118–19, LNR.

35. Frey, *Water from the Rock*, 142; Egerton, *Death or Liberty*, 151.

36. Soderlund, *Quakers and Slavery*.

37. Ibid., 29–31; Slaughter, *Beautiful Soul of John Woolman*, 233–36.

38. Woolman, *The Journal of John Woolman*, 110–13; Worrall, *Quakers in the Colonial Northeast*, 160–62.

Appendix Two

1. Transcriptions may be found in Donnan, *Documents*, 3:158–59.

BIBLIOGRAPHY

Primary Sources

Unpublished

Charleston, S.C.
 South Carolina Historical Society
  Ball Family Papers
  Fraser Papers
  John Guerard Letter Book
  Manigault Family Papers
Columbia, S.C.
 South Carolina Department of Archives and History
  Charleston Wills
  Colonial Plat Books
  Miscellaneous Records
  Records of the Public Treasurer
  Petitions to the General Assembly
  Probate Inventories
  South Carolina Council Journal
 South Caroliniana Library, University of South Carolina
  Alexander Fraser Receipt Book
  Ball Papers
  Paul Cross Papers
  Vernon Letters
Cooperstown, N.Y.
 New York State Historical Association Library
  Isaac Carr Nautical Logbook, 1773–1775
Edinburgh, Scotland
 National Archives of Scotland
  GD 345/1180/1762, Grant of Monymusk Papers
Hartford, Conn.
 Connecticut State Library
  Logbook of Slave Traders between New London and Africa, 1757–58
Kew, England
 British National Archives
  ADM 7, Registers of Passes
  ADM 33, Navy Board: Ships' Pay Books
  ADM 36, Royal Navy Ships' Musters

ADM 51, Admiralty, Captain's Logs
CO 267, Original Correspondence of the Secretary of State
CO 388, Minutes of the Board of Trade
CO 700, Sierra Leone 1a
EXT 1, Extracted Items
PRO 30, Gifts
T70, Records of the Royal African Company
London, England
British Library
Add Ms 4213
Add Ms 12,131
Add Ms 59777, West Africa
Eg. 1162A
New Haven, Conn.
Beinecke Rare Books Library, Yale University
Austin & Laurens Account Book, 1753–1758
Henry Baker Correspondence
Letters to Richard Oswald
Newport, R.I.
Newport City Hall
Newport Probate Record
Records of the Newport Town Council
Newport Historical Society
Dr. William Hunter Physician's Account Book, 1765–1770
John Sherman Horoscope Book
Newport Town Records, Land Evidence
Tax Books
Thomas Richardson Account Book, 1740–1754
Vernon Papers
Redwood Library and Athenæum
Ezra Stiles, "Map of the City and Harbor of Newport," 1758
Roderick J. Terry, Jr., Autograph Collection
New York, N.Y.
New-York Historical Society
Samuel and William Vernon Papers, Slavery Collection
Trade Book of the Sloop *Rhode Island*, 1748–49
New York Public Library
Log of the *Louisa*
Pawtucket, R.I.
Rhode Island State Supreme Court Judicial Archives
Godfrey v. Vernon, case no. 14,159
Providence, R.I.
Rhode Island Historical Society

John Banister Daybook
Malbone Family Collection
Rhode Island State Archives
Admiralty Papers
Land and Notarial Records
Rate Assessment List, Newport, 1760
Waltham, Mass.
National Archives at Boston
RG 36: Account of Duties Received Under Acts of Parliament, 1768–1772
Worcester, Mass.
American Antiquarian Society
John Chaloner Account Book
Samuel West Memoirs
Slave Journal, 1789–1792
Unidentified Diary, 1760

Published

MICROFILM COLLECTIONS

Coughtry, Jay, ed. *Papers of the American Slave Trade*. Bethesda, Md.: University Publications, 1998.

Stampp, Kenneth, ed. *Records of the Antebellum Plantations from the Revolution to the Civil War*. Frederick, Md.: University Publications of America, 1985.

NEWSPAPERS

American Weekly Mercury
Boston Evening Post
Boston Gazette
Boston News-Letter
Boston Post Boy
Boston Weekly News Letter
New London Gazette
Newport Mercury
New York Gazette Revived in the Daily Post-Boy
New York Mercury
Pennsylvania Gazette
South Carolina and American General Gazette
South Carolina Gazette
South Carolina Gazette and Country Journal
Virginia Gazette

BOOKS AND ARTICLES

Abstract of the Evidence Delivered before a Select Committee of the House of Commons, in the Years 1790 and 1791; on the Part of the Petitioners for the Abolition of the Slave Trade, 2nd ed. London: R. Hayworth, 1791.

Africa Pilot: Or Sailing Directions for the West Coast of Africa, Part I, from Cape Spartel to the River Cameroon, Including the Azores, Madeira, Canary and Cape Verde Islands, 3rd ed. London: Hydrographic Office, Admiralty; J. D. Potter, 1880.

American Husbandry: Containing an Account of the Soil, Climate, Production and Agriculture of the British Colonies in North-America and the West-Indies. London: J. Bew, 1778.

The Charter, Granted by His Majesty, King Charles II, to the Governor and Company of the English Colony of Rhode Island and Providence-Plantations in New England in America. Newport: Samuel Hall, 1767.

Considerations on the Present Peace as Far as It Is Relative to the Colonies and African Trade. London: W. Bristow, 1763.

Drums and Shadows: Survival Studies among the Georgia Coastal Negroes. Athens: University of Georgia Press, 1940.

The English Pilot, 7th ed. 5 vols. London: W. and J. Mount and T. Page, 1766.

Journal of the Commissioners for Trade and Plantations. 14 vols. London: Stationery Office, 1933.

Journals of the House of Commons. House of Commons, 1803.

New England Historical and Genealogical Register. Vol. 33. Boston: New England Historical, Genealogical Society, 1879.

The North American and the West-Indian Gazetteer. London: G. Robinson, 1778.

Periodical Accounts Relating to the Missions of the Church of the United Bretheren, Established among the Heathen. Vol. 2. London: Bretheren's Society, 1797.

Practical Considerations, Founded on the Scriptures, Relative to the Slave Population of South Carolina. Charleston: A. E. Miller, 1823.

Short Description of the Province of South Carolina, with an Account of the Air, Weather, and Diseases, at Charles Town, Written in the Year 1763. London: John Hinton, 1770.

A Short History of Barbados, from Its First Discovery and Settlement to the Present Time, new ed. London: J. Dodsley, 1768.

A Treatise Upon the Trade from Great-Britain to Africa, Humbly Recommended to the Attention of the Government. London, 1772.

Adams, Charles Francis, Edwin Francis Gray, George Peabody Wetmore, and Worthington Chauncey Ford, eds. *Commerce of Rhode Island, 1726–1774*. Boston: Massachusetts Historical Society, 1914.

Adanson, Michel. *A Voyage to Senegal, the Isle of Goreé and the River Gambia*. London: J. Nourse and W. Johnston, 1759.

Afzelius, Adam. *Sierra Leone Journal, 1795–1796*. Uppsala: Almqvist & Wiksells, 1967.

Alryyes, Ala, ed. *A Muslim American Slave: The Life of Omar Ibn Said*. Madison: University of Wisconsin Press, 2011.

Arnold, James, ed. *Vital Records of Rhode Island, 1636–1850*. First Series: Births, Marriages, and Deaths. 21 vols. Providence: Narragansett Historical Publishing Company, 1891.

Atkins, John. *A Voyage to Guinea, Brasil, and the West-Indies, in His Majesty's Ships, the Swallow and Weymouth*. London: Caesar Ward and Richard Chandler, 1735.

Aubrey, T. *The Sea-Surgeon, or the Guinea Man's Vade Mecum*. London: John Clarke, 1729.

Austin, Allan D., ed. *African Muslims in Antebellum America: A Sourcebook*. New York: Garland, 1984.

Ball, Charles. *Fifty Years in Chains*. 1837. Reprint, New York: Dover, 1970.

Barber, John W. *History of the* Amistad *Captives*. New Haven: E. L. and J. W. Barber, 1840.

Bartlett, John, ed. *Census of the Colony of Rhode Island and Providence Plantations Taken by Order of the General Assembly, in the Year 1774*. Providence: Knowles, Anthony, and Co., 1858.

———, ed. *Records of the Colony of Rhode Island and Providence Plantations in New England*. 10 vols. Providence: Knowles, Anthony, & Co., 1860.

Birket, James. *Some Cursory Remarks Made by James Birket in His Voyage to North America, 1750–1751*. New Haven: Yale University Press, 1916.

Blaskowitz, Charles. "A Plan of the Town of Newport in Rhode Island," 1777. American Memory Collection, Library of Congress. Online at http://www.loc.gov/item/74692105 (accessed September 7, 2015).

Blassingame, John W., ed. *Slave Testimony: Two Centuries of Letters, Speeches, Interviews, and Autobiographies*. Baton Rouge: Louisiana State University Press, 1977.

Bolzius, Johan Martin. "Reliable Answer to Some Submitted Questions Concerning the Land Carolina." *William & Mary Quarterly*, 3d ser., Vol. 14, no. April (1957): 223–61.

Bosman, Willem. *A New and Accurate Description of the Coast of Guinea, Divided into the Gold, the Slave, and the Ivory Coasts*. Second ed. London: J. Knapton, D. Midwinter, 1705.

Bruchey, Stuart, ed. *The Colonial Merchant: Sources and Readings*. New York: Harcourt, Brace, & World, Inc., 1966.

Butterworth, William. *Three Years Adventures of a Minor in England, Africa, the West Indies, South Carolina, and Georgia*. Leeds: Edward Baines, 1823.

Carretta, Vincent, ed. *Olaudah Equiano: The Interesting Narrative and Other Writings*. New York: Penguin, 1995.

———, ed. *Unchained Voices: An Anthology of Black Authors in the English-Speaking World of the 18th Century*. Expanded ed. Lexington: University Press of Kentucky, 2004.

Catesby, Mark. *The Natural History of Carolina, Florida and the Bahama Islands : Containing Two Hundred and Twenty Figures of Birds, Beasts, Fishes, Serpents, Insects and Plants*. Savannah: Beehive Press, 1974.

Churchill, Awnsham, and John Churchill, eds. *A Collection of Voyages and Travels, Some Now First Printed from Original Manuscripts*. London: Churchill, 1732.

Clarke, Robert. *Sierra Leone: A Description of the Manners and Customs of the Liberated Africans; with Observations upon the Natural History of the Colony and a Notice of the Native Tribes*. London: James Ridgway, 1843.

Clarkson, Thomas. *An Essay on the Slavery and Commerce of the Human Species, Particularly the African*. Second ed. London, 1788. 1785.

———. *Substance of the Evidence of Sundry Persons on the Slave-Trade*. London: James Phillips, 1789.

Cooper, Thomas, and James McCord, eds. *The Statutes at Large of South Carolina*. 10 vols. Columbia: A. S. Johnston, 1837.

Corry, Joseph. *Observations on the Windward Coast of Africa*. London: G. and W. Nicol; James Aspen, 1807.

Cremer, John. *Ramblin' Jack: The Journal of Captain John Cremer, 1700–1774*. Edited by R. Reynell Bellamy. London: Jonathan Cape, 1936.

Crèvecoeur, J. Hector St. John. *Letters from an American Farmer and Sketches of Eighteenth-Century America*. New York: Penguin, 1981.

Cugoano, Ottobah. "Narrative of the Enslavement of Ottobah Cugoano, a Native of Africa; Published by Himself, in the Year 1787." In *The Negro's Memorial; or, Abolitionist's Catechism; by an Abolitionist*, edited by Thomas Fisher, 120–27. London: Hatchard & Co., 1825.

Curtin, Philip D., ed. *Africa Remembered: Narratives by West Africans from the Era of the Slave Trade*. Madison: University of Wisconsin Press, 1967.

Dampier, William. *A Voyage to New Holland, &c. In the Year 1699*. London: James Knapton, 1703.

Davies, K. G., ed. *Calendar of State Papers, Colonial Series: America and the West Indies*. 45 vols. London: Stationery Office, 1994.

Dexter, Franklin Bowditch, ed. *Extracts from the Itineraries and Other Miscellanies of Ezra Stiles, D.D., Ll.D., 1755–1794, with a Selection from His Correspondence*. New Haven: Yale University Press, 1916.

———, ed. *The Literary Diary of Ezra Stiles, D.D., L.L.D.* New York: Charles Scribner and Sons, 1901.

Donnan, Elizabeth, ed. *Documents Illustrative of the History of the Slave Trade to America*. 4 vols. Washington, D.C.: Carnegie Institution, 1930; reprint, Octagon, 1965.

Easterby, James, R. Nicholas Olsberg, and Terry Lipscomb, eds. *Journal of the Commons House of Assembly of South Carolina*. 16 vols. Columbia, S.C.: Historical Commission of South Carolina, 1989.

Falconbridge, Alexander. *An Account of the Slave Trade on the Coast of Africa*, 2nd ed. London: James Phillips, 1788.

Falconbridge, Anna Maria. *Two Voyages to Sierra Leone, During the Years 1791–2–3, in a Series of Letters*, 2nd ed. London: Anna Maria Falconbridge, 1794.

Falconer, William. *Universal Dictionary of the Marine*. London: T. Cadell, 1769.

Fisher, Ruth A., ed. *Extracts from the Records of the Royal African Companies*. Washington, D.C.: Association for the Study of Negro Life and History, 1930.

Fiske, Jane Fletcher, ed. *Gleanings from Newport Court Files*. Boxford, Mass.: Jane Fletcher Fiske, 1998.

Fyfe, Christopher, ed. *Sierra Leone Inheritance*. London: Oxford University Press, 1964.

Glen, James. "A Description of South Carolina; Containing, Many Curious and Interesting Particulars Relating to the Civil, Natural, and Commercial History of That Colony." In *Colonial South Carolina: Two Contemporary Descriptions*, edited by Chapman J. Milling. Columbia: University of South Carolina Press, 1951.

Golberry, Silvestre Meinrad Xavier. *Travels in Africa*. 2 vols. London: W. Flint, 1808.

Greene, Jack P., ed. *Selling a New World: Two Colonial South Carolina Promotional Pamphlets*. Columbia: University of South Carolina Press, 1989.

Griffin, Patricia C., ed. *The Odyssey of an African Slave*. Gainesville: University Press of Florida, 2009.

Hair, P. E. H., Adam Jones, and Robin Law, eds. *Barbot on Guinea: The Writings of Jean Barbot on West Africa, 1678–1712*. London: Hakluyt Society, 1992.

Hall, Richard, ed. *Acts Passed in the Island of Barbados, from 1643 to 1762, Inclusive, Carefully Revised, Innumerable Errors Corrected; and the Whole Compared and Examined, with the Original Acts*. London: Richard Hall, 1764.

Hamer, Philip M., George C. Rogers, Peggy J. Wehage, David R. Chesnutt, and James C. Taylor, eds. *The Papers of Henry Laurens*. 10 vols. Columbia: University of South Carolina Press, 1968–2002.

Harrison, T. P., ed. "Journal of a Voyage to Charlestown in So. Carolina by Pelatiah Webster in 1765." *Southern History Association Publications* 2 (January 1898): 131–48.

Hawkins, John. *A History of a Voyage to the Coast of Africa, and Travels into the Interior of That Country*. Troy, New York: Luther Pratt, 1797.

Hewatt, Alexander. *An Historical Account of the Rise and Progress of the Colonies of South Carolina and Georgia*. 2 vols. London: Alexander Donaldson, 1779.

Hooker, Richard J., ed. *The Carolina Backcountry on the Eve of the Revolution: The Journal and Other Writings of Charles Woodmason, Anglican Itinerant*. Chapel Hill: University of North Carolina Press, 1953.

House of Commons. "Abridgement of the Minutes of Evidence Taken before a Committee of the While House, to Whom It Was Referred to Consider of the Slave Trade." House of Commons, 1791.

———. "Papers Laid before the Honourable House of Commons by the Commissioners for Trade and Plantations, Pursuant to an Address of the House of Lords to His Majesty, the 8th of June 1749, for the Better Securing, Improving, and Extending, the Trade to Africa." House of Commons, 1750.

Houstoun, James. *Some New and Accurate Observations Geographical, Natural and Historical, Containing a True and Impartial Account of the Situation, Product, and Natural History of the Coast of Guinea*. London: J. Peele, 1725.

Hoxse, John. *The Yankee Tar: An Authentic Narrative of the Voyages and Hardships of John Hoxse*. Northampton: John Metcalf, 1840.

Hunter, Michael, and Annabel Gregory, eds. *An Astrological Diary of the Seventeenth Century: Samuel Jeake of Rye, 1652–1699*. Oxford: Clarendon Press, 1988.

Jefferys, Thomas. *The West-India Atlas*. London: Robert Sayer and John Bennett, 1775.

Jones, E. Alfred, ed. "The Journal of Alexander Chesney, a South Carolina Loyalist in the Revolution and After." *Ohio State University Bulletin* 26 (October 1921): iii–166.

Jones, George Fenwick, ed. *Detailed Reports on the Salzburger Emigrants Who Settled in America*. 18 vols. Athens: University of Georgia Press, 1968–95.

Kelsey, R. W. "Swiss Settlers in South Carolina." *South Carolina Historical Magazine* 23 (July 1922): 85–91.

Laing, A. G. *Travels in the Timannee, Kooranko, and Soolima Countries*. London: John Murray, 1825.

Lambert, Sheila, ed. *House of Commons Sessional Papers of the Eighteenth Century*. 145 vols. Wilmington, Del.: Scholarly Resources, 1975.

Law, Robin, and Paul E. Lovejoy, eds. *The Biography of Mahommah Gardo Baquaqua: His Passage from Slavery to Freedom in Africa and America*. Princeton: Markus Wiener, 2001.

Loewald, Klaus, Beverly Starika, and Paul S. Taylor. "Johann Martin Bolzius Answers a Questionnaire on Carolina and Georgia." *William and Mary Quarterly*, 3d ser., 14 (April 1957): 218–22.

———. "Johann Martin Bolzius Answers a Questionnaire on Carolina and Georgia, Part I I." *William and Mary Quarterly*, 3d ser., 15 (April 1958): 228–52.

Macgunnigle, Bruce C. *A Short Description of the Province of South-Carolina, with an Account of the Air, Weather, and Diseases, at Charles-Town, Written in the Year 1763*. London: John Hinton, 1770.

MacSparran, James. *A Letter Book and Abstract of Our Services, Written during the Years 1743–1751*. Boston: D. B. Updike, 1899.

Martin, Bernard, and Mark Spurrell, eds. *The Journal of a Slave Trader (John Newton) 1750–1754, with Newton's Thoughts Upon the African Slave Trade*. London: Epsworth Press, 1962.

Martin, Evaline, ed. *Journal of a Slave Dealer: A View of Some Remarkable Axcedents in the Life of Nics. Owen on the Coast of Africa and America from the Year 1746 to the Year 1757*. Boston: Houghton Mifflin, 1930.

Martin, Wendy, ed. *Colonial American Travel Narratives*. New York: Penguin, 1994.

Mason, George Champlin. "The African Slave Trade in Colonial Times." In *The American Historical Record, Vol. I*, edited by Benson J. Lossing, 311–19; 338–45. Philadelphia: Chase and Town, 1872.

———. *Annals of Trinity Church, Newport, Rhode Island, 1698–1821*. Philadelphia: Evans Printing House, 1890.

Mathews, John. *A Voyage to the River Sierra Leone, on the Coast of Africa; Containing an Account of the Trade and Productions of the Country, and of the Civil and Religious Customs and Manners of the People*. London: B. White and Son, 1788.

Maxwell, John Irving, ed. *The Spirit of Marine Law; or, a Compendium of the Statutes Relating to the Admiralty*. London: Chapman, 1800.

Merrens, H. Roy, ed. *The Colonial South Carolina Scene: Contemporary Views, 1697–1774*. Columbia: University of South Carolina Press, 1977.

Moore, Francis. *Travels into the Inland Parts of Africa Containing a Description of the Several Nations for the Space of Six Hundred Miles up the River Gambia*. London: E. Cave, 1738.

Mouser, Bruce L., ed. *Journal of James Watt: Expedition to Timbo Capital of the Fula Empire in 1794*. Madison: African Studies Program, University of Wisconsin, 1994.

———, ed. *A Slaving Voyage to Africa and Jamaica: The Log of the Sandown, 1793–1794*. Bloomington: Indiana University Press, 2002.

Newton, John. *An Authentic Narrative of Some Remarkable and Interesting Particulars in the Life of *******, 3rd ed. London: S. Drapier, T. Hitch, P. Hill, 1765.

———. *Letters to a Wife*. London: J. Johnson, 1793.

———. *Thoughts upon the African Slave Trade*. London: J. Buckland and J. Johnson, 1788.

Park, Mungo. *Journal of a Mission to the Interior of Africa in the Year 1805*, 2nd ed. London: John Murray, 1815.

———. *Travels in the Interior Districts of Africa, Performed under the Direction and Patronage of the African Association, in the Years 1795, 1796, and 1797*, 5th ed. London: W. Bulmer, 1807.

Postlethwayt, Malachy. *A Short State of the Progress of the French Trade and Navigation*. London: J. Knapton, 1756.

Quincy, Josiah. "Journal of Josiah Quincy, Junior, 1773." *Proceedings of the Massachusetts Historical Society* 49 (1916): 424–81.

Quincy, Samuel. *Twenty Sermons on the Following Subjects . . . Preach'd in the Parish of St. Philip, Charles-Town, South-Carolina*. Boston: John Draper, 1750.

Ramsay, David. *History of South Carolina, from its First Settlement in 1670 to the Year 1808*. 1809. Reprint, Charleston: W. J. Duffie, 1858.

Robinson, Samuel. *A Sailor Boy's Experience Aboard a Slave Ship in the Beginning of the Present Century*. Hamilton: Wm. Naismith, 1867. G.C. Book Publishers, 1996.

Sigourney, Lydia H. *Sketch of Connecticut, Forty Years Since*. Hartford: Oliver D. Cooke and Sons, 1824.

Smith, Venture. *A Narrative of the Life and Adventures of Venture, a Native of Africa: But Resident above Sixty Years in the United States of America; Related by Himself*. New London, 1798.

Smith, William. *A New Voyage to Guinea*. London: John Nourse, 1744.

Snelgrave, William. *A New Account of Some Parts of Guinea and the Slave-Trade*. London: James, John, and Paul, 1734. Frank Cass, 1971.

Stock, Leo Francis, ed. *Proceedings and Debates of the British Parliaments Respecting North America*. 5 vols. Washington, D.C.: Carnegie Institution, 1941.

Tattersfield, Nigel, ed. *The Forgotten Trade: Comprising the Log of the Daniel and Henry of 1700 and Accounts of the Slave Trade from the Minor Ports of England, 1698–1725*. London: Pimlico, 1998.

Taylor, G. *A Voyage to North America, Performed by G. Taylor, of Sheffield, in the Years 1768, and 1769*. Nottingham: S. Creswell, 1769.

Thompson, Edward. *Sailor's Letters, Written to His Select Friends in England, During His Voyages and Travels in Europe, Asia, Africa, and America, from the Year 1754 to 1759*. Dublin: J. Potts, 1767.

Thompson, Thomas. *An Account of Two Missionary Voyages, by the Appointment of the Society for the Propagation of the Gospel in Foreign Parts*. Society for Promoting Christian Knowledge, 1937. First published 1763, London: Benj. Dodd.

Thornely, Samuel, ed. *The Journal of Nicholas Cresswell, 1774–1777*. New York: Dial Press, 1924.

Torrington, F. William, ed. *House of Lords Sessional Papers, 1798–99*. 60 vols. Dobbs Ferry, N.Y.: Oceana, 1974.

Towle, Dorothy S., ed. *Records of the Vice-Admiralty Court of Rhode Island, 1716–1752*. Vol. 3, American Legal Records. Washington, D.C., 1936.

Trenchard, John. *An Argument Shewing, That a Standing Army Is Inconsistent with Free Government*. London: n.p., 1697.

Tweed, James. *Considerations and Remarks on the Present State of Trade to Africa*. London, 1771.

Vernon, Thomas. *Reminiscences of Thomas Vernon, an American Loyalist: Royal Postmaster, at Newport, from About 1745 to 1775, and for Twenty Years Registrar of the Court of Vice-Admiralty*. New York: n.p., 1880.

Wadstrom, C. B. *Observations on the Slave Trade, and a Description of Some Part of the Coast of Guinea, During a Voyage Made in 1787, and 1788, in Company with Dr. A. Sparrman and Captain Arrehenius*. London: James Phillips, 1789.

Weekes, Nathaniel. *Barbados: A Poem*. London: R. and J. Dodsley, 1754.

Williamson, Karina, ed. *Contrary Voices: Representations of West Indian Slavery, 1657–1834*. Kingston, Jamaica: University of the West Indies Press, 2008.

Windley, Lathan A., ed. *Runaway Slave Advertisements: A Documentary History from the 1730s to 1790*. 4 vols. Westport, Conn.: Greenwood Press, 1983.

Winter, Kari J., ed. *The Blind African Slave, or Memoirs of Boyrereau Brinch, Nicknamed Jeffrey Brace*. Madison: University of Wisconsin Press, 2004.

Winterbottom, Thomas. *An Account of the Native Africans in the Neighbourhood of Sierra Leone, to Which Is Added an Account of the Present State of Medicine among Them*. 2 vols. London: C. Whittingham, 1803.

Withington, Lothrop. "South Carolina Gleanings in England." *South Carolina Historical Magazine* 5 (October 1904): 218–28.

Wood, Trist. "Prince-Wood and Brenton Bible Records." *New England Historical and Genealogical Register* 63 (1913): 158–60.

Woolman, John. *The Journal of John Woolman, and a Plea for the Poor*. John Greenleaf Whittier Text. Philadelphia: Joseph Cruikshank, 1774. Reprint, Corinth, N.Y, 1961.

——. *Some Considerations on the Keeping of Negroes, Recommended to the Professors of Christianity of Every Denomination*. Philadelphia: James Chattin, 1754.

Young, Sir William. "A Tour through the Several Islands of Barbadoes, St. Vincent, Antigua, Tobago, and Grenada, in the Years 1791 and 1792." In *An Historical Survey of the Island of Saint Domingo*, edited by Bryan Edwards, 259–301. London: John Stockdale, 1801.

Secondary Sources

Rules of the Society, List of Officers and Members from 1729 to 1892, Centennial and other Addresses, Poems and Historical Sketch. Charleston: Walker, Evans, and Cogswell, 1892.

Addoun, Yacine Daddi, and Paul E. Lovejoy. "Muhammad Kaba Saghanughu and the Muslim Community of Jamaica." In *Slavery on the Frontiers of Islam*, edited by Paul E. Lovejoy, 201–20. Princeton: Markus Wiener, 2004.

Alie, Joe A. D. *A New History of Sierra Leone*. Oxford: Macmillan, 1990.

Allen, Kacie. "Looking East: Muslim Identity in the Archaeological Record of American Enslavement." *African Diaspora Archaeology Newsletter* 12 (September 2009): 1–109.

Anderson, Fred. *Crucible of War: The Seven Years' War and the Fate of Empire in British North America, 1754–1766*. New York: Knopf, 2000.

Austin, Allan D. *African Muslims in Antebellum America: Transatlantic Stories of Spiritual Struggles*. New York: Routledge, 1997.

Bailey, Anne C. *African Voices of the Atlantic Slave Trade: Beyond the Silence and the Shame*. Boston: Beacon, 2005.

Bailey, Ronald. "The Slave(ry) Trade and the Development of Capitalism in the United States: The Textile Industry in New England." *Social Science History* 14 (Autumn 1990): 373–414.

Bailyn, Bernard. *Atlantic History: Concepts and Contours*. Cambridge: Harvard University Press, 2005.

———. *The New England Merchants in the Seventeenth Century*. Cambridge: Harvard University Press, 1955.

———. "Slavery and Population Growth in Colonial New England." In *Engines of Enterprise: An Economic History of New England*, edited by Peter Temin, 253–59. Cambridge: Harvard University Press, 2000.

———. *Voyagers to the West: A Passage in the Peopling of America on the Eve of the Revolution*. Vintage, 1988. New York: Random House, 1986.

Baker, William A. *Sloops and Shallops*. Barre, Mass.: Barre Publishing, 1966.

Ball, Edward. *Slaves in the Family*. New York: Ballantine Books, 1998.

Barry, Boubacar. *Senegambia and the Atlantic Slave Trade*. Translated by Ayi Kwei Armah. Cambridge: Cambridge University Press, 1998.

Battey, H. V. *Samson Battey of Rhode Island: The Immigrant Ancestor and His Descendants*. Council Bluffs, Iowa: 1932.

Beckles, Hilary McD. *Natural Rebels: A Social History of Enslaved Black Women in Barbados*. New Brunswick: Rutgers University Press, 1989.

Behrendt, Stephen D. "Crew Mortality in the Transatlantic Slave Trade in the Eighteenth Century." In *Routes to Slavery: Direction, Ethnicity and Mortality in the Atlantic Slave Trade*, edited by David Eltis and David Richardson, 49–71. London: Frank Cass, 1997.

———. "Human Capital in the British Slave Trade." In *Liverpool and Transatlantic Slavery*, edited by David Richardson, Suzanne Schwarz, and Anthony Tibbles, 66–97. Liverpool: Liverpool University Press, 2007.

———. "Markets, Transaction Cycles, and Profits: Merchant Decision Making in the British Slave Trade." *William and Mary Quarterly*, 3d ser., 58 (January 2001): 171–204.

Behrendt, Stephen D., David Eltis, and David Richardson. "The Costs of Coercion: African Agency in the Pre-Modern Atlantic World." *Economic History Review* 54 (August 2001): 454–76.

Bellman, Beryl Larry. *The Language of Secrecy: Symbols & Metaphors in Poro Ritual*. New Brunswick: Rutgers University Press, 1984.

Benson, J. Lossing, ed. *American Historical Record*. Vol. I. Philadelphia: Chase & Town, 1872.

Berlin, Ira. "From Creole to African: Atlantic Creoles and the Origins of African-American Society in Mainland North America." *William and Mary Quarterly*, 3d ser., 53 (April 1996): 251–88.

———. *Generations of Captivity: A History of African American Slaves*. Cambridge: Harvard Belknap, 2003.

———. *Many Thousands Gone: The First Two Centuries of Slavery in North America*. Cambridge: Harvard Belknap, 1998.

Beyan, Amos J. "Transatlantic Trade and the Coastal Area Pre-Liberia." *Historian* 57, no. 4 (1995): 757–68.

Bigelow, Bruce M. "Aaron Lopez: Colonial Merchant of Newport." *New England Quarterly* 4 (October 1931): 757–76.

Bird, Charles S. "The Development of Mandekan (Manding): A Study of the Role of Extra-Linguistic Factors in Linguistic Change." In *Language and History in Africa*, edited by David Dalby, 146–59. New York: Africana Publishing Company, 1970.

Bolster, W. Jeffrey. *Black Jacks: African American Seamen in the Age of Sail*. Cambridge: Harvard University Press, 1997.

Bolton, Charles S. *Southern Anglicanism: The Church of England in Colonial South Carolina*. Westport, Conn.: Greenwood Press, 1982.

Botte, Roger. "Les Rapports Nord-Sud, la Traite Négrière et le Fuuta Jaloo à la Fin du 18e Siècle." *Persee* 46, no. 6 (1991): 1411–35.

Bowden, Martyn J. "The Three Centuries of Bridgetown: An Historical Geography." *Journal of the Barbados Museum and Historical Society* 49 (2003): 1–137.

Brathwaite, Edward. *The Development of Creole Society in Jamaica*. Oxford: Oxford University Press, 1971.

Breen, T. H. "Baubles of Britain: The American and Consumer Revolutions of the Eighteenth Century." *Past and Present* 119 (May 1988): 73–104.

———. "Creative Adaptations: People and Cultures." In *Colonial British America: Essays in the New History of the Early Modern Era*, edited by Jack P. Greene and J. R. Pole. 195–232. Baltimore: Johns Hopkins University Press, 1984.

Bridenbaugh, Carl. *Cities in Revolt: Urban Life in America, 1743–1776*. New York: Knopf, 1955.

Bridges, Anne Baker Leland, and Roy Williams III. *St. James Santee Plantation Parish: History and Records, 1685–1925*. Spartanburg, S.C.: Reprint Company, 1997.

Brooks, George E. *Eurafricans in Western Africa: Commerce, Social Status, Gender, and Religious Observance from the Sixteenth to the Eighteenth Century*. Athens, Ohio: Ohio University Press, 2003.

———. *Landlords and Strangers: Ecology, Society, and Trade in West Africa, 1000–1630*. Boulder, Colo.: Westview Press, 1994.

Brown, Ras Michael. *African-Atlantic Cultures and the South Carolina Lowcountry*. Cambridge: Cambridge University Press, 2012.

Brown, Vincent. *The Reaper's Garden: Death and Power in the World of Atlantic Slavery*. Cambridge: Harvard University Press, 2008.

Bruyns, Willem, and F. J. Mörzer. "The Development of Navigational Methods and Techniques, 1740–1815." In *Maritime History, Volume 2: The Eighteenth Century and the Classic Age of Sail*, edited by John B. Hattendorf, 95–100. Malabar, Fla.: Krieger, 1997.

———. "Sources of Knowledge: Charts and Rutters." In *Maritime History, Volume 2: The Eighteenth Century and the Classic Age of Sail*, edited by John B. Hattendorf, 69–77. Malabar, Fla.: Krieger, 1997.

———. "Techniques and Methods of Navigation before 1740." In *Maritime History, Volume 2: The Eighteenth Century and the Classic Age of Sail*, edited by John B. Hattendorf, 57–66. Malabar, Fla.: Krieger, 1997.

Bryan, Evelyn McDaniel Frazier. *Colleton County, S.C.: A History of the First 160 Years, 1670–1830*. Jacksonville, Fla.: Florentine Press, 1993.

Burnard, Trevor, and Kenneth Morgan. "The Dynamics of the Slave Market and Slave Purchasing Patterns in Jamaica, 1655–1788." *William & Mary Quarterly*, 3d ser., 58 (January 2001): 205–28.

Butel, Paul. *The Atlantic*. London: Routledge, 1999.

Butler, Jon. *Awash in a Sea of Faith: Christianizing the American People*. Cambridge: Harvard University Press, 1990.

Byrd, Alexander X. *Captives and Voyagers: Black Migrants across the Eighteenth-Century British Atlantic World*. Baton Rouge: Louisiana State University Press, 2008.

———. "Eboe, Country, Nation, and Gustavus Vassa's *Interesting Narrative*." *William and Mary Quarterly*, 3d ser., 58 (January 2006): 123–48.

Byrd, Michael D. "The First Charles Town Workhouse, 1738–1775: A Deterrent to White Pauperism." *South Carolina Historical Magazine* 110 (Jan.–April 2010): 35–52.

Carney, Judith. *Black Rice: The African Origins of Rice Cultivation in the Americas*. Cambridge: Harvard University Press, 2001.

———. "With Grains of Rice in Her Hair: Rice in Colonial Brazil." *Slavery & Abolition* 25 (April 2004): 1–27.

Caron, Peter. "'Of a Nation Which the Others Do Not Understand': Bambara Slaves and African Ethnicity in Colonial Louisiana, 1718–1760." *Slavery and Abolition* 18 (1997): 98–121.

Carretta, Vincent. *Equiano, the African: Biography of a Self-Made Man*. New York: Penguin, 2005.

Challenger, Denise, Luther Johnson, John Bannister, and Arlene Waterman. "The Streets of Bridgetown Circa 1765." *Journal of the Barbados Museum and Historical Society* 45 (December 1999): 76–87.

Chambers, Douglas B. *Murder at Montpelier: Igbo Africans in Virginia*. Jackson: University Press of Mississippi, 2005.

———. "'My Own Nation': Igbo Exiles in the Diaspora." *Slavery & Abolition* 18, no. 1 (1997): 72–97.

———. "The Significance of Igbo in the Bight of Biafra Slave-Trade: A Rejoinder to Northrup's 'Myth Igbo.'" *Slavery & Abolition* 23, no. 1 (2002): 101–20.

Champlin, Richard S. "The Art, Trade, or Mystery of the Ropemaker." *Newport History* 46, no. 4 (1973): 81–95.

Chapelle, Howard I. *History of American Sailing Ships*. Bonanza, 1960. New York: Norton, 1935.

Chapin, Howard M. *Rhode Island in the Colonial Wars: A List of Rhode Island Soldiers & Sailors in King George's War, 1740–1748*. Providence: Rhode Island Historical Society, 1920.

Chaplin, Joyce E. *Anxious Pursuit: Agricultural Innovation and Modernity in the Lower South, 1730–1815*. Chapel Hill: University of North Carolina Press, 1993.

Childs, Matt D. *The 1812 Aponte Rebellion and the Struggle against Atlantic Slavery*. Chapel Hill: University of North Carolina Press, 2006.

Chireau, Yvonne P. *Black Magic: Religion and the African American Conjuring Tradition*. Berkeley: University of California Press, 2003.

Christopher, Emma. *Slave Ship Sailors and Their Captive Cargoes, 1730–1807*. Cambridge: Cambridge University Press, 2006.

Clute, Robert F. *The Annals and Parish Register of St. Thomas and St. Denis Parish in South Carolina, from 1680 to 1884*. Reprint, 1974 ed. Charleston, 1884.

Coclanis, Peter A. "How the Low Country Was Taken to Task: Slave-Labor Organization in Coastal South Carolina and Georgia." In *Slavery, Secession, and Southern History*, edited by Robert Louis Paquette and Louis Ferleger. Charlottesville: University of Virginia Press, 2000.

Coclanis, Peter A. *Shadow of a Dream: Economic Life and Death in the South Carolina Low Country, 1670–1920*. New York: Oxford University Press, 1989.

Cody, Cheryll Ann. "There Was No 'Absalom' on the Ball Plantations: Slave Naming Practices in the South Carolina Low Country, 1720–1865." *American Historical Review* 92 (June 1987): 563–96.

Coggeshall, Charles Pierce, and Thellwell Russell Coggeshall. *The Coggeshalls in America*. Boston: C. E. Goodspeed, 1930.

Cohen, Robin, and Paola Toninato, eds. *The Creolization Reader: Studies in Mixed Identities and Cultures*. London: Routledge, 2010.

Colman, Peter J. "The Insolvent Debtor in Rhode Island, 1745–1828." *William & Mary Quarterly*, 3d ser., 22 (July 1965): 413–34.

Condé, Maryse. *Segu*. New York: Viking/Penguin, 1987.

Conrad, David C. *Status and Identity in West Africa: Nyamakalaw of Mande*. Bloomington: University of Indiana Press, 1995.

Coughtry, Jay. *The Notorious Triangle: Rhode Island and the African Slave Trade, 1700–1807*. Philadelphia: Temple University Press, 1981.

Crane, Elaine Forman. *A Dependent People: Newport, Rhode Island in the Revolutionary Era*. New York: Fordham University Press, 1985.

———. "The First Wheel of Commerce: Newport, Rhode Island, and the Slave Trade, 1760–1776." *Slavery & Abolition* 1, no. 1 (1980): 178–98.

Creel, Margaret Washington. *"A Peculiar People": Slave Religion and Community-Culture among the Gullahs*. New York: New York University Press, 1988.

Crouse, Maurice A. "Gabriel Manigault: Charleston Merchant." *South Carolina Historical Magazine* 68 (October 1967): 98–109.

Curry, Patrick. *Prophecy and Power: Astrology in Early Modern England*. Princeton: Princeton University Press, 1989.

Curtin, Philip D. *The Atlantic Slave Trade: A Census*. Madison: University of Wisconsin Press, 1969.

———. *Cross-Cultural Trade in World History*. Cambridge: Cambridge University Press, 1984.

———. *Economic Change in Precolonial Africa: Senegambia in the Era of the Slave Trade*. 2 vols. Madison: University of Wisconsin Press, 1975.

Dalby, David. "Levels of Relationship in the Comparative Study of African Languages." *African Language Studies* 7 (1966): 171–79.

———. "Mel Languages in the Polyglotta Africana: Part I: Baga, Landuma, and Temne." *Sierra Leone Language Review* 4 (1965): 129–35.

———. "Mel Languages in the Polyglotta Africana: Part II: Bullom, Kissi, and Gola." *Sierra Leone Language Review* 5 (1966): 139–51.

———. "The Mel Languages: A Reclassification of Southern 'West Atlantic.'" *African Language Studies* 6 (1965): 1–17.

Davids, Karel. "The Development of Navigational Techniques, 1740–1815: General Background." In *Maritime History, Volume 2: The Eighteenth Century and the Classic Age of Sail*, edited by John B. Hattendorf. 87–93. Malabar, Fla.: Krieger, 1997.

————. "Sources of Knowledge: Journals, Logs, and Travel Accounts." In *Maritime History, Volume 2: The Eighteenth Century and the Classic Age of Sail,* edited by John B. Hattendorf, 79–85. Malabar, Fla., 1997.

Davies, K. G. *The Royal African Company.* London: Longman, 1957. Reprint, Atheneum, 1970.

Davis, David Brion. *The Problem of Slavery in the Age of Revolution, 1770–1823.* Ithaca, N.Y.: Cornell University Press, 1975.

Davis, Ralph. *The Rise of the English Shipping Industry in the Seventeenth and Eighteenth Centuries.* London: St. Martin's Press, 1962.

Davis, Ronald W. *Ethnohistorical Studies on the Kru Coast.* Newark, Delaware: Liberian Studies Association, 1976.

Deutsch, Sarah. "The Elusive Guineaman: Newport Slavers, 1735–1774." *New England Quarterly* 55 (June 1982): 229–53.

Deyle, Steven. "'By Farr the Most Profitable Trade': Slave Trading in British Colonial North America." *Slavery & Abolition* 10, No. 2 (1989): 107–25.

Diouf, Sylviane A. "Devils or Sorcerers, Muslims or Studs: Manding in the Americas." In *Trans-Atlantic Dimensions of Ethnicity in the African Diaspora,* edited by Paul E. Lovejoy and David V. Trotman, 139–57. London: Continuum, 2003.

————. *Dreams of Africa in Alabama: The Slave Ship* Clotilda *and the Story of the Last Africans Brought to America.* New York: Oxford University Press, 2007.

————. *Servants of Allah: African Muslims Enslaved in the Americas.* New York: New York University Press, 1998.

————, ed. *Fighting the Slave Trade: West African Strategies.* Athens, Ohio: Ohio University Press, 2003.

Diptee, Audra A. *From Africa to Jamaica: The Making of an Atlantic Slave Society, 1775–1807.* Gainesville: University Press of Florida, 2010.

Dorjahn, V. R., and Christopher Fyfe. "Landlord and Stranger: Change in Tenancy Relations in Sierra Leone." *Journal of African History* 3, no. 3 (1962): 391–97.

Duncan, T. Bentley. *Atlantic Islands: Madeira, the Azores and the Cape Verdes in Seventeenth-Century Commerce and Navigation.* Chicago: University of Chicago Press, 1972.

Dunn, Richard S. *Sugar and Slaves: The Rise of the Planter Class in the English West Indies, 1624–1713.* Norton, 1973. Chapel Hill: University of North Carolina Press, 1972.

Dye, Ira. "Early American Merchant Seafarers." *Proceedings of the American Philosophical Society* 120 (October 1976): 331–60.

Earle, Peter. *Sailors: English Merchant Seamen, 1650–1775.* London: Methuen, 1998.

Edelson, S. Max. *Plantation Enterprise in South Carolina.* Cambridge: Harvard University Press, 2006.

Edelson, S. Max, Gwendolyn Midlo Hall, Walter Hawthorne, David Eltis, Philip D. Morgan, and David Richardson. "AHR Exchange: The Question of Black Rice." *American Historical Review* 115 (February 2010): 123–71.

Edgar, Walter, and N. Louise Bailey, eds. *Biographical Directory of the South Carolina House of Representatives.* Columbia: University of South Carolina Press, 1977.

Egerton, Douglas R. *Death or Liberty: African Americans and the Revolutionary Era.* Oxford: Oxford University Press, 2011.

Ellery, Harris, and Thomas Vernon. "The Vernon Family and Arms: A Communication to the New England Historical and Genealogical Register, for July, 1879." *Rhode Island Historical Tracts* 13, no. 1 (1879): 117–40.

Eltis, David. "African Agency and Resistance." Online at *Voyages: The Transatlantic Slave Trade Database*, http://www.slavevoyages.org/tast/assessment/essays-intro-03.faces (accessed August 21, 2015).

———. *The Rise of African Slavery in the Americas*. Cambridge: Cambridge University Press, 2000.

———. "Tales from the Ships." *William & Mary Quarterly*, 3d ser., vol. 61 (January 2004): 161–66.

———. "The U.S. Transatlantic Slave Trade, 1644–1867: An Assessment." *Civil War History* 54 (December 2008): 347–78.

———. "The Volume and Structure of the Transatlantic Slave Trade: A Reassessment." *William & Mary Quarterly* 58 (January 2001): 17–46.

Eltis, David, Stephen D. Behrendt, David Richardson, and Herbert S. Klein. *The Trans-Atlantic Slave Trade: A Database on CD-Rom*. Cambridge: Cambridge University Press, 1999.

Eltis, David, Philip D. Morgan, and David Richardson. "Agency and Diaspora in Atlantic History: Reassessing the African Contribution to Rice Cultivation in the Americas." *American Historical Review* 112 (December 2007): 1329–58.

Eltis, David, and David Richardson. *Atlas of the Transatlantic Slave Trade*. New Haven: Yale University Press, 2010.

———. *Extending the Frontiers: Essays on the New Transatlantic Slave Trade Database*. New Haven: Yale University Press, 2008.

———. "Prices of African Slaves Newly Arrived in the Americas, 1673–1865: New Evidence on Long-Run Trends and Regional Differentials." In *Slavery in the Development of the Americas*, edited by David Eltis, Frank D. Lewis, and Kenneth L. Sokoloff, 181–218. Cambridge: Cambridge University Press, 2004.

———. "Productivity in the Transatlantic Slave Trade." *Explorations in Economic History* 32 (1995): 465–84.

Esposito, John L., ed. *The Oxford History of Islam*. Oxford: Oxford University Press, 1999.

Falola, Toyin, and Matt D. Childs. *The Yoruba Diaspora in the Atlantic World*. Bloomington: University of Indiana Press, 2004.

Falola, Toyin, and Paul E. Lovejoy. "Pawnship in Historical Perspective." In *Pawnship, Slavery, and Colonialism in Africa*, edited by Paul E. Lovejoy and Toyin Falola. Trenton: Africa World Press, 2003.

———, eds. *Pawnship in Africa: Debt Bondage in Historical Perspective*. Boulder, Colo., 1994.

Ferguson, Leland. *Uncommon Ground: Archaeology and Early African America, 1650–1800*. Washington, D.C.: Smithsonian Institution Press, 1992.

Ferreira, Roquinaldo. *Cross-Cultural Exchange in the Atlantic World: Angola and Brazil in the Era of the Slave Trade*. Cambridge: Cambridge University Press, 2012.

Fett, Sharla M. *Working Cures: Healing, Health, and Power on Southern Slave Plantations*. Chapel Hill: University of North Carolina Press, 2002.

Fields-Black, Edda L. *Deep Roots: Rice Farmers in West Africa and the African Diaspora*. Bloomington: University of Indiana Press, 2008.

Finley, M. I. *Ancient Slavery and Modern Ideology*. New York: Viking, 1980.

Frazier, E. Franklin. *The Negro in the United States*. New York: Macmillan, 1949.

Frey, Sylvia R. "The Visible Church: Historiography of African American Religion since Raboteau." *Slavery & Abolition* 29 (March 2008): 83–110.

———. *Water from the Rock: Black Resistance in a Revolutionary Age*. Princeton: Princeton University Press, 1991.

Frey, Sylvia R., and Betty Wood. *Come Shouting to Zion: African American Protestantism in the American South and British Caribbean to 1830*. Chapel Hill: University of North Carolina Press, 1998.

Fyfe, Christopher. *A History of Sierra Leone*. London: Oxford, 1962.

Galenson, David W. *Traders, Planters, and Slaves: Market Behavior in Early English America*. Cambridge: Cambridge University Press, 1986.

Garraty, John A., and Mark C. Carnes, eds. *American National Biography*. 24 vols. New York: Oxford University Press, 1999.

Georgia Writers' Project. *Drums and Shadows: Survival Studies among the Georgia Coastal Negroes*. Athens: University of Georgia Press, 1940. 1986.

Glover, Beulah. *Narratives of Colleton County: The Land Lying between the Edisto and Combahee Rivers*. Walterboro, S.C.: n.p., 1962.

Goldenberg, Joseph A. *Shipbuilding in Colonial America*. Newport News and Charlottesville: Mariner's Museum and University Press of Virginia, 1976.

Gomez, Michael A. "Africans, Culture, and Islam in the Lowcountry." In *African American Life in the Georgia Lowcountry*, edited by Philip D. Morgan, 103–30. Athens: University of Georgia Press, 2010.

———. *Black Crescent: The Experience and Legacy of African Muslims in the Americas*. Cambridge: Cambridge University Press, 2005.

———. *Exchanging Our Country Marks: The Transformation of African Identities in the Colonial and Antebellum South*. Chapel Hill: University of North Carolina Press, 1998.

———. *Pragmatism in the Age of Jihad: The Precolonial State of Bundu*. Cambridge: Cambridge University Press, 1992.

———. *Reversing Sail: A History of the African Diaspora*. Cambridge: Cambridge University Press, 2005.

Graham, Sandra Lauderdale. "Being Yoruba in Nineteenth-Century Rio de Janeiro." *Slavery & Abolition* 32 (March 2011): 1–26.

Gray, Lewis Cecil. *History of Agriculture in the Southern United States to 1860*. 2 vols. Washington, D.C.: Carnegie Institution, 1933. Peter Smith, 1958.

Green, Toby. *The Rise of the Trans-Atlantic Slave Trade in Western Africa, 1300–1589*. Cambridge: Cambridge University Press, 2012.

Greene, Jack P. *Pursuits of Happiness: The Social Development of Early Modern British Colonies and the Formation of American Culture*. Chapel Hill: University of North Carolina Press, 1988.

Greene, Jack P., and Philip D. Morgan. *Atlantic History: A Critical Appraisal*. New York: Oxford University Press, 2009.

Greene, Lorenzo J. *The Negro in Colonial New England, 1620–1776*. New York 1942.

Hair, P. E. H. *Africa Encountered: European Contacts and Evidence, 1450–1700*. Aldershot: Variorum, 1997.

———. "Ethnolinguistic Continuity on the Upper Guinea Coast." *Journal of African History* 8, no. 2 (1967): 247–68.

Hall, David D. *Worlds of Wonder, Days of Judgment: Popular Religious Belief in Early New England*. Cambridge: Harvard University Press, 1989.

Hall, Gwendolyn Midlo. *Africans in Colonial Louisiana: The Development of Afro-Creole Culture in the Eighteenth Century*. Baton Rouge: Louisiana State University Press, 1992.

———. *Slavery and African Ethnicities in the Americas: Restoring the Links*. Chapel Hill: University of North Carolina Press, 2005.

Hancock, David. *Citizens of the World: London Merchants and the Integration of the British Atlantic Community, 1735–1785*. Cambridge: Cambridge University Press, 1995.

Handler, Jerome S. "Life Histories of Enslaved Africans in Barbados." *Slavery & Abolition* 19 (April 1998): 129–41.

Harms, Robert. The *Diligent: A Voyage through the Worlds of the Atlantic Slave Trade*. New York: Basic Books, 2003.

Harris, J. William. *The Hanging of Thomas Jeremiah: A Free Black Man's Encounter with Liberty*. New Haven: Yale University Press, 2009.

Harris, Joseph Earl. "The Kingdom of Fouta-Diallon." Ph.D. diss., University of Illinois, 1965.

Hart, Emma. *Building Charleston: Town and Society in the Eighteenth-Century British Atlantic World*. Charlottesville: University of Virginia Press, 2010.

Hartman, Saidiya. *Lose Your Mother: A Journey along the Atlantic Slave Route*. New York: Farrar, Straus, and Giroux, 2007.

Hattendorf, John B., ed. *Maritime History, Volume 2: The Eighteenth Century and the Classic Age of Sail*. Malabar, Fla.: Krieger Publishing Co., 1997.

Hawthorne, Walter. "'Being Now, as It Were, One Family': Shipmate Bonding on the Slave Vessel *Emilia*, in Rio de Janeiro, and Throughout the Atlantic World." *Luso-Brazilian Review* 45 (Spring 2008): 53–77.

———. *From Africa to Brazil: Culture, Identity, and an Atlantic Slave Trade, 1600–1830*. Cambridge: Cambridge University Press, 2010.

———. *Planting Rice, Harvesting Slaves: Transformations along the Guinea-Bissau Coast, 1400–1900*. Portsmouth, N.H.: Heinemann, 2003.

Heine, Bernard, and Derek Nurse, eds. *African Languages: An Introduction*. Cambridge: Cambridge University Press, 2000.

Heitzler, Michael J. *Goose Creek, a Definitive History, Volume 1: Planters, Politicians and Patriots*. Charleston: The History Press, 2005.

Herman, Bernard L. "Slave and Servant Housing in Charleston, 1770–1820." *Historical Archaeology* 33, no. 3 (1999): 88–101.

Herndon, Ruth Wallis. "The Domestic Cost of Seafaring: Town Leaders and Seamen's Families in Eighteenth-Century Rhode Island." In *Iron Men, Wooden Women: Gender and Seafaring in the Atlantic World, 1700–1920*, edited by Margaret S. Creighton and Lisa Norling, 55–69. Baltimore: Johns Hopkins University Press, 1996.

———. *Unwelcome Americans: Living on the Margin in Early New England*. Philadelphia: University of Pennsylvania Press, 2001.

Herskovits, Melville J. *The Myth of the Negro Past*. With a new introduction by Sidney W. Mintz. Boston: Beacon Books, 1990.

Heyward, Duncan Cinch. *Seed from Madagascar*. Chapel Hill: University of North Carolina Press, 1937.

Heywood, Linda M., ed. *Central Africans and Cultural Transformations in the American Diaspora*. Cambridge: Cambridge University Press, 2002.

Heywood, Linda M., and John K. Thornton. *Central Africans, Atlantic Creoles, and the Foundation of the Americas, 1585–1660*. Cambridge: Cambridge University Press, 2007.

Higgins, Robert W. "Charles Town Merchants and Factors in the External Negro Trade, 1735–1775." *South Carolina Historical Magazine* 65, no. 4 (1964): 205–17.

Hill, Lawrence. *Someone Knows My Name*. New York: W. W. Norton & Co., 2007.

Hoffer, Peter Charles. *Cry Liberty: The Great Stono River Slave Rebellion of 1739*. New York: Oxford University Press, 2012.

Hogerzeil, Simon J., and David Richardson. "Slave Purchasing Strategies and Shipboard Mortality: Day-to-Day Evidence from the Dutch African Trade." *Journal of Economic History* 67 (March 2007): 160–90.

Howard, Allen M. "Mande Identity Formation in the Economic and Political Context of North-West Sierra Leone, 1750–1900." *Paideuma* 46 (2000): 13–35.

———. "Nineteenth-Century Coastal Slave Trading and the British Abolition Campaign in Sierra Leone." *Slavery & Abolition* 27 (April 2006): 23–50.

———. "Trade and Islam in Sierra Leone, 18th-20th Centuries." In *Islam and Trade in Sierra Leone*, edited by Alusine Jalloh and David E. Skinner. Trenton, N.J.: Africa World Press, 1997.

Howe, George. *History of the Presbyterian Church in South Carolina*. Columbia: Duffie & Chapman, 1870.

Hudson, Nicholas. "From 'Nation' to 'Race': The Origin of Racial Classification in Eighteenth-Century Thought." *Eighteenth-Century Studies* 29 (Spring 1996): 247–64.

Huggins, Nathan Irvin. *Black Odyssey: The Afro-American Ordeal in Slavery*. Vintage ed. New York: Random House, 1977.

Jackson, Harvey Hardaway. *Lachlan Mcintosh and the Politics of Revolutionary Georgia*. Athens, Ga.: University of Georgia Press, 1979.

Jalloh, Alusine, and David E. Skinner, eds. *Islam and Trade in Sierra Leone*. Trenton, N.J.: Africa World Press, 1997.

James, Sydney V. *Colonial Rhode Island: A History*. New York: Scribners, 1975.

———. "Of Slaves and Rum." *Reviews in American History* 10 (June 1982): 168–72.

Jarvis, Michael. "'The Fastest Vessels in the World': The Origin and Evolution of the Bermuda Sloop, 1620–1800." *Bermuda Journal of Archaeology and Maritime History* 7, no. 1 (1995): 31–50.

———. *In the Eye of all Trade: Bermuda, Bermudians, and the Maritime Atlantic World, 1680–1783*. Chapel Hill: University of North Carolina Press, 2010.

Johnson, George Lloyd. *The Frontier in the Colonial South: South Carolina Backcountry, 1736–1800*. Westport, Conn.: Greenwood Press, 1997.

Jones, Adam, and Marion Johnson. "Slaves from the Windward Coast." *Journal of African History* 21, no. 1 (1980): 17–34.

Jones, Denise. "The British Slave Trade in Sierra Leone: A Case Study of Robert Bostock, 1769–92." In *Empire, Slave Trade and Slavery: Rebuilding Civil Society in Sierra Leone, Past and Present*. Hull, U.K., 2008.

Joyner, Charles. *Down by the Riverside: A South Carolina Slave Community*. Urbana: University of Illinois Press, 1984.

Kaye, Anthony E. *Joining Places: Slave Neighborhoods in the Old South*. Chapel Hill: University of North Carolina Press, 2007.

Kea, Ray A. "'I Am Here to Plunder on the General Road': Bandits and Banditry in the Pre-Nineteenth Century Gold Coast." In *Banditry and Social Protest in Africa*, edited by Donald Crummey, 109–32. London: James Currey, 1986.

Kelley, Sean. "The Dirty Business of Panyarring and Palaver: Violence and the Slave Trade on the Upper Guinea Coast in the Eighteenth Century." In *Slavery, Abolition, and the Transition to Colonialism in Sierra Leone,* edited by Paul E. Lovejoy and Suzanne Schwarz, 89–108. Trenton, N.J.: Africa World Press, 2014.

———. "People of Business: The Vernon Brothers and the Rhode Island Slave Trade." Paper presented at the Conference on Africa & the World, University of Texas at Austin, March 2011.

———. "Scrambling for Slaves: Captive Sales in Colonial South Carolina." *Slavery & Abolition* 34 (March 2013): 1–21.

Klein, Herbert S. *The Atlantic Slave Trade*. Cambridge: Cambridge University Press, 1999.

———. *The Middle Passage: Comparative Studies in the Atlantic Slave Trade*. Princeton: Princeton University Press, 1978.

Koger, Larry. *Black Slaveowners: Free Black Slave Masters in South Carolina, 1790–1860*. Columbia: University of South Carolina Press, 1985.

Konadu, Kwasi. *The Akan Diaspora in the Americas*. New York: Oxford University Press, 2010.

Kup, Alexander Peter. *A History of Sierra Leone, 1400–1787*. Cambridge: Cambridge University Press, 1961.

Landers, Jane. *Black Society in Spanish Florida*. Urbana: University of Illinois Press, 1999.

———. *Atlantic Creoles in the Age of Revolutions*. Cambridge: Harvard University Press, 2011.

Law, Robin. "On Pawning and Enslavement for Debt in the Precolonial Slave Coast." In *Pawnship, Slavery, and Colonialism in Africa*, edited by Paul E. Lovejoy and Toyin Falola. Trenton: Africa World Press, 2003.

———. *Ouidah: The Social History of a West African Slaving 'Port,' 1727–1892*. Athens: Ohio University Press, 2004.

Lawrence, A. W. *Trade Castles and Forts of West Africa*. Stanford: Stanford University Press, 1964.

Lemons, J. Stanley. "Rhode Island and the Slave Trade." *Rhode Island History* 60, no. 4 (2002): 94–104.

Leopold, Anita M., and Jeppe S. Jensen, eds. *Syncretism in Religion: A Reader*. London: Equinox, 2004.

Leventhal, Herbert. *In the Shadow of the Enlightenment: Occultism and Renaissance Science in Eighteenth-Century America*. New York: New York University Press, 1976.

Levtzion, Nehemia. "The Early Jihad Movements." In *Cambridge History of Africa*, edited by Richard Gay. Cambridge: Cambridge University Press, 1975.

———. "Notes on the Origins of Islamic Militancy in the Futa Jallon." In *Islam in West Africa*, 1–4. Aldershot, U.K.: Variorum, 1994.

———. "Patterns of Islamization in West Africa." In *Islam in West Africa*. 207–16. Aldershot, U.K.: Variorum, 1994.

———. "Slavery and Islamization in Africa: A Comparative Study." In *Islam in West Africa*. 182–98. Aldershot, U.K.: Variorum, 1994.

Levtzion, Nehemia, and J. O. Voll. "The Eighteenth Century: Background to the Revolutions in West Africa." In *Eighteenth Century Renewal and Reform in Islam*. Syracuse: Syracuse University Press, 1987.

Lin, Rachel Chernos. "The Rhode Island Slave-Traders: Butchers, Bakers and Candlestick-Makers." *Slavery & Abolition* 23 (December 2002): 21–38.

Littlefield, Daniel C. "Charleston and Internal Slave Redistribution." *South Carolina Historical Magazine* 87, no. 2 (1986): 93–105.

———. *Rice and Slaves: Ethnicity and the Slave Trade in Colonial South Carolina*. Urbana: University of Illinois Press, 1981.

———. "The Slave Trade to Colonial South Carolina: A Profile." *South Carolina Historical Magazine* 91, no. 2 (1990): 68–99.

Lofkranz, Jennifer, and Paul E. Lovejoy. "Maintaining Network Boundaries: Islamic Law and Commerce from Sahara to Guinea Shores." *Slavery and Abolition* 26 (June 2015): 211–32.

Lovejoy, Paul E. "The African Diaspora: Revisionist Interpretations of Ethnicity, Culture and Religion under Slavery." *Studies in the World History of Slavery, Abolition and Emancipation, II* 1, no. 1 (1997): 1–23, http://www.yorku.ca/nhp/publications/Lovejoy_Studies%20in%20the%20World%20History%20of%20Slavery.pdf (accessed September 8, 2015).

———. "Ethnic Designations of the Slave Trade and the Reconstruction of the History of Trans-Atlantic Slavery." In *Trans-Atlantic Dimensions of Ethnicity in the African Diaspora*, edited by Paul E. Lovejoy and David V. Trotman. 9–42. London: Continuum, 2003.

———. "Extending the Frontiers of Transatlantic Slavery, Partially." *Journal of Interdisciplinary History* 40 (Summer 2009): 57–70.

———. "The Impact of the Atlantic Slave Trade on Africa: A Review of the Literature." *Journal of African History* 30, no. 3 (1989): 365–94.

———. *Transformations in Slavery: A History of Slavery in Africa*, 2nd ed. Cambridge: Cambridge University Press, 2000.

———. "The Urban Background of Enslaved Muslims in the Americas." *Slavery & Abolition* 26 (December 2005): 349–76.

———, ed. *Slavery on the Frontiers of Islam*. Princeton: Markus Wiener, 2004.

Lovejoy, Paul E., and Toyin Falola, eds. *Pawnship, Slavery, and Colonialism in Africa*. Trenton: Africa World Press, 2003.

Lovejoy, Paul E., and David Richardson. "The Business of Slaving: Pawnship in West Africa, 1600–1810." *Journal of African History* 42, no. 1 (2001): 67–89.

———. "Trust, Pawnship, and Atlantic History: The Institutional Foundations of the Old Calabar Slave Trade." *American Historical Review* 104 (April 1999): 333–55.

Lovejoy, Paul E., and David V. Trotman, eds. *Trans-Atlantic Dimensions of Ethnicity in the African Diaspora*. London: Continuum, 2003.

Macgunnigle, Bruce C., ed. *Rhode Island Freemen: A Census of Registered Voters*. Baltimore: Genealogical Publishing, 1977.

Manning, Patrick. *The African Diaspora: A History through Culture*. New York: Columbia University Press, 2009.

———. *Slavery and African Life: Occidental, Oriental, and African Slave Trades*. Cambridge: Cambridge University Press, 1990.

Mark, Peter. *"Portuguese" Style and Luso-African Identity*. Bloomington: University of Indiana Press, 2002.

Martin, Evaline C. *The British West African Settlements, 1750–1821*. London: Longman, Green, & Co., 1927. Negro Universities Press, 1970.

Mason, George Champlin. *Reminiscences of Newport*. Newport, R.I.: Charles E. Hammett, Jr., 1884.

Massing, Andreas W. "The Mane, the Decline of Mali, and Mandinka Expansion towards the South Windward Coast." *Cahiers d'Etudes Africaines* 25 (1985): 21–55.

Masur, Louis P. "Slavery in Eighteenth-Century Rhode Island: Evidence from the Census of 1774." *Slavery & Abolition* 6, no. 2 (1985): 139–50.

Mathias, Peter. "Risk, Credit and Kinship in Early Modern Enterprise." In *The Early Modern Atlantic Economy*, edited by John J. McCusker and Kenneth Morgan. 15–35. Cambridge: Cambridge University Press, 2000.

Matson, Cathy. "Imperial Political Economy: Ideological Debate and Shifting Practices." *William & Mary Quarterly*, 3d ser., 69 (January 2012): 35–40.

———. *Merchants and Empire: Trading in Colonial New York*. Baltimore: The Johns Hopkins University Press, 1998.

McCandless, Peter. *Slavery, Disease, and Suffering in the Southern Lowcountry*. Cambridge: Cambridge University Press, 2011.

McCusker, John J. *How Much Is That in Real Money?: A Historical Commodity Price Index for Use as a Deflator of Money Values in the Economy of the United States*. Worcester, Mass.: American Antiquarian Society, 2001.

———. *Money and Exchange in Europe and America, 1600–1775*. Chapel Hill: University of North Carolina Press, 1978.

———. *Rum and the American Revolution: The Rum Trade and the Balance of Payments of the Thirteen Continental Colonies, 1650–1775*. New York: Garland Publishing, 1989.

———. "The Rum Trade and the Balance of Payments of the Thirteen Continental Colonies, 1650–1775." *Journal of Economic History* 30 (March 1970): 244–47.

McCusker, John J., and Russell R. Menard. *The Economy of British America, 1607–1789*. Chapel Hill: University of North Carolina Press, 1985.

McMillin, James. *The Final Victims: The Foreign Slave Trade to North America, 1783–1810*. Columbia: University of South Carolina Press, 2004.

Meillassoux, Claude. *The Anthropology of Slavery: The Womb of Iron and Gold*. Translated by Alide Dasnois. Chicago: University of Chicago Press, 1991.

Meinig, Donald W. *The Shaping of America: A Geographical Perspective on 500 Years of History. Volume 1: Atlantic America, 1492–1800*. New Haven: Yale University Press, 1986.

Melish, Joanne Pope. *Disowning Slavery: Gradual Emancipation and 'Race' in New England, 1780–1860*. Ithaca: Cornell University Press, 1998.

———. "Reconsidering Rhode Island History." *Rhode Island History* 64 (Summer 2006): 49–60.

Mell, Dr. and Mrs. P. H. *The Genealogy of the Mell Family in the Southern States*. Auburn, Ala., 1897.

Meriweather, Robert L. *The Expansion of South Carolina, 1729–1765*. Kingsport, Tenn.: Southern Publishers, 1940.

Millar, John Fitzhugh. *Early American Ships*. Williamsburg: Thirteen Colonies Press, 1986.

Mintz, Sidney W., and Richard Price. *The Birth of African-American Culture: An Anthropological Perspective*. Boston: Beacon Press, 1992. Originally published as *An Anthropological Approach to the Afro-American Past*, 1976.

Misevich, Philip. "In Pursuit of Human Cargo: Philip Livingston and the Voyage of the Sloop *Rhode Island*." *New York History* 86 (Summer 2005): 185–204.

———. "On the Frontier of 'Freedom': Abolition and the Transformation of Atlantic Commerce in Southern Sierra Leone, 1790s–1860s." Ph.D. diss., Emory University, 2009.

———. "The Origins of Slaves Leaving the Upper Guinea Coast in the Nineteenth Century." In *Extending the Frontiers: Essays on the New Transatlantic Slave Trade Database*, edited by David Eltis and David Richardson, 155–75. New Haven: Yale University Press, 2008.

Montgomery, Michael, ed. *The Crucible of Carolina: Essays in the Development of Gullah Language and Culture*. Athens: University of Georgia Press, 1994.

Morgan, Jennifer L. *Laboring Women: Reproduction and Gender in New World Slavery*. Philadelphia: University of Pennsylvania Press, 2004.

Morgan, Kenneth. "The Organization of the Colonial American Rice Trade." *William and Mary Quarterly*, 3d. ser., 52 (July 1995): 433–52.

———. *Slavery and the British Empire: From Africa to America*. Oxford: Oxford University Press, 2007.

———. "Slave Sales in Colonial Charleston." *English Historical Review* 113, no. 453 (1998): 905–27.

Morgan, Philip D. "Black Life in Eighteenth-Century Charleston." *Perspectives in American History* 1 (1984): 187–232.

———. "Black Society in the Lowcountry, 1760–1810." In *Slavery and Freedom in the Age of the American Revolution*, edited by Ira Berlin and Ronald Hoffman, 83–142. Urbana: US Capitol Historical Society and the University of Illinois Press, 1983.

———. "Colonial South Carolina Runaways: Their Significance for Slave Culture." *Slavery & Abolition* 6, no. 3 (1985): 57–78.

———. "The Cultural Implications of the Atlantic Slave Trade: African Regional Origins, American Destinations, and New World Developments." *Slavery & Abolition* 18 (April 1997): 122–45.

———. "Lowcountry Georgia and the Early Modern Atlantic World, 1733–Ca. 1820." In *African American Life in the Georgia Lowcountry: The Atlantic World and the Gullah Geechee*, edited by Philip D. Morgan, 13–47. Athens: Unviversity of Georgia Press, 2010.

———. *Slave Counterpoint: Black Culture in the Eighteenth-Century Chesapeake and Lowcountry*. Chapel Hill: University of North Carolina Press, 1998.

————, ed. *African American Life in the Georgia Low Country*. Athens, Ga.: University of Georgia Press, 2010.

Morgan, Philip D., and George D. Terry. "Slavery in Microcosm: A Conspiracy Scare in Colonial South Carolina." *Southern Studies* 21 (Summer 1982): 121–45.

Mouser, Bruce L. *American Colony on the Rio Pongo: The War of 1812, the Slave Trade, and the Proposed Settlement of African Americans, 1810–1830*. Trenton, N.J: Africa World Press, 2013.

————. "A History of the Rio Pongo: Time for a New Appraisal?" *History in Africa* 37 (2010): 329–54.

————. "Iles de Los as a Bulking Center in the Slave Trade, 1750–1800." *Revue Française d'Histoire d'Outre-Mer* 83 (1996): 77–90.

————. "Landlords-Strangers: A Process of Accommodation and Assimilation." *International Journal of African Historical Studies* 8 (1975): 425–40.

————. "Rebellion, Marronage, and *Jihad*: Strategies of Resistance to Slavery on the Sierra Leone Coast, c. 1783–1796." *Journal of African History* 48, no. 1 (2007): 27–44.

————. "Trade, Coasters, and Conflict in the Rio Pongo from 1790 to 1808." *Journal of African History* 14, no. 1 (1973): 45–64.

————. "The Voyage of the Good Sloop 'Dolphin' to Africa 1795–1796." *American Neptune* 38, no. 4 (1978): 249–61.

————. "'Walking Caravans' of Nineteenth Century Fuuta Jaloo, Western Africa." *Mande Studies* 12 (2010): 19–104.

————. "Who and Where Were the Baga?: European Perceptions from 1793–1821." *History in Africa* 29 (2002): 337–64.

Mullin, Gerald W. *Flight and Rebellion: Slave Resistance in Eighteenth-Century Virginia*. Oxford: Oxford University Press, 1972.

Mullin, Michael. *Africa in America: Slave Acculturation and Resistance in the American South and the British Caribbean, 1736–1831*. Urbana: University of Illinois Press, 1992.

Nash, Gary B. *The Urban Crucible: Social Change, Political Consciousness, and the Origins of the American Revolution*. Cambridge: Harvard University Press, 1979.

Newell, Margaret Ellen. "The Birth of New England in the Atlantic Economy: From Its Beginning to 1770." In *Engines of Enterprise: An Economic History of New England*, edited by Peter Temin, 11–68. Cambridge: Harvard University Press, 2000.

————. *From Dependency to Independence: Economic Revolution in Colonial New England*. Ithaca: Cornell University Press, 1998.

Newson, Linda A., and Susie Minchin. *From Capture to Sale: The Portuguese Slave Trade to Spanish South America in the Early Seventeenth Century*. Leiden: Brill, 2007.

Northrup, David. "Igbo and Myth Igbo: Culture and Ethnicity in the Atlantic World, 1600–1850." *Slavery & Abolition* 21 (December 2000): 1–20.

Nwokeji, G. Ugo, and David Eltis. "Roots of the African Diaspora: Methodological Considerations in the Analysis of Names in the Liberated Africans Registers of Sierra Leone and Havana." *History in Africa* 29 (2002): 365–79.

Ogot, B. A., ed. *General History of Africa, Vol. 5: Africa from the Sixteenth to the Eighteenth Century*. Abridged ed. Berkeley: University of California/UNESCO, 1999.

Olwell, Robert A. *Masters, Slaves, and Subjects: The Culture of Power in the South Carolina Low Country, 1740–1790*. Ithaca: Cornell, 1998.

O'Malley, Gregory E. "Beyond the Middle Passage: Slave Migration from the Caribbean to North America, 1619–1807." *William & Mary Quarterly*, 3d ser., 66 (January 2009): 125–72.

———. *Final Passages: The Intercolonial Slave Trade of British America, 1619–1807*. Chapel Hill: University of North Carolina Press, 2014.

Opala, Joseph A. *The Gullah: Rice Slavery, and the Sierra Leone Connection*. Freetown, Sierra Leone, 1986.

Ostrander, Gilman M. "The Colonial Molasses Trade." *Agricultural History* 30 (April 1956): 77–84.

———. "The Making of the Triangular Trade Myth." *William & Mary Quarterly*, 3d ser., 30 (October 1973): 635–44.

Palmié, Stephan. "Creolization and Its Discontents." *Annual Review of Anthropology* 35 (2006): 433–56.

———. "Is There a Model in the Muddle? 'Creolization' in African Americanist History and Anthropology." In *Creolization: History, Ethnography, Theory*, edited by Charles Stewart, 178–200. Walnut Creek, Calif.: Left Coast Press, 2007.

———. *Wizards and Scientists: Explorations in Afro-Cuban Modernity and Tradition*. Durham: Duke University Press, 2002.

Pares, Richard. *War and Trade in the West Indies, 1739–1763*. London: Frank Cass, 1963.

———. *Yankees and Creoles: The Trade between North America and the West Indies before the American Revolution*. London: Longman, 1956.

Patterson, Orlando. *Slavery and Social Death: A Comparative Study*. Cambridge: Harvard University Press, 1982.

Pearson, Edward A. "A Countryside Full of Flames: A Reconsideration of the Stono Rebellion and Slave Rebelliousness in the Early Eighteenth-Century South Carolina Lowcountry." *Slavery & Abolition* 17 (August 1996): 22–50.

Perinbam, B. Marie. "Notes on Dyula Origins and Nomenclature." *Bulletin de l'Institut Fondamental d'Afrique Noir* 36, no. 4 (1974): 676–90.

Phillips, Caryl. *Cambridge*. New York: Alfred A. Knopf, 1992.

Pincus, Steve. "Rethinking Mercantilism: Political Economy, the British Empire, and the Atlantic World in the Seventeenth and Eighteenth Century." *William & Mary Quarterly*, 3d ser., 69 (January 2012): 3–34.

Pincus, Steve, Cathy Matson, Christian J. Koot, Susan D. Amussen, Trevor Burnard, and Margaret Ellen Newell. "Forum: Rethinking Mercantilism." *William & Mary Quarterly*, 3d ser., 69 (January 2012): 3–70.

Platt, Virginia Bever. "'And Don't Forget the Guinea Voyage': The Slave Trade of Aaron Lopez of Newport." *William & Mary Quarterly*, 3d ser., 32 (October 1975): 601–18.

———. "Tar, Staves, and New England Rum: The Trade of Aaron Lopez of Newport, Rhode Island, with Colonial North Carolina." *North Carolina Historical Review* 48 (January 1971): 1–22.

———. "Triangles and Tramping: Captain Zebediah Story of Newport, 1769–1776." *American Neptune* 33, no. 4 (1973): 294–303.

Pollitzer, William S. *The Gullah People and Their African Heritage*. Athens: University of
Georgia Press, 1999.

Porter, Roy. *English Society in the Eighteenth Century*, rev. ed. London: Penguin Books, 1990.

Poston, Jonathan. *The Buildings of Charleston: A Guide to the City's Architecture*. Columbia:
University of South Carolina Press, 1999.

Potvin, Ronald M. "John Sherman's Book of Horoscopes." *Newport History* 66 (Spring 1995):
185–93.

Preston, Howard Willis. *Rhode Island and the Sea*. Providence: Rhode Island State Bureau of
Information, 1932.

Price, Jacob. "The Imperial Economy, 1700–1776." In *The Oxford History of the British Empire*,
edited by Wm. Roger Louis, P.J. Marshall and Alaine Low. Oxford: Oxford University Press,
1998.

Price, Richard. *Alabi's World*. Baltimore: Johns Hopkins University Press, 1990.

———. "The Concept of Creolization." In *The Cambridge World History of Slavery*, edited by
David Eltis and Stanley L. Engerman, 3:513–537. Cambridge: Cambridge University Press,
2011.

Rappleye, Charles. *Sons of Providence: The Brown Brothers, the Slave Trade, and the American
Revolution*. New York: Simon and Schuster, 2007.

Rashid, Ismail. "'A Devotion to the Idea of Liberty at Any Price': Rebellion and Antislavery
in the Upper Guinea Coast in the Eighteenth and Ninenteenth Centuries." In *Fighting the
Slave Trade: West African Strategies*, edited by Sylviane A. Diouf, 132–51. Athens: Ohio
University Press, 2003.

Rathbone, Richard. "Some Thoughts on Resistance to Enslavement in West Africa." *Slavery &
Abolition* 6, no. 1 (1986): 11–22.

Rawley, James A. "Henry Laurens and the Atlantic Slave Trade." In *London, Metropolis of the
Slave Trade*. Columbia, Mo.: University of Missouri Press, 2003.

———. *London, Metropolis of the Slave Trade*. Columbia, Mo.: University of Missouri Press,
2003.

Rawley, James A., and Stephen D. Behrendt. *The Transatlantic Slave Trade: A History*. Lincoln:
University of Nebraska Press, 2005.

Rediker, Marcus. *Between the Devil and the Deep Blue Sea: Merchant Seamen, Pirates, and the
Anglo-American Maritime World, 1700–1750*. Cambridge: Cambridge University Press, 1989.

———. *The Slave Ship: A Human History*. New York: Viking, 2007.

———. *Villains of All Nations: Atlantic Pirates in the Golden Age*. Boston: Beacon Press, 2004.

Rees, J. F. "Mercantilism and the Colonies." In *The Cambridge History of the British Empire*,
edited by J. Holland Rose, A. P. Newton, and E. A. Benians, 561–602. Cambridge:
Cambridge University Press, 1929.

Reis, Jõao José. *Slave Rebellion in Brazil: The Muslim Uprising of 1835 in Bahia*. Translated by
Arthur Brakel. Baltimore: Johns Hopkins University Press, 1993.

Rhode Island Historical Preservation Commission. *The Southern Thames Street Neighborhood in
Newport, Rhode Island*. Providence: Rhode Island Historical Preservation Commission, 1980.

Richardson, David. "The British Slave Trade to Colonial South Carolina." *Slavery and Abolition*
12 (December 1991): 125–72.

———. "Prices of Slaves in West and West-Central Africa: Toward an Annual Series." *Bulletin of Historical Research* 43 (January 1991): 21–56.

———. "Shipboard Revolts, African Authority, and the Atlantic Slave Trade." *William and Mary Quarterly* 58 (January 2001): 69–92.

———. "Slavery, Trade, and Economic Growth in Eighteenth-Century New England." In *Slavery and the Rise of the Atlantic System*, edited by B. L. Solow, 237–64. Cambridge: Cambridge University Press, 1991.

Rivière, Claude. "Sociologie des Guerres au Fouta-Djalon Precolonial." *Cultures et Développement* 16, no. 3–4 (1984): 552–81.

Roberts, Gary Boyd. *Genealogies of Rhode Island Families from the New England Historical and Genealogical Register.* 2 vols. Baltimore: Genealogical Publishing, 1989.

Roberts, Richard L. "Production and Reproduction of Warrior States: Segu Bambara and Segu Tokolor, c. 1712–1890." *International Journal of African Historical Studies* 13, no. 3 (1980): 389–419.

Rodger, N. A. M. *The Wooden World: An Anatomy of the Georgian Navy.* Norton ed. London: William Collins, 1986.

Rodney, Walter. *A History of the Upper Guinea Coast, 1545–1800.* Oxford: Oxford University Press, 1970.

———. "Jihad and Social Revolution in Futa Djalon in the Eighteenth Century." *Journal of the History Society of Nigeria* 4 (June 1968): 269–84.

———. "Upper Guinea and the Significance of the Origins of Africans Enslaved in the New World." *Journal of Negro History* 54 (October 1969): 327–45.

Rogers, George C. *Charleston in the Age of the Pinckneys.* Columbia: University of South Carolina Press, 1980.

———. *History of Georgetown County.* Columbia: University of South Carolina Press, 1970.

Roland, Alex, W. Jeffrey Bolster, and Alexander Keyssar. *The Way of the Ship: America's Maritime History Reenvisioned.* Hoboken, New Jersey: John Wiley & Sons, 2008.

Rowland, Lawrence S., Alexander Moore, and George C. Rogers. *The History of Beaufort County, South Carolina, Volume 1: 1514–1861.* Columbia: University of South Carolina Press, 1996.

Rucker, Walter C. *The River Flows On: Black Resistance, Culture, and Identity Formation in Early America.* Baton Rouge: Louisiana State University Press, 2006.

Rudolph, Richard H. "Eighteenth Century Newport and Its Merchants." *Newport History* 51, no. 2 (1978): 21–38.

———. "Eighteenth Century Newport and Its Merchants." *Newport History* 51, no. 3 (1978): 45–60.

Ryan, William R. *The World of Thomas Jeremiah: Charles Town on the Eve of the American Revolution.* New York: Oxford University Press, 2010.

Schafer, Daniel L. *Anna Madgigine Kingsley: African Princess, Florida Slave, Plantation Slaveowner.* Gainesville: University Press of Florida, 2003.

Schaffer, Matt. "Bound to Africa: The Mandinka Legacy in the New World." *History in Africa* 32 (September 2005): 321–69.

Scott, Kenneth. "George Scott: Slave Trader of Newport." *American Neptune* 12 (July 1952): 222–28.

Searing, James F. *West African Slavery and Atlantic Commerce: The Senegal River Valley, 1700–1860*. Cambridge: Cambridge University Press, 1993.

Sellers, Leila. *Charleston Business on the Eve of the American Revolution*. Chapel Hill: University of North Carolina Press, 1934.

Sharafi, Mitra. "The Slave Ship Manuscripts of Captain Joseph B. Cook: A Narrative Reconstruction of the Brig *Nancy*'s Voyage of 1793." *Slavery & Abolition* 24, no. 1 (2003): 71–100.

Shaw, Rosalind. *Memories of the Slave Trade: Ritual and the Historical Imagination in Sierra Leone*. Chicago: University of Chicago Press, 2002.

Shepherd, James F., and Gary M. Walton. *Shipping, Maritime Trade, and the Economic Development of Colonial North America*. Cambridge: Cambridge University Press, 1972.

Shields, David S. "Mean Streets, Mannered Streets: Charleston." *Common-Place: The Interactive Journal of Early American Life* 3 (2003). http://www.common-place.org/vol-03/no-04/charleston/ (accessed August 21, 2015).

Shumway, Rebecca. "Castle Slaves of the Eighteenth-Century Gold Coast (Ghana)." *Slavery and Abolition* 35 (March 2014): 84–98.

———. *The Fante and the Transatlantic Slave Trade*. Rochester: University of Rochester Press, 2011.

Sidbury, James. *Becoming African in America: Race and Nation in the Early Black Atlantic*. Oxford: Oxford University Press, 2007.

Sidbury, James. "Globalization, Creolization, and the Not-So-Peculiar Institution." *Journal of Southern History* 73 (August 2007): 617–30.

Sidbury, James, and Jorge Cañizares-Esguerra. "Mapping Ethnogenesis in the Early Modern Atlantic." *William and Mary Quarterly*, 3d ser., 68 (April 2011): 181–208.

Singleton, Theresa A., ed. *The Archaeology of Slavery and Plantation Life*. Orlando, Fla.: Academic Press, 1985.

———, ed. *"I, Too, Am America": Archaeological Studies of African American Life*. Charlottesville: University of Virginia Press, 1999.

Skinner, David E. "Islam and Education in the Colony and Hinterland of Sierra Leone (1750–1914)." *Canadian Journal of African Studies* 10, no. 3 (1976): 499–520.

———. "Islam in the Northern Hinterland and Its Influence on the Development of the Sierra Leone Colony." In *Islam and Trade in Sierra Leone*, edited by Alusine Jalloh and David E. Skinner. Trenton, N.J.: Africa World Press, 1997.

———. "Mande Settlement and the Development of Islamic Institutions in Sierra Leone." *International Journal of African Historical Studies* 11, no. 1 (1978): 32–62.

Slaughter, Thomas P. *The Beautiful Soul of John Woolman, Apostle of Abolition*. New York: Hill and Wang, 2008.

Smallwood, Stephanie E. "African Guardians, European Slave Ships, and the Changing Dynamics of Power in the Early Modern Atlantic." *William and Mary Quarterly*, 3d ser., 64 (October 2007): 679–716.

———. *Saltwater Slavery: A Middle Passage from Africa to American Diaspora*. Cambridge: Harvard University Press, 2006.

Smith, Mark M. "Remembering Mary, Shaping Revolt: Reconsidering the Stono Rebellion." *Journal of Southern History* 67 (August 2001): 513–34.

————, ed. *Stono: Documenting and Interpreting a Southern Slave Revolt*. Columbia: University of South Carolina Press, 2005.

Smith, Robert. "Peace and Palaver: International Relations in Pre-Colonial West Africa." *Journal of African History* 14, no. 4 (1973): 599–621.

Smith, S. D. "Gedney Clarke of Salem and Barbados: Transatlantic Super-Merchant." *New England Quarterly* 76 (December 2003): 499–549.

————. *Slavery, Family, and Gentry Capitalism in the British Atlantic: The World of the Lascelles, 1648–1834*. Cambridge: Cambridge University Press, 2006.

Sobel, Mechal. *The World They Made Together: Black and White Values in Eighteenth-Century Virginia*. Princeton: Princeton University Press, 1987.

Soderlund, Jean R. *Quakers and Slavery: A Divided Spirit*. Princeton: Princeton University Press, 1985.

St. Clair, William. *The Door of No Return: The History of Cape Coast Castle and the Atlantic Slave Trade*. New York: Blue Bridge, 2007.

Steele, Ian K. *The English Atlantic, 1675–1740*. New York: Oxford University Press, 1986.

Stine, Linda F., Martha Zierden, Lesley M. Drucker, and Christopher Judge, eds. *Carolina's Historical Landscapes: Archaeological Perspectives*. Knoxville: University of Tennessee Press, 1997.

Stuckey, Sterling. *Slave Culture: Nationalist Theory and the Foundations of Black America*. New York: Oxford University Press, 1987.

Stumpf, Stuart. "South Carolina Importers of General Merchandise, 1735–1765." *South Carolina Historical Magazine* 84, no. 1 (1983): 1–10.

Sweet, James H. "Defying Social Death: The Multiple Configurations of the Slave Family in the Atlantic World." *William and Mary Quarterly*, 3d ser., (April 2013): 251–72.

————. *Domingos Alvares, African Healing, and the Intellectual History of the Atlantic World*. Chapel Hill: University of North Carolina Press, 2010.

————. "Mistaken Identities? Olaudah Equiano, Domingos Alvares, and the Methodological Challenges of Studying the African Diaspora." *American Historical Review* 114 (April 2009): 279–306.

————. *Recreating Africa: Culture, Kinship, and Religion in the African-Portuguese World, 1441–1770*. Chapel Hill: University of North Carolina Press, 2003.

Sweet, John Wood. *Bodies Politic: Negotiating Race in the American North, 1730–1830*. Baltimore: Johns Hopkins University Press, 2003.

Taylor, Eric Robert. *If We Must Die: Shipboard Insurrections in the Era of the Atlantic Slave Trade*. Baton Rouge: Louisiana State University Press, 2006.

Terry, George D. "'Champaign Country': A Social History of an Eighteenth-Century Lowcountry Parish in South Carolina, St. John's Berkeley County." Ph.D. diss., University of South Carolina, 1981.

Thomas, Hugh. *The Slave Trade: The Story of the Atlantic Slave Trade, 1440–1870*. New York: Simon & Schuster, 1999.

Thomas, Keith. *Religion and the Decline of Magic*. New York: Scribner's, 1971.

Thornton, John K. "African Dimensions of the Stono Rebellion." *American Historical Review* 96 (October 1996): 1101–13.

————. *Africa and Africans in the Making of the Atlantic World, 1400–1680*. Cambridge: Cambridge University Press, 1992.

————. *Warfare in Atlantic Africa, 1500–1800*. London: Routledge, 1999.

Trinkley, Michael, Debi Hacker, and Sarah Fick. "Investigation of an Eighteenth Century Overseer Site (38ch1278), Christ Church Parish, Charleston County, South Carolina." *Chicora Foundation Research Series* 64 (May 2005): 23–45.

Turner, Lorenzo Dow. *Africanisms in the Gullah Dialect*. Columbia: University of South Carolina Press, 2002. First published 1949.

Twining, Mary A., and Kenneth E. Baird. *Sea Island Roots: African Presence in the Carolinas and Georgia*. Trenton, N.J.: Africa World Press, 1991.

Unsworth, Barry. *Sacred Hunger*. New York: W. W. Norton & Co., 1992.

U.S. Census Bureau. *Historical Statistics of the United States, Colonial Times to 1970*. 2 vols. Washington, D.C.: General Printing Office, 1975.

Vezeau, Susan Lynne. "The Mepkin Abbey Shipwreck: Diving into Mepkin Plantation's Past." Master's thesis, Texas A&M, 2004.

Vickers, Daniel, and Vince Walsh. "Young Men and the Sea: The Sociology of Seafaring in Eighteenth-Century Salem, Massachusetts." *Social History* 24 (January 1999): 17–38.

————. *Young Men and the Sea: Yankee Seafarers in the Age of Sail*. New Haven: Yale University Press, 2005.

Vignols, M. Léon. "La Campagne Négrière de *La Perle* (1755–1757)." *Revue Historique* 163 (1930): 51–78.

Vydrine, Valentin. "Who Speaks 'Mandekan'?: A Note on Current Use of Mande Ethnonyms and Linguinyms." *MANSA (Mande Studies Association) Newsletter* 25 (1995): 6–9.

Walker, Sheila S., ed. *African Roots/American Cultures: Africa in the Creation of the Americas*. Lanham, Md.: Rowman and Littlefield, 2001.

Wallace, David Duncan. *Life of Henry Laurens*. New York: Russell & Russell, 1915.

Walsh, Lorena S. "The Chesapeake Slave Trade: Regional Patterns, African Origins, and Some Implications." *William & Mary Quarterly*, 3d ser., 58 (January 2001): 139–70.

————. *From Calabar to Carter's Grove: The History of a Virginia Slave Community*. Charlottesville: University of Virginia Press, 1997.

Walvin, James. *The Zong: A Massacre, the Law, and the End of Slavery*. New Haven: Yale, 2011.

Warren, Mary Bondurant. *South Carolina Jury Lists, 1718 through 1783*. Danielsville, Ga.: Heritage Papers, 1977.

Wax, Darold D. "The Browns of Providence and the Slaving Voyage of the Brig 'Sally,' 1764–1765." *American Neptune* 32, no. 3 (1972): 171–79.

————. "Thomas Rogers and the Rhode Island Slave Trade." *American Neptune* 35 (October 1975): 289–301.

Wedderburn, Alexander. *The Wedderburn Book: A History of the Wedderburns in the Counties of Berwick and Forfar*. 2 vols. n.p.: Privately published, 1898.

Weir, Robert M. *Colonial South Carolina: A History*. Columbia: University of South Carolina Press, 1983.

Welch, Pedro L. V. *Slave Society in the City: Bridgetown, Barbados, 1680–1834*. Oxford: James Currey Publishers, 2004.

Williamson, Kay, and Roger Blench. "Niger-Congo." In *African Languages: An Introduction*, edited by Bernd Heine and Derek Nurse, 11–42. Cambridge: Cambridge University Press, 2000.

Withey, Lynne. *Urban Growth in Colonial Rhode Island: Newport and Providence in the Eighteenth Century*. Albany: State University of New York Press, 1984.

Wolff, H. Ekkehard. "Language and Society." In *African Languages: An Introduction*, edited by Bernd Heine and Derek Nurse, 298–347. Cambridge: Cambridge University Press, 2000.

Wood, Betty. *Slavery in Colonial Georgia, 1730–1775*. Athens: University of Georgia Press, 1984.

———. *Women's Work, Men's Work: The Informal Slave Economies of Lowcountry Georgia*. Athens: University of Georgia Press, 1995.

Wood, Peter. *Black Majority: Negroes in Colonial South Carolina from 1670 through the Stono Rebellion*. New York: Knopf, 1974.

Woodbridge, George. "The Vernon House." *Newport History* (Winter 1987): 28–39.

Woodson, Carter G. *The African Background Outlined*. Washington, D.C.: Association for the Study of Negro Life and History, 1936.

Worrall, Arthur J. *Quakers in the Colonial Northeast*. Hanover, N.H.: University Press of New England, 1980.

Wright, Donald R. "Darbo Jula: The Role of a Mandinka Jula Clan in the Long-Distance Trade of the Gambia River and Its Hinterland." *African Economic History* 3 (Spring 1977): 33–45.

———. "'What Do You Mean There Were No Tribes in Africa?': Thoughts on Boundaries—and Related Matters—in Precolonial Africa." *History in Africa* 26 (1999): 409–26.

Wylie, Kenneth C. "The Influence of the Mande on Temne Political Institutions: Aspects of Political Acculturation." *International Journal of African Historical Studies* 7 (1974): 255–71.

Young, Jason R. *Rituals of Resistance: African Atlantic Religion in Kongo and the Lowcountry South in the Era of Slavery*. Baton Rouge: Louisiana State University Press, 2007.

Zacek, Natalie. "'A People So Subtle': Sephardic Jewish Pioneers of the English West Indies." In *Bridging the Early Modern Atlantic World: People, Products, and Practices on the Move*, edited by Caroline A. Williams, 97–112. Bristol: Ashgate, 2009.

Online Databases and Tools

Church of Jesus Christ and the Latter Day Saints. *FamilySearch*. Online at https://familysearch.org/.

Eltis, David, and Martin Halbert. *Voyages: The Transatlantic Slave Trade Database*. Online at www.slavevoyages.org.

MeasuringWorth.com. Online at http://www.measuringworth.com/.

INDEX

France, 50, 51, 61, 63, 69, 88, 127–28
Fraser, Alexander, 137, 150, 155, 162
Frazier, E. Franklin, 2
French and Indian War, 44, 51, 90, 124, 185–87, 192, 195, 229 (n. 64)
Fryer, George, 64, 65
Futa Jallon, 68, 93; Futa Jallon Jihad, 85, 95–97, 103, 106, 166, 169, 173, 185; Muslims and, 82, 84–85, 106, 185; slave trade and, 82, 96–102, 103, 106, 166, 169, 173, 185

Garden, Alexander, 154
Gardner, Caleb, 34
Gardner, George, 34, 225–26 (n. 59)
Georgia, 157, 189; Muslims and, 179, 180; slavery and, 137–38, 146, 193; slave trade and, 7, 207
Glen, James, 121, 123
Godfrey, Caleb, 15, 34, 67, 226 (nn. 9–10), 227 (n. 16), 236 (n. 77); Barbados and, 114, 115, 116–17, 186–87, 239 (n. 44); captive sales and, 119, 120, 132, 184, 188; "coast commission" and, 127, 183–84, 190; communications and, 61, 72, 82, 87, 106, 115, 119; crew and, 14, 35, 40, 43, 44, 70–71, 72, 104–5, 106, 116–18, 182–83, 238 (n. 33), 239 (nn. 36–37); detaining captives and, 38, 39, 103–4, 116, 131, 132, 182; earlier life of, 36–39; *Hare* second voyage and, 90, 185, 186–87, 190, 201–2, 229–30 (n. 7); later years of, 190–91; merchant instructions and, 38, 49–50, 187; navigation and, 82–83, 121; obtaining captives and, 1, 12, 62, 70, 72, 78, 81, 83–84, 85–88, 89–92, 101, 102–4, 111, 194, 234 (n. 22); obtaining captives on second voyage and, 90, 186–87; outgoing voyage and, 51, 53, 54–55, 57, 58, 59, 229–30 (n. 7); provisioning and, 63, 70, 89, 106–7, 108; remittances (return cargo) and, 182, 183; return voyage and, 110–11, 112, 120, 201, 239 (n. 44); Vernon brothers and, 14, 36, 38, 39, 49, 184, 190; voyage preparations and, 14, 35, 43, 48
Godfrey, Caleb, Jr., 36, 191
Godfrey, John, 38, 227 (n. 16)
Gold Coast, 27, 32, 50, 63, 130–31, 163, 185, 188, 201, 229 (n. 60)

Gomez, Michael, 151, 180
Good Hope (ship), 111
Grant & Oswald (Grant, Oswald, & Co.), 64, 67, 69, 74, 78, 83, 87, 231 (n. 32)
Great Britain: astrology and, 45, 46, 48; Atlantic trade and, 19–20, 21; slavery and, 113–14; slave ships and, 9, 39, 41, 61, 70, 72, 77, 83, 105, 110, 187; slave trade and, 7, 73, 181, 219 (n. 15), 229 (n. 60), 244 (n. 4); slave trade at Bance Island and, 63, 64–67, 69–70, 72, 74, 75, 78, 83, 87, 186, 190, 231 (n. 32)
Greegrees, 176
Gromettos, 66–67, 79, 89, 106, 231 (n. 37)
Gullah culture, 7, 9, 167, 175, 178, 180

Hall, Richard, 89–90, 235 (n. 44)
Hammond, John Arnold, 35, 40, 41, 55, 70, 104, 105, 117, 118, 191–92, 248 (n. 29)
Hammond, Nathaniel, 25, 27
Hare captives in South Carolina: captive sales and, 5–6, 12, 122, 126–27, 130–31, 132–33, 134–35, 137, 190, 201; cattle raising and, 157–58; in Charles Town, 138, 139, 145, 146, 147, 156, 162; children and, 145, 146, 150, 155, 160, 163, 187, 194, 244 (n. 33); communications and, 7, 103, 160, 162, 172, 173–74, 193; deaths and, 145, 146, 160, 161, 193–94; female vs. male, 134–35, 145, 146, 147, 148, 150, 155, 156, 163, 173–74, 244 (n. 33); indigo plantations and, 138, 155–57, 159, 165, 243–44 (n. 30), 244 (n. 33); in "Middle Country," 140, 155; rice plantations and, 7, 138, 141, 142, 150–58; shipmates and, 159–61, 162; slave names and, 1, 13. *See also* Slaves in South Carolina
Hare demise, 192–93
Hare first voyage: communications and, 5–6, 49–50, 219 (n. 12); gunpowder tax and, 131–32, 241 (n. 19); insurance and, 14, 28, 49, 119–20; merchant instructions and, 49–50, 227 (n. 25); navigation and, 82–83, 121; Newport and, 14, 16, 18, 184; outgoing cargo of, 14, 29, 30, 31–35, 49, 52, 56–57, 61, 62–63, 224–25 (n. 51), 226 (n. 60); outgoing voyage, 9, 10, 50–51, 52–53, 54–55, 56–57, 58–59, 201,

229 (n. 62); provisions for, 35, 58, 61–62, 63, 70, 89, 106–7, 108, 110; remittances (return cargo) and, 181–82; return voyage, 9, 107, 108, 110–11, 113, 119, 120, 122, 124, 126, 129, 201; ship type and, 27–30, 223 (n. 41), 223–24 (n. 42), 224 (nn. 43, 46), 241 (n. 19); violence and, 105–6, 109; voyage preparations for, 12, 14, 35; weapons and armaments and, 29, 107; weather at sea and, 108, 110, 112, 121; weather in Africa and, 61–62, 92. *See also* Godfrey, Caleb

Hare first voyage, captives on board: ages of, 41, 102–3; branding and, 91–92; communication and relationship and, 7, 93–94, 102, 103, 112–13; captive sales and, 49–50, 119, 120, 189; deaths of, 49, 111, 115, 120; children and, 182; detaining captives, 103–4, 110, 116, 119–20, 132, 182; disease and, 49, 111, 112, 115–16, 119, 120, 129; female vs. male, 41, 109; provisions for, 107, 108; quarantine of, 129–30, 131, 186

Hare first voyage, crew: captives on board and, 62, 92, 109, 110; desertion and, 70–71, 72, 116–18, 120, 238 (n. 33), 238–39 (n. 35); officers and, 40–41, 55, 104–5, 191–92; "privilege slaves" and, 40, 49, 111; punishments and, 70–71, 104–6; seamen and, 43–45, 55, 182–83, 192, 232 (n. 49), 238 (n. 34), 239 (nn. 36–37); voyage preparations for, 14, 29, 35, 229 (n. 62); wages of, 40, 41, 43–44. *See also* Godfrey, Caleb

Hare first voyage, obtaining captives: Bance Island and, 70, 78, 87–88, 91; children and, 1, 62; female vs. male, 1, 81, 90, 91, 102; Northern Rivers and, 82–83, 84, 85–88, 96, 101; Sherbro and, 90–91, 96, 99, 101; slave dealers and, 5, 70, 78, 81, 82, 83, 84, 85–87, 88, 89, 90, 91, 101, 206; Upper Guinea and, 8, 9, 11, 12, 50, 93, 96, 185, 201

Hare first voyage, ports of call: Bance Island, 61, 64, 67, 70, 78, 87–88, 91, 107, 230 (n. 30); Cape Verde, 56–57, 58, 201, 229–30 (n. 7); Isles de Los, 59, 81, 85, 86, 91, 104, 110, 131, 201; merchant instructions and, 49–50; Northern

Rivers and, 81, 82–83, 84, 85–88, 91; passengers and, 119; Plantain Islands and, 89; Sherbro and, 89, 90–91, 99; Sierra Leone and, 58, 59, 88, 110, 164, 201. *See also* Barbados

Hare second voyage, 40, 97, 190; captive sales and, 49, 187, 189; captives in South Carolina and, 154, 164, 187–88; merchant instructions and, 49, 50, 227 (n. 25); obtaining captives and, 90, 185, 186–87; ports of call and, 58, 86, 90, 186, 187, 188, 201–2, 229–30 (n. 7)

Harleston family, 164
Harrison, John, 53
Harrison, William, 86
Harriss, William, 87
Hartwick, Barnt, 71, 117, 232 (n. 49), 238 (nn. 33–34)
Harvey, Robert, 183, 192
Harvey, William, 183, 192
Hawk (ship), 192
Herskovits, Melville J., 2
Hicks, Benjamin, 46
Hill, Lawrence, 13
HMS *Assurance*, 88
Holman, John, 85–86
Holman, John, Jr., 86, 91
Holson, Christopher, 168
Honorable Friend (ship), 70
Hope (ship), 191
Hopkins, Stephen, 192
Hore, Benjamin, 79
Horry, Daniel, 140
Horry, Elias, 140, 160, 162
Hoxse, John, 42
Huguenots, 127–28, 136, 140
Hunter, William, 191
Hutchinson, Anne, 23

Indigo, 20, 129, 138, 152, 155–57, 159, 165, 243–44 (n. 30), 244 (n. 33)
Insurance, 14, 22, 25, 35, 38, 49, 52, 119–20
Islam. *See* Muslims
Isles de Los: *Hare* first voyage and, 59, 81, 85, 86, 91, 104, 110, 131, 201; *Hare* second voyage and, 86, 186, 188; slave dealers and, 81, 83, 85, 86; slave ships and, 111; slave trade and, 78, 83, 185

Jamaica, 57, 113, 114, 132, 238 (n. 22); *Hare* demise and, 192; *Hare* first voyage and, 49–50, 115, 118; Newport trade and, 24, 32, 33, 37

Jolly Hanna (sloop), 37

Jones, William, 43, 71, 72, 192

Joyner, Charles, 7

Jumonville, Joseph Coulon de Villiers de, 51

Juula, 82, 98, 99, 100, 101, 103, 104, 171, 235 (n. 56)

Kalteisen, Michael, 168

King George's War (1748), 15, 24, 31, 32, 43, 44, 88, 155

Kissi people, 169, 172

Landlord-stranger relationship, 73–74

Langton, Jonathan, 86–87

Langton, Shepherd, & Co., 87

Languages, 92–94, 197–200. *See also* Mande peoples

Laurens, Henry, 168, 193, 243–44 (n. 30); rice plantations and, 141, 142, 145–46, 150, 190; as slave purchaser, 138, 139, 140, 141, 142, 145–46, 160, 163–64, 189, 208; slave trade and, 86, 87, 141, 142, 155, 161, 165, 184, 187, 188, 189–90, 241 (n. 35), 244 (n. 9)

Laurens, John, 142, 190

Lessesne, Daniel, 140, 160

Lightning, 38, 39, 51, 61

Lindsay, David, 47, 61, 62

Little Betsey (sloop), 46

Little George (sloop), 37, 226 (n. 10)

Little Will (ship), 80

Lloyd, William, 137, 145, 146, 147, 156

Longitude, 53, 54–55

Lopez, José, 63, 72, 75

Lorimer, Charles, 137, 152, 155–56, 157, 161, 244 (n. 33)

Low, James, 67, 69

Malbone, Evan, 19

Malbone, Godfrey, 22, 24, 32, 37, 38

Mali Empire, 12, 94–95, 171

Mande peoples: in Africa, 12, 62, 80, 82, 85, 95, 98; defined, 11–12; greegrees and, 176, 177; jihad and, 82, 85, 95, 103,

126; languages and, 6, 12, 93–94, 102, 160, 166, 169–74, 197–200, 235 (n. 56), 245 (nn. 13, 16); secret rituals and, 80, 178; slave trade and, 102, 103, 126, 187; in South Carolina, 126, 160, 162, 166, 167, 169–74, 178, 187, 193

Mane people, 95, 103, 171

Manigault, Gabriel, 24, 25, 193, 239 (n. 44), 240 (n. 9); captive sales and, 120, 122, 126–29, 130, 131, 132, 134–35, 181, 189, 201; "coast commission" and, 183–84, 190; remittances (return cargo) and, 181, 182, 184

Manigault, Peter, 128

Manigault, Pierre, 127–28

Marabouts, 82, 95, 176, 177, 180

Mary (ship), 24

"Masseboy King of Nunko," 84, 234 (n. 22)

Matheny, Daniel, 183

Mathews, Robert, 76

Mawdo, Sori. *See* Sori, Ibrahima

McCulloch, Hance, 137, 157

McIntosh, Lachlan, 146, 162, 189, 193

Mell, Thomas, 136, 150, 165

Methuen Treaty of 1703, 26

Minnick, Christian, 137, 140, 157–58

Mintz, Sidney, 2, 4

Mohammed, Bilali, 179, 180

Molasses, 20, 21, 24

Mongo Dandi, 85

Morgan, Philip D., 162

Moroney, William, 118, 192

Morrison, Andrew, 87–88

Mountain, Francis, 119, 239 (n. 42)

Mozambique, 189

Muslims: in Africa, 62, 82, 84–85, 94, 102, 103, 106, 176, 177, 180, 185, 236 (n. 58); jihad and, 95–96, 98–99, 103, 106, 126, 166, 173, 185, 236 (n. 58), 247 (n. 13); slavery and, 84, 95, 96, 102, 236 (n. 58); slave trade and, 2, 82, 96, 102, 103, 126, 166, 179–80, 218 (n. 2), 236 (n. 58), 246 (n. 33); in South Carolina, 151, 174, 179–80, 246 (n. 33)

Navigation, 28, 53–55, 59, 82–83, 113, 115; Charles Town and, 121, 122, 129

Navigation Acts, 19–20, 21

(n. 18), 243 (n. 24); "task system" and, 152–53, 175, 243 (n. 21)
Richardson, Thomas, Jr., 33–34, 195
Richardson, Thomas, Sr., 33–34
Rivers of Guinea. *See* Northern Rivers
Ruff, John, 77, 90
Ross, Alexander, 87
Royal African Company, 63, 64, 65, 72, 75, 79, 90, 229 (n. 60)
Rum, 20, 21, 24, 128; African trade and, 30–31, 62–63, 87, 108, 221 (n. 15); Newport and, 15, 18, 25, 32, 33–34; slave trade and, 35, 56, 61, 62, 78, 84, 85, 86, 88, 89, 90, 91, 202, 224 (n. 44)

Said, Omar Ibn, 174
Sally (sloop), 191
Salt, 58
Sande society, 178
Sankoh, Buri Lahi, 99
Scarcies, The, 81, 82, 83, 84, 85, 87, 104, 234 (n. 22)
Scarcies Rivers, 83, 98, 99, 185, 186
Scott, Mary, 40
Scottish migrants, 137
Senegal, 50, 56
Senegambia, 50, 58, 95, 131, 161, 172, 173, 185
Seven Years' War, 46, 192
Sherbro, 81, 85, 89, 90, 91, 99, 101, 102, 103, 186
Sherman, John, 46, 48
Sidbury, James, 4
Sierra Leone, 60, 68; culture and, 11, 178; *Hare* first voyage and, 58, 59, 88, 110, 164, 201; *Hare* second voyage and, 186–87, 188; history of, 11, 92, 93, 94–95; indigo and, 157; map of, 60; rice-growing and, 153, 240–41 (n. 18); slave dealers and, 79–80, 81, 83, 87; slaves returning to, 194; slave trade and, 47, 62, 63, 70, 78, 90, 91, 173, 184–85, 233 (n. 1), 235 (n. 44); and slave trade with South Carolina, 1, 10, 50, 83–84, 131, 146, 172, 207, 248 (n. 33); weather and, 61, 82
Sierra Leone (sloop), 24
Sierra Leone Company, 74

Simons, Samuel, 150
Simson, Robert, 87
Siraloon (ship), 61, 230 (n. 24)
Sitiki, 99, 101
Skinner, William, 91, 235 (n. 46)
Slave purchasers, 134–42, 143–44, 147–48, 193, 208–9, 210–11, 241 (nn. 31, 35); cattle ranging and, 157–58; indigo and, 129, 138, 152, 155–57, 165, 243–44 (n. 30), 244 (n. 33); later lives and, 189–90; rice plantations and, 138, 139, 141, 142, 145–46, 149–55, 163–64, 165; runaway slaves and, 167–68; and slavery views, 140–42; slaves from Upper Guinea and, 161–62, 163, 164, 187–88, 212–13, 244 (n. 9); slave shipmates and, 159–61
Slave rebellions, 151, 154, 191, 243 (n. 27); in Africa, 66, 97; slave ships and, 49, 71, 72–73, 109–10, 226 (n. 10); Stono Rebellion, 8, 125, 143, 245 (n. 22)
Slavery: in Africa, 96–98, 101, 102; African culture and, 2–4, 6, 7–8; Africans in North America and, 5, 6, 9, 219 (n. 13); Bance Island and, 65, 66–67, 176, 231 (nn. 37, 39); Barbados and, 113–14, 115–16, 120; Cape Verde and, 56, 58; Caribbean and, 5, 143; Catholic Church and, 4, 219 (n. 10); Creolization theories and, 2–4, 11, 218 (nn. 3–5); emancipation and, 190, 194–95; Muslims and, 84, 95, 96, 102, 236 (n. 58); Newport and, 18–19, 23, 32, 33, 36, 195, 221 (n. 12); North American studies and, 4–5, 185, 219 (n. 10); patriarchalism and, 142–43; Revisionist theories and, 2–4, 6, 218 (n. 5); runaways and, 167–71, 172–73, 216; violence and, 143–44. *See also* Slaves in South Carolina; South Carolina
Slave ships: accidents and, 38, 39, 64, 70, 106; astrology and, 45–48; attacks and, 50, 63, 73, 105, 106, 229 (n. 61), 236 (n. 77), 248 (n. 29); Brazil vs. North America and, 7, 219 (n. 15); captive communication and relationship and, 112–13, 238 (n. 18); captives dying and, 28, 38, 39, 78; captives on board, 111–12, 237 (nn. 10, 15–16), 238 (n. 17);

communications and, 5, 219 (n. 12); crew and, 39, 41–43, 48, 55–56, 71–72, 92, 118–19, 227 (n. 23), 228 (n. 44); detaining captives and, 100–101, 114, 115, 116; disease and, 41, 72, 108–9, 129; insurance and, 22, 38, 52; navigation and, 28, 53–55, 59, 113, 115; New England vs. Great Britain and, 9, 39, 41, 110; Newport and, 15, 18, 24, 61, 77, 184, 248 (n. 29); obtaining captives and, 3, 7, 8, 11, 49, 73, 76, 80, 98, 99, 101–2, 201, 205, 244 (n. 4); outgoing cargo and, 30–31, 224 (n. 44); ports of call and, 201–2, 229–30 (n. 7); preparations and, 22, 23–24; "privilege slaves" and, 39, 42, 92, 227 (n. 23); provisions and, 35, 59, 101, 110, 113, 114; return voyages and, 85, 86, 111; Rhode Island and, 1, 15, 22, 24, 41–42, 61; sails and, 27–28, 55; ships' masters and, 27, 36–37, 38, 39, 40, 43, 62, 76, 77, 80; ship types and, 27–30, 223 (n. 41), 223–24 (n. 42), 224 (nn. 43–46); slave rebellions and, 49, 71, 72–73, 109–10, 226 (n. 10); studies on, 5, 219 (n. 11); violence and, 38, 41, 52–53; wages and, 39, 42; weapons and armaments and, 224 (n. 46). *See also* Great Britain; *Hare* first voyage; *Hare* second voyage; Slave trade

Slaves in South Carolina, 193, 210–11; African culture and, 6, 162, 166–67, 174–80, 193, 245 (n. 22); amulets and charms and, 175–77; from Central Africa, 8, 125, 126, 162, 165, 177; Christianity and, 178, 179, 180; as "countrymen," 159, 161, 165–66, 172, 193; deaths and, 160, 163, 193–94; disease and, 151, 154, 160; "drivers" and, 151, 152–53, 156, 157; indigo and, 129, 155–57, 165, 243–44 (n. 30), 244 (n. 33); languages and, 166, 168–69, 170–74; Mande peoples and, 126, 160, 162, 166, 167, 169–74, 178, 187, 193; Muslims and, 151, 174, 179–80, 246 (n. 33); overseers and, 150–51, 152, 156, 157, 193; return to Africa of, 194; rice plantations and, 8, 125, 131, 145–46, 149–55, 158, 175, 240–41 (n. 18); runaways and, 148, 167–71, 172–73, 216; skilled male laborers and, 147, 152, 154–55, 156,

157, 243 (n. 20); skilled women laborers and, 147, 152, 243 (n. 20); slave names and, 164, 168, 169, 170, 177, 179, 187–88, 244 (n. 8); social gatherings and, 149, 155, 162; Stono Rebellion of, 8, 125, 143, 245 (n. 22); "task system" and, 152–53, 243 (n. 21); from Upper Guinea, 7–9, 126, 148, 149, 161–62, 163, 164–66, 168–70, 172–73, 175, 212–13, 214, 216; violence and, 151, 154; women and, 146, 148–49, 153, 154, 173–74; workhouses and, 168–71, 172–73, 214, 216. *See also* Charles Town; *Hare* captives in South Carolina

Slave trade: African geography of, 6, 7, 8, 11–12, 131, 219 (n. 13); African landlord-stranger relationship and, 73–74; American Revolution and, 188–89, 190; Barbados and, 50, 61, 85, 125; captive sales and, 122, 130–31, 132–35, 139, 161, 181, 184, 187, 195; Central Africa and, 7, 8, 125, 126, 165; Charles Town and, 122, 132, 137, 138, 187, 190, 241 (n. 21); costs and profits and, 22, 80, 83, 184, 185, 188, 204, 233 (n. 9), 247 (n. 9); detaining captives and, 65–67, 80, 91, 98, 99–100, 101, 103, 104; vs. free migrants, 1–2, 218 (n. 2); Futa Jallon and, 82, 96–102, 103, 106, 166, 169, 173, 185; legal end of, 2, 4–5, 9, 86, 185, 189, 195; Muslims and, 2, 82, 96, 102, 103, 126, 166, 179–80, 218 (n. 2), 236 (n. 58), 246 (n. 33); New England and, 2, 9–10, 12, 15, 21–22, 195, 204, 220 (n. 23), 222 (nn. 19–20); Newport and, 15, 16, 17, 18, 22, 184, 188, 195; obtaining captives and, 52, 53, 69–70, 76, 79–80, 97–98; "palaver" and, 66, 74–75, 76, 101–2; "panyarring" and, 75, 77, 90; pawnship and, 75–76, 80; Quakers and, 194, 195; "refuse" slaves and, 133, 135, 136, 187; slave names and, 1, 13, 104; violence in Africa and, 10, 50, 52–53, 72–73, 74, 76–77, 97, 105–6. *See also* Great Britain; Rhode Island; Rum; Sierra Leone; Slave purchasers; Slave ships; South Carolina; Upper Guinea

Slave trade dealers, 73, 76, 89–91, 97–98, 99–100, 103, 104, 233 (n. 12); Bance Island and, 78, 79–80, 83, 90, 91, 99;

184, 185; communications and, 26–27, 52, 61, 70, 71, 106, 108, 229 (n. 61); crew and, 43, 104, 105, 118, 239 (nn. 37–38); Godfrey and, 14, 36, 38, 39, 49, 184, 190; *Hare* second voyage and, 185, 188, 189; insurance and, 14, 25, 28, 119–20; merchant instructions and, 38, 49–50, 115, 227 (n. 25); obtaining captives and, 87, 111; outgoing cargo and, 31, 32–33, 34, 35, 52; "privilege slaves" and, 40, 49, 92; slaving voyages and, 14–15, 22, 27, 188–89
Vernon Galley (ship), 24
Vesey, Denmark, 179
Vickers, Daniel, 45
Virginia, 5, 219 (n. 13)

Wallace, John, 83, 85
Walsh, Vince, 45
Wanton (ship), 37
Wanton, William, 37, 226 (n. 9)

Washington, George, 51, 186, 190, 229 (n. 64)
Washington, Margaret, 7
Watt, James, 96–97
Webster, Pelatiah, 183
Wedderburn, Susannah, 137, 152, 156, 161, 244 (n. 33)
Welch, Francis, 117, 192, 248 (n. 33)
Westcott, Priscilla, 44
White, William, 44, 70–71, 72, 192
Whitefield, George, 51, 229 (n. 64)
William (ship), 76
William Johnston & Co., 61
"Windward Coast," 50, 229 (n. 60), 244 (n. 4). *See also* Upper Guinea
Wonkopong, 84, 85, 98
Woolman, John, 194–95
Workhouses, 168–69, 170–71, 172–73, 214, 216
Wright, Robert, 88